Modern Japan

Modern Japan

Second Edition

Peter Duus

STANFORD UNIVERSITY

HOUGHTON MIFFLIN COMPANY   Boston   New York

Address editorial correspondence to:

Houghton Mifflin Company
College Division
222 Berkeley Street
Boston, MA 02116-3764

Editor-in-Chief: *Jean Woy*
Assistant Editor: *Keith A. Mahoney*
Project Editor: *Julie Lane*
Associate Production Coordinator: *Deborah Frydman*
Manufacturing Coordinator: *Andrea Wagner*
Marketing Manager: *Sandra McGuire*

Cover Design: Tony Saizon

Cover Image: *SUWA, Kanenori (1897–1932):* Asakusa Rokku, *1930. The British Museum, Department of Japanese Antiquities.*

Photograph Credits: *p. 24,* "Cattle Sheds at Takanawa" from the series "Tokaido Highway" by Kawanabe Kyosai. Kawanabe Kyosai Memorial Museum; *p. 46,* The British Museum; *p. 68,* Corbis-Bettmann; *p. 88,* Courtesy Peabody Essex Museum, Salem, MA; *p. 106,* Asian Art & Archaeology, Inc./Corbis; *p. 124,* Library of Congress/Corbis; *p. 163,* Corbis-Bettmann; *p. 192,* Hulton Deutsch Collection/Corbis; *p. 212,* From *A Century of Japanese Photography* by Japan Photographers Association. Photographs Copyright © 1971 by Japan Photographers Association. Reprinted by permission of Pantheon Books, a division of Random House; *p. 247,* From *A Century of Japanese Photography* by Japan Photographers Association. Photographs Copyright © 1971 by Japan Photographers Association. Reprinted by permission of Pantheon Books, a division of Random House; *p. 255,* The National Archives/Corbis; *p. 258,* AP/Wide World Photos; *p. 279,* UPI/Corbis-Bettmann, *p. 306,* Michael S. Yamashita/Corbis; *p. 321,* World Wide Photos; *p. 367,* Michael S. Yamashita/Corbis

Printed in the U.S.A.

Library of Congress Catalog Number: 97-72463

ISBN: 0-395-74604-3

11 12 13-DC-10 09 08 07

Contents

Preface to the
Second Edition

When the first edition of this book appeared two decades ago, Japan was still *terra incognita* to most Westerners. Today, that is no longer the case. As Japanese economic and cultural ties with the West have deepened, few Westerners are unaware that Japan is one of the most advanced, productive, and prosperous societies in the world. Indeed, it has become nearly impossible for Westerners to avoid coming in contact with Japan in their everyday lives. Whether they gulp down instant noodles for lunch, listen to a CD player while studying, or drive to work in a compact automobile, the chances are that by the end of the day they will have used or consumed something Japanese. Today *sushi, judo, karate,* and even *karaoke* all have fit into the great mosaic of Western popular culture. For young Westerners in particular, Japan has become familiar in a way that it was not to their parents or their grandparents.

This book is an attempt to bring this newly familiar Japan into better focus. While most Westerners take for granted that Japan is an economic superpower, it was not always so. It has taken four or five generations for the Japanese to arrive at where they are today. In the middle of the nineteenth century, the Japanese were poorer and less technologically advanced than the newly industrializing Western societies who abruptly intruded upon them. The Japanese feared the Westerners but admired them too, and for the next several decades sought to "catch up" with them: first as assiduous students of Western cultural and institutional models, then as their competitors in the imperialist game, and finally as the creators of a rapidly developing economic giant.

Compressing a century and a half of human experience between the covers of a book is a presumptuous task, and doubly so in a book so short as this one. It is little bit like pruning a vigorous sapling into a dwarf *bonsai* tree. The academic term is brief, however, and demands on students are many, so trimming the narrative to essentials will allow instructors to assign other historical and cultural writings from the rich literature on modern Japan. This book is meant to whet an appetite for the study of modern Japanese history, not to satisfy it.

Like the first edition, the book focuses on major political, economic, and social trends, but it also examines the lives of ordinary peasants, workers and farmers, the social and political position of women, the structure of the family, and popular culture more closely than the previous edition did. I have tried to incorporate new perspectives and material from the enormous body of historical and social science research done on modern Japan during the past two decades. There is more coverage of industrialization and its consequences, and new material has been included on Japan's emergence as an imperialist power. The chapters on the late Tokugawa period have been broadened and deepened, and the chapters on the post-World War II period have been expanded considerably to cover recent developments. This edition is longer than the first one, but the addition of new maps, charts, and photographs should also make it more readable for students.

The romanization of Japanese words and names follows the Hepburn system, the standard in the English-speaking world. With some exceptions, Chinese words and names have been romanized according to the *pinyin* system, but the older Wade-Giles romanization is also included at the first mention of a Chinese term. Following the practice of all the East Asian cultures, the surnames or family names of individuals are placed before their personal names.

In writing this volume, I have relied on the help of others. My most important collaborators are my students, who continually force me to refine my own understanding of modern Japanese history. Other more immediate assistance came from the following reviewers who commented on the manuscript throughout the revision process: Steven Ericson, Dartmouth College; Gail Bernstein, University of Arizona; Parks Coble, University of Nebraska; Ann Walthall, University of California–Irvine; Jeff Hanes, University of Oregon; Sharon Minnichiello, University of Hawaii, Manoa; Louise Young, New York University; John Henderson, Louisiana State University; Donald Clark, Trinity University; Andrew Gordon, Duke University; and Sally Hastings, Purdue University. To all who have helped me in one way or another, I wish to express my thanks.

P.D.

Introduction

When Commodore Matthew Perry sailed into Uraga Bay in July 1853, he carried a letter assuring the emperor of Japan that the United States had no intention of disturbing the tranquility of his realm. This comforting assurance could hardly have been wider of the mark, for Perry's arrival ushered in a century and more of rapid and bewildering change that profoundly altered the course of Japanese history. Within the space of a generation, the Japanese transformed their country into the first modern nation state outside the West, began to build a modern industrial economy, and plunged into the exciting but uncertain waters of great power politics. As one foreign observer noted in 1900, Japan was like a bright comet suddenly tracing a path across the sky, exploding into the vision of an outside world that for centuries had hardly taken notice of it.[1]

This remarkable transformation has always fascinated Western historians. Although the Japanese came from a radically different cultural and historical background, it was striking that they underwent the same kinds of changes that Western societies have experienced since the mid-eighteenth century. The questions were: why and how? Until the end of World War II, many historians regarded Japan as a unique case, very different from China, India, and other "backward" societies that were unable to make a breakthrough into modernity. Some advanced the peculiar argument that a "capacity for imitation" had allowed the Japanese to model themselves on the West, just as a millennium earlier their ancestors had modelled themselves on China. But as the brilliant Canadian historian E. H. Norman suggested in 1940, traditional Japanese society was undergoing profound changes even before the advent of Perry, and it was these changes more than any "capacity for imitation" that accounted for Japan's modern transformation.[2]

After World War II, Japan's modern experience was placed in a new perspective. The emergence of dozens of "new nations" in the postwar world made Japan seem less a unique case than the first instance of a more general phenomenon: the modernization of the non-Western world. Indeed, many historians used the Japanese case as a testing ground for larger theories about what constituted "modernization" and "modern society." More often than not these theories fit Japan poorly—or so loosely as to be platitudinous. Equally seductive was the idea that Japan might serve as an example for other non-Western nations to follow. During the Cold War, defenders of the "free world" tried to gain advantage in ideological debates by pointing out that Japan had not only modernized itself early on but had done so within the framework of a free-enterprise economy under a non-Communist leadership. If Japan could do it, so could the rest of the developing world.

Until the last decade or so, the prevailing image of modern Japanese history stressed its positive aspects. Indeed, there was a strong inclination to view modern Japanese history as a kind of success story, particularly as Japan challenged the United States in the world marketplace. To be sure, there was much to commend this point of view. After all, in the late 1960s Japan became the world's third-largest industrial economy, and its population enjoyed a degree of material comfort and security unknown to their great-grandparents or even to their neighbors in East Asia. As Japanese economic growth rolled on, Japan came to be measured by standards of Western experience rather than by those of the non-Western world. Indeed, many observers inside and outside Japan argued that perhaps the Westerners had a thing or two to learn from the Japanese about how to manage an economy and maintain a stable society.

But it is wise to remember that there has always been a darker side to Japan's modern experience. While the economy grew steadily since the late nineteenth century, the benefits of growth were not always distributed evenly, particularly during the early phases of industrialization. The process of economic growth produced losers as well as winners, and the disparity generated frequent conflict. The persistence of older habits of mind also meant that politics were often authoritarian, oppressive, and reactionary in character. It was only after World War II that democratic practices became firmly established and that the general population found themselves free of constraints over public speech and action. And finally, the success of the Japanese in modernizing while their neighbors remained less developed tempted the country's leaders to embark on wars of aggression and expansion in East Asia. For many Asians, as well as those Japanese who still remember World War II, the prime lesson of Japan's modern history is how *not* to modernize.

It is clear that Japan's path to the present has been strewn with both failures and successes. To sweep aside the failures, as the price inevitably paid for the long-run achievements, makes no more sense than to suggest that these achievements are nothing compared with the sufferings Japan has undergone. In any case, before offering judgements on the meaning or significance of Japan's modern experience, it is wise to try understanding what happened and why. Not to do so tempts us to judge the past by anachronistic standards. To be sure, it is not possible to observe the past with any more objectivity than it is to look at any human activity. History, like human life, is filled with ambiguities and uncertainties, and its meaning can be as varied as its observers are numerous. But surely we can not understand Japan and the Japanese today unless we confront that history ourselves. In the end we all have to be our own historians.

ENDNOTES

1. The foreign observer was Gustav Lebon, whose remarks are quoted in the introduction to Yosaburo Takekoshi, *The Economic Aspects of the History of the Civilization of Japan*, 3 vols. (London: George Allen and Unwin, 1930).

2. Norman's classic work is E. Herbert Norman, *Japan's Emergence as a Modern State* (New York: Institute of Pacific Relations, 1940). A selection of Norman's most important writings has been anthologized in *Origins of the Modern Japanese State: Select Writings of E. H. Norman*, ed. John W. Dower (New York: Pantheon Books, 1975).

CHINA

RUSSIA

Hokkaidō

Sapporo

Hakodate

Aomori
AOMORI

AKITA
IWATE

Sea
of
Japan

YAMAGATA
MIYAGI
Sendai

Sado
Honshū

NIIGATA
FUKUSHIMA

TOCHIGI
Mito
GUMMA
IBARAKI
TOYAMA
SAITAMA
ISHIKAWA
NAGANO
TŌKYŌ
Tokyo
FUKUI
YAMANASHI
CHIBA
GIFU
Yokohama
SHIGA
KYŌTO
KANAGAWA
TOTTORI
AICHI
SHIZUOKA
Nagoya
SHIMANE
HYŌGO
Kyōto
OKAYAMA
Kobe
MIE
HIROSHIMA
Osaka
NARA
Hiroshima
KAGAWA
OSAKA
YAMAGUCHI
TOKUSHIMA
WAKAYAMA
EHIME
Kōchi
FUKUOKA
Shikoku
Fukuoka
KŌCHI
NAGASAKI
SAGA
ŌITA
Nagasaki
KUMAMOTO
Kyūshū
KAGOSHIMA
MIYAZAKI

Kagoshima

Tanegashima

PACIFIC
OCEAN

Modern Japan

I

The Fall of the Tokugawa Order, 1800–1868

1

Late Tokugawa Society

Modern Japanese society did not spring into being full-blown with the arrival of Western gunboats in the mid-nineteenth century: it grew out of a complex historical and cultural context that has shaped its transformation to the present day. This transformation required a head-on assault on long-standing customs, institutions, and ideas; naturally enough, habits of heart and mind changed slowly. It was one thing to adopt new technology like steam engines and telegraph lines, but quite another to alter the way people felt or thought about such things as family, gender, or status. And often the country's leaders, out of nostalgia or design, sought to reinvent older social practices or at least to recast them in new molds. As the essayist Okakura Tenshin wrote in 1904, a generation after the transformation of the country began, "One who looks beneath the surface can see, in spite of her modern garb, that the heart of Old Japan is still beating."[1] The residue of the past has persisted even in contemporary Japan, making it distinctly different from other industrialized societies. To understand why Japan became a modern society in the particular way that it did, one must begin by looking at what Japanese society was like on the eve of its modernization in the late Tokugawa period (1600–1868).

CULTURAL UNITY AND DIVERSITY

To a degree unusual among the large and complex societies of the pre-industrial world, Japan developed in relative physical isolation from neighboring societies. At the end of the ice age, when rising seas covered land bridges to the Asian mainland, the inhabitants of the Japanese archipelago were cut off from sustained contact with outside peoples. The Straits of Tsushima, a formidable maritime barrier more than five times as wide as the English Channel, separated northern Kyushu from the tip of the Korean peninsula by 115 miles of open water. While that did not prevent either cultural contacts or trading relations with China, the historic center of East Asian civilization, it did serve as a buffer against outside invasion and checked most impulses to expand abroad. Save for two abortive invasion attempts by Mongol armadas in the late thirteenth century, no foreign attack ever challenged indigenous Japanese authority, nor except for two expeditions launched against Korea in the 1590s and the conquest of the Okinawan kingdom in 1609 did a Japanese ruler attempt to establish control over peoples across the sea.

Nor were there any major in-migrations by continental peoples during historic times. When the early Japanese state was taking shape in the fourth, fifth, and sixth centuries, artisans, scholars, monks, and noblemen arrived in Japan from Korea and China to help build the new society. A thousand years later, Korean artisans were brought back as captives by Japanese armies in the late sixteenth century. But these were exceptional episodes, and the migrants were ultimately assimilated into the indigenous society. By the late Tokugawa period, the only culturally distinctive people living in the archipelago were the Ainu, an indigenous ethnic group displaced to the northern island of Hokkaido (then known as Ezo) by the spread of Japanese settlers into the northeastern parts of Honshu over several centuries. These "hairy people," as the Japanese called them, were regarded as primitive barbarians whose lives the Japanese thought little better than those of the wild animals they hunted. By the middle of the eighteenth century, however, even the Ainu were coming under the influence of the dominant culture as Japanese merchants sought to expand trade in furs and marine products on the northern frontier.

The relative isolation of the Japanese archipelago has given rise to the notion that Japan has enjoyed a tradition of cultural unity. It is common for Japanese today to speak of themselves as a "homogeneous people" unencumbered by the religious, linguistic, and ethnic differences that have so often troubled their Asian neighbors. Certainly there is much to support this view. Historically, Japan was free of the deep religious divisions that divided Hindu from Moslem in India, the complex ethnic mixtures created by the movement of peoples in Southeast Asia, or even the linguistic differences that separated the people of north China from those in the South. The people inhabiting the Japanese archipelago, by and large, shared a common racial heritage, spoke a common language, and worshipped a common set of gods. From early times, social and political elites have stressed the relatively homogeneous character of the population, and its relatively uniform culture. For example, it was common for them to distinguish between what was authentically Japanese (*wa*) from things of continental origin (*kara*) or to celebrate "Japanese spirit" (*wagokoro*) as distinctive from "continental" or "Chinese spirit" (*karagokoro*).

It would be a mistake, however, to overemphasize the cultural or social homogeneity of Japan. To late Tokugawa Japanese, what would have been most noticeable when they traveled away from their native places was not similarity or familiarity but immense diversity and variety. From one province to another, a traveler would notice striking variations in the words people used, the houses they lived in, the way their villages were laid out, and the food they ate. Certainly this was the case with Kita and Yaji, the roguish heroes of the early nineteenth century novel *Hizakurige (Shank's Mare)*, as they make their way along the Tokaido, the main highway linking the city of Edo with western Japan. At an inn along the way, for example, Yaji burns his feet badly when he leaps into a bathtub with a heated bottom, common in western Japan but unfamiliar to an inhabitant of Edo like him; reluctant to ask the inn keeper what to do, he climbs in again wearing a pair of wooden clogs—somewhat like wearing sneakers in the shower.[2]

The most important cultural boundary—the one that confounded Kita and Yaji—separated the eastern and western parts of the country. Since the thirteenth century, the region west of the barrier station at Ōtsu became known as Kantō ("east of the barrier") in contrast to the Kansai region ("west of the barrier"). While this political boundary lost significance over time, as a cultural boundary it remained an important dividing line on mental maps of the country. Even after the balance of political, economic, and cultural power moved eastward with the establishment of a new regime under the Tokugawa shoguns in 1600 (see Chapter 2), people of the Kyoto-Osaka area continued to consider themselves as more refined in taste, behavior, and high culture than the upstarts in the east.

A less noticeable but perhaps more important boundary was an economic one separating the more prosperous and developed parts of the country from the poorer and less developed. Cutting across the east-west cultural division was a geographical zone stretching from northern Kyushu along both sides of the Inland Sea through the Kansai region to the Kantō Plain in the east. It was along this corridor that a core economic region took shape. From early times, the Inland Sea had functioned much as great river systems did in other advanced pre-industrial societies, providing a highway for commerce as well as a conduit for outside influences, but the development of the Tōkaidō, a highway linking Osaka with the Tokugawa capital at Edo, extended this important transportation artery eastward. (Even today this zone contains all the major metropolitan centers, the main railway artery, and the most heavily travelled superhighways.) Trade, population and production flourished in the core region while the coast of the Japan Sea, with its heavy rainfall, long and gloomy winters and snowbound villages, along with the northeastern part of Honshu, remained less densely populated and far less affluent. By the late nineteenth century it became common to contrast "back door Japan" (*ura Nihon*) with the country's more prosperous "front door" (*omote Nihon*) along the Pacific coast.

Even more important, the inhabitants of late Tokugawa Japan lived in a society that was divided by class and status, age and gender, community and province. It was these cleavages that impinged most directly on their daily lives, shaped their attitudes toward society, and even determined their livelihoods. Ordinary folk were much more likely to think of themselves as the member of a particular class, the inhabitant of a particular community, or the member of a particular household than as a "Japanese." Indeed, it was these narrower social boundaries that Japanese leaders sought to overcome in their attempt to reshape Japan as a modern nation state in the late nineteenth century. It was only when that had been accomplished that the relatively ethnic, cultural, and linguistic cohesiveness of the society gave birth to the idea that the Japanese had always been a "homogeneous people."

CLASS AND STATUS

When the first Japanese diplomatic mission arrived in the United States in 1860, its members were astonished to find that the American president dressed in clothes no different from those of an ordinary merchant, took walks unattended by guards and retainers, and chatted casually with his "subjects." In their own society, where consciousness of status and respect for rank were deeply embedded, this would have been unthinkable. When the procession of a daimyo, or regional lord, marched along the main highway to or from the capital at Edo, for example, peasants had to cease their work in the nearby fields to pay their respects by squatting along the roadside with their heads bowed; and when high officials met with one another, they observed a scrupulous dress code that sharply distinguished different ranks. The social distance between people of different status was enormous, as unimaginable to Americans today, as American informality and egalitarianism were to the members of the 1860 mission.

In early nineteenth-century Japan the most basic social division was between commoners and *samurai,* the warrior elite ruling class. This division had its origins in the late sixteenth century when Toyotomi Hideyoshi, who had brought most of the country under this control, attempted to suppress local civil disorder by assigning people to their proper stations in society. The common people were disarmed; the right to carry weapons was restricted to the samurai; and the commoners, most of whom were peasants, were forbidden to leave their fields for military or other adventure. Under a new line of shoguns founded by Hideyoshi's political successor, Tokugawa Ieyasu, these regulations were reinforced and elaborated. The right to carry two swords became the most visible badge of samurai status, and sumptuary regulations meticulously regulated distinctions separating samurai from commoners in every sphere of daily life, from hairstyles to house plans. Samurai were allowed to wear silk, but commoners could not; farmers were enjoined to eat coarse grains like barley and millet while the samurai were permitted to eat rice; and townspeople were forbidden to build dwellings as handsome or ostentatious as those of the samurai. The distinction extended even to criminal law, which established a double standard for the two classes. Gambling, for example, was only a mild misdemeanor for commoners, but for samurai it was a serious offense that compromised the dignity of the class.

The ideas of Confucianism, which dominated elite social and political discourse in Tokugawa Japan, provided justification for this basic division of society. Moralists, high and low, propagated the conventional Confucian view that society ought to be divided into a hierarchy of four estates or four classes, each with its own special function. Ogyū Sorai, an early eighteenth-century Confucian scholar, put it succinctly: "The peasant cultivates the fields and so nourishes the people; the artisan makes utensils and has the people use them; the merchant exchanges what one has for what one has not and so helps the people; the samurai rules so that disorders will not arise. Though each performs only his own job, he is helping the other."[3] In other words, people were to be ranked according to their social utility. The samurai stood at the top because they guaranteed the basic stability of society; next came the peasants who produced the basic essential, food; then the artisans who produced less necessary goods; and last the merchants who produced nothing at all.

Moralists also conceived of the four-class model as a hierarchy of virtue. Confucian discourse made an important distinction between the "cultivated man," who pursued his own moral development through study and learning, and the "petty man," who thought only of his own immediate interest or profit. In the Confucian view, society would function harmoniously only if the morally cultivated, who committed themselves to the common good, were put in charge, setting an example for the rest of the population. In late Tokugawa Japan, the ascendancy of the samurai class was often justified in these terms, and the samurai were portrayed as occupying the moral high ground. This idea was potentially subversive, or at least the source of social criticism, since it held the samurai elite to a higher standard than the commoner but often found them wanting.

In actuality, the four-class model did not provide an accurate picture of later Tokugawa society. For one thing, many kinds of people—Buddhist monks, Shinto priests, court aristocrats, beggars, and an outcaste group known as *eta*—did not fit into it at all. For another, the four-class model obscured the many subtle and not so subtle distinctions within both the commoner and the samurai classes. But most important, it ignored the fact that social status in late Tokugawa society was determined not by an individual's moral cultivation or education but by his or her birth. Everyone knew that society was based on heredity. While mobility between the samurai and commoner classes was not completely unknown, normally samurai children remained in the samurai class and commoner children grew up to be commoners. In this respect Tokugawa Japan differed not only from our own society but from Qing (Ch'ing) China, where a commoner could become a member of the privileged scholar-official elite by passing the official examinations. Even though many political thinkers and moralists paid lip service to the idea that the samurai elite owed its position to moral or cultural merit,[4] Japanese society fundamentally discouraged interclass mobility.

The rigid social pecking order made it nearly impossible for anyone but samurai to enter the ruling class. By the same token, it provided strong motivation for commoners to perform as well as they could in whatever place the accident of birth had put them. If they could not rise to a higher status outside their class, they could at least rise to the first rank among peers. Personal achievement was not so closely linked with upward social mobility as it is in American society, nor did ambition mean rising above one's station. Rather, it was important for commoners to do their best in their own walk of life. A carpenter could not hope to become a samurai, but he could hope to become a master artisan whose work was admired by all. It was this kind of success in which the commoners took pride. "No matter how poor you are, you must not be beguiled into another trade," warned a book of advice to craftsmen. "If you ply your craft unchangingly and with complete devotion, the time may come when you will prosper."[5] All people had their own places in society and they were expected to do their best within those places. Moralists often spoke of this as a *shokubun* ("calling") with its own set of duties and functions to be fulfilled. A person's worth was measured by his or her success in fulfilling them.

In a society that placed such heavy emphasis on status and hierarchy, rank determined how people behaved toward one another, creating a kind of situational social ethic. As Fukuzawa Yukichi, a later critic of the Tokugawa order, noted: "[The Japanese] make a clear distinction between the moral codes that apply to people above them and to people below, and an equally clear distinction in the field of rights and duties. As a result every individual is in

Population by Status Group–c. 1868

Imperial court nobles (*kuge*)	2,000	.01%
Samurai	1,925,597	6.4%
Religious persons	374,398	1.25%
Buddhist priests	(146,950)	
Shinto priests	(227,448)	
Commoners	27,265,628	90.62%
Peasants/farmers		(80–85%)
Artisans and merchants		(5–10%)
Outcastes (*eta*) and nonpersons (*hinin*)	520,451	1.72%
	30,089,391	100.00%

Source: Susan B. Hanley and Kozo Yamamura, *Economic and Demographic Change in Pre-Industrial Japan, 1600–1868* (Princeton, NJ: Princeton University Press, 1987).

one capacity the victim of coercion, while in another he metes out coercion to his fellow men."[6] While Fukuzawa's critique overstated the case, his observation underlines how far late Tokugawa society was from any liberal conception of society. It offered little room for any notion of "equality of opportunity" or any recognition of basic human equality. Conventional wisdom assumed that there would always be social superiors and social inferiors, and that each would be treated by a different standard.

This society may sound grim to contemporary Americans but it would be wrong to characterize late Tokugawa Japan as a place of untrammeled social oppression. Even within elite Confucian discourse those at the top of the social hierarchy were constrained by *noblesse oblige* to treat their inferiors benevolently and justly. A regional lord would open himself to rebuke if he were cruel, irresponsible or dissolute, and an official might be punished if he were corrupt or arbitrary in his dealing with the people. In practice, of course, the legal system offered little recourse for commoners to redress grievances against samurai who shirked their duty, since the courts would entertain suits by people of low status against their superiors only with the superiors' consent. But the notion that the high born and the powerful should not take advantage of the poor and the weak provided a check on gross abuses of privilege and authority. Authoritarian excess was contained, not by a sense of rights, but by a web of mutual and interlocking social obligations.

It should also be remembered that the status ethic was observed more carefully by the samurai class, and perhaps by the more affluent commoners class, than it was by most ordinary commoners. The lower orders had little choice but to show deference to the samurai but often they were skeptical of their pretensions. "Even a lord with a million," as one comic verse put it, "journeys to the other world alone." Fiction covertly spoofing the samurai was not at all uncommon, and even satirical prints subtly poked fun at them. Commoners were also inclined to measure their peers by their merits rather than by their birth. A humble hierarchy of talent and ability existed alongside the official hierarchy of status. For townspeople, material success established a person's worth. "Birth and lineage mean nothing," proclaimed one tract for merchants. "Money is the only family tree for the townsman. A man may be descended from the noblest of the Fujiwara (an ancient aristocratic family), but if he dwells among shopkeepers and lives in poverty he is lower than a vagabond monkey-trainer."[7] Peasants too were more likely to earn the respect of their neighbors by display of hard work than by their parents' pedigree.

COMMUNITY AND SOLIDARITY

If the late Tokugawa obsession with status and rank seems strange to those brought up on a diet of egalitarianism, so too does willingness of individuals to subordinate personal interest to the claims of the group or collectivity.

Rugged individualism was not highly prized in early nineteenth-century Japan. On the contrary, independent individuals stubbornly pursuing their own goals or following the dictates of their own consciences were more likely to be regarded as eccentrics, crackpots, or rebels than as heroes, and nonconformity often invited social rejection. "The nail that sticks out gets hammered down," went a popular saying. What one sociologist has called a "collectivity ethic"[8] made paramount the goals of the group, whether family, village, or domain, and equated the pursuit of individual desires with selfishness. Indeed, "individualism" was so alien a concept that a word had not yet been invented for it in the Tokugawa period.

The most extreme form of "collectivity ethic" was to be found in the samurai class, whose members were constantly enjoined to sacrifice themselves for their daimyo and their domain. By precept and example young samurai were taught that their highest duty was personal loyalty (chū) to their lord. Military romances and moral tracts written for the class took as their heroes medieval warriors who fought to the death in the services of their lords, throwing away their lives without hesitation. One of the most popular dramas of the period was Chūshingura (The Storehouse of Loyalty) the story of forty-seven samurai who devoted their lives to avenging the unjust death of their young lord. It was based on an incident that took place in the early eighteenth century, when a band of former retainers of Akō domain, defying a ban against private vendettas, broke into the heavily guarded residence of a high shogunal official who had provoked their former daimyo into drawing his sword within the shogun's castle, an offense that cost him his life.[9] After decapitating their lord's tormentor, the loyal retainers marched to their lord's grave and presented him with the severed head. Other historical plays celebrated the theme of self-sacrifice in the name of feudal loyalty but none captured the public imagination so tenaciously.

Few samurai in late Tokugawa Japan were called on to sacrifice their lives for their lords, but the idea of "duty to one's lord" remained a powerful moral imperative. The lord was at the pinnacle of the domain, the collectivity they were to serve all of their lives. In practice, the daimyo's band of samurai retainers (kashindan) was more like a corporate bureaucracy than a warrior army bound by personal vassalage. The daimyo was thought of as a symbol of the domain rather than as a personal charismatic leader. The layout of the castle towns where the samurai lived constantly reminded them not only of their lord's authority but their own place in the domain hierarchy. At the center was the daimyo's castle, a multi-storeyed structure whose towering keep loomed over the town as cathedral spires did in Western Europe, and the town plan meticulously reflected the ranking system. Near the castle moat were the sprawling villas of high-ranking samurai who served as the domain elders and confidants of the daimyo, while the lesser ranks resided farther from the center, the lowest often on the edges of town even beyond the commercial neighborhoods.

The collectivity ethic within the peasant villages, where most of the population lived, rested on a sense of community created by common economic interests, the need to cooperate in daily life, and a sense of togetherness over time. The system of wet rice agriculture practiced in most of the country created interdependence among village households. The timely flow of water to the villager's rice paddies could mean the difference between prosperity and hardship, and the sharing of water resources placed a premium on cooperation with other villagers. Too little water in the paddy could spoil the harvest, and a peasant family that got more than its fair share could hurt the welfare of its neighbors. In most villages, rigid customs governed the flow of irrigation water, so that no family gained at the expense of others. But villagers shared other resources such as the common lands and common forest where they collected firewood, picked wild herbs and mushrooms, or gathered grass and twigs for mulch. Neighboring households also helped each other in certain important tasks—such as transplanting rice seedlings from seed beds to the main paddies, cultivating and weeding fields, thatching roofs and repairing houses, or preparing for funerals. The impulse toward cohesion and cooperation was deeply rooted in the daily and yearly processes of production.

The relative stability of village communities reinforced social solidarity. Compared to modern Japan, population movement in the countryside was slight. At the beginning of the Tokugawa period, the political authorities tried to discourage travel and migration by requiring peasants to get special permission to make religious pilgrimages, visits to hot springs, or other long trips. Although younger sons and daughters often left their villages to work for a time in nearby towns or cities, most households stayed put, remaining in their village as far back as family memory stretched. Only poorer peasant households were likely to move during the course of a generation. This population stability created a sense of local roots that is difficult to imagine in our own highly mobile society, where people change houses, jobs, and spouses with little hesitation. Membership in the village was almost a birthright and villagers knew their neighbors' history as well as they knew their own. A dispute or other episode that happened a generation or two before might remain as fresh in the collective memory of the village as one a week or two old. This rootedness of the villagers made them distrustful of outsiders and strangers, whom they could not know or trust as they did one another.

An annual cycle of festivals brought the villagers together as a collectivity throughout the year. Not surprisingly, festivals were associated with the annual agricultural cycle, on which the whole community's survival depended. The cultivation of rice was thought to involve collaboration between humans and the gods (*kami*), and at every important turning point in the growing cycle a ritual brought the two together. Just before spring planting came festivals to welcome the return of the "god of the field" (thought to descend from a nearby mountain where it spent the rest of the year); then came another festival when the seedlings were transferred to main fields; during late summer village rituals were performed to ward off insects or typhoons that might damage the crop; and finally in the fall the villagers held a harvest festival to thank the "god of the field" and send him off until the following year. The ostensible purpose of these festivals was to protect crops from natural harm, but they also served to reinforce a sense of common purpose and community.

In many villages age-based groups cutting across kin or economic ties pulled villagers together along generational lines. Most common were "youth groups" (*wakamonoguni*), made up of young unmarried men who lived in a separate residence until they found wives and started their own families. These groups played an important role in village life, fighting fires, reinforcing dikes along streams, or carrying the portable shrine at festival time. Membership wove bonds among men of the same age that lasted the rest of their lives. In some regions, it was also possible to find "young women's associations" (*musumegumi*) or "old people's associations" (*rojingumi*), but usually these groups did not involve separate residence, nor did they play as important a role in village affairs, which remained a male prerogative.

Commitment to the village community was just as strong (and perhaps even stronger) than samurai loyalty to the domain. It rested on the notion that decisions affecting the whole village should be based on the consensus of all concerned and should be obeyed by all. Village custom affected the most minute aspects of daily life, from the number of sake cups one could drink at a family wedding to the conversion of a dry field to a rice paddy. This produced strong pressures for personal conformity to village opinion. The oppressive side of village life in the village was brilliantly described by the novelist, Tokutomi Kenjirō, who wrote,

> There's as much freedom in the country as in a prison, believe me. Drop a pebble in a bowl and you set up a tidal wave. Stretch your arms in the country, and you bump old Tagobei's front door—your legs, and they get caught in Gonsuke's back gate. If your daughter so much as changes the neckband of her kimono, the whole village must be talking about it. A hermit can live in the middle of any town, and in the capital nobody bothers about anything—but in the country you can't even sneeze without wondering what people will say.[10]

The sanctions for defying village custom or consensus could be harsh. In extreme cases households who breached the village code, and their families as well, were punished by a kind of communal ostracism (*murahachibu*) that cut them off from most human contacts for a period of years—and sometimes indefinitely. To be denied participation in village life and rites was not only emotionally painful, it deprived a household of cooperative support and endangered its livelihood.

Despite the need for cooperation, cohesiveness, and consensus, the late Tokugawa village was not immune to conflict. As we shall see, competition over possession of land was common, and so was conflict over status, especially when newly prosperous families vied with declining older ones for village honors. Rarer but no less important than intravillage antagonism were riots or risings against samurai authorities or rich peasants. All were part of the social landscape. But conflict was not thought of as positive force, as it often is in our own society, which celebrates adversarial relationships as protection against oppression. Rather conflict was regarded as socially destructive. In both elite discourse, and in the conventional wisdom of the commoners, the best society was thought to be a harmonious one, and conflict was seen as a sign that not all was well with the world. In practice, every effort was bent to resolve potential conflict without resort to law or litigation (really a continuation of conflict by other means), often through conciliation by go-betweens. Peasants angry at the arbitrariness of samurai officials sometimes appealed (albeit illegally) over their heads by petition to the domain lord, and merchants involved in a dispute over debts negotiated through some third party to achieve a reasonable compromise. When grievances were not redressed or differences were left unresolved, violence often occurred, but the authorities punished its perpetrators severely if they had the means to do so.

HOUSEHOLD AND GENDER

In late Tokugawa Japan, people were known not simply as members of a particular class or community but as members of a particular household (*ie*). Indeed, the household not the individual was seen as the basic building block of society. The authorities held households rather than individuals responsible for paying taxes, and if an individual committed an offense against law or violated village custom, male household members often suffered punishment along with the offender. On the Tokugawa domains, commoner households were organized into groups (*goningumi* or "five-man groups"), consisting of anywhere from a couple to a dozen households, charged with joint responsibility to keep up the roads, supply labor, maintain waterways, or carry on other important economic functions.

The household developed first as an institution of the samurai class, then spread to the rest of the population, modified everywhere by local custom and circumstance. The household was not quite the same thing as "family" in the sense we understand it today, as a group of people directly related by blood. It was defined by residence as well as by biological affinity, and its members were those who "shared the same roof" or "cooked meals in the same pot." The household could include two or three generations of lineal kin (grandparents, parents, and children) as well as servants, indentured laborers, apprentices, and others who contributed to the household economy. Since the household was expected to endure over generations, its deceased and unborn members were linked across time with its living members. Indeed, preserving the household was the most important responsibility of the household head, who regularly reported its fortunes to his ancestors (or asked for their help) at the family altar or family grave. The household was not simply a reproductive body but one that had important ritual, work, and property-holding functions.

The household head, usually a married male, was its most powerful and important member, whose word was to be feared like "earthquake, thunder, and fire." He represented the household to the outside world, controlled its property and other assets, and managed the household economy, whether it was based on farming, craft production, or trade. To ensure continuity across generations, the household headship and property were usually passed on to a single heir rather than divided among several. Among the samurai, this practice was required by law. To prevent disputes the succession usually took place while the incumbent household head was still alive, so that he could supervise and guide the new household head from retirement. Among commoners, other siblings were expected to leave and set up households of their own, sometimes as a branch (*bunke*) of the main household (*honke*). The successor to the family headship was usually but not necessarily the eldest son, but in some parts of the country it might be a younger son or even the eldest daughter. If the household head had no sons, it was common practice to adopt the eldest daughter's husband or the male offspring of a brother, cousin, or uncle as a successor, and a childless household might even adopt a younger married couple as ready-made "son" and "daughter." Needless to say, this occasionally led to some very complicated family relationships, with household heads ending up as uncles of their biological brothers and sisters.

Since marriage was important to household continuity, it was not a matter left to romantic attraction, sexual appeal, or even the wishes of the prospective bride and groom. Among the samurai and well-to-do commoners, marriages were arranged between households, with other kinfolk or friends acting as go-betweens, to enhance the family fortunes. Ambitious household heads tried to marry their offspring up the social hierarchy, but usually marriages were arranged between households of relatively equal resources and status so that exchanges between them would be balanced and fair. For the samurai, forging social alliances or the production of an heir to carry on the family name were most important in choosing a bride or groom, but for the commoners other considerations were often at work. Peasants were also more inclined to pay attention to sexual compatibility, and in some regions peasant couples were betrothed only after "night visits" (*yobai*) by the prospective groom led to the bride's pregnancy. (In general, sexual relations were much freer among the peasants, where young men bedded down several possible partners before marriage, and where female virginity was prized less highly than among the samurai.)

For the peasant household, marriage was a way of recruiting a permanent member of the household work force. The young bride's labor was as important to the peasant family as her ability to bear children. Indeed, some historians now suggest that work rather than "motherhood" was the defining role of married peasant women. The wife was expected not only to get up early in the morning, start the fire, make the morning meal for the family, prepare food for the rest of the day, and take care of washing and other household chores, she also had to work in the fields alongside her husband and in-laws. From the household's point of view, a healthy and hardworking bride was the ideal daughter-in-law, no matter what her looks and personality might be. Since the groom's family was acquiring such a valuable economic asset, it usually paid for the costs of the wedding and shared the cost of the bride's clothing, bedding, and furniture. Among urban commoners, women were also an important economic resource for the household, working at hand production such as spinning or weaving, or waiting on customers in the family shop. In some merchant households the wife and daughters helped to manage the family business—and in a few rare cases, a widow might be in full charge.

Since no one thought that marriages were made in heaven, divorce was not uncommon in late Tokugawa Japan. The usual causes were infertility or incompatibility. Among the samurai class, the husband could simply send his wife back to her family, an event more embarrassing to her and her family than to the husband. Needless to say, in such a patriarchical society, the reverse was not true. The widely read eighteenth-century advice manual, *The Great Learning for Women (Onna daigaku)*, enjoined the wife to be dutiful, chaste, obedient, respectful, and subservient toward her husband and her in-laws and listed as grounds for divorce not only bad health or barrenness but disobedience, jealousy, and even talkativeness. While the position of wives was probably similar among wealthy merchant families or large rural land-owning households, among the mass of the population—poor and middling peasants, ordinary artisans, and urban laborers—marital relations were more egalitarian. Divorce was often initiated by women, who found it much less difficult to return to their natal households.

In conventional Confucian discourse, women were thought to be as naturally subordinate to men as the moon was to the sun or the earth was to the sky. As *The Great Learning for Women* observed, "[The wife] must look to her husband as her lord, and must serve him with all worship and respect." In reality, the position of the wife within the household depended on her class, her personality, and the nature of her marriage. The main difference was between the women of the samurai class, who had limited economic functions, and those of the peasant, artisan, and laboring classes, who made important contributions to family income and production. While most samurai women tried to fit the ideal laid out in the *Great Learning*, assertive spouses were not uncommon among the lower orders. In the popular stories and comic prints of the late Tokugawa period, the loud-mouthed harridan in a back-street tenement who screamed at her husband for making too many babies and too little money or the randy housewife with a penchant for infidelity were often stock characters. The nature of the marriage also affected the wife's position. If a bride came from another household, her position was generally weak, and often she had to endure hazing by her mother-in-law, who usually got her son to side with her. But in households where a son-in-law was adopted, the wife's position was much stronger. Indeed, the Japanese term for "adopted son-in-law" can also connote a "hen-pecked husband." Even an outside bride gained power over time, often subjecting her own daughter-in-law to the same petty harassments she had endured when young, and when her husband died, she became the ranking family elder.

Since age conveyed privilege and status within the household, children and youths were at the bottom of the family hierarchy. From infancy, samurai children were taught to show deference to social superiors, and above all to their parents. The widely read *Classic of Filial Piety,* a Confucian text on family morality, was filled with instructive tales of model children who went to extremes of self-sacrifice to show respect for their parents. One paragon of filial piety, even though well into middle age, gamboled like an infant in front of his seventy-year-old parents so they would think themselves still young, and another drenched himself with rice wine (sake) and lay naked by his parents' bed at night to draw away mosquitoes. Similarly, Kaibara Ekken, who authored a work on child-rearing, enjoined parents,

> The way of man is to observe the virtues of filial piety and obedience, and the children must be taught that all goodness in life emanates from these two virtues. . . .
> If parents permit their children to hold other people in contempt, and take pleasure in their antics, the children will lose a sense of distinction between good and evil . . . and will not shed their bad habits even after they become adults.[11]

The model behavior prescribed for the young was submissiveness to the authority of their elders, an appropriate message for those growing up in a society that placed such strong emphasis on maintaining one's proper place.

Hierarchical morality was less explicitly articulated among commoners, but everyone spoke a language woven through with honorific words that were to be used toward elders and social superiors—and familiar ones to be used toward juniors and social inferiors. A mother addressed her child with a familiar form of *you,* like the French *tu,* but when she spoke with her husband (and master) she used a more formal second-person pronoun like the French *vous.* Younger siblings called older ones by terms that meant "elder brother" or "elder sister," and all siblings deferred to the eldest brother if he were expected to become the household heir. Sometimes he was more resented than respected, especially if he flaunted his authority, but since social convention usually prevailed over private feelings, there was little that younger siblings could do about it.

HUMANS AND GODS

While our own society makes a clearcut boundary between the natural and the supernatural, in late Tokugawa Japan a sense of continuity between the visible world of humans and the invisible one of the gods was very strong.

The dead, the divine, and the supernatural were as real to people as their kin and neighbors. The Tokugawa peasant lived in a world populated by unhappy ghosts and human spirits, magical foxes able to turn themselves into seductive women, half-human half-birdlike winged *tengu* living in the dark depths of the forest, and amphibious saucer-headed *kappa* waiting to pull unsuspecting bypassers into the streams where they dwelt. Even the better educated, more secularized and skeptical members of the samurai class felt strong and tangible bonds with their deceased ancestors.

Unlike religion in the Judeo-Christian-Islamic tradition, religious practices in late Tokugawa Japan were neither highly institutionalized nor tightly compartmentalized into separate sects and denominations. Dealing with gods and other superhuman forces was much more diffuse, and religious beliefs were much more syncretic. Indeed, a Japanese of the time would probably have found the question, "What is your religion?" rather puzzling since his complicated bundle of beliefs would have been difficult to give a name. Ritual and practice, in any case, were more important than personal creed, and religious feelings were more likely to be rooted in a particular sacred site than in a particular doctrine. Indeed, the household itself was an important site for ritual and worship. Religious affiliation was inclusive rather than exclusive, and most people had no qualms about participating in rituals that had their origins in quite different belief systems. In the course of their lives, all people participated in religious rites that we would now call "Buddhist" or "Shinto," and few would have difficulty reconciling either with a commitment to conventional Confucian morality.

If there was anything like an "official religion" or "established religion" it was Buddhism, a faith that arrived in Japan a millennium or so earlier. From the early seventeenth century, the political authorities had promoted its expansion among the mass of the population as a way of checking the spread of heterodox religious ideas, especially Christianity, which Catholic missionaries had introduced into the country with great success in the sixteenth century. In the mid-seventeenth century, the Tokugawa authorities ordered all the domains to have every household registered as a "parish household" (*danka*) at a local Buddhist temple as a means of checking the spread of Christianity. The local domain lords often built new temples and granted land to support them, and the local parishioners took responsibility for their upkeep. Large temples in Kyoto, Edo and the castle towns enjoyed the patronage of the upper classes—the court aristocracy, the shogun, and the daimyo—who lavished contributions on them. The political authorities encouraged local temples to become "branch temples" of the "main temples" in the urban areas, creating the kind of hierarchical organizational network officials were so fond of. Some Buddhist sects, like the Pure Land (*Jōdo shinshū*) or Sōtō Zen sects, used the system to expand into powerful religious corporations.

Intellectual ferment with the Buddhist establishment was less vigorous than in early centuries, and the Buddhist priesthood had become quite worldly. Rural priests, who were permitted to marry, usually led lives not so very different from their peasant parishioners, and the abbots who headed the great urban temple complexes enjoyed many of the comforts of their aristocratic patrons. The "meat-eating priest," who ignored the Buddhist taboo against consuming animal flesh or spent his evenings in brothels, was the object of popular satire, and so was the mercenary priest greedy for fees. "In his mouth the sutra [i.e. scripture]," went one comic poem about a Buddhist priest, "In his heart, 'How much will they give me.'" Nevertheless Buddhism rooted itself among the mass of the population as it had not in earlier times. Samurai and commoner households alike maintained family graves at nearby Buddhist temples, and the most important function of the priests was to preside over funerals and other rituals to commemorate deceased ancestors. The more affluent households kept family altars (*butsudan*) with memorial tablets (*ihai*) at home, and the household head and other family members paid homage to the ancestral spirits or sought their help in daily prayers.

The popular morality associated with Buddhism reinforced the values of diligence, frugality, and achievement celebrated in conventional Confucian discourse. Hard work and worldly success were seen as a way of repaying the blessings bestowed by deceased parents and ancestors, and these ideas found support among all strata of society. As the peasant moralist Ninomiya Sontoku wrote, "The wealth of our parents depends on the industry of their ancestry, and our wealth depends on the accumulated good deeds of our parents. Our descendants' wealth depends on us and our faithful discharge of duty."[12] Such advice found acceptance not only among the peasantry, whose lives demanded a morality of hard work as a matter of necessity, but town dwellers and samurai as well, and the sense of obligation toward society, collectivity, and family remained a powerful source of individual motivation even after much of late Tokugawa society had been swept away. The practices and beliefs of Buddhism, which emphasized that all human beings faced death and possible rebirth, also reminded people that the hierarchical society in which they lived was a transitory one.

If the Buddhist temple served the needs of the individual and the fortunes of the household, the local Shinto shrine was linked more closely to the village or community. Buddhist temples were by no means ubiquitous, but shrines and local sacred local sites could be found in every hamlet, village, and urban neighborhood. The deities (*kami*) worshipped at shrines were not transcendent powers omnisciently presiding over the human world from on high but rather local forces immanent in the landscape and the cyclical processes of nature. Indeed, it was not uncommon for huge trees, imposing rocks, or even waterfalls to be marked off by sacred ropes as residences of local *kami*. As we have already seen, peasants believed that these local deities could help them reap a bountiful harvest, and the community carried out periodic propitiatory ceremonies aimed at keeping them in a good mood. Individual villagers also went to the shrine to pray for personal help—successful childbirth, curing an illness, a safe journey, or some other worldly concern.

Festivals conducted with the local deities reminded villagers of their common interests and reinforced the local social hierarchy. The local shrine priest took charge of performing the rituals, but they were presided over by shrine organizations (*miyaza*) made up of the heads of wealthier or older village families. In form, festivals put the villagers in active communion with the *kami*, through offerings of sake, rice, and other local produce, which were consumed in a ritual meal. To reacquaint the local deity with his local bailiwick, the young men of the community would carry it in a portable shrine on a procession through the village or neighborhood, shouting and singing to the accompaniment of drums and flutes. The usual rules of behavior were suspended at festival time, and the annual cycle of ritual had a playful side. Villagers could find release from the drudgery of work in dancing, singing, and drinking, and they could work off (or act out) intravillage hostilities in boat races or tug-of-wars. Indeed, festivals were such an important part of village life that many Tokugawa villagers probably took more "time off" for them than workers in contemporary Japan take for vacation.

By the early nineteenth century, popular religious activity spilled beyond the boundaries of household and community. Although the political authorities restricted travel for ordinary folk, an exception was made for pilgrimages to famous temples or shrines. Pilgrims, clad in special ritual clothes, traveled in groups along regular religious routes such as the circuit of eighty-eight Buddhist temples on the island of Shikoku, enjoying a chance for tourism as well as devotion. More dramatic and frenzied were the periodic "thanksgiving pilgrimages" (*okage mairi*) to the great shrine at Ise, where the sun goddess Amaterasu was worshipped. In 1771 and again in 1830, millions took to the roads to Ise over a period of several months, inspired by rumors that magical amulets had fallen from heaven. Many departed on these massive pilgrimages to secure the special blessing and protection of the sun goddess, but a festival atmosphere prevailed. Pilgrims caroused in the temporary inns, drinking huts, teahouses and brothels that sprang up along the route, and the boundary between devotion and dissent often dissolved when pilgrims demanded free food from wealthy peasant and merchant households or asked local authorities to forgive their debts.

Perhaps more significant was the emergence of new sects or "new religions" based not on the village community or on the individual household but on the commitment of individual believers. People joined these new sects and engaged in their religious practices not as a matter of obligation to their neighbors or their ancestors but because they were attracted to their preachings. Founded by charismatic leaders, often women, the new sects promised relief from everyday cares and suffering and promised good health, long life, and success in worldly endeavors. Typical was Tenrikyō, founded in the 1830s by a pious and long suffering peasant woman, Nakayama Miki, who was possessed by a powerful *kami* that revealed how to deliver humankind from evil, suffering, and disease and to create an orderly, blissful world where everyone would live in harmony. Coming at a time of widespread famine and rural hardship in the late 1830s, this revelation quickly gained Tenrikyō a large following in central Japan, much to the distress of local authorities, who regarded unorthodox religions with much suspicion. Appeals to individuals to reform and purify themselves, and promises of a millenarian future, were common to other new sects, suggesting that cultural and social changes were producing a spiritual malaise not assuaged by established religious practices. Some historians suggest that the millennial element in many "new religions," which promised the coming of a "new age" of peace and prosperity, was a sign that the hierarchical society of late Tokugawa society was showing signs of severe strain.

ENDNOTES

1. Okakura Kakuzō, *The Awakening of Japan* (New York: The Century Co., 1905), 187.

2. Ikku Jippensha, *Shanks' Mare,* trans. Thomas Satchell (Rutland, Vt.: Charles E. Tuttle, 1966), 41–44.

3. A brief discussion of the four-class theory may be found in Eijirō Honjo, *The Social and Economic History of Japan* (New York: Russell and Russell, 1965), 188–202.

4. The "ideology of merit" is discussed in Thomas C. Smith, " 'Merit' as Ideology in the Tokugawa Period," in *Aspects of Social Change in Modern Japan,* ed. R. P. Dore (Princeton, N.J.: Princeton University Press, 1967), 71–90.

5. The quotation from the craftsman's handbook may be found in Charles J. Dunn, *Everyday Life in Traditional Japan* (London: B. T. Batsford, 1969), 92.

6. Fukuzawa Yukichi is quoted in Masao Maruyama, *Thought and Behaviour in Modern Japanese Politics* (New York: Oxford University Press, 1963), 18.

7. The quotation is from Ihara Saikaku, *The Japanese Family Storehouse, or the Millionaires' Gospel Modernised,* trans. G. W. Sargent (Cambridge: Cambridge University Press, 1959), 144.

8. Dore's comments on the "collectivity ethic" may be found in R. P. Dore and Tsutomu Ōuchi, "Rural Origins of Japanese Fascism" in *Dilemmas of Growth in Modern Japan,* ed. James W. Morley (Princeton, N.J.: Princeton University Press, 1971), 181–209.

9. A famous puppet play based on this tale has been translated by Donald Keene: *Chūshingura: The Tragedy of Loyal Retainers* (New York: Columbia University Press, 1971).

10. The quotation is from Kenjirō Tokutomi, *Footsteps in the Snow,* trans. Kenneth Strong (London: George Allen and Unwin, 1970), 67.

11. Kaibara Ekken is quoted in David John Lu, *Sources of Japanese History,* vol. 1 (New York: McGraw-Hill, 1974), 248–249.

12. Quoted in Robert N. Bellah, *Tokugawa Religion: The Values of Pre-Modern Japan* (New York: Free Press, 1957), 128.

2

The Political Heritage

Modern nation states are the product of conscious political decisions, and so are their borders. They were constructed by political leaders driven by the idea of "nationality" or "nationhood," who believed that people sharing a distinctive common culture, language, or ethnicity ought to be joined in a single political community that safeguards their welfare, interests, and security. In the early nineteenth century, many educated Japanese, especially among the samurai, would have agreed that Japan had a distinctive culture, perhaps one superior to the rest of the world, but few would have had a sense of common interest or common dependence as a nation. Despite its well-defined geographical boundaries, late Tokugawa Japan was not yet a nation state. Political authority was fragmented and so was political allegiance. Although a sense of cultural identity was spreading, it had not yet found a political expression. In the same sense that neither "Germany" nor "Italy" existed in the early nineteenth century, neither was there a "Japan."

EMPEROR, SHOGUN, AND DAIMYO

Although it was common to speak of the whole country as "the realm" (*tenka*), "the land of the gods" (*shinshū*), or some other abstract word, these were cultural or historical terms rather than political ones. In late Tokugawa Japan, no single government or state structure guaranteed order throughout the country, nor was there any political center to which people gave their undivided loyalty. After Tokugawa Ieyasu, the dynasty's founder, led a coalition of daimyo, or local territorial lords, to victory over a rival coalition at the battle of Sekighara in 1600, he chose not to construct a unified state. Save for those rivals whom Ieyasu wished to destroy, the daimyo were allowed to retain control over the territories they had built by warfare, intrigue, and marriage, and they continued to maintain their armies of samurai retainers. Neither Ieyasu nor his successors sought to crush the daimyo or obliterate their domains. Instead they chose to rule as shoguns, or feudal overlords, demanding loyalty from the daimyo and exercising direct control only over their own territorial domains, major cities and ports, and gold and silver mines.

The title of shogun, sought by warrior hegemons since the late twelfth century, was conveyed on Ieyasu and his successors by the emperor (*tennō*), the semidivine civil monarch living at the old imperial capital at Kyoto. The imperial institution had been defunct as an effective political force for centuries, having become the pawn first of ambitious factions of court aristocrats (*kuge*), then later of great feudal barons. The myth of divine descent, which claimed that the imperial lineage had been spawned by the sun goddess Amaterasu, however, established the emperor as the ultimate source of political authority and surrounded the imperial throne with a thicket of taboos that protected it from usurpation. Even during the fifteenth and sixteenth centuries, when warring regional lords rode roughshod over other inherited institutions, they competed for honors and ranks from the imperial court to validate their social respectability and their political legitimacy. So did Tokugawa Ieyasu, who quickly consolidated his military victory by seeking bestowal of the shogunal title.

In justifying their ascendancy, the Tokugawa shoguns propagated a "theory of delegation" (*ininron*), expressed succinctly by Yamaga Sokō, a seventeenth-century scholar:

> The throne descends—fearful to say—from the Sun Goddess. Its lineage is eternal. Though the shogun wields power and governs the country, in truth he is only rectifying things for the imperial court. The shogun's greatest obligation as a subject to his sovereign is to carry out the affairs of the imperial court tirelessly in every detail.[1]

It might seem strange that the Tokugawa shoguns embraced a theory that subordinated them to the emperor, but in fact this provided powerful justification for their rule. It established, first of all, that the shogun was not a "tyrant" (*ha*) who had usurped power by sheer military force but a rightfully appointed ruler; it denied the emperor any role in actual governance, leaving that to the shogun; and finally, it suggested that the shogun, acting as a loyal and reverent vassal to his lord, the emperor, provided a model for the rest of the ruling class. The "theory of delegation" affirmed the authority of the imperial court, but it placed power in the hands of the shogun. All roads literally led to the shogun's capital in Edo, where he presided over an administrative regime known as the *bakufu* (literally, "government under a tent").

Except for those living near the imperial capital at Kyoto, the emperor remained a remote figure, known mainly through literature and drama, never as a political presence. No one doubted the shogun was the paramount force in the country. So confident were the shoguns of their ascendancy that from the 1630s until the 1850s no shogun visited his "lord" at Kyoto but instead received imperial emissaries at their own court in Edo. The imperial household, moreover, was dependent for its income on lands granted by the shogun, and the imperial capital at Kyoto was governed by deputies dispatched by the bakufu to make sure that the emperor did not become involved in real politics. By the late Tokugawa period, the emperor lived secluded in his palace, presiding over a small court of aristocrats. Most of his activities—granting court ranks and titles, performing propitiatory ceremonies, and acting as patron of poets, artists, and classical dances—were remote from the world of real politics.

In theory, just as the emperor had delegated the "realm" to the shogun, the shogun in turn delegated basic functions of government to the local daimyo. The shoguns made no attempt to establish a monopoly of state power as many early modern monarchs did in Europe. The power to raise taxes, issue laws, raise military forces, and dispense justice was widely dispersed. The Tokugawa family itself administered only about one quarter of the country's landed wealth, and the rest was divided up into a patchwork of daimyo domains (*han*). The political order, usually called the *bakuhan* system (i.e., bakufu-han system) was designed to curb the daimyo and contain territorial fragmentation. Its central mechanisms were feudal in form. Even though their ancestors might have won all or part of their territory in battle, the daimyo held their domains as fiefs from the shogun, and whatever the size or origin of their domains, all were treated as the personal vassals of the shogun, bound to him by an oath of personal allegiance. The oath was renewed each time a new shogun was installed, and when a daimyo's heir took office, he was obliged to undergo an investiture ceremony in the shogun's presence. To be sure, the vassalage bond between shogun and daimyo, renewed more or less automatically, was largely pro forma, but it justified the right of the shogun to reward or punish the daimyo.

The Tokugawa dynasty consolidated its power firmly only in 1614–1615, after crushing a force of disgruntled samurai who rallied around Toyotomi Hideyori, the son of Ieyasu's political predecessor. The greatest fear of the Tokugawa rulers continued to be the possibility of insurrection by powerful vassals. To make sure that individual daimyo or a coalition of daimyo did not plot a similar uprising, Ieyasu and his successors promulgated laws that enjoined the daimyo to maintain surveillance on one another, limited the number of their samurai retainers, restricted the number and size of their fortifications, required approval of marriages with other daimyo families, and limited their autonomy in other ways. The sanctions for disobedience were severe. As a feudal lord, the shogun could reduce or even confiscate a daimyo's domain, and he was free to move the daimyo around the territorial

An 1863 woodblock print showing a shogun's procession marching through the streets of Edo. Note the commoners kneeling on the roadside to show their respect (as well as the little boys in the stable trying to peek over the wall).

chessboard if he found good cause to do so. By the early nineteenth century, punitive transfers or confiscations were rarer than they had been in the turbulent half-century following the battle of Sekigahara, but this reflected not so much a weakening of the shogun's powers as the growing docility of the daimyo.

This docility was due not simply to the cooling of ancient antagonisms; it was encouraged by the *sankin-kōtai* or alternate attendance system. At first by custom and then by law, all the daimyo were required to spend every other year in Edo, where their families were required to live at all times and a specified number of domain officials, retainers, and guards were to be maintained. This system grew out of the feudal practice of using hostages to control powerful vassals, as Ieyasu himself had been in his childhood. While the original purpose of the system was to keep an eye on the daimyo, in the long run it worked to transform the daimyo from fractious provincial warlords into pliant and free-spending courtiers, often more engrossed in ceremonies at the shogunal court and the pleasures of life at Edo than in the affairs of their own domains. The system weakened the daimyo financially as well. The costs of several mansions at Edo, the elegant progresses to and from the capital, and the conspicuous consumption demanded by attendance at the shogun's court made it increasingly difficult for many daimyo to make ends meet. In some domains, from 70 to 80 percent of the daimyo's income went toward defraying these costs.

While the daimyo were all subject to the same laws, their domains varied widely in size, and so did their political influence. In the seventeenth century, the daimyo had been divided into three main groups: the *fudai* or vassal daimyo, the *shimpan* or collateral daimyo, and the *tozama* or outside daimyo. This division reflected not wealth, strength, or prestige but political reliability. The fudai daimyo, descended from members of the original Tokugawa vassal band or men who had been made daimyo by Ieyasu and his successors, identified most closely with the interests of the bakufu. Their territories frequently abutted Tokugawa lands, protecting their flanks, and the bakufu's highest officials were drawn from their ranks. Not surprisingly, the fudai daimyo, as one historian has suggested, were more Tokugawa than the Tokugawa themselves.

The tozama or outer daimyo were descended from allies of Ieyasu too strong to be considered his direct vassals or from daimyo who submitted to his suzerainty only after the battle of Sekigahara. Their domains were large, on average twice the size of the fudai daimyo, and usually located on the periphery of the archipelago. The bakufu was anxious to keep them at arm's length. The farther the tozama were from Edo, the more difficult it was for them to mount a surprise attack. Since the tozama were the object of deep distrust, they were barred from holding offices in the bakufu administrative structure. So were the shimpan daimyo, but their political influence was not quite so limited. Newly created by the Tokugawa dynasty, the shimpan daimyo houses were branch houses set up to placate the sons of early shoguns who did not inherit the office and to provide collateral successors to the main line. Although formally excluded from office in the bakufu, the opinions of the shimpan daimyo, particularly the older and more prestigious houses such as Mito, Kii, and Owari, carried great informal weight, and when a shogun died without heirs, a successor was recruited from their ranks.

The fragmented nature of the *bakuhan* system had several long-run implications for political attitudes and behavior. First, since everyone, from the samurai on down, realized that their social and economic well-being depended on the daimyo rather than on the shogun, political loyalties were local not "national." Indeed, the modern Japanese term for "state" (*kokka*) referred not to the whole bakuhan system but to the individual domains. Second, political division kept alive a sense of rivalry among the domains. Not only did they compete for the favors of the shogun, but by the late Tokugawa they were often economic competitors as well. Beneath the apparently placid surface of the *pax Tokugawa* roiled a continual struggle among the domains to advance their own interests, often at the expense of others. And finally, political fragmentation made it difficult for the bakufu and the domains to take concerted action in the face of common crises such as natural disasters or country-wide famines. The exquisite balance between the centripetal and centrifugal impulses of the daimyo could produce stalemate at times when decisive action was needed. Indeed, it was only the appearance of an extraordinary outside threat, the arrival of Western gunboats, that finally forced the ruling elite to think of Japan as a single political body. Until this intrusion, any emerging sense of "nationalism" or "nationhood" remained confined to the realm of cultural identity.

THE WEB OF GOVERNMENT

With such a clutter of local jurisdictions, one might think that government in late Tokugawa Japan was in a state of unimaginable confusion. Paradoxically, political fragmentation did not weaken government. Rather it enabled political authority to reach far deeper into the daily lives of the people than in most pre-industrial societies. Despite its outwardly feudal structure, Japan was in many respects a model bureaucratic state. Most daimyo domains were small enough that every village and every peasant lived no more than two or three days' journey from the castle town; the same was true of the Tokugawa lands in the hinterland of Edo. Officials, who kept meticulous account of everything that went on in their domains, stacked their offices high with records and documents of every conceivable kind, from land surveys to population registers, which recorded all of the population in some way or other. (In the domain of Morioka, a horse-breeding area, even the pregnancies of mares were recorded.) To scrutinize the comings and goings of travellers, the bakufu set up checkpoints (*sekisho*) along all the main highways, and peasants had to carry permits when they went on pilgrimages to distant temples or shrines. While government was much "smaller" than in any modern state, the density of the administrative network was remarkable for a pre-industrial society.

The daimyo, responding to pressure from Edo, modelled their domain governments on the bakufu. Leadership was collective, conciliar and oligarchic. By the late Tokugawa period, neither the daimyo nor the shogun normally made major political decisions by themselves. Usually, they were mere figureheads who accepted decisions made by personal favorites or small groups of advisors. In the bakufu, the decision-making role was played by the *rōjū* (council of elders), a body made up of middling-size fudai daimyo, informally dominated by a chief elder (*rōjū shūseki*). These high officials controlled bakufu finances, promoted and demoted lower officials, and made critical policy decisions. In the domains, the same role was played by the domain elders (*karō*) recruited from the highest ranks of the daimyo's retainers. This conciliar style protected the bakufu (and the domains as well) against the possibility of weak or incompetent hereditary leaders, who were all too common. For example, the shoguns who reigned after the middle of the eighteenth century were often incompetent, inattentive, or immoral—and in at least one case, incontinent as well.

The politics of the bakufu, like those of the domains, were cliquish, secretive, and personal. Within the bakufu, the prestige and the power of the elders, especially the chief elder, enabled them to build up personal cliques and factions knitted together by friendship, patronage, marriage, and money. Astute clique leaders gathered round them able and reliable cohorts, and intrigued to secure backing among the shogun's direct retainers, other fudai daimyo, and the shimpan houses. The women of the "great interior," the living quarters set aside for the shogun's mother, nurses, wife, and concubines (along with their several thousand personal attendants), were also deeply involved in shogunal palace politics. Invariably, the palace women worked behind the scenes to influence disputes over the shogunal succession, and they promoted the careers of their fathers, brothers, uncles, or other male relatives whenever they could. So did the wives and consorts of the daimyo.

The day-to-day business of government was carried on by the shogun's petty liege vassals (*hatamoto* and *gokenin*) or by the daimyo's samurai retainers, who were recruited to serve as civil officials. In medieval times, the samurai had been warriors, living on the landed fiefs and answering the summons of the daimyo in time of war, but after the establishment of the bakuhan system the daimyo had moved them off the land into castle towns where they were supported by annual stipends. Instead of serving their lords solely as fighting men, they served them by collecting taxes, overseeing domain finances, settling civil disputes, enforcing criminal laws, managing economic enterprises, maintaining roads and fortifications, or performing some other kind of official service. By late Tokugawa, the samurai were no more swashbuckling fighting men than the daimyo were battle-hardened generals.

The most important task of the civil officials was collecting the land taxes that provided the samurai their stipends and financed the daimyo's household. The basic tax was collected in rice, the staple crop of the peasantry and the main standard of value for the ruling class. (For example, the size of domains, the ranks of retainers, and the salaries of officials were all reckoned in so many *koku* [about five bushels] of rice.) The machinery for collecting taxes was small, efficient, and economical. Instead of taxing individual farmers or households, the shogun and daimyo levied taxes on the whole village and let the villagers decide among themselves how much each household should pay. As long as the proper quotas were delivered to samurai district intendants (*daikan*), and or in some domains to the castle town itself, the ruling authorities did not concern themselves with how it was collected. The district intendant usually worked with a small staff of clerks, recorders, and guards drawn from the lower samurai ranks and paid for their services. Although petty corruption and bribery were not unusual, the system avoided the abuses of tax-farming common in countries like China and India, where taxes were collected by private individuals or contractors, who made personal profit by squeezing as much as possible from the peasants and forwarding as little as possible to the government. Save for a small amount added for administrative and transportation costs, nearly all of the tax revenues reached bakufu or domain treasuries. The result was a very high effective tax rate, perhaps 25 to 30 percent of the harvest, according to one estimate.

Military forces were also recruited from the ranks of the samurai. The bakufu had its own fighting force of direct vassals, but it required the daimyo to maintain armies and arsenals as well. In theory, by calling on the daimyo, the shogun could summon a host of several hundred thousand samurai in time of emergency. In fact, however, no major civil wars or rebellions occurred after the 1630s, and these samurai forces served primarily as a constabulary. The shogun's direct vassals stood guard at his castles or manned small garrisons at key strategic points, and the fudai and shimpan daimyo provided men to perform the vestigial function of protecting the outer perimeters of the Tokugawa domain against attacks from domestic rivals. Such attacks never came, and by the late Tokugawa period membership in the guard forces was a matter of hereditary prestige, with little relation to military skill or prowess. Rutherford Alcock, first English Minister to Japan, noted in the 1850s that the guard houses throughout Edo were "generally occupied by boys or superannuated old men, who spend their whole time squatting on their knees and heels and either dozing or smoking the pipe of apathetic idleness."[2]

A meticulous concern for privilege, protocol, and prerogative guided high bakufu and domain officials. Most saw themselves as stewards of ancestral traditions stretching back to the days of Ieyasu. One eighteenth-century daimyo, for example, enjoined his officials to "rest upon the respectful adherence to the laws of the previous generation and to their elaboration."[3] Policies might change, he said, and old usages might no longer fit new situations, but every effort should still be made that "basic laws and important precedents shall not be put aside." Samurai officials tended to be conservative, reluctant to challenge precedent, and inclined to take refuge in "ancestral customs"—which they occasionally invented—but these attitudes by no means inoculated domain or bakufu politics against conflict or change. There was constant factional infighting among official cliques, which occasionally erupted into public disputes, and practically every domain went through periods of reform when conscientious officials attempted to strengthen the domain or set its finances aright by advocating bold new measures.

The rhetoric of reform revolved around the notion of "benevolent government" (*jinsei*), a term that embodied the prevailing view of the purpose of government. In Confucian discourse, "benevolence" referred to the basic human altruism, the instinct to help, protect, and nurture other human beings. The Confucian classic, the *Mencius*, for example, pointed out that when a stranger saw a small child teetering on the edge of a well his natural impulse was to save it. By extension, "benevolent rule" meant that the ruler should protect and nurture the whole society, putting aside private or personal interests to serve the "people" or the "realm." As one eighteenth-century daimyo wrote,

> The state [*kokka*] is inherited from one's ancestors and passed on to one's descendants; it should not be administered selfishly. The people belong to the state; they should not be administered selfishly. The lord exists for the state and for the people; the state and the people do not exist for the sake of the lord.[4]

Reform-minded officials who saw their lords straying from this ideal could remind them that the failure to rule benevolently would invite "Heaven's punishment"—personal misfortune, removal from office, popular rebellion, or even assassination.

Although late Tokugawa government was hardly representative or democratic, it was flexible enough to respond to problems when it needed to. In times of crisis, the system remained flexible enough to produce visionary samurai officials, with little patience for convention or precedent, who quickly rose to positions of leadership when the times called for radical change. Factional struggles brought shifts in domain policy and turnover in domain leadership. To be sure, the domains tried to avoid public confrontations, since the bakufu could seize on local unrest as an excuse to confiscate a domain or remove its daimyo from power, and more often than not, factional disputes were resolved by negotiation or mediation. The losers were often dismissed and sent into retirement on grounds of malfeasance, corruption, or some other charge. The late-eighteenth-century bakufu leader, Matsudaira Sadanobu, for example, was forced out of office for his alleged affront of a member of the imperial family, but the real reason was opposition to his stringent policy of reducing bakufu expenditures.

THE SAMURAI ELITE

The samurai elite were a relatively large group. If their families are included, the samurai class amounted to about 6 percent of the population, a proportion very much larger than any European aristocracy and larger even than the non-aristocratic scholar-official class in China. Within the samurai class, however, the range of wealth and prestige was wide. The great retainers of the large daimyo often enjoyed incomes as large as those of small daimyo, while country samurai (*gōshi*) or foot soldiers (*ashigaru*) had to survive on stipends barely sufficient to sustain their families. In some domains, high-ranking samurai families had retainers or rear-vassals (*baishin*) of their own, adding further complexity to the class. In many cases, the social distance between the lower samurai ranks and the upper was as great as it was between lower samurai and commoners. (In the domain of Nakatsu, when lower samurai met high-ranking retainers, they were required to prostrate them-selves on the ground, and children of lower samurai families used less elegant language than upper samurai children.)

Historians have long debated where to draw the precise divisions among the upper, middle, and lower strata of the class, but the important thing to note is that such distinctions signified enormous differences in wealth, polit-ical influence, access to office, opportunities for education, and feelings of self-respect. The upper samurai, usually no more than a handful of families in most domains, served as domain elders, lived in splendid villas at the cen-ter of the castle town, and married their sons and daughters to the daimyo's offspring. By contrast, the lower samurai, far and away in the majority, lived in crowded dwellings on the edge of the commoner quarters, often with little or no contact with the daimyo, serving as petty guards, runners, messengers, or clerks. In between lay the middle ranks who had the right of audience with their lord and who occupied posts as officers in the daimyo's guard, as magistrates in the central domain administrative offices, or district intendants.

Samurai rank was hereditary, passed on from father to son, and normally office was linked to rank, with the higher posts reserved for the upper and middle samurai. But within this framework there was room for competition and upward mobility. Since there were usually more samurai in a particular rank than offices to fill, selectivity in recruiting was possible. If an individual samurai showed special talent, he could often work his way a step or two be-yond the offices normally open to him. Rising on the ladder of preferment brought an extra stipend (*tashidaka*), and it could also mean temporary pro-motion to higher rank. Although the samurai class never became a meri-tocracy like the Chinese scholar-official class or the modern civil servant, a samurai could be rewarded for special skills or accomplishments.

The ethos of the samurai, sometimes called "the way of the warrior" (*bushidō*) or "the way of the samurai" (*shidō*), blended an older ethic of vio-lence with a newer ethic of merit. The image of the samurai as a warrior ready to lay down his life in the service of his lord persisted into Tokugawa times. One side of the samurai ethic celebrated all the virtues the medieval samurai had needed on the battlefield—fearlessness, physical prowess, mag-nanimity, self-sacrifice, and indifference to death. *Hagakure (Under the Shadow of Leaves)*, an early eighteenth-century moral tract, called upon the samurai to "educate themselves for death" and to serve their lords with the same pas-sion and devotion as they would a lover. The other side of the samurai ethic, however, rested on an image of the samurai as a model Confucian "man of virtue" who provided moral leadership for the rest of society. It stressed the civic virtues—literacy, industry, fortitude, prudence, and austerity—needed by samurai in their roles as officials. While the two sides of the samurai ethic might seem contradictory, they were regarded as complementary, and the house codes of the daimyo urged their samurai retainers to cultivate both the civil (*bun*) and martial (*bu*) sides of their lives.

As many historians have pointed out, the samurai ethic proved to be a positive asset for mid-nineteenth-century Japan. It shaped a ruling elite keenly sensitive to military threat and endowed with a strong sense of public purpose. At the time, however, the high standards set by the samurai ethic were the source of political and social criticism as well. The majority of the samurai lived quiet and routine lives, punctuated by an occasional trip to Edo in the daimyo's procession or attendance at official ceremonies. Samurai were rarely if ever called upon to display the battlefield virtues of fearlessness and bravery, and they acquired martial skills—archery, swordsmanship, and horsemanship—more as personal accomplishments than out of necessity. This seemed to many a sign of samurai decadence. As one late eighteenth-century writer noted, most samurai had lost the "true martial spirit," and in time of crisis "seven or eight out of ten would be as weak as women and their morale as mean as merchants."[5] The image of the samurai as "man of virtue" or "cultivated man" also collided with social reality. It was clear that authority went to the well-born, who often had no particular capacities, moral or otherwise. Complaints that the highest leaders of the land were weak, ignorant, stupid, ostentatious, self-indulgent, extravagant, and arrogant were common among late Tokugawa samurai writers, who lamented that the most able and virtuous people were not exercising the influence that was their due. A feeling that leaders did not live up to their ideals was at the base of much social and political criticism in the early nineteenth century, and so was uneasiness at the discrepancy between the samurai ethic and the actual behavior of the class.

Still, such criticism was not sufficient to bring the whole samurai class to the point of open political dissent. In the end, most samurai realized that they were dependent on the bakuhan system and its leaders for both income and status. Unlike the rebellious gentry in seventeenth-century England, they were cut off from the land, and unlike the restive bourgeoisie of eighteenth-century France they were an established class enjoying hereditary privilege. Although discontent might move a minority to what one historian has called a "revolutionary rage"[6] the majority accepted their lot in life, comforted by their family pride, their sense of pedigree, and their outward badges of status. Far from wanting to overthrow the bakuhan system, even those samurai who criticized their society wanted it to live up to its stated ideals. They were less future-oriented radicals than backward-looking fundamentalists.

VILLAGE POLITICS

From the perspective of the samurai, the mass of the population were passive actors in the processes of governing. The commoners, frequently referred to as "the ignorant people" (*gumin*), were described as selfish, superstitious, and indifferent to the public good. As one Confucian scholar put it: "The common people were too busy attending to their own business . . . to have any time to cultivate themselves in the ways of virtue and morality, so among them avarice knows no bounds, the stronger preying on the weak, . . . just like so many birds and beasts battling with each other."[7] The commoners needed to be guided, disciplined, and regulated—but not consulted. To be sure, in many domains (and on bakufu territory as well) the samurai authorities recognized the right of commoners to complain, and public petition boxes were a valuable source of information about what was going on in the domain. If commoners petitioned for tax relief because of crop failure, that alerted the castle town authorities to impending food shortages, and if they complained about official corruption, that was a signal to bring officials back into line. The use of petition boxes appears to have increased by the early nineteenth century, though often they were used by disgruntled samurai as well as townsmen and villagers. But nothing remained more disturbing to the authorities than the prospect of aroused commoners taking concerted action to press their grievances. Indeed, the laws of the bakufu prohibited the commoners from any kind of collective political activity—banding together, distributing broadsides, or staging demonstrations.

In major towns and cities, samurai officials controlled the highest administrative level. Needless to say, the samurai inhabitants in the castle town and in Edo were under the domain authorities, who organized them into military-style units, but a city magistrate (*machi bugyō*) assisted by a small staff was placed in charge of the commoner sections. Much of the actual work of governing the commoner sections—keeping censuses, fighting fires, patrolling the streets, and pursuing criminals—was in the hands of the townspeople themselves. Rich merchants, artisans, and urban landlords served as city elders, acting as go-betweens for samurai officials and ordinary commoners; and in larger cities ward elders were appointed too. Ordinary commoners performed more practical tasks. In Edo, for example, commoners set up fire brigades to protect their neighborhoods and hired local constables to keep an eye out for suspicious characters and watch for fires. By the late Tokugawa period, these local functionaries sometimes made as much trouble as they fixed. Firemen who demolished houses and other buildings to make fire breaks were especially notorious for their rowdy ways, and often they seemed more interested in betting how fast the fires would spread than in putting them out.

While the commoners had only limited involvement in governance at the domain or bakufu level, villagers were not innocent of politics. As long as the peasants committed no crimes, avoided disputes with other villages, and paid their taxes, the samurai authorities left them to their own devices. Within these constraints, the political culture of the village took shape. Village politics centered mainly on the question of how to share assets and divide obligations. The most important issue was the allocation of land tax and labor service levies among the village households, but decisions had to be made about other questions affecting daily life and livelihood—the distribution of water rights, the marking of field boundaries, the punishment of disruptive villagers, the upkeep of the local Shinto shrine, the use of common meadow and forest land, and the keeping of village accounts.

Village government was dominated by "full-fledged peasants" (*hon-byakusho*), who held land and were responsible for paying taxes. Not only did they carry greater weight in village deliberations than landless peasants or tenant farmers, it was from their ranks that came the formal village leadership. A headman, usually assisted by a small number of other village officers, represented the village to outside authority. In some villages, the post was hereditary, handed down within one household over the generations; in others it was rotated among a small group of households; and in still others it was chosen by ballot. But the headman, who had to be confirmed by the district intendant, often enjoyed privileges reserved for the samurai, such as the right to wear silk, live in a large house, or wear a short sword. Since village decision-making was collegial and consensual, the headman had to enjoy the trust and confidence of the other villagers and he spent a good deal of time pouring oil on troubled waters, trying to ensure harmony, cooperation, and solidarity within the community. According to a set of instructions one early nineteenth-century headman left to his successor, "It is essential that a headman have wisdom, benevolence, bravery, and integrity; if he lacks any one of these qualities, he can not perform his duties."[8]

While the views of the wealthier households were important, discussion, negotiation, and conciliation were at the heart of village politics. Since economic competition was far more intense among the villagers than among the samurai, whose incomes were stable, disputes over everything from loans to land tenure were common. Villagers often quarrelled with the village headman over tax assessments and other matters, and in many villages a "peasant spokesman" (*hyakushodai*) was selected to check the headman's decisions and to ensure that all villagers were treated fairly. When harmony broke down, quarrels among peasant households could sometimes linger for generations. The domain authorities, who preferred to have villages settle their own differences, discouraged law suits or other recourse to legal action. Disputes were mediated within the village, often resolved by written agreements claimed to have been reached after "mature and harmonious discussion." The language of harmony belied the prevalence or squabbling among the villagers, but it reminded them of how important the collective stability of the community was. Although these agreements could not be enforced in any court of law, they recorded a consensus that bound the signers and their descendants into the future.

The sense of community that bound villagers in normal times continued to work when villagers found themselves in conflict with higher authorities. Peasant disturbances (called *ikki*) occurred frequently during the late Tokugawa period. Between 1770 and 1871, more than 1800 cases, or an average of about 18 a year, were recorded. Despite the widespread aversion toward conflict, peasant protest had become a normal part of the political culture, as strikes and demonstrations have in twentieth-century Japan. Just as the villagers paid taxes collectively, they aired their grievances collectively too. Headmen occasionally made direct appeals to the authorities on behalf of the villagers, but more often the villagers presented petitions or appeals signed by all the village household heads. Often their signatures were in a circle so that no villager could be ranked above any other, nor any singled out as a leader. As one historian has pointed out, "In the eyes of the peasants and the townspeople, . . . acting as a group gave their demands a legitimacy that transcended prohibitions on united and concerted action."[9]

Peasant protests often began with legal appeals or petitions through regular channels, then escalated into boisterous confrontation when higher authorities turned a deaf ear. If their grievances were ignored by the district intendant, the peasants might go over his head to appeal to the daimyo, or in dramatic cases to high bakufu officials, in defiance of official prohibitions. To show their anger, large bands of peasants, sometimes in the thousands, simply fled from their villages to neighboring domains to call attention to how badly they were governed. In handling peasant protests, the authorities were usually patient and rarely resorted to force unless the protestors themselves turned to violence, venting their anger by attacking the district intendant's office or trashing the houses and storehouses of well-to-do local peasants and merchants.

The rash of peasant disturbances in late Tokugawa Japan, in the eyes of some historians, demonstrates the existence of widespread peasant discontent. Discontent no doubt there was, especially when harvests were poor and famine was widespread, but few disturbances lasted more than a week or so, and usually they were resolved by concessions from the authorities. When crowds of peasants descended on a domain office, samurai officials tried to disperse them with appeals to act reasonably and promises of concessions, and only if that failed did they resort to force or threat of punishment. For their part, the peasants did not speak a language of defiance, proclaiming their rights, but rather a language of persuasion, calling on the daimyo and his officials to act "benevolently" or reminding them that conditions were once better in the "good old days" under their ancestors. The peasants often appealed to the daimyo's economic interests as well, pointing out that if taxes were so high that the peasants could not eat or plant seed for the following year, the domain would lose the basic source of its wealth. At the core of most peasant disturbances was not revolution but negotiation.

It should be remembered, however, that once disturbances had subsided the samurai authorities meted out harsh reprisals to remind peasants that however reasonable or grievous their complaints might be civil disobedience would not be tolerated. The village ringleaders were punished, often by death; fines were levied on the village; and the villagers were forced to promise never to be disorderly again. These tactics seem to have succeeded. Rarely did a village or locality become involved in a serious disturbance more than once, and seldom did a village produce leaders for more than one. Although the ruling elite was willing to accept that the lord should act "benevolently," they also insisted that the "foolish people" should respond by fulfilling their own obligations—leading frugal and orderly lives, paying their taxes, and showing respect for authority.

THE BAKUFU AND THE OUTSIDE WORLD

While the bakufu was not a "national government" in the modern sense, the Tokugawa shoguns took charge of relations with the outside world. As many historians have pointed out, by regulating contacts with foreign countries the bakufu was able to enhance its prestige and to block dangerous liaisons between the daimyo and foreigners. Like many pre-modern regimes, including Qing China and Yi Korea, the bakufu maintained several portals open to foreign trade, but limited access to the country and placed foreign sojourners under tight supervision. Although this policy is often referred to as a "seclusion" or "closed country" policy, the Japanese did not think of it in those terms until the early nineteenth century when they learned that was the way the Europeans described it.

Ironically, in the sixteenth century the Japanese at first welcomed the Europeans, whom they called "southern barbarians," because they sailed to Japan from the south through the China Sea. In the western island of Kyushu, local daimyo cultivated contacts with the Portuguese, whose ships brought in profitable trade goods and highly coveted firearms. In a canny effort to monopolize trade, several daimyo converted to Catholicism and ordered their samurai vassals to do so as well. By 1600, the Jesuit mission in Japan claimed 300,000 Japanese converts, and indigenous priests and proselytizers were being trained in Jesuit seminaries. The success of the foreign religion excited the suspicion of the newly established Tokugawa regime, and so did the activities of the "southern barbarians" elsewhere in the world. When Protestant traders from England and Holland arrived in Japan at the turn of the seventeenth century, they pointed to the Spanish conquest of the Philippines and Mexico as the true measure of the intentions of the Catholic countries. Bakufu leaders, worried that native Christians might be more loyal to the pope in Rome than to the bakufu, took these warnings to heart.

Shortly before his death, Tokugawa Ieyasu issued decrees prohibiting the practice of Christianity on bakufu domains, but only under his grandson, Tokugawa Iemitsu, did a systematic campaign to suppress the religion begin. European missionaries were expelled, and native converts forced to recant or face torture and execution. To quarantine the country against further contact with the foreign religion, in the early 1630s the bakufu issued edicts that forebade Japanese to leave the country without permission and promised death for those living abroad if they returned. It also tightened controls over European ships putting into Japanese ports and placed a ban on the construction of vessels capable of navigating the high seas. The bakufu's anti-Christian policy took final shape after a major rebellion broke out in Kyushu at Shimabara, a region earlier under the control of a Christian daimyo. The rebellion began in 1637 as a popular protest over harsh taxes, but the rebels took as their leader a young Christian samurai, Amakusa Shirō, whom they proclaimed to be a "Heavenly angel." Rumors spread that the Portuguese were helping the rebels. After a ruthless crackdown that slaughtered tens of thousands of men, women, and children, the bakufu forbade Portuguese ships from entering Japanese ports and required all other foreign vessels to put in only at the port of Nagasaki.

The anti-Christian seclusion policy was aimed at crushing potential subversion but it was not intended to cut off economic ties with the outside world. The bakufu wanted to maintain and control the lucrative trade that had developed with the rest of Asia. It allowed the Dutch East India Company, whose agents had assured bakufu authorities that they had no interest in propagating their religion, to continue trading at Nagasaki. In 1641, the Dutch agents were confined to Deshima, a small man-made island, where bakufu officials could keep an eye on them, but the Dutch did not seem to mind as long as they were able to make money. Nagasaki was also host to a community of several thousand Chinese merchants, who were also restricted to their own quarter but allowed to maintain their own temples and markets. The Dutch and the Chinese linked Japan with a wider regional market, bringing in goods from the Philippines, the Dutch East Indies, and other parts of Southeast Asia as well as from China.

The bakufu opened other trade routes to the continent as well. Shortly after banning the Portuguese, the bakufu urged the daimyo of Tsushima, an island in the Korean straits, to establish trading ties with Korea. The Tsushima domain was eager to do so, since there was not enough land on the island to feed its population, and trade provided income for the daimyo. The bakufu also encouraged Satsuma to continue its trade with the kingdom of Okinawa in the Ryukyu Islands, which the domain had conquered in the early seventeenth century. Chinese silks, Korean ginseng, and other luxury goods flowed into the country through both Tsushima and Satsuma. Although the Ryukyu route was shut down in the late seventeenth century, a clandestine smuggling trade with Satsuma continued.

By the early eighteenth century, bakufu officials began to doubt the desirability of trade. The Japanese paid for their imports with silver and copper dug from bakufu-controlled mines. The exhaustion of silver ore veins made it more and more difficult to mint silver coins, and some bakufu officials concluded that the outflow of silver was the root cause of the problem. Arai

Hakuseki, an advisor to the shogun, recommended severe restrictions on trade:

> Let us think of our national products in terms of the human body. Our agricultural products are like hair; it continues to grow no matter how we cut it. Our mineral wealth is like the skeleton, however; once gone it cannot be replaced. . . . To exchange mineral wealth that we ourselves need for useless trifles from other lands is to ignore the far-reaching interests of our country.[10]

These ideas were not very different from those of contemporary mercantilist thinkers in Europe, who measured a country's national wealth and strength not by its trade or productivity but by its store of gold and silver. In any case, by the early eighteenth century the Japanese had begun domestic production of many luxury import goods such as fine silk yarn and silk brocades. Trading relations with the Dutch, Chinese, Koreans, and Ryukyu Islanders continued, but since the bakufu banned the export of silver by the late eighteenth century the volume of trade had dropped appreciably.

The bakufu maintained few formal or ceremonial ties with its neighbors. Relations with Korea had been poisoned in the 1590s when Hideyoshi, Tokugawa Ieyasu's predecessor, had mounted two invasions against the peninsula, at considerable cost to the Koreans. To restore friendly ties, Ieyasu adopted an uncharacteristically humble position. He admitted that the Japanese had been at fault and repatriated Korean prisoners captured during Hideyoshi's campaigns. In 1607, the Korean court restored friendly relations by sending missions to Edo every several years. The court at Seoul did not regard the shogun as the peer of the Korean king, nor did the Korean authorities permit Japanese envoys to visit their capital, but few Japanese were aware of this asymmetry. The leisurely progresses of the Korean missions through Japan on their way to Edo left the impression that the Korean envoys came to pay court to the shogun. For all practical purposes, the Korean missions ceased after 1764, perhaps because trade with Japan was declining in importance. But the daimyo of Tsushima continued to serve as a conduit for official greetings and salutations between Edo and Seoul.

Neither did the bakufu maintain direct diplomatic exchanges with the Chinese. Although the Ming court, which helped the Koreans to repel Hideyoshi's invasions, refused to restore trading ties with the Tokugawa bakufu when the fighting ended, it called on the bakufu for military help during the Manchu invasion in the 1640s. The bakufu debated whether to send a military force but finally decided not to. When the Ming dynasty fell, a few loyalist Ming officials and scholars found refuge in Japan, where they were welcomed by Japanese Confucian scholars. Eventually the newly established Manchu Qing dynasty permitted trade to resume, but the bakufu declined to become a tributary state like most other countries on the periphery of China. Safely beyond the reach of Chinese armies, the Japanese elite had always shown a staunch independence toward China, and the Tokugawa shoguns, like most of their predecessors, refused to be drawn into a ceremonial relationship that subordinated them to the Chinese emperor. On the contrary, in a cunning manipulation of the Chinese tribute system, the daimyo of Satsuma not only required the Ryukyu kingdom to send tribute missions to the castle town of Kagoshima, it permitted them to send a mission to the Qing court as a way of acquiring Chinese trade goods.

By the late Tokugawa period, elite attitudes toward the outside world were strongly ethnocentric, though no more so than in Korea and China, or indeed anywhere else in the world. Like their neighbors, the Japanese had regarded the "southern barbarians" (which sometimes included Indians and Southeast Asians as well as Europeans) as crude and exotic peoples, whose manners and morals placed them beyond the pale of civilization. Popular lore even suggested that the Dutch belonged to another species. It was widely reported that the Dutch urinated like dogs, wore shoes with high heels because they had none on their feet, and were unable to bend their legs like ordinary humans. Nevertheless, the bakufu authorities remained curious about the Dutch, and the Dutch *kapitan* at Deshima was regularly summoned to Edo to appear before the shogun, who might call on him to dance a jig or sing a song. By the early eighteenth century, many bakufu officials and scholars were also beginning to show interest in the scientific and technical knowledge of the Dutch.

Attitudes toward China, to which Japanese culture owed a heavy debt, were more complicated. Just as a mastery of Latin or a knowledge of the Greek classics was the mark of an educated man in eighteenth-century Europe, so too a knowledge of Chinese and a mastery of the Confucian classics was the sign of a cultivated man in eighteenth-century Japan. Chinese metaphors and images filled the essays and poetry of the educated elite, and their discussions of political and social affairs were replete with allusions to Chinese history or Chinese culture heroes, such as Yao and Shun, the mythical founders of the Chinese state. In the seventeenth century, many Japanese scholars and intellectuals accepted the Chinese evaluation of the world, namely that Chinese wisdom and morality, embodied in the Confucian tradition, was the apex of civilized discourse. Hayashi Razan, who sought official bakufu patronage for Confucian learning, argued that Japan had been founded by refugees from China, and the early eighteenth-century Confucian scholar Ogyū Sorai referred to himself as a "stupid Eastern barbarian."

After the Ming dynasty was overthrown by Manchu invaders, cultural respect for China declined. Many Confucian scholars began to assert that Japan rather than China was the apex of civilization. Indeed, some claimed that Japan should be regarded as the "central kingdom" and contrasted the high moral purity of Japanese culture with the decadence of China's. The durability of the imperial institution was cited as proof that the Japanese embraced the Confucian ideals of "loyalty" and "filial piety" more faithfully than the Chinese did. While dynasties rose and fell in China, only one imperial family had ruled Japan. "Japan is praised even more than China as a land of superior men," wrote Kumazawa Banzan. "This is because except for China there is no other country in the world where the [Confucian] Way . . . is practiced with such purity and refinement. And *this* is because of the Imperial Court."[11] By the eighteenth century, the view that the Japanese followed the "Way" of Confucius more faithfully than the Chinese was commonplace. Indeed, Matsudaira Sadanobu, a bakufu official who sought to ban "heterodox" non-Confucian points of view from public discourse, remarked that even in the days of Yao and Shun China had not been able to surpass Japan in the benevolence of its rulers and the harmoniousness of its society.

The development of nativist thought or *kokugaku* ("national learning") in the eighteenth century was an even more potent expression of cultural ethnocentrism. Reacting to the heavy influence of Confucian ideas on Japanese culture, nativist thinkers tried to discover a Japanese "Way" that antedated the influx of morals, ideas, and institutions from China. By searching through the myths, legends, and semi-legendary history set down in the *Kojiki* ("Record of Ancient Matters") and the *Nihongi* ("Chronicle of Japan"), they hoped to find out what the Japanese had been like before they were warped by Chinese learning and Chinese culture. Scholars like Motoori Norinaga, for example, argued that the Japanese people had been much more spontaneous, emotional, and aesthetically sensitive before their contacts with the hard rational moralism of Confucianism. In this reading of the ancient Japanese texts, China became a corrupting force not a civilizing one.

During the early nineteenth century, another nativist thinker, Hirata Atsutane, used the Japanese foundation myths to argue that the Japanese were a kind of chosen people, whose country had been founded by the Sun Goddess and who enjoyed the special protection of the gods (*kami*). "Our country," he wrote,"as a special mark of the heavenly gods was begotten by them, and there is thus so immense a difference between Japan and all the other countries of the world as to defy comparison."[12] Indeed, Hirata regarded all other countries, Western and Asian alike, as inferior and contemptible. While other students of kokugaku confined themselves to literary or scholarly studies, Hirata sought a following among the common people, especially the more educated peasants and village leaders, and he propounded an elaborate cosmology that explained the links between the world of human beings and the world of the *kami*. By the early nineteenth century, nativism was developing deep roots in popular consciousness.

Although the stirrings of cultural nationalism had spread beyond the samurai elite, the strong sense of Japan's uniqueness or sacredness was always tempered by an awareness that more powerful countries, including China, existed in the outside world. Even though Japan might be at the moral center of the world it was by no means invulnerable. Indeed, the Japanese elite, living as they were on an island exposed to the sea at every point, remained sensitive to the possibility of outside attack by "barbarians." Both ethnocentrism and strategic anxiety proved to be assets in face of "threats from without." Unlike the Chinese scholar-official class, whose spongelike cosmopolitanism prevented them from realizing that their culture was not universally accepted and whose continental complacence made them indifferent to seaborne threats, the Japanese elite came to understand the cultural, technological, and military threat posed by the West relatively quickly, and their sense of cultural distinctiveness helped to mobilize political forces to deal with them.

ENDNOTES

1. Yamaga Sokō is quoted in Herschel Webb, *The Japanese Imperial Institution in the Tokugawa Period* (New York: Columbia University Press, 1968), 174.

2. Sir Rutherford Alcock, *The Capital of the Tycoon: A Narrative of a Three Years' Residence in Japan,* 2 vols. (New York: Harper & Bros., 1868), 152–153.

3. See John W. Hall, "The Nature of Traditional Society," in *Political Modernization in Japan and Turkey* (Princeton: Princeton University Press, 1964), 34.

4. Quoted in Mark Ravina, "State Building and Political Economy in Early Modern Japan," *Journal of Asian Studies,* 54, no. 4 (Nov. 1995), 997.

5. Quoted in John W. Hall, *Tanuma Okitsugu: Forerunner of Modern Japan* (Cambridge, Mass.: Harvard University Press, 1955), 112.

6. See Harry D. Harootunian, *Toward Restoration: The Growth of Political Consciousness in Tokugawa Japan* (Berkeley: University of California Press, 1970), 403–410.

7. Ryusaku Tsunoda et al. (comp.), *Sources of Japanese Tradition* (New York: Columbia University Press, 1965), 172.

8. Fujii Joji, "Nihon no kinsei," *Shihai no shikumi 3* (Tokyo: Chūōkōronsha, 1991), 268–270.

9. Anne Walthall, *Social Protest and Popular Culture in Eighteenth-Century Japan* (Tucson: The University of Arizona Press, 1986), 19.

10. Quoted in Tashiro Kazui, "Foreign Relations During the Edo Period: *Sakoku* Reexamined," *Journal of Japanese Studies,* 8 (Summer 1982), 299.

11. Kumazawa Banzan quoted in Herschel Webb, *The Japanese Imperial Institution in the Tokugawa Period* (New York: Columbia University Press, 1968), 171.

12. Hirata is quoted in Ryusaku Tsunoda et al. (comp.), *Sources of Japanese Tradition* (New York: Columbia University Press, 1965), 544.

3

Economic and Social Change

By modern standards, late Tokugawa Japan, like any pre-industrial country, was poor and backward, but by the standards of the time its economy was prosperous and thriving. In the late eighteenth century, Carl Peter Thunberg, a Swedish doctor and botanist stationed at the Dutch trading post in Nagasaki and a man who had seen a good bit of the world, was so impressed that he wrote, "Of all the countries that inhabit the three largest parts of the globe, the Japanese deserve to rank the first, and to be compared with the Europeans."[1] Economic historians today agree that pre-industrial economic growth during the Tokugawa period produced institutions, attitudes, and behavior that facilitated building a modern economy rapidly once Japan imported modern industrial technology. By the early nineteenth century, they argue, the economy was already in a state of potential change that needed only an outside stimulus to produce full-blown modern economic growth. But the social dislocations that accompanied these economic changes were matters of grave concern to the ruling elite, who saw their own position declining while others in society were gaining. What seem the marks of progress from today's perspective were seen as signs of moral decline by many late Tokugawa observers.

POPULATION INCREASE, URBANIZATION, AND DEMAND

Tokugawa officials, hungry though they were for information, were not as efficient as their great-great-grandchildren in gathering economic statistics, so the actual scale of economic growth during Tokugawa times is hard to measure with precision. This has not stopped economic and demographic historians from coaxing land registers, population censuses, tax records, and other documents to yield evidence of just how well developed the late Tokugawa economy was. One economic historian, for example, has estimated that per capita GNP in Japan during the early 1870s, before significant industrialization took place, was not so very different from that of England on the eve of its "industrial revolution," and that both the Japanese and the English had reached levels of economic well-being significantly higher than countries like India.[2] If true, this estimate suggests that Japan had a healthy head start toward industrialization over its Asian neighbors.

Although the Japanese carried on some trade with the outside world, the economy achieved growth without the stimulus of overseas markets. As one contemporary Dutch observer noted, the Japanese economy seemed to thrive without extensive international contacts:

> Ever since the Empire hath been shut up, nature, that kind mistress, taught them, and they themselves readily own it, that they wholly subsist upon what it affords, and that they have no need of being supplied by foreigners with the necessities of life.[3]

What drove economic change was an expansion of domestic demand. As the population rose and more people moved into towns and cities, domestic producers found new and better ways to satisfy basic needs for food, clothing, and other basic necessities. The economy did not grow evenly nor in linear fashion, and it experienced no dramatic technological breakthroughs, but by fits and starts small institutional and technical changes produced significant increase in output.

The dimension of population growth during the Tokugawa period is a matter of some dispute. No reliable population figures exist until 1721, when the bakufu ordered censuses to be taken at six-year intervals. It is not surprising that guesses about the size of the population at the beginning of the Tokugawa period vary widely, from as high as 18 million to as low as 9.8 million. The most widely accepted current estimates, however, suggest that the population doubled from 12 million in 1600 to 27.7 million in 1700, then fluctuated from a high of 32 million in 1730 to a low of 30.6 million in 1800. The seventeenth-century population explosion is not hard to explain. With the political unification of the country after a long period of civil war, human and natural resources were no longer squandered in combat, and people were no longer dying in battle or suffering from famine that came in its wake. Warring daimyo, who had built up their material strength by constructing irrigation systems, reclaiming waste land, and other large economic projects, found that their domains could support larger populations once peace came. Indeed, an increase in population—which meant an increase in peasant producers—was welcome because it meant yet more land could be brought under cultivation.

The slowdown of population growth in the eighteenth century is more puzzling. According to one argument, demographic stagnation was the result of Malthusian pressures: too many mouths to feed and too little land to feed them. Since the size of the population had reached the point where it could no longer expand on the existing resources base, the argument goes, periodic famines killed off potential parents or forced peasants to practice infanticide (called *mabiki*, literally "thinning out"), particularly of female babies. This argument has been challenged by economic historians who suggest that by the eighteenth century many peasant families limited family size not to reduce their poverty but to maintain or improve living standards. Instead of "thinning out" babies at birth, pregnancies were often terminated by herbal medicines and other methods. And these economic historians argue that other factors may have been at work as well: late marriages reduced the fertility period of married women; male family members who inherited no land often remained bachelors; and migration to urban areas, where death rates were usually higher, also checked population growth.

It may not be necessary to choose among these arguments. Demographic change is a complicated process, and there were wide variations in local and regional patterns of population growth. For example, the southwestern parts of the country, particularly the large domains in Kyushu, tended to grow during the eighteenth century, while the domains in the northeast, with its harsher winters and shorter growing season, experienced a decrease. There is no doubt that bad weather, heavy floods, or bad harvests checked population growth. In the mid-1780s, such natural calamities led to the deaths of several hundred thousand people (from 200,000 to 900,000, depending on the estimate) by famine and disease, particularly in the northeastern Honshu. In 1784, for example, thirty domains in the region reported no harvest at all, and in other parts of the country yields were less than half of normal. In areas hit most hard, the effects of these famine deaths were felt for decades. But there is also evidence that in the more developed and affluent parts of the country rich and poor peasants alike chose to limit the size of their families in order to husband assets and resources. In other words, depending on the time and place, the eighteenth-century slowdown in population growth may have resulted either from economic desperation or economic affluence.

Urban population growth, especially in the seventeenth and early eighteenth centuries, was as dramatic as the overall demographic change. In 1600 Kyoto, the old imperial capital, was the only major urban center in Japan, but by 1800 perhaps 10 percent of the population lived in large towns and cities, making Japan one of the most urbanized societies in the world. Urbanization resulted from the political reorganization of the country under the Tokugawa dynasty. As the daimyo moved their samurai retainers off the land and into their castle towns, urban centers grew in size and importance. By the eighteenth century, there were more than 200 castle towns, ranging in size from 10,000 to 60,000 persons. The largest castle town of all, the shogun's capital at Edo, had become a metropolis, boasting a population of one million by the middle of the century, surpassing London, Paris, Vienna, and St. Petersburg in size. In the Kansai region, the great commercial city of Osaka, south of Kyoto, had grown to about 400,000 persons. Post towns sprang up along the great highways linking Edo to the rest of the country and catered to the needs of daimyo processions and other travelers, and scores of ports with populations in the 10,000s emerged to service a lively coastal shipping trade.

The growth of castle towns and other urban settlements stimulated economic development in a way that rural villages could not. The samurai households and their servants, who accounted for a majority of the population in the castle towns, neither produced their own food nor fashioned their own goods. Instead they lived on annual stipends that came from the agricultural surpluses flowing into the castle towns as tax payments. The castle towns thus became important centers of consumption, providing concentrated markets for basic goods that the samurai class did not produce for itself. The middle and upper samurai, who spent much of their income on official functions, private rituals like weddings and funerals, complicated protocols of gift-giving, and other forms of conspicuous consumption also created demand for luxury goods, and so did town merchants anxious to display their wealth, albeit often clandestinely. As a consequence, urban markets grew steadily.

The establishment of the bakuhan system provided the initial impulse for urbanization, but urban centers continued to grow by attracting migrants from surrounding rural areas. The castle towns were powerful generators of employment, particularly for sons of peasants unable to find work as farmers. Construction workers, carpenters, plasterers, and stone masons were needed to build the growing towns and cities—and rebuild them after devastating fires that periodically leveled them. In the commercial and entertainment sections, there was work as well for day laborers, shop clerks, apprentices, porters, waitresses, and prostitutes. Often, employment was seasonal, and the size of the commoner population fluctuated throughout the year. While urban commoners did not enjoy guaranteed incomes as the samurai households did, they, too, contributed to the steady expansion of demand, spending most of their income on food and the rest on clothing, furniture, and daily utensils.

By the early nineteenth century, Japan was on its way to becoming a nation of avid consumers. As the woodblock prints and illustrated guide books of the times make vividly clear, the streets in the commoner sections were clogged with shoppers buying everything from kimonos and swords to patent medicines and cheap toys. Itinerant peddlers wandered through residential districts hawking bean curd and cooking oil with their distinctive cries, and upscale merchants carried samples of porcelain and brocade to samurai mansions, discreetly offering credit that could be settled at the end of the year. Even peasant villagers in the more developed areas were able to spend cash on goods that would have seemed outlandish luxuries to their great grandfathers a century before, and small shops selling sundry goods could be found in many villages. Fujita Yūkoku, an advisor to the Mito daimyo, complained, "High and low compete in ostentation and luxury while government becomes more and more lax. This is an age when money buys anything."[4]

AGRICULTURAL GROWTH

Growth of output in the agricultural sector—which fed the whole society, employed 80 to 85 percent of its members, and produced most of its surplus wealth—was at the base of overall growth. Although its share of output probably diminished over time, even in the early 1870s agriculture still accounted for more than 60 percent of total production. According to conventional Confucian discourse, agriculture was the foundation of society, without which it could not survive. During the seventeenth century, many daimyo financed large-scale projects to expand arable land or improve irrigation systems: flood control projects tamed many of the country's short and shallow rivers; dikes and reservoirs were built to hold irrigation water; and marshy lowlands near the coast were reclaimed by drainage. In many parts of the country, along the coastline and in former flood plains villages appeared on "new fields" (*shinden*) reclaimed from marginal land.

A spurt of agricultural output took off in the seventeenth century, but estimates suggest that not until the eighteenth century did it begin to keep pace with the growing number of mouths. As population growth slowed down, however, the productivity of the soil overtook the reproductivity of its inhabitants, and the per capita food supply grew slowly. It has been estimated that rice production rose from 19.7 million koku in 1600 to 30.6 million in 1700 and 37.6 million in 1800. The production of other cereal crops like barley, wheat, millet and buckwheat probably showed similar gains, and the humble sweet potato, which arrived from the New World, became a staple for poorer peasant households in Kyushu and western Japan. Requiring no irrigation, it flourished on dry upland fields where it was difficult to grow rice.

Unlike Europe or Latin America with their great estates, haciendas, or manors, the agricultural economy in Tokugawa Japan was dominated by small-scale cultivators. Most farming was done by individual peasant households who worked small land holdings with occasional outside help. Peasants relied mainly on human muscle. Draft animals were expensive to keep and feed, and land was too valuable to be given over to grazing pasture. Although farm animals could be found in most villages, probably fewer than 10 percent of the peasant households owned them. Women household members worked in the fields alongside their husbands, sons, fathers, or fathers-in-law, providing an important part of household labor, and households with more land than they could manage by themselves hired laborers by the day or year. With human muscle so abundant, there was little need to rely on animals, and the application of human labor to the land became more intensive as farming technology improved.

Scenes of peasants at work. At the top, they dam up a water course to irrigate the rice fields; two women sort rice seed, while the men below them fertilize a seed bed; at the bottom, a man and horse plow a flooded rice field.

While peasants worked with the simplest hand tools, the sickle and the hoe, the increase in agricultural production owed much to improved farming techniques. By the early eighteenth century, handbooks for farmers showed how to make two stalks of rice grow where one grew before. Small mechanical innovations such as a three-toed hoe and a "thousand-tooth" thresher speeded up cultivation and harvesting, making it possible for peasants to plant second crops or work in agricultural by-employments. The development of new varieties of rice, some early ripening and some late ripening, permitted more intensive use of the land. Not only did this make double-cropping possible, it reduced the peasants' risk. With different rice paddies ripening at different times, the entire crop was less likely to be devastated by patches of bad weather. The use of commercial fertilizers increased the productivity of the soil. In western and central Japan, Osaka merchants marketed dried sardines or herring shipped from the north, and around Edo,

Osaka, and many castle towns vendors sold "night soil" collected from urban privies to spread on the fields. (Night soil from samurai households, thought to be of better quality, fetched a higher price.)

By the middle of the eighteenth century, many peasant households in the more urbanized areas along the Inland Sea and the Pacific coast, responded to new market opportunities by producing commercial crops as well as food. As cotton garments replaced coarser hemp linen among the commoner class, whole villages in the Kansai region devoted their fields to raising cotton, often in rotation with other crops, and gradually its cultivation spread eastward. The demand for silk textiles, worn by the samurai class and by rich commoners, stimulated the spread of sericulture. In remote upland or mountain villages, where it was difficult to grow rice, peasants planted mulberry trees, whose leaves silk worms munched at an astonishing rate before spinning their cocoons. Poorer regions, like the highland of central Honshu, found sericulture a welcome new local source of wealth. And in the hinterlands of the large cities and castle towns, peasant farmers raised fruits and vegetables for the urban marketplace and raised crops such as tobacco, rape seed, indigo, and safflower that could be turned into consumer goods.

By the early nineteenth century, agriculture had moved well beyond the subsistence farming in most areas, and peasants produced ever larger surpluses beyond their consumption needs. While the domains and the bakufu captured some of the new surpluses in the form of taxes, most fattened the pockets of peasant households, drawing them into the cash economy as they had not been in the early Tokugawa period. For peasants accustomed to producing for the market, money was no mystery. To be sure, the commercialization of the economy was most advanced in the core region stretching along the Inland Sea to the hinterland of Edo in the east, but it affected all but the most remote mountain villages, where some subsistence farming remained.

To prosper in the commercial economy, the rural population needed to keep records, issue bills and invoices, and compute gains and losses. As a result, literacy and numeracy were on the rise, not only in the towns and cities, but in rural areas as well. It goes without saying that the samurai and rich merchants were literate, and so were village leaders, who had to keep track of tax receipts, draft documents resolving disputes, and enforce official regulations. But more and more ordinary peasants were acquiring these skills too. Many successful peasant farmers, for example, kept diaries noting the times to plant and fertilize, and recording the size of the harvest yield. By 1800, many villages could boast a primary school or *terakoya* (literally "temple school"), often housed in a Buddhist temple or Shinto shrine, where the local priest, a village scholar or perhaps an impecunious samurai, led children through their lessons. According to one estimate, by the end of the Tokugawa period, perhaps 40 percent of all boys and 10 percent of all girls had experienced some formal schooling.

Literacy allowed well-to-do peasants and village leaders, especially in the hinterland of great cities like Edo, Osaka, and Kyoto, to share in the flourishing popular urban culture. They bought and read "best sellers" written by popular writers, such as Shikitei Samba's comic vignettes about lives of the urban lower classes or Takizawa Bakin's tales of warrior chivalry and adventure. Traveling jugglers, itinerant story tellers, or other popular performers had always traveled through the countryside, but by the early nineteenth century, *kabuki* and puppet troupes from the city put on local performances as well. In a few places, villagers even spent the long winter months preparing performances of their own, using scripts bought in the city and costumes following urban models. The wealthiest peasants, with large land holdings and ample leisure time, indulged in more elegant pursuits—poetry, tea ceremony, calligraphy, and collecting art objects—that mimicked the ways of the samurai elite, and their sons sometimes produced local histories or gazetteers recording peasant rebellions, floods and fires, or other dramatic local events.

But for all their involvement in the commercial economy and urban culture, most peasant households still lived by an ethic of scarcity, constantly aware that they were at the mercy of the weather and other accidents of nature. Only so much could be squeezed from the land. Conventional peasant morality stressed the values of perseverance, diligence, and frugality and warned against the dangers of indolence, indulgence, and extravagance. Regulations drafted by peasants in a late eighteenth-century village, for example, not only enjoined villagers to rise at six in the morning, stay sober, and abstain from quarrels with their neighbors; it also forbade young people from congregating in large numbers, prohibited villagers from "unsuitable entertainments," and set a curfew for the return of those who had left the village for "business or pleasure." Ninomiya Sontoku, an early nineteenth-century agricultural reformer and peasant moralist, advised farmers: "Work much, earn much, and spend little."[5] It was these qualities that could mean the difference between prosperity and ruin.

PROTO-INDUSTRIALIZATION

By the late Tokugawa period, what some economic historians call "proto-industrialization" was well underway. The term, borrowed from European economic history, refers to the production of goods for distant markets by small groups of workers using traditional technologies. Representing a transition to an "industrial revolution" based on mechanical power, proto-industrialization differed both from household production, where families made clothing and tools for their own use, and from artisanal production, where skilled craftsmen—cobblers, silversmiths, blacksmiths, and the like—produced goods for local markets. Proto-industrial production, moreover, was based not in the towns but in the countryside where labor was abundant and cheap. It was organized by small capitalist entrepreneurs interested in profit rather than satisfying their own needs. In a sense, proto-industrialization represented the halting first step toward mass production for a broad market. It corresponded to what other historians call "the stage of commercial capitalism."

In late Tokugawa Japan, the making of ordinary consumer goods—and luxury goods as well—relied on handicraft technology. Little mechanization of production had taken place, and nearly all the energy applied to production was supplied by human muscle. Neither wind power nor animal power were much used, nor was the water wheel very important. The limited use of water power is perhaps surprising given the hundreds of small rivers that descended swiftly to the sea, full of potential energy. Water wheels were used to polish rice or turn oil presses but the heavy dependence of rice agriculture on irrigation may have discouraged the use of water power for other purposes. Peasants were reluctant to share water with millers. Often rice polishing mills were allowed to operate only in the winter months when the rice paddies were dry. The abundance of human labor, providing readily available animate energy, may also have discouraged the spread of new power technology or labor-saving machinery dependent upon it.

Nevertheless, as in any economy where profit could be made by producing more or better goods at lower prices, there were strong incentives to improve materials, tools, and efficiency. There were few dramatic technological breakthroughs such as the invention of the steam engine or the spinning jenny, but small yet important technical advances took place in every kind of production from iron smelting to book publishing. With the exception of some traditional luxury handicraft production, no technology was exactly the same in 1800 as it had been a century or two before. In weaving, for example, the shift from a seated loom to a tall loom allowed weavers to work two or three times more rapidly, and in iron smelting the use of a man-powered bellows to force air through the furnace not only increased the output of pig iron but improved its quality as well. Technological change was a slow and anonymous process, often the work of several generations rather than the discovery of an individual inventor who made a sudden breakthrough. Change came as the result of trial and error, an ongoing process of experimentation, carried on in the workplace and not driven by scientific discovery. The technological innovators were master workers, experienced farmers, or craftsmen who were intimately familiar with the processes and materials at hand. No legal structure, such as a patent system, protected innovations, and technical secrets could not be hidden forever, so it was not uncommon for new technologies to spread.

Central to proto-industrialization were new ways of organizing production. While nothing like the modern-style factory emerged in late Tokugawa Japan, enterprises employing a dozen to several dozen workers under one roof and organized into a complex division of labor became more and more common. In most rural areas, small mills and breweries supplied the local population with such staple food products as soy sauce, bean paste, sake, or vegetable oil. By the early nineteenth century, such local enterprises accounted for a substantial proportion of all non-agricultural output. Since production was seasonal, young men from local farm families or neighboring districts were hired as temporary unskilled laborers to do much of the manual labor—hauling, lifting, and loading—while a handful of specialized workers supervised them. Iron smelting and mining, which also required a concentrated work force, kept workers employed more or less permanently, and productivity often improved as workers became more experienced. Indeed, if anything resembling a modern factory force had emerged by the early nineteenth century, it was to be found in these industries.

Side by side with these concentrated work places, more dispersed production similar to the "putting out" system of cottage industry in pre-industrial Europe developed in cotton textile production, especially in the Kansai region and along the Inland Sea. In the early seventeenth century, peasant women spun cotton yarn and woven cotton cloth for their own families, but as demand grew, a more complex division of labor emerged. Individual farm households began to specialize. As raw cotton was moved from one household to another, it was slowly transformed into cloth: raw cotton was carded in one household; the carded cotton spun into yarn in another; the yarn woven into cloth in the home of still another; and the cloth dyed or finished in a fourth. This chain of small household work places functioned like the assembly line of a modern factory. The entrepreneurs who financed the operation were often wealthier peasant households who invested in spinning wheels or looms and hired other villagers to work them on a part-time or full-time basis. Town and city-based merchants (*ton'ya*) became involved too, buying up raw cotton and then hiring peasant households to process it. By the early nineteenth century, whole villages had come to specialize in spinning or weaving, with the village inhabitants working for wages instead of tilling their fields.

The concentration of proto-industrial production in rural areas appears to have slowed migration to castle towns and large cities. As Thomas C. Smith has noted, not only did the population of large cities like Osaka begin to decline, but so did the populations of many older market centers. Instead, small country towns close to the rural market and the supply of rural labor grew in importance. The authorities in one castle town complained:

> People used to come into the castle town from the surrounding areas to shop or take goods on consignment in order to sell them in the country. But people from the castle town go to the country to shop, and town shopkeepers send agents to the country to arrange to receive goods on consignment. Thus the distinction between front and back, town and country has been lost; farmers and tradesmen have changed position.[6]

While this shift worked to the disadvantage of urban shopkeepers, merchants, and craftsmen, it provided new opportunities for peasant families. Well-to-do families who invested in non-agricultural production obviously profited, but so did the less well off, who had new opportunities to earn extra income through by-employments like spinning and weaving or work as manual or semi-skilled laborers in local breweries or mills. Indeed, the development of rural proto-industrialization all over Japan, but particularly in the core region, provided an economic cushion for villagers with little or no land. As a result, it created new agricultural surpluses that could be turned to consumption or even investment in small enterprises.

MERCHANTS AND MARKETS

In the early seventeenth century, the Tokugawa bakufu did what it could to encourage economic development. The authorities in Edo abolished the customs barriers that local daimyo had set up to tax goods traveling through their domains, and they tried to replace a confusing welter of local weights and measures with units standard throughout the country. The construction of highways linking the remotest extremities of the islands with the shogun's capital at Edo were intended not only to serve the daimyo processions but to provide avenues for trade, and new shipping routes were developed along the country's long coastline. Economic unification, which accelerated despite the lack of a parallel political unification, meant that goods could travel from one part of Japan to another in relative security and that commercial transactions could be carried on under more uniform conditions in all parts of the country. These institutional changes created the ligatures of a national market network, which the bakufu did its best to regulate and control.

At the highest level, this countrywide marketing network was shaped by the economic needs of the daimyo. All the domains, except for a few small ones, faced the problem of turning local resources into revenues. The most basic need was to convert tax rice into cash to defray the costs of the daimyo's castle, his residences in Edo, and his travels back and forth between them. Instead of marketing surplus tax rice locally, domains in western Japan began to send it for sale to Osaka, and those in the eastern part of the country to Edo. By the early eighteenth century, lumbering rice boats plied regular routes along the coasts of the Pacific and the Sea of Japan, picking up tax rice shipments headed for both cities. The Osaka market, which became the earliest center of the national rice trade, set national prices, influencing local rice markets throughout the country. As rural production became more diverse, domains began to ship other food products and fashioned goods to both Edo and Osaka. Between 1736 and 1840, for example, the value of trade flowing into Osaka grew enormously, but the most striking increase was in goods like cotton, salt, charcoal, and other non-agricultural products, which were "re-exported" to other parts of the country.

Many great merchant houses, which served as bankers, financiers, or fiscal agents for the domains or the bakufu, got their start with wealth accumulated in the rice trade. Turning their capital to new financial ventures, they went into the business of converting silver currency used in the Osaka rice market for gold currency used in official transactions, or earned commissions transferring funds between Osaka and Edo through paper credit transactions. The most lucrative, if not the most secure, profits for these wealthy merchants came from advancing funds to the daimyo or the shogun against their future tax revenues. Often these advances, in effect long-term loans, amounted to several years' worth of domain taxes, and since interest rates ran 15 to 20 percent per year, the profits were enormous. Occasionally, a great merchant house might find its wealth confiscated if it ran afoul of its political patron, but most continued to serve as fiscal agents for the daimyo, earning even a stipend and the right to wear a sword.

The largest and best known merchant houses, many originally from the Kansai region, survived over many generations. The house of Mitsui, for example, began as a dry goods business with shops in Kyoto and Edo, and later branched out into money lending and money exchange, but its fortunes took off in the 1690s when the bakufu chartered family members as official agents for transmitting to Edo receipts from the sale of bakufu rice in Osaka. In the domains, castle town merchants who developed close ties with the local daimyo were sometimes entrusted with the supervision of domain finances. Cautious to a fault, the household heads of these long-established merchant firms saw themselves less as entrepreneurs than as stewards of the family fortunes. A sense of obligation to their forebears, reinforced by custom, made them reluctant to risk the fortunes bequeathed to them by their ancestors, and merchant house codes stressed not only frugality and diligence, but also placed a high premium on following precedent and tradition. As the Mitsui house code put it succinctly, "Do not put your hand to any type of activity that has not been done before."[7] Since such injunctions focused on safe and secure profits rather than on adventurous innovation, it encouraged what economists call a "rentier" or "rent-seeking" mentality rather than an "entrepreneurial" one.

Urbanization promoted interregional trade in goods besides rice. Every conceivable kind of consumer good, from vegetables and pickles to crockery and ironware, flowed into the huge urban markets of Edo and Osaka. The teeming fish market at Nihonbashi, the vast drapery showrooms of the Echigoya, and the fashionable shops in downtown Edo teemed with buyers and sellers. If the great merchant princes of Osaka and Edo dominated the rice trade, wholesale merchants specializing in a particular product or in the products of a particular region played a central role in regional trade. To ensure a steady flow of goods into Edo and Osaka (and also to raise additional revenues), the bakufu began giving charters to associations (*kabu-nakama*) of such wholesale merchants—iron mongers, dry goods dealers, cotton merchants, tea dealers, silversmiths, and so forth—in the early eighteenth century. In return for a fee paid to the bakufu, members of the association were granted a monopoly over the sale of their particular goods within the city. The associations had the power to regulate prices, enforce standards of quality, and guarantee credit—and some also pooled funds to insure losses of individual members. As the volume of trade grew, the bakufu created many new associations in the 1760s and 1770s. Privileged merchants bought goods from local or regional wholesalers, then sold them to urban jobbers or retail shops, using their exclusive rights over the trade to buy as cheaply as possible and to sell as dear as possible. While not so closely tied with the ruling authorities as great merchant houses like Mitsui, their interests and fortunes were clearly linked with the bakufu.

Not all town merchants enjoyed inside political connections or built up vast fortunes passed from one generation to the next. The major towns and cities were filled with retail merchants, small shopkeepers, money lenders, jobbers, restaurant proprietors, fishmongers, and landlords who succeeded by dint of clever business practices, hard work, or just plain parsimony. In his *Tales from the Bathhouse (Ukiyoburo)* Shikitei Sanba provides a savage portrait of a petty money lender:

> All year around, he had gruel boiled in tea for breakfast, and just a little soup for lunch. At night all he had with his rice was pickled radish, but that takes a lot of salt to make, so he limited himself to just two slices for the whole meal, right up through his hot water at the end. . . . The only thing he ever had for a snack between meals was a little salted fried rice, with maybe a few soybeans somebody had sent him from the country—but not so many, you understand, that you could find them without a search party. . . . He honored his ancestors, and he kept a close watch on everybody's comings and goings, so it's no wonder he did so well for himself. Money makes money, . . . and before long he was a very rich man.[8]

Unfortunately the fictional skinflint's son, like many sons in real life, dissipated the family fortune by too many trips to teahouses and brothels.

By the early nineteenth century, many domain governments became deeply involved in trade. As heavy spending and heavy borrowing plunged domain finances deeper and deeper into the red, domain officials sought a piece of the profits merchants enjoyed by marketing local products through domain-controlled monopolies. By the late 1830s, perhaps one third of domains, including most of the larger ones (over 100,000 koku) set up marketing offices to "export" local products such as indigo, paper, wax, or sugar outside the domain or to monopolize the sale of "imports" of products from other domains. In 1830, for example, the domain of Awa earned a million gold pieces (ryo) from its indigo monopoly. Samurai officials managed these monopolies, often with the help of well-to-do castle town merchants, and sometimes they invited artisans from the outside to train local workers in new kinds of production. In larger domains, inspection stations were set up along the main roads and highways to stop the illicit movement of goods, but smugglers and clever merchants who distributed "gifts" to domain officials did not find them difficult to elude.

The ability of the bakufu to control trade was breaking down by the early nineteenth century. The domains by-passed the privileged kabu nakama merchant associations in Osaka and Edo in dealing with other domains, and so did aggressive provincial merchants. When a series of bad harvests brought famine and inflation in the 1830s, the bakufu finally put an end to the kabu nakama system, and the prohibition was extended to the domains the following year. The bakufu leader who instituted these changes, Mizuno Tadakuni, hoped to contain rising prices by laws controlling consumption and prices but he fell from power before he was able to do so. Even if he remained in office, it seems doubtful that he would have succeeded. By the mid-nineteenth century, the volume of trade and the complexity of the marketing system had simply grown beyond the capacity of any central authority to control.

THE SOCIAL IMPACT OF ECONOMIC GROWTH

A growing economy brought general prosperity, but it also brought social change, dislocation, and tension. The impact was as profound in the countryside as in urban areas. At the outset of the Tokugawa period, the elite had regarded the peasants as tax-producing machines whose surplus crops were to be gobbled up by the country's rulers. As one of Ieyasu's advisors put it, "It is fit that the peasants be treated so that they have neither too much nor too little."[9] Taxes were to take as much of the peasants' harvest as possible, leaving just enough for subsistence. If peasants tried to improve their lot by keeping aside some of their crops for capital, samurai officials feared that the social equilibrium would be upset: rulers would be deprived of revenue and invidious distinctions between rich and poor would create conflict among the commoners. To keep peasants from accumulating wealth, the law forbade them to buy or sell land, and taxes were fixed at high rates.

By the early nineteenth century, however, this exploitative view of the peasantry no longer fit social reality. Although agricultural production grew, tax rates did not change much over the years, and peasants often resisted by force official attempts at new land surveys. By the middle of the nineteenth century, taxes in many areas were based on assessments a century and a half old, even though the productivity as well as the amount of land under cultivation had increased enormously in the meantime. The new agricultural surpluses remained in the villages, increasing incomes and fueling the commercialization of the rural economy, but they also produced what the founders of the Tokugawa had feared: a growing gap between the rich peasants and the poor.

In the early seventeenth century, villages tended to be made of households with more or less the same landholdings, but as agriculture shifted away from subsistence farming to commercial production, aggressive and enterprising peasant households who realized that land could turn a profit did their best to increase yields or shifted to lucrative cash crops. As they accumulated profits, these entrepreneurial peasants accumulated more land as well. Clearing new fields or terracing hillsides for rice paddies was one way to do this, but another was to acquire land already under cultivation from their less enterprising or less fortunate neighbors. An active land market, made possible by various legal devices to circumvent the prohibition of land sales, generated inequalities in land holdings. An astute and acquisitive peasant who had put aside a small reserve would make loans to fellow villagers, often at rates of 10 to 20 percent a year. In return, the borrowers would put up their land as collateral or promise a portion of their harvest to the lender over an agreed period of years. But when a borrower found himself unable to repay the loan due to a crop failure, a drop in the rice price, death or sickness in the family, or simple laziness, the lender would either take the borrower's land in payment or turn him into a sharecropping tenant on his own land. In many villages, this process concentrated land holdings in the hands of a few households. The number of middling-size landholders dwindled, and the number of small holders, tenant farmers, and sharecroppers grew. Wealthy peasant landlords, living off income from rents, branched out into other profit-making enterprises such as pawnbroking or money lending, sake brewing, or cotton and silk textile production.

Widening stratification within the village community, accelerating as the economy grew more commercial, led to new kinds of social tension. In the early days of the Tokugawa period, when the exactions of corrupt officials or rapacious daimyo provoked peasant discontent, whole villages rose united in protest under village leaders, but by the late eighteenth century a new pattern appeared in peasant disturbances. Angry villagers, led by middling-size or poorer peasant leaders, vented their hostilities against village landlords and money-lenders by looting their storehouses or trashing their homes. These intravillage conflicts, common during the famines of the 1780s and the 1830s, worried the political authorities, but they did little to check the rising affluence and power of the wealthy peasants. On the contrary, both bakufu and domain governments often found it useful to raise money from rich villagers by levying forced loans (*goyōkin*) from them or by selling them the privilege of wearing swords or taking surnames. This practice accelerated the erosion of status boundaries between the commoners and the samurai. Many samurai observers deplored this. "The most lamentable abuse of the present day among the peasants," noted one anonymous writer, "is that those who have become wealthy forget their status and live luxuriously like city aristocrats."[10] Not only were such critics alarmed that the rich peasants acquired their wealth at the expense of fellow villagers, they resented the presumptions of the wealthy peasants.

Needless to say, economic growth had made life more difficult for the samurai class. In contrast to the wealthy town merchants or well-to-do peasant landlord-entrepreneurs, the class as a whole suffered a relative economic decline. Samurai stipends had been fixed generations before, so samurai households suffered absolute decline in income as commodity prices rose.

Many samurai households found it impossible to maintain a lifestyle congruent with their station in life, and some had difficulty making ends meet. In the small domain of Nakatsu, for example, an income of twenty to thirty *koku* of rice per year was necessary for a samurai household just to get along, but many had incomes of less than half that amount.

To make matters worse, bakufu and domain governments often sought to solve financial problems at the expense of their samurai retainers. The fluctuating price of rice, subject to the vagaries of the market in Osaka and Edo, made the flow of revenues unstable. While the amount of tax rice collected remained fairly steady, its value did not, and daimyo might find their incomes sufficient one year but not the next. As daimyo expenditures grew more lavish over the years, domains were less and less able to balance their budgets. Even the bakufu, as one historian has pointed out, was "caught between a more or less fixed income and a practically unlimited capacity for consumption."[11] To tide themselves over, the domains and the bakufu borrowed money from rich merchant-financiers of Edo and Osaka but interest payments only deepened their financial straits, so they reduced samurai stipends to cut their expenditures. Usually this took the form of "borrowing" perhaps a third or a quarter of their samurai-retainers' stipends. In practice, the "borrowing" often became a permanent loan.

By the early nineteenth century, many samurai, particularly those in the middling and lower ranks, scrambled to find ways of supplementing their incomes. The more fortunate pursued genteel by-employments such as teaching calligraphy, giving instruction in swordsmanship, taking in roomers, or perhaps raising *bonsai* ("dwarf trees") for sale. Others tried to marry their daughters into well-to-do commoner families. In Edo, marriage brokers would arrange such alliances for a fee. The truly desperate sold family heirlooms or ran up debts with town merchants in the hope, perhaps, that domain government would eventually cancel their indebtedness by fiat. But for lower samurai, whom money lenders regarded as poor risks, the only alternative was to earn money through handicraft labor, making cricket cages, paper fans or umbrellas, spinning silk into cloth, or some other menial work. This was particularly distasteful since it meant haggling over money with the commoner merchants for whom they worked.

It is little wonder that by the early nineteenth century the pretentious but impecunious samurai had become the object of popular satire and that commoner respect for the class, if not for its authority, had begun to dwindle. Even the direct retainers of the bakufu could not escape scorn. In 1856, for example, three village leaders rebuked a bakufu retainer who lived on their taxes and loans for his spendthrift ways.

> Your brother is an immoral idler. As long as such a person is supported by your household, there is little chance of reducing your expenditures. Last winter, we asked that some actions be taken against your brother. What is your plan? You have more than six servants including maids and horsemen. Some should be dis-

missed. . . . Even if a low interest loan were to be made to you, it would be of little use as long as you have your useless brother. . . . As far as we can determine, you are sufficiently provided for, [but] to keep your brother is uneconomical. If no action is taken, we intend to resign our post as village leaders.[12]

To be sure, this was an extreme case, but it is difficult to imagine that peasant leaders would have risked such a harsh rebuke a few generations before—or that a self-respecting samurai would have tolerated it.

ECONOMIC THOUGHT, SOCIAL CRITICISM, AND REFORM

Since education in the Confucian classics inclined the samurai toward anti-mercantile views, many scholars and officials viewed the expansion of trade and production with alarm and confusion. To be sure, they recognized that material prosperity was essential to a well-ordered society. But Confucian economic thought, which assumed that agriculture was the foundation of society's wealth, insisted the realm would prosper as long as grain production was ample. This view allowed little room for any notion of economic progress. Conventional commentators, who thought that the social division of labor and the size of the economy were fixed, argued that the role of "benevolent government" was to ensure an equitable distribution of wealth and to provide ordinary people with enough to survive. The goal of economic policy was to encourage production while discouraging consumption as much as possible.

By the late eighteenth century, a handful of scholars had begun to question orthodox Confucian economic views. Early in the century, Dazai Shundai, who held no particular brief for the merchant class and their pursuit of profit, argued that commerce was as essential to the economy as agriculture and argued that the daimyo should take advantage of trade. A few years later, Kaiho Seiryō, a canny scholar who had traveled widely throughout the country observing the frugality, ingenuity, and perseverance of peasant entrepreneurs and town merchants, took this view a step further by questioning the anti-mercantile prejudices of orthodox Confucian thought. The pursuit of profit, he argued, should not be disdained or disparaged since the whole society rested on the principles of exchange and profit. Rice tax was a form of profit for the daimyo, and the samurai's stipend was like a wage paid for his service. The domains, he said, should pursue profit by exporting local products to other parts of the country, and samurai should be encouraged to work in trade and production. Yamagata Bantō, a merchant scholar from Osaka who helped reform the finances of the Sendai domain, went even farther, urging the authorities not to regulate prices or tamper with the activities of the merchants since they transported goods from where they were scarce to where they were needed. A number of other commoner scholars echoed his criticisms, pointing out that expedients such as debasing the currency, canceling samurai debts, or extracting forced loans from rich commoners, were not only futile but likely to disrupt the economy.

By the late eighteenth century, a few visionaries called for more active official promotion of national wealth and strength. Honda Toshiaki, a polymath who had learned a bit about the West, thought Japan should learn from the example of England, another island country whose society seemed to be flourishing as the result of trade and overseas colonization. In 1798, he wrote a tract proposing that the country focus on four goals: the production of gunpowder, the smelting of iron and other metals, the building of a merchant fleet, and settlement of the northern territory of Ezo. An even more radical set of proposals was put forward by Satō Nobuhiro, who called for a reorganization of the country into a highly centralized state devoted to promoting general prosperity through central control. In place of the four-class system described in the Confucian tradition, he proposed that society be organized on the basis of occupational groups, and in order to build national strength he suggested that a central ministry of state should direct all economic activities. But these new ideas remained outside mainstream political discourse, less significant for their immediate influence than as harbingers of things to come.

To orthodox Confucians the relentless pursuit of profit, which upset the social hierarchy, remained the cause of troubles within the realm. Economic change, the growth of trade, and the growing prosperity of commoners signified to them a decline in public morals, not an advance in public well-being. Outbursts of peasant discontent, such as those in the 1780s, were taken as signs that all was not well. Even the nativist scholar Motoori Norinaga observed, "If there is good government, there will be no rioting, no matter how poverty-stricken the peasants may be."[13] During the long reign of the shogun Tokugawa Ienari (1786–1841), a spendthrift whose advisors preferred to muddle through rather than undertake serious reforms, such criticism was heard with greater frequency. The failure of the bakufu or the domains to arrest the social dislocations brought by economic change created doubts about their leaders. In the Confucian view, only virtuous rulers could guarantee political stability and social harmony. "Whose fault is it that the people starve and good fields turn to waste?" wrote one reformer in the late eighteenth century. "These evils can not be blamed on laziness or disloyalty [of the people] but are owing to the crimes of the rulers."[14] Instead of tending the affairs of state, the shogun and daimyo, closeted themselves in their mansions surrounded by sycophants and showed little concern for their people or their retainers.

In 1837, such sentiments prompted Ōshio Heihachirō, a minor bakufu retainer living in Osaka, to raise the banner of rebellion. During the mid-

1830s, a series of bad harvests had brought widespread famine and distress to the region. When Ōshio learned that the local city magistrate had ordered rice in bakufu storehouses to be shipped to Edo, he urged that it be distributed to hungry local inhabitants instead. After his plea fell on deaf ears, he gathered together a small band of followers, sold his books to buy them weapons, and issued a summons to commoners in the Osaka area to wreak "Heaven's punishment" on corrupt local officials and greedy merchants. The rebellion failed, but fires set by Ōshio's followers to divert the attention of the authorities destroyed nearly a third of Osaka and disrupted the trade networks centering on the city. Rumors spread that the official charged with putting down the rising had fallen off his horse at the first sound of gunfire, prompting a satiric verse that began,

> Off his horse he fell,
> His heels up over his hat.
> Never had heard tell
> Of a samurai wimpy as that.

The Ōshio affair was a tremendous embarrassment to the bakufu, not simply because he was one of their own, but because he quickly became a popular hero for other discontents, who held him up as a "sage" or "man of righteousness" who sacrificed his life to "save the people."

In response to the Ōshio rebellion as well as to perennial financial problems, Mizuno Tadakuni, who became bakufu chief elder in 1841, launched reforms to balance the bakufu budget and restore the social equilibrium. Unable to escape the confines of conventional economic thinking, Mizuno pursued conservative measures that tried to turn the clock back by issuing sumptuary laws, fixing prices by regulation, curtailing the privileges of merchant associations, and instituting an austerity program in the shogun's household. At best such reform measures were weakly palliative, at worst they disrupted trade, making the rise of prices even more acute. Neither did they have an impact on the direction of economic change. Quite the contrary, when Mizuno proposed to reestablish claims to easily accessible fertile lands in the hinterlands of Edo and Osaka, direct bakufu retainers whose vested economic interests were threatened by the move succeeded in bringing about his resignation.

Reform programs undertaken in many domains were more successful. Instead of evoking platitudes about the prosperity of the people, officials in these domains spoke of pursuing "domain profit" (*kokueki*), and instead of restricting trade and merchants, they attempted to mobilize them in the service of the domain. During the 1830s and 1840s, officials in Mito, Satsuma, and elsewhere succeeded in revitalizing domain finances by strengthening control over domain monopolies or by expanding them. In Satsuma, for example, domain debt was wiped out by profits from a lucrative monopoly over Ryukyu sugar. By contrast, Chōshū, Saga, and several other large domains pursued more conventional remedies not unlike Mizuno's reforms. But even the most innovative reformers did not question the basic economic structure nor the shape of the political economy. It was only the appearance of a new problem, pressure from the Western countries to end restrictions on outside trade, that forced the country's leaders to consider new ways of generating wealth and strength.

Endnotes

1. Thunberg's observations on Japan may be found in his *Travels in Europe, Africa, and Asia,* vol. IV (London: F. and C. Rivington, 1795).

2. Yasuba Yasukichi, "The Tokugawa Legacy: A Survey," *Economic Studies Quarterly* 38, no. 4 (Dec. 1987), 290–308.

3. Englebert Kaempfer, *History of Japan,* trans. J. G. Scheuchzer, vol 3 (Glasgow: James MacLehose and Sons, 1896), 313.

4. Fujita is quoted in Harry D. Harootunian, *Toward Restoration: The Growth of Political Consciousness in Tokugawa Japan* (Berkeley: University of California Press, 1970), 78.

5. Ninomiya is quoted in Robert N. Bellah, *Tokugawa Religion: The Values of Pre-Modern Japan* (New York: Free Press, 1957), 128.

6. Thomas C. Smith, "Pre-Modern Economic Growth: Japan and the West," *Past and Present* 43 (1973), 138.

7. Quoted in Johannes Hirschmeier, *The Origins of Entrepreneurship in Meiji Japan* (Cambridge, Mass.: Harvard University Press, 1964), 23.

8. Robert Leutner, *Shikitei Samba and the Comic Tradition in Late Edo Period Popular Fiction* (Cambridge, Mass.: Harvard University Press, 1985), 156–157.

9. See Eijirō Honjo, *Economic Theory and History of Japan in the Tokugawa Period* (New York: Russell and Russell, 1965), 31–32.

10. Quoted in Thomas C. Smith, *The Agrarian Origins of Modern Japan* (Stanford, Cal.: Stanford University Press, 1959), 176.

11. Conrad Totman, *Politics in the Tokugawa Bakufu* (Cambridge, Mass.: Harvard University Press, 1967), 77.

12. Kozo Yamamura, *A Study of Samurai Income and Entrepreneurship: Quantitative Analyses of Economic and Social Aspects of the Samurai in Tokugawa and Meiji Japan* (Cambridge, Mass.: Harvard University Press, 1974), 47–48.

13. For Motoori's views, see Shigeru Matsumoto, *Motoori Norinaga, 1730–1801* (Cambridge, Mass.: Harvard University Press, 1970), 144–156.

14. Honda Toshiaki is quoted in Thomas C. Smith, "'Merit' as Ideology in the Tokugawa Period," in *Aspects of Social Change in Modern Japan,* ed. R. P. Dore (Princeton, N.J.: Princeton University Press, 1967), 89.

4

The Fall of the
Old Order

By the early nineteenth century, the social stress created by the growth of the market, the impoverishment of the samurai, and the emergence of rich commoners was beginning to strain confidence in the existing social and political structure. Some historians argue that these long-term trends were pushing Japan in the direction of radical, perhaps even revolutionary change. Whether such was the case is a question not easily answered, since pressures toward change from within were suddenly overwhelmed by a series of decisive shocks from without. From the turn of the century, but especially in the 1840s, the Western countries demanded more and more insistently that Japan end its isolation from the West and open up its markets wider to their goods. The failure of the bakufu to resist these demands cast doubt on the nerve of the bakufu leadership and revealed deep lines of fracture in the bakuhan system. Tensions and contradictions generated by long-term social change contributed to the crisis, but in the end the Meiji Restoration, the palace coup that finally brought down the old order in 1868, was less a social revolution than a nationalist one. However widespread discontent had been, the foreign threat had quickened feeling that the whole society had a common interest in strengthening the country against it.

THE FOREIGN THREAT

The policy of limiting access to the outside world worked as well as it did for nearly two centuries because the Western countries had showed little interest in renewing contacts with Japan. Unlike India and China, long the object of

European interest, Japan remained outside the imagination of most Western-ers, a dimly known country with little exotic or commercial appeal. (Even Gulliver, Jonathan Swift's well-traveled creation, who stopped briefly on his way home to England from Lilliput and other ports of call, found little or nothing to say about the country.) Knowledge about Japan was restricted to the reports of physicians and natural scientists temporarily stationed at the Dutch trading post at Deshima, and these often devoted as much attention to local flora and fauna as to Japanese society and institutions. The Westerners saw in Japan a "forbidden land," stubbornly conservative and wrapped in mystery, that had changed little since the Europeans first arrived in the six-teenth century. As one foreign observer noted, "having thus cut off from al-most all intercourse for such a long period, it is not to be expected that . . . the manners, habits, and customs of the Japanese should have materially al-tered during that time."[1]

In fact, the Japanese seemed to have been far more interested in European culture than the Westerners were interested in Japan's. While few Japanese had any direct contact with the foreigners, a small but growing number of scholars and officials were acquiring Western practical knowledge through the development of "Dutch learning" (*rangaku*), the study of Dutch scientific and technical works. In 1720, the shogun Yoshimune, who hoped that Euro-pean astronomical, calendrical, and climatic knowledge might help to in-crease domestic production, lifted the ban on the import of foreign books that did not deal with Christianity. By the late eighteenth century, Dutch trading ships regularly brought shipments of Dutch books ordered by the bakufu, and a cadre of several dozen scholars painstakingly translated the odd "sideways letters"* of the "red-haired barbarians" into Japanese. Many daimyo employed resident rangaku scholars, who often served as physicians too, to study natural sciences such as botany, anatomy, and pharmacology in hopes of contributing to the prosperity and welfare of their domains. As Sugita Gempaku, a prominent rangaku scholar observed, Dutch learning was "like a drop of oil, which when dropped on a pond, spread across its whole surface."[2]

Although Western science and practical learning attracted the interest of the ruling elite, old fears of Christianity and foreign invasion remained strong. "When those barbarians plan to subdue a country not their own, they start by opening commerce and watch for a sign of weakness," warned one early nineteenth-century writer. "If an opportunity is presented, they will preach their alien religion to captivate the people's hearts."[3] In the 1790s, these fears had been rekindled by the Russians, whose explorers were charting the icy waters off Hokkaido and whose trappers were moving into the sparsely in-habited islands of Sakhalin and the Kurile chain. What was simply the end of a century-long march of Russian settlers across the Siberian subcontinent

---

*The Japanese wrote vertically from right to left, while the Europeans wrote horizontally from left to right.

presaged a new foreign threat to the Japanese authorities. When the Russian court sent a peaceful mission to Hokkaido to ask for trade in 1792, the bakufu leadership turned them away with evasive politeness, offering hospitality but no concessions. Indeed, the bakufu reaffirmed that it was the country's "ancestral policy" to restrict relations with foreign countries.

As the intrusions of the Westerners became more strident—and on occasion more violent—the apprehensions of the bakufu became more intense. In 1807, when another Russian mission was turned away, its frustrated members attacked Japanese settlements in Sakhalin and the Kuriles, arousing great alarm in Edo. The following year in 1808, the British frigate *Phaeton* entered Nagasaki in pursuit of Dutch merchant ships, then enemies in the Napoleonic wars, and its nineteen-year-old captain, a hotheaded adolescent, threatened to burn all the Chinese and Dutch ships in the harbor if he were not supplied with provisions and water. These incidents, the first in a series of more frequent intrusions by Western vessels, deepened a paranoid image of the Western "barbarians." In 1825, after sailors from an English whaling vessel landed at a fishing village in the Mito domain in search of provisions, the bakufu ordered local authorities to destroy all foreign vessels that came close to Japanese shores and to arrest or kill any surviving crew members with "no second thoughts." Shooting first and asking questions later might seem an unrealistic policy, but it was enforced with moderate rigor over the next fifteen years. In 1837, for example, the *Morrison*, a merchant vessel dispatched by an American trading company in China, was driven out of Edo Bay, and Kagoshima Bay as well, under a hail of cannon balls.

The fears of the authorities were misplaced. The Westerners had no sinister designs on Japan or its territory, and certainly no desire to turn the country into a colony, but powerful economic forces were driving them ever closer to Japanese shores. As the industrial revolution gathered momentum, the Western search for foreign markets accelerated. Great Britain, well on the way to becoming the "workshop of the world," was steadily expanding into Asian markets such as India, where the British East India Company had established its dominion, and China, where British merchants traded manufactured goods legally—and opium illegally. As early as 1793, the British government had proposed that Lord McCartney, who headed a mission to negotiate better conditions for English merchants in China in 1793, visit Japan too. As his instructions noted, "It is not impossible that the competition of the Japanese market with that of China might render the commodities of both places cheaper to the purchaser."[4]

As the gyre of British trade widened, the doctrine of free trade gained support among British merchants, politicians, and scholars. It was based on the assumption that competition in the marketplace, unimpeded by government legislation or interference, would ensure consumers the best products at the lowest price. When applied to trade among nations, this assumption was reformulated as the concept of comparative advantage: if each nation in the world sold what it produced best and most cheaply, and bought from other nations what was costly to produce at home, all nations would benefit; any legal, institutional, or tariff barriers that interfered with the free flow of goods among nations were therefore a threat to their mutual prosperity. During the 1830s, the British government, with the strong backing of merchants and parliament, began to press for the "opening" of markets across the globe.

It was with such intentions that the British went to war with China in 1839, after a Chinese official appointed to stop the opium trade confiscated large stocks of the drug and threatened to arrest a British merchant. For the British, the conflict was not a "war on drugs," as it was for the Chinese, but a fight to win new conditions of trade. In 1842, after a series of successful skirmishes with Chinese naval and land forces, the British negotiated a treaty that opened five new ports to trade, fixed tariffs at levels agreed upon by the British, and gave British consular officials full legal jurisdiction (called "extraterritorial rights") over British citizens in the treaty ports. News of the Opium War, brought to Japan by Dutch and Chinese traders at Nagasaki, shattered any easy confidence that the Westerners might be put off by force, and by the mid-1840s accounts of the war circulated widely. The shocking defeat of the Chinese by a small British naval and military force shattered the traditional image of Chinese strength, and it also raised the question of whether a similar fate might be in store for Japan. "How can we know," remarked one writer, "whether the mist gathering over China might not come down as frost on Japan."[5]

The sense of threat from without, smoldering since the 1790s, was fanned into fear by the Opium War. Scholars, officials, and bakufu leaders debated how best to deal with the "barbarians." Nearly all who participated in the debate were agreed that the Westerners were probably up to no good but there was no consensus on how best to respond to their predatory advances. The most ardent advocates of resisting the foreigners were to be found in the domain of Mito, where anti-foreign scholars like Fujita Tōko and Aizawa Seishisai emerged as a driving force for domain reform. Moved in part by conventional economic ideas, in part by visceral xenophobia, and in part by realistic fears, these men defended a rigid policy of seclusion. To them, the foreigners were violent in nature, ignorant of "true morality," absorbed in the pursuit of profits, and carriers of the "false doctrines" of Christianity. Should Japan open itself to trade with the outside, they said, commerce with the foreigners would not only drain Japan of its gold and silver, it would accelerate the moral decline of the country already evident in widespread habits of luxury, moral laxity, and social corruption. Profit-grubbing merchants would enrich themselves at the expense of their fellow commoners, and the "ignorant people" would be seduced by the subversive religious beliefs of the foreigners.

These radical seclusionists urged that the Western threat be met by the moral reinvigoration of the country. The Westerners, they argued, posed a threat because they arrived in a Japan made flabby and weak by two centuries of peace and idleness. Informed by the historical experience of China, where weakened dynasties were often overthrown by barbarian invasion, they saw an inextricable link between "troubles at home" (*naiyū*) and "threats from without" (*gaikan*). Unless the old spirit of discipline and martial vigor was restored among the samurai class, and unless the people regained their old habits of frugality and obedience, it would be difficult to save Japan from being overwhelmed by its enemies or from slipping into moral decay through exposure to the Westerners. In good Confucian fashion, the Mito scholars called on the bakufu leaders and the daimyo to put an end to official laxity and corruption, to stop spending lavishly on concubines, entertainments, and other luxuries, and to devote themselves to improving the welfare of the people.

While the Mito school was backward-looking in many respects, it also represented the stirrings of proto-nationalism. Like the nativist scholars of the eighteenth century, the Mito writers thought of Japan, the "land of the gods" (*shinkoku*), as the moral center of the world, and they introduced the notion of Japan as a hierarchical "national body" (*kokutai*) with the emperor at it pinnacle. Within this structure everyone, from the humblest commoner to the monarch himself, had a proper role, and only if all pursued their proper roles would society function harmoniously. What these writers had in mind was a more unified bakuhan system, bound by links of loyalty from the bottom to the top, but their emphasis on the importance of the imperial institution as the ultimate object of popular respect introduced a potentially subversive idea into political discourse.

The ideas of the Mito scholars attracted many followers during the 1840s and 1850s, but others felt that the best way to prepare against the foreign threat was to accelerate acquisition of Western knowledge. Scholars of Dutch learning like Sakuma Shōzan, Takashima Shūhan, and Takano Chōei were no less anti-foreign than the Mito scholars and no less convinced of Japan's moral superiority, but they had a more acute appreciation of the country's military backwardness and less confidence that Japan could maintain its independence by moral or political means alone. To be sure, they agreed that domestic reforms were necessary—few concerned scholars and officials did not—but they thought that the main task in dealing with the foreign threat was to acquire Western science, Western technology, and Western guns. Without these, no matter how valiant and determined its people, Japan would be incapable of defending itself. As Sakuma Shōzan put it, "Why did an upright and righteous great country like China lose to an insolent, unjust, and contemptible country like England? It is because the [rulers of China] prided themselves on their superiority, regarded the outside world with contempt, and paid no heed to the progress of machinery in foreign countries." It was necessary, he argued, to bring "Western skills" to the defense of "Eastern morality."[6]

The scholars' debate over the foreign threat was echoed in the council chambers of Satsuma, Tosa, Echizen, and Mito, several large strategically located coastal tozama and shinpan domains, which were normally excluded from the bakufu decision-making but likely to bear the brunt of a foreign attack. Their daimyo, supported by reform-minded officials, experimented with different strategies to deal with the looming foreign threat. The most militant defender of seclusion was Tokugawa Nariaki, the blunt, persistent, nearly fanatical lord of Mito. Already in the 1830s, under the influence of men like Fujita Yūkoku and Fujita Tōko, he undertook a reform program ranging from smallpox inoculations to forging cannon from temple bells in preparation for a military clash with the foreigners. When he suggested in an excess of zeal that the shogun cut down his household spending and abandon his effete life of luxury in Edo castle, he fell out of favor with the bakufu, but his fortunes rose once more in the 1850s. Unlike Tokugawa Nariaki, Shimazu Nariakira, daimyo of Satsuma, who had studied Dutch and gathered around him a group of low-ranking samurai officials, felt that it would be impossible to keep the country closed as it had been in the past. The only realistic policy for the country, he thought, was to build up military and economic strength to keep the foreigners in line once they came into the country for trade. When British and French ships demanded in 1846 that the kingdom of the Ryukyus, a "tributary" of Satsuma, sign treaties of friendship and commerce, he urged the bakufu to give permission to do so, and a few years later he ordered the construction of Western-style iron smelting furnaces and arsenals to manufacture Western-style artillery and machinery.

By the early 1850s then, the Japanese ruling elite had taken measure of the foreign threat. The contrast with other Asian counties, particularly China, is striking. To some extent, the Japanese profited from the bad example of the Qing dynasty, whose defeat at the hands of the English demonstrated the foolhardiness of failing to take the demands of the Westerners seriously. No doubt their sense of vulnerability was also heightened by a realization that an island country like Japan was harder to defend than a continental one like China, but political culture probably played a role as well. The identification of the samurai with their warrior origins may have made them more sensitive to outside military threats, and the long-standing competition among the domains may have prepared them for the dog-eat-dog international politics of the Westerners. But the most important influence on their thinking was an embryonic notion of national interest that had emerged in the debate over the foreign threat. However men like Mito Nariaki and Shimazu Nariakira or Aizawa Seishisai and Sakuma Shōzan may have disagreed, all of them had begun to think of Japan not simply as a culture but as a body politic as well. The seeds of modern nationalism were beginning to sprout.

THE TREATY SETTLEMENTS

Although the bakufu continued to insist that its "ancestral law" of isolation forbade treaty relations with the Western countries, it retreated from the obdurate militancy adopted in the 1820s. In the wake of the Opium War, the bakufu prudently rescinded the "no second thought" expulsion order in 1842, and local authorities were urged to give water, provisions, and fuel to Western ships in distress who requested them peacefully. An even greater shift in bakufu policy came under Abe Masahiro, the chief elder of the bakufu from 1845 to 1855, who realized the urgency of undertaking military and institutional reforms. In 1844, the Dutch king sent the bakufu a letter warning that the British would soon be knocking on their door and that if the bakufu did not accept their demands for trade, Japan might well find itself at war with them.

Taking charge of a new office of coastal defense, established to prepare for Western probes, Abe launched plans to build up coastal fortifications, particularly along sea approaches to Edo, which was fatally vulnerable to gunboat attacks, and he ordered direct bakufu retainers to train with Western-style weaponry. While his efforts were hamstrung by bakufu financial difficulties and some conservative resistance, awareness of the need for preparedness spread through all levels of the bakufu. To forestall the danger that the country might fly apart under foreign pressure, Abe broke with the long-standing practice of keeping the daimyo divided and weak. Not only did he try to win the personal trust and confidence of men like Tokugawa Nariaki and Shimazu Nariakira, who had begun to strengthen their own defenses, he also permitted Satsuma, Saga, and other domains to build new coastal fortifications or to experiment with Western technology. It was clear that Japan could not face the Westerners successfully unless the inherent weaknesses of the decentralized political structure were overcome, and he tried to hold together an informal coalition of allies that included the profoundly anti-foreign Mito domain and the innovative Satsuma domain. It was not an easy task.

The Russians, and then the British, were the first Westerners to have shown interest in "opening" Japan, but by the 1840s the Americans were becoming involved as well. The opening of the treaty ports in China aroused new American interest in the China trade, and the outbreak of the war with Mexico, which led to the acquisition of California in 1848, kindled new American ambitions to become a commercial power in the Pacific. Like the British, the Americans wished to increase trade with Japan as well as China, but they had other interests as well. Since the 1820s, New England whaling vessels, having exhausted whaling stocks in the Atlantic, had pursued their huge quarries in the northern Pacific. Whale boats blown away from their ships by winds and high sea sometimes washed up on Japanese shores, and the allegedly harsh treatment of their crews by the local Japanese authorities stirred public sentiment in favor of protecting them. The American navy was also interested in acquiring coaling stations in the western Pacific to supply its growing steam fleet. Since Japan, which was rumored to have abundant supplies of coal, lay on the main sea routes between the Pacific coast and the Asian mainland, it was an ideal place to secure ports of refuge. As Commodore Matthew Calbraith Perry, a champion of steam power, urged, it was important to establish a presence there before the "unconscionable government" of England did.

The arrival of four American gunboats under Perry's command in July 1853 was hardly a surprise to the Japanese authorities. In 1846, the bakufu

The Landing of Perry in 1854. A contemporary print of the treaty negotiations in 1854. As Commodore Perry marched to the negotiating place, his fleet of seven "black ships" (three of them steam powered) rode confidently at anchor in Edo Bay. Japanese officials stand in the foreground.

had turned away an American expedition under Commodore Biddle, and the Dutch at Deshima kept Edo fully informed about American plans to open negotiations with the Japanese. But the tactics of polite obfuscation and delay, used so successfully in the past to deflect earlier Western probes, did not work with Commodore Perry. The dogged, humorless, and imperious American commander, who regarded the Japanese authorities as vindictive and deceitful, was determined to stand them down.[7] With a promise to return within a few months for a reply to President Millard Fillmore's request for a treaty, he blithely steamed his flotilla of "black ships" past bakufu coastal forts guarding Edo. The message was clear: if the Americans did not get a positive response from the bakufu they were prepared to use force.

Not surprisingly, rumors that war was imminent spread quickly. The bakufu ordered daimyo responsible for defending the coastline to strengthen their forces and appear in full battle armor. In Edo, constables and fire fighters were put on alert, and households living near the shoreline were ordered to withdraw in the event of hostilities. The streets soon filled with panic-stricken residents, young and old, hauling their furniture, kitchenware, and family heirlooms to stay with friends or relatives on the landward outskirts of the city. The price of rice, oil, and pickled plums skyrocketed as consumers hoarded them in anticipation of war. A few helpful townsmen, aware of how ill prepared their samurai superiors were for war, also suggested novel ways of fending off the Americans. A lumber merchant, mindful of potential sales, suggested floating a huge wooden raft mounted with cannon on Edo Bay to repel an American attack, and a brothel owner proposed blowing up the American ships after getting their crews drunk at a welcoming party.

Faced with Perry's firmness and aware of their own lack of military preparedness, the bakufu leaders chose not to fight to preserve the isolation policy, but they did so with the tacit acquiescence of the daimyo. Abe Masahiro, who knew that he would have to rely on the domains for military and financial support in the event of war, broke precedent again by asking all the daimyo how to respond to the American demands. The extant replies, sixty-one out of two hundred-odd, indicate that most daimyo urged the bakufu to reject American demands for trade but wished to avoid hostilities as well. Only a handful were willing to go to war. Given this uncertain mandate the bakufu leaders felt they had no choice but to compromise with the Americans. The bakufu refused to open up the country to American trade, but in March 1854 it signed a treaty opening the remote ports of Shimoda and Hakodate to American ships and providing for the repatriation of shipwrecked sailors, the provisioning of American ships, and the establishment of American consulates at the newly opened ports. In short order, the other Western powers—the British, the Russians, and the Dutch—negotiated similar treaties. Anti-foreign daimyo like Tokugawa Nariaki were shocked at the extent of the concessions to the foreigners, but the bakufu leadership was happy to have weathered the crisis without resorting to war and without having given the foreigners the right to trade.

For the Americans, however, the "wood and water treaty" was just the first step. In late 1856, Townsend Harris, the first American consul, arrived at the port of Shimoda with instructions to negotiate a trade treaty. Unlike Perry, he had no fleet to back him, but he was able to play on the bakufu's anxieties. At once cajoling and intimidating, Harris argued that trade would be more beneficial to Japan than harmful, and he also suggested that it would be better for the Japanese to reach an agreement with him than with a fleet of British gunboats. The bakufu, under the new leadership of Hotta Masayoshi, who became chief elder after daimyo criticism forced Abe Masahiro from office, realized it had little choice but to accept the inevitable, and so did most of the daimyo. In late 1857, in response to another inquiry from the bakufu, the majority agreed that it was impossible to avoid either trade or diplomatic relations with the foreigners. With a much clearer mandate than Abe had enjoyed, in January 1858 Hotta signed a draft treaty with the United States providing for the opening of new treaty ports, the establishment of customs duties by treaty, the right of American traders and other nationals to be tried by consular courts rather than by Japanese courts, and the right of the Americans to dispatch a minister to Edo. Although the Japanese adamantly refused to permit the import of opium as the Chinese had, the terms were essentially the same as the Westerners had extracted from the Qing court a decade and a half before.

The majority of the daimyo accepted the Harris treaty, but political consensus was fracturing on another issue: who was to succeed ailing shogun Iesada, a sickly young man with no children of his own. The reformist daimyo of

Satsuma, Echizen, Mito, and Date, who had become outspoken in their demands that the bakufu set its finances in order and build up its military strength, backed the candidacy of Tokugawa Yoshinobu, the seventh son of Tokugawa Nariaki, an attractive young man with a reputation for unusual intelligence. Educated by Mito scholars like Aizawa Seishisai, Yoshinobu had become the daimyo of Hitotsubashi, one of the shimpan domains. To his backers, he seemed the strong leader the country needed in a time of crisis. The fudai daimyo, who feared losing their long-standing dominance of the bakufu, put forward their own candidate, the daimyo of Kii, a twelve-year-old boy who would be easy for them to control. The result was a potentially dangerous split between the fudai daimyo who wanted to protect the political status quo and reform-minded daimyo who wanted to enlarge their role in bakufu decisions.

Conflict over the shogunal succession became entangled with the bakufu's effort to secure broad support for bakufu foreign policy. In the spring of 1858, Hotta Masayoshi, responding to the urging of many daimyo, decided to submit the Harris treaty to the emperor for ratification. Confident that imperial approval would be forthcoming, Hotta made an unprecedented visit to Kyoto, bearing lavish gifts for the emperor and the court aristocracy. The trip proved disastrous. Not only were the emperor Kōmei and his closest advisors anti-foreign in outlook, but the conservative Tokugawa Nariaki and other reformist daimyo secretly urged the court to back the candidacy of Yoshinobu as successor to the shogun. To the shock of the bakufu delegation, the emperor expressed his disapproval of the treaty and urged the bakufu to reconsider it after consulting again with the daimyo. This radical departure from the emperor's usual custom of tamely submitting to the bakufu's requests was a severe blow to the bakufu's authority.

To replace the hapless Hotta, the shogun appointed Ii Naosuke, daimyo of Hikone, to the rarely filled office of Great Elder (*tairō*), a position second in prestige only to the shogun himself. A strong and intelligent man, Ii Naosuke, backed by the fudai daimyo officials, was determined to reassert bakufu initiative both in foreign policy and domestic politics. Like the reformist daimyo, he was aware of the need for strong leadership but he was not prepared to accept it on untraditional terms. In July 1858, Ii decided to sign the Harris treaty without imperial approval, and soon negotiated similar agreements with the Dutch, the Russians, the British, and the French. To end outside meddling in the bakufu affairs, he declared the shogunal succession a purely internal matter of the Tokugawa house, in which neither tozama daimyo nor the emperor had a right to interfere, and he had the child candidate of the fudai named as the shogun's heir. To put down domestic opposition, he forced into retirement most of the reform-minded daimyo who had backed the Hitotsubashi candidacy, and he arrested and punished their retainers who had expressed opposition to the Harris treaty or the appointment of the new shogun.

"REVERE THE EMPEROR AND EXPEL THE BARBARIANS"

Although the bakufu had adopted a policy generally backed by the daimyo that probably saved Japan from a clash with foreign gunboats, it had done so at the tremendous cost to its authority and legitimacy. The "ancestral law" of isolation was dead, and the bakufu had killed it. In a bitterly ironic poem the anti-foreign Yanagawa Seigan chided the shogun:

> You, whose ancestors in mighty days
> Roared at the skies and swept across the earth
> Stand now helpless to drive off the wrangling foreigners—
> How empty your title, "Queller of the Barbarians"![8]

By contrast, the emperor, who had taken a resolute stand against the Harris treaty, emerged as a rallying point for anti-foreign elements. In defying the emperor's wishes by signing the Harris treaty, the bakufu had also betrayed its trust as delegate of the imperial power. With some justice the shogun could be branded as a disloyal vassal, who no longer deserved the loyalty of others.

The opening of the new treaty ports in 1859 accelerated the decline of political confidence in the bakufu. A steady stream of Western traders, most employed by British firms with experience in India or China, set up shop in Yokohama, Nagasaki, Niigata, Hakodate, and eventually Hyogo (Kobe). The new treaty ports were securely in the grip of the foreigners, who controlled 90 percent of Japan's trade with the outside world. They soon became the spout of a funnel through which foreign trade poured. Happily enough, however, the Japanese enjoyed a favorable balance of trade throughout the 1860s, finding a ready market for raw silk in Europe, where French and Italian silk worms had been stricken by disease, and for green tea in the United States, where the middle classes had become addicted to its consumption.

But foreign trade generated short-term economic disruptions too. The most serious was rapid and demoralizing inflation. When foreign traders discovered that the value of gold was lower in Japan than in the world market, they rushed to buy up Japanese gold pieces for sale abroad. As soon as the bakufu authorities discovered what was going on, they attempted to withdraw gold coins from circulation, then remint them with the same face value but a smaller gold content. The effects of the Western "gold rush" was a de facto devaluation of the currency and a sudden increase in the money supply. Compounding these inflationary pressures was a shift of domestic production toward the foreign market, where prices were higher and profits greater. The price of raw silk, for example, tripled during the early years of trade, and when a series of bad harvests hit the country in the mid-1860s, things grew even worse. According to one estimate, price levels in 1866 were four times higher than they had been before the opening of the ports.

Popular woodblock prints and broadsides likened the upward spiral of prices to pilgrims hiking up Mt. Fuji or New Year's kites soaring the sky, but for many it was no joking matter. Inflation made life harder for samurai families, particularly among the lower ranks, and it hurt poorer urban commoners as well. Not surprisingly, urban riots or "trashings" (*uchikowashi*) erupted with greater frequency than since the hard times of the 1830s. In many commercially developed rural areas, where foreign trade disrupted commodity prices, imports of cotton textiles created unemployment; traditional marketing networks were upset; and peasant uprisings erupted as well. In the summer of 1866, for example, thousands of peasants in the silk-producing areas west of Edo wreaked their fury against village headmen, money lenders, pawnshop owners, rich landlords, and wholesale merchants by tearing down their houses or breaking open their storehouses. Interestingly, however, xenophobia seems to have played only a small role in these disturbances.

Such was not the case with the anti-foreign "loyalist" or *sonnō-jōi* ("revere the emperor and repel the barbarians") movement, which drew into its ranks men roused by the contamination of the "divine land" by the foreigners or by fear for the country's independence. The emperor's opposition to the Harris treaty in 1858 forged a firm link between anti-foreignism and veneration for the emperor, and the imperial capital at Kyoto became a magnet for anti-foreign activists angered by the disloyalty of the emperor's "rebellious vassal," the shogun. Some loyalists rallied around the emperor because they thought of him as the divine embodiment of the Japanese identity, while others saw him as the apex of the chain of loyalty that cemented the *kokutai*. But all were gripped by a sense of fear and humiliation roused by the intrusion of the foreigners.

Fairly typical of the loyalist movement was Yoshida Shōin, a young samurai from Chōshū, who had shown early concern about the foreign threat. Even before the arrival of Perry, he had traveled throughout the country making a study of its coastal defenses and acquainting himself with scholars like Sakuma Shōzan. In 1854, bakufu authorities arrested him for attempting to stow away on one of Perry's vessels in hopes of going to see the West at first hand. Fearful that trade would open the country to foreign subversion, Yoshida ferociously attacked both the shogun and the daimyo for failing to stand up to the foreigners. His anti-foreign patriotism attracted a devoted following of young lower samurai to his small private academy in Hagi, the castle town of Chōshū, but when he became involved in an abortive plot to assassinate a high bakufu official he was executed on orders of the bakufu. Shortly before his death in 1859, he called for a rising of "humble heroes," ready to trade their domain loyalties for direct service to the emperor in the struggle against the foreigners and corrupt bakufu leaders.

Like Yoshida and his students, most of those who flocked to the loyalist movement came from the middle and lower ranks of the samurai class. It also attracted an admixture of commoners, especially the educated sons of wealthy peasants or well-to-do townsmen who were influenced by samurai ideals.

Pockets of loyalists were to be found all over the country, but they were concentrated in large domains like Satsuma, Mito, and Chōshū, whose daimyo had been advocates of reform or anti-foreign sentiments in the 1850s. Most were angry young men in their late teens or twenties, outraged by the failure of their elders to deal with the foreign threat or with the country's weakness. Being young and of low status, they had little influence on domain politics and often they condemned "black-hearted officials" out of frustration at their own political impotence. In most domains, conservative officials did indeed oppose the emergence of vocal and undisciplined factions that challenged tradition, but in a few, notably Satsuma and Mito, the daimyo or high-ranking domain officials were often sympathetic to loyalist views.

The loyalists drew inspiration from the older samurai ethic of decisiveness, daring, and indifference to death. Nurtured on tales of medieval warrior exploits, they took as heroes men like Kusunoki Masashige, a fourteenth-century general who committed suicide after unsuccessfully defending the imperial court against Ashikaga Takauji, a rebellious general who had betrayed the emperor and founded a line of shoguns. Many loyalists, who styled themselves as "men of high purpose" (*shishi*) devoted to the "whole realm" (*tenka*), cut ties to their domains, trading pro forma loyalty to their daimyo for a more intense personal commitment to the emperor. Like many earlier critics, loyalists deplored the decline in the martial morale and vigor of the samurai class, which they saw as the cause of the bakufu's feckless and pusillanimous response to the foreigners. Reckless, confident in their own virtue, and committed to decisive action, the loyalists took quickly to the tactics of terror in hopes that heroic violence would drive the foreigners away or bring the country's leaders to their senses. Shibusawa Eiichi, a young loyalist firebrand who later became a prominent business leader, recalled his mood at the time: "What did it matter that the foreigners possessed huge gunboats and cannons? We had our samurai swords, we had honed our skills, and we would cut them down, one by one, mercilessly."[9]

A wave of loyalist terrorism began in 1860 when a band of Mito loyalists assassinated Ii Naosuke, the symbol of bakufu tyranny and weakness, as he made his way out of Edo castle on a snowy February morning. Attempts on the lives of other high bakufu officials soon followed, and loyalist bands in Kyoto cut down bakufu informers, bakufu police officials, and merchants thought to be dealing with the foreigners. In a bizarre episode, loyalist followers of Hirata Atsutane decapitated the images of four Ashikaga shoguns, accused by some of disloyalty to the throne in the fourteenth century. The severed wooden heads, displayed on a riverbank in the middle of the city, were festooned with warnings that "traitors" like the Ashikaga could expect to be "rectified" by men of high purpose if they did not repent their ways. The incident, which occurred just before the visit of the young shogun Iemochi to Kyoto, was ominous in its symbolism.

The foreigners in Japan also came under attacks by loyalist assassins. In 1861, Henry Heuskens, Townsend Harris' Dutch interpreter, was cut down as he made his way back at night to the American legation quarters in Edo, and a band of loyalists from Chōshū attacked the British legation, wounding two diplomats and killing several Japanese servants. The most troublesome attack occurred at Namamugi on the outskirts of Yokohama, when Charles Richardson, an English merchant from Shanghai, was killed after he rode his horse in front of the Satsuma daimyo's procession. The British government, lodging a strong protest, demanded indemnities from both Satsuma and the bakufu, and Westerners in Yokohama took to sleeping with weapons at their bedsides in case of attack. But in the age of gunboat diplomacy, random acts of violence did not discourage the foreigners, who were willing to take some risk as they made quick fortunes.

When terrorism failed to wreck the treaty settlement, loyalists from the domain of Chōshū allied with anti-foreign elements in the imperial court persuaded the emperor Komei in 1863 to order expulsion of the foreigners by force. Chōshū, whose government had come under the control of pro-loyalist officials, was the only domain to obey. In June, domain shore batteries, which commanded the Straits of Shimonoseki, fired on an American cargo ship headed for Shanghai, and bombardments of other foreign ships continued for several weeks. In response, the foreigners protested, and troops from Satsuma drove the Chōshū loyalists from Kyoto under orders from the bakufu. But loyalists continued to control the Chōshū domain government, and in 1864 Chōshū activists returned to Kyoto in hopes of staging a coup to "free" the emperor to command a military expedition expelling the foreigners from Japan. Led by Kusaka Gensui and Maki Izumi, two ardent loyalist leaders, the plan was the first attempt to displace the shogun as the country's political leader. This bold attempt was put down by troops from Satsuma, Aizu, and other domains led by Shimazu Hisamitsu, the daimyo of Satsuma, who had struck a deal with the bakufu to encourage cooperation with the court but whose ultimate goals was to increase his domain's influence over bakufu policy.

The loyalist movement was, as one historian has put it, merely "a rehearsal for Restoration."[10] The movement, which ended in failure, shared few concrete goals beyond the expulsion of the barbarians. Some loyalist leaders expected the bakuhan system to remain intact, while others envisaged the creation of a new structure modeled on Confucian principles. But the movement's basic weakness was that its goal of expelling the barbarians was a practical impossibility. A few loyalists who had managed to travel abroad, where they saw with their own eyes the fullness of Western power, realized this early on. When Itō Hirobumi, a student of Yoshida Shōin traveling secretly (and illegally) in England, heard of Chōshū's plans to bombard foreign ships, he immediately rushed home to dissuade domain leaders from this rash action. After the British bombarded the Satsuma capital of Kagoshima in September 1863 to force payment of an indemnity for the murder of Richardson, and after a joint Western fleet bombarded Chōshū shore batteries in September 1864 in retaliation for their attacks on Western vessels, all but the most obtuse anti-foreign loyalists realized that expulsion was futile.

The coup de grace for the loyalist movement came when the bakufu finally decided to crack down on the loyalist-dominated domain of Chōshū, whose officials and activists had repeatedly violated bakufu laws and orders. Having reestablished its control over the imperial court, the bakufu managed to have the emperor declare Chōshū an enemy of the court and mobilized samurai levies from all over the country for a military expedition to chastise the rogue domain. In late 1864, Chōshū surrendered without a fight. Meanwhile, in the domain of Mito, another center of anti-foreign agitation, a rebellion led by loyalist activists, including the son of Fujita Tōko, was crushed by joint bakufu and domain forces, and its leaders were ruthlessly punished. With its leadership decimated and its influence at Kyoto destroyed, the back of the loyalist movement had been broken. The center of political action shifted from acts of heroic violence in Kyoto and Edo to more ominous efforts by powerful domains to restructure the old order.

THE MEIJI RESTORATION

Ironically, the crushing of the loyalist movement proved no salvation for the bakufu, which was doing its best to strengthen the country. Since the late 1850s, the bakufu had accelerated efforts to acquire new weapons and military technology from the West. Beginning with an embassy to ratify the Harris treaty in Washington in 1860, the bakufu sent several missions to the West not only to establish formal diplomatic exchanges but to gather knowledge from the Westerners. It invited experts from Holland and other Western countries to help build new arsenals and shipyards to manufacture steamships and modern-style weapons. In a search for talent, the bakufu also recruited a cadre of "Western experts" from various domains, many of them graduates of private rangaku academies, and it began sending promising young direct retainers abroad to study in Holland. Conservative bakufu officials, reluctant to abandon traditional practices, even in the face of domestic unrest and foreign pressure, grumbled about these innovations but low-ranking retainers like Katsu Kaishū, who had trained with Dutch instructors in Nagasaki, pushed them forward as best they could.

During the early 1860s, the bakuhan system continued to crumble even as the bakufu tried to patch up its tattered relations with the imperial court at Kyoto by conciliatory gestures. Before his assassination, Ii Naosuke had hoped to promote "unity between court and bakufu" (*kōbu gattai*) by arranging a marriage between the boy shogun, Tokugawa Iemochi, and the Kōmei emperor's sister, Princess Kazunomiya. Like the earlier bakufu attempt to secure approval of the Harris treaty, the move was intended to bolster bakufu authority of the bakufu. The marriage finally took place in 1862, but powerful reformist daimyo in Satsuma, Mito, Echizen, and Tosa used the kōbu-gattai slogan to broaden their own influence over both the court and the bakufu. If a direct conflict with the foreigners were to come, it was they who would bear the brunt of the defense. Not only did they urge the bakufu to tighten its belt, they called for an end to the sankin kotai system, arguing that the money saved by abandoning these costly progresses could be used to build up their own military and coastal defenses. In 1862, the bakufu agreed to relax the system, and it lifted a long-standing ban on the construction of ocean-going vessels. The reformist daimyo also extracted a promise from the bakufu to appoint three of their number (Shimazu Hisamitsu of Satsuma, Matsudaira Shungaku of Echizen, and Tokugawa Yoshinobu of Hitotsubashi) as special high advisors to the shogun. The bakufu was willing to make these concessions not only to build national strength but because it needed allies to crush the loyalist movement.

The bakufu's success in chastising Chōshū and crushing the rebellion in Mito rested on the cooperation of Satsuma and other key domains, but the loosening of traditional controls over the daimyo unleashed the centrifugal tendencies inherent in the bakuhan system. Not only were large domains like Satsuma, Tosa, and Echizen experimenting with Western machinery and manufacturing methods, they were building arsenals of Western ships and weapons. In the mid-1860s, it was clear to most domain leaders that it was cheap to buy Western guns, munitions, and steamships—mostly surplus from recent Western conflicts like the Crimean War—directly from eager foreign merchants in the treaty ports. By 1868, roughly 200,000 firearms and more than one hundred Western-style vessels, many barely seaworthy, had been brought in through the treaty ports at a cost of $7.8 million. The country was slowly breaking up into regional armed camps.

In Chōshū, former loyalists regained control of the domain government through military coup, and in Satsuma and Tosa, they won the personal support of the daimyo. Chastened by the failure of terrorism and expulsion, the former loyalists adopted radical but more pragmatic tactics than they had earlier. Since it was impossible to drive the Westerners out of the country, the only sensible alternative was to make Japan as strong as the foreigners through a policy of "national wealth and strength" (*fukoku kyōhei*, literally, "rich country and strong army"). But to do that required not only technological change but unification of the country. New leaders like Ōkubo Toshimichi (Satsuma), Kido Takayoshi (Chōshū), Sakamoto Ryōma (Tosa), and Iwakura Tomomi (imperial court) were becoming convinced that the great domains should unite to supplant the faltering bakufu. Sakamoto Ryōma, who in his days as a loyalist intended to assassinate the Westernizing bakufu official Katsu Kaishū, even drafted a plan for a national consultative assembly of daimyo inspired by the English parliamentary system.

As the bakufu moved forward slowly with its own military Westernization, distrust of its intentions was deepening among the domains, who worried that Edo was preparing to clamp down on domestic dissidents rather than fend off foreign attacks. In March 1866, through the mediation of Sakamoto Ryōma, Satsuma made a secret pact with Chōshū, promising support if the bakufu mounted another military expedition against its radical leadership. This was precisely this sort of alliance that the bakuhan system was intended to prevent. In the summer of 1866, when the shogun Iemochi personally led a second anti-Chōshū campaign, Satsuma and other key domains declined to supply troops. Faced with resistance by a stronger and more unified Chōshū, the bakufu campaign bogged down, and when Iemochi suddenly died, the bakufu army withdrew ignominiously. This military failure was one more blow to the bakufu's dwindling authority, and the army's retreat along the main highways exposed bakufu weakness even to the common people. A wave of protests by peasants, disgruntled at the bakufu's extraordinary tax levies and labor service to support the second Chōshū expedition, swept across the bakufu domains in late 1866 and 1867.

Ironically, the bakufu made a desperate new attempt at reform under the leadership of Tokugawa Yoshinobu, long the favorite of the reformist daimyo. Hoping to patch the bakuhan system together, he at first proposed that a new shogun be elected by a council of daimyo, who would assist him in initiating a reform program. Meeting with little positive response from the daimyo, Yoshinobu took office as shogun in early 1867, determined not to be a mere figurehead like his predecessors. Relying on officials like Oguri Tadamasa, a high-ranking bakufu retainer, who advocated eliminating the domains completely, and turning for advice and promises of financial support to Leon Roches, the French minister to Edo, Yoshinobu moved ahead with sweeping reform plans. The new shogun envisaged major institutional changes: the council of elders was to be recast into a Western-style cabinet with functional ministries; bakufu finances were to be restored through the levy of new taxes, the opening of mines, and the promotion of industry; and the military forces of the bakufu were to be transformed from a feudal samurai levy into a professional standing army equipped with Western weapons and financed by taxes on the shogun's direct retainers. In effect, Yoshinobu was planning to transform the bakuhan system into a highly centralized modern-style state. Little wonder that Kido Takayoshi, an anti-bakufu leader in Chōshū, said his appointment as shogun was like "the rebirth of Ieyasu."

This belated reform effort was the last straw for anti-bakufu elements in Chōshū, Satsuma, and Tosa. By mid-1867 leaders in these domains had decided to establish a new imperial government to replace the bakufu. As Iwakura Tomomi, a loyalist court noble, wrote in 1866, "To [reassert our national prestige and overcome the foreigners] requires that the country be united. For the country to be united, policy and administration must have a single source. And for policy and administration to have a single source, the Court must be made the center of the national government."[11] The only remaining question was whether to end Tokugawa rule by peaceful means or by force.

As political certainties collapsed, commoners sensed that major change was in the air. In late 1867, residents of towns and villages along the main highways linking Edo with the Kansai region were swept up in a popular frenzy of dancing and celebration. When rumors spread that amulets from the great shrine at Ise, where the sun goddess was enshrined, were falling from the skies over Nagoya, the original base of the Tokugawa family, people poured into the streets in festive attire chanting "Hey, what the hell!" ("*Ee ja nai ka!*"). In many places, despite official orders to ban them, the revels lasted for weeks with throngs dancing, drinking, and carousing, as crowds on the great Ise pilgrimages had. These popular outbursts were buoyed by an abundant harvest that promised to end high rice prices, but they bespoke an awareness of political turmoil at the top. The revelers sang songs hinting at Chōshū's success in holding off the bakufu and tweaking bakufu leaders for their incompetence. In Fujisawa, a post town to the south of Edo, the raucous inhabitants even held a mock funeral for the bakufu, carrying a coffin bearing the honorific name of Tokugawa Ieyasu.

The actual demise of the Tokugawa regime began in July 1867 when the domains of Tosa and Echizen put forward a proposal for a peaceful transfer of power: the abolition of the shogunate, the demotion of the Tokugawa house to daimyo status, and the establishment of a bicameral national assembly made up of an upper house of court nobles and daimyo and a lower house of samurai and even of commoners. The Tosa proposal, which meshed with the ideas of bakufu reformers like Katsu Kaishū, was preferable to civil war. In November, after several months of negotiation, the shogun Yoshinobu agreed to formally return "sovereign power" to the imperial court. The change was more formal than substantive. Under the new arrangement, Yoshinobu held considerable power, serving as head of both the executive and legislative branches of the new government and retaining the power to appoint judicial officials as well. The Tokugawa family was also left in control of its ancestral territories, an extensive domain that allowed the Tokugawa to remain an *imperium in imperio,* powerful enough to challenge imperial authority.

The leaders of Satsuma and Chōshū, fearing that the Tokugawa house would continue pursuing its selfish interests, finally decided to stage a military coup to destroy its economic base and its last vestiges of political power by military force. In early December 1867, contingents of Satsuma and Chōshū troops moved into Kyoto to seize control of the imperial court and put a final end to Tokugawa supremacy. On January 3, 1868, military units from Satsuma, Chōshū, and Tosa seized control of the imperial palace gates. The young emperor Meiji, who had succeeded to the throne after the sudden death of his anti-foreign father, the emperor Kōmei, issued a decree formally abolishing all the traditional offices of the court and bakufu, establishing a new imperial government staffed with high-ranking court nobles, daimyo, and their retainers, and promising to sweep away past evils. After two and a half centuries, the Tokugawa bakufu had come to an end, brought down by an alliance of rebellious domains.

Typical of the secretive style of traditional politics, this revolutionary declaration was kept secret from the daimyo for nearly a week. The implications of the palace coup were clear enough to the former shogun Yoshinobu, who

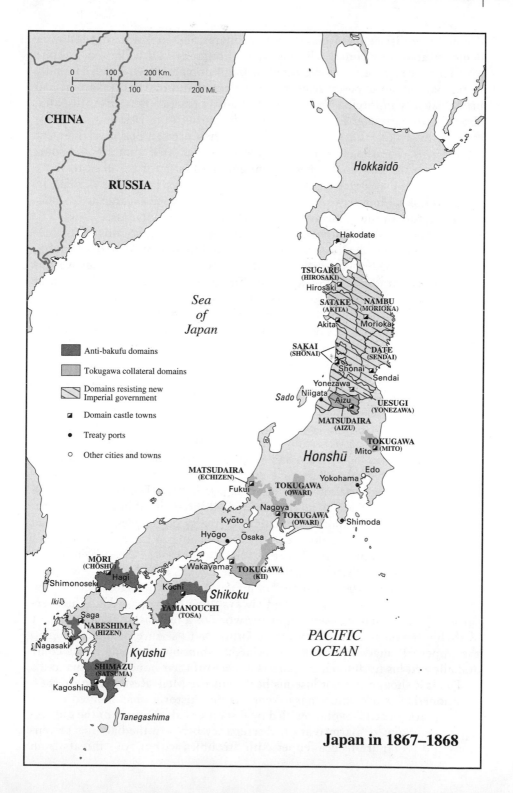

Japan in 1867–1868

Anti-bakufu domains

Tokugawa collateral domains

Domains resisting new Imperial government

Domain castle towns

Treaty ports

Other cities and towns

decided to resist at the urging of his retainers. The civil war that followed demonstrated how completely Tokugawa authority had collapsed. Despite the fact that bakufu forces retreated through domains traditionally friendly to the bakufu, an imperial army under the command of Saigō Takamori had little difficulty in forcing Yoshinobu all the way back to Edo. In April 1868, choosing to surrender Edo castle peacefully rather than risk destruction of the city, the bakufu forces finally laid down their arms, albeit on rather generous terms. The shogun's direct retainers were granted amnesty and some soon joined the new government. Although Yoshinobu was forced to retire as head of the Tokugawa family, his successor was granted a domain of 700,000 koku, about equal in size to Satsuma and twice as large as Chōshū. The departure of the Tokugawa had proven relatively bloodless.

Resistance to the new imperial government, however, continued for several months in the northeast, especially in the domains of Aizu and Nambu, which had decided to cast their lot with the bakufu. Their resistance was inspired less by traditional loyalty to the Tokugawa than by apprehension at the power acquired by the southwestern daimyo. Provincial loyalty and sectionalism died harder than the authority of the Tokugawa, and fighting in the north did not end until six months after the fall of Edo. The final gasp of the old regime came in Hokkaido, where a rump of bakufu retainers under Enomoto Takeaki, second-in-command of the bakufu's new navy, had fled to establish an independent "republic." In June 1869, after heavy fighting, Enomoto finally surrendered, after graciously sending his adversary his book on Western military science.

Few had rallied to the cause of the Tokugawa. The direct retainers, the fudai daimyo, and the great collateral houses, all of whom might have been expected to defend the dynasty, had remained neutral in the fighting for reasons that are not hard to guess. Despite Yoshinobu's last-minute reform efforts, the decline in bakufu prestige had not halted. The shogun was no longer respected or feared, and the bakufu had shown itself unable to control the country. As the economic difficulties of the samurai class, including the bakufu's direct retainers, mounted after the opening of the ports, many had lost faith in the ability of the Tokugawa house to provide "benevolent rule." Finally, of course, the leaders of the Satsuma and Chōshū had wisely wrapped themselves in the "brocade banner" of imperial authority, as founders of new dynasties and new governments had always done in the past. Had the overthrow of the Tokugawa been simply the work of a few disgruntled daimyo it probably would not have gone so smoothly. But "seizure of the jewel [i.e., the emperor]" made it possible to declare Yoshinobu an enemy of the court and allowed his traditional supporters to cast off their bonds of allegiance.

The last shogun did not lose his head, but the Meiji Restoration of 1868 was nonetheless a revolutionary event. As one historian has pointed out, it was "an aristocratic revolution" led by discontented members of the old ruling class who were alarmed at the discrepancy between the bakufu's pretensions and its failure to deal either with "troubles within" or "threats from without."[12] In this respect, it was similar to most other modern revolutions, which overthrew weak regimes of demonstrated incompetence rather than powerful and tyrannical states. The fall of the bakufu differed only in that the revolutionaries used traditional rhetoric—the "restoration of imperial rule"—to justify their actions. But it was soon to become clear that this conservative goal masked a fundamental urge to reshape the country from top to bottom, transforming it into a modern nation. As an imperial decree noted in late 1868, "The rapid march of civilization demands the concentration of the governing power in a single center and identity of feeling in the national mind in order to preserve the state and insure the execution of the laws."

ENDNOTES

1. Quoted in Toshio Yokoyama, *Japan in the Victorian Mind: A Study of Stereotyped Images of a Nation, 1850–1880* (Houndsmill, Basingstoke, Hampshire: Macmillan, 1987), 4.

2. For a slightly different translation, see Sugita Gempaku, *Dawn of Western Science in Japan (Rangaku kotohajime)* (Tokyo: Hokuseido Press, 1969), 69.

3. Aizawa Seishisai is quoted in Ryusaku Tsunoda et al., *Sources of Japanese Tradition* (New York: Columbia University Press, 1958), 602.

4. Sir Stamford Raffles, *Report on Japan to the Secret Committee of the English East India Company* (Kobe, Japan: J.L. Thompson and Co.), 160.

5. *Meiji ishin,* Yomiuri shimbunsha, Tokyo, 1968, 19–20.

6. The comment is quoted in Konishi Shirō, *Kaikoku to jōi* (Tokyo: Chūō kōronsha, 1966), 8.

7. Perry's views on the Japanese are dealt with in Samuel Eliot Morison, *"Old Bruin": Commodore Matthew Calbraith Perry* (Boston: Little, Brown and Co., 1967).

8. Donald Keene (ed.), *Anthology of Japanese Literature* (New York: Grove Press, 1955), 439.

9. Shibusawa Eiichi, *The Autobiography of Shibusawa Eiichi From Peasant to Entrepreneur,* trans. Teruko Craig (Tokyo: University of Tokyo Press, 1994), 20–21.

10. See Harry D. Harootunian, *Toward Restoration: The Growth of Political Consciousness in Tokugawa Japan* (Berkeley: University of California Press, 1970), Chapter 6.

11. Quoted in W. G. Beasley, *The Meiji Restoration* (Stanford, Cal.: Stanford University Press, 1972), 261.

12. See Thomas C. Smith, "Japan's Aristocratic Revolution," *Yale Review* 50, no. 3 (Spring 1961), 370–383.

II

The Pursuit of Wealth
and Power, 1868–1905

5

Revolution from Above

The Meiji Restoration brought to power new leaders not so very different from those they had overthrown. Enjoying neither broad popular support nor representing a cross-section of society, nearly all of them came from the old samurai elite. Loyalist court nobles like Iwakura Tomomi and Sanjō Sanetomi and reforming daimyo like Shimazu Hisamatsu held the highest posts in the new imperial government, but its middle and lower echelons were filled by samurai activists and officials from the domains of Satsuma, Chōshū, and Tosa. Neither did the country's new leaders stand for a radically new set of policies. Beneath the complex maneuvering of the 1860s, a consensus emerged among all camps that Japan should overcome "national humiliation" at the hands of the foreigners by building a "rich country and a strong army" (*fukoku kyōhei*). Anti-foreign sentiment had been transformed from crude expulsionism into an ambition to strengthen Japan by mastering Western technology and adopting Western institutions. The bakufu leaders, already moving in that direction under the leadership of Tokugawa Yoshinobu, might well have continued such policies had the Restoration not occurred.

THE CENTRALIZATION OF POWER

It is difficult to associate any systematic ideology with the new regime. Its leaders were not intellectuals but pragmatic men of action, who neither embraced a philosophical position like "the doctrine of the rights of man" nor proposed a utopian vision of a new and perfect social order. Driven by a determination to "restore the imperial honor" through national self-strengthening, they did nevertheless have a clear set of goals. These were outlined in the Imperial Oath (usually called the Charter Oath) proclaimed by the young Meiji emperor in April 1868.[1] The oath was intended to rally the country behind a common effort and to assure people that the new regime was not going to be a new bakufu dominated by a few domains. It promised (1) the convocation of a national assembly and submission of matters of state to "public discussion," (2) the unity of "all classes high and low" in promoting the national welfare, (3) the abolition of "absurd customs of olden times," and (4) the pursuit of "knowledge from all over the world" in order to "strengthen the foundations of imperial rule." All but the most rabid antiforeign elements could embrace these goals, but they were broad and ambiguous enough to conceal disagreement over how best to realize them.

In the early days of the new regime, an outward facade of unity masked deep cleavages within the ranks of the government. It was, as one historian has put it, a "community of strangers."[2] Even outsiders could detect the lack of political cohesion and stability. "There was a restlessness, I might almost say an irritability perceptible in the management of public business that showed all was not working smoothly," noted a foreign journalist. "Men had not yet found their proper grooves."[3] Provincial hostilities, suspicions, and jealousies were never far below the surface. In 1868, rumors swept the new imperial capital at Tokyo (the new name for Edo) that fighting would shortly break out between Satsuma and Chōshū now that the bakufu had been overthrown. Uncertainty over future direction intensified political restlessness. The coalition that overthrew the bakufu had been united by a common enemy, but once the Tokugawa were gone, its members began to debate among themselves what to do next.

Like all revolutionary governments, the new imperial regime gave first priority to consolidating control over the rest of the country. Its territorial base was limited to the new capital at Tokyo and territory confiscated from the Tokugawa bakufu. But in the rest of the country the domains remained intact, and so did their fighting forces, many now equipped with Western weapons. Any attempt to encroach on domain autonomy ran the risk of renewed civil war. To create a sense of national unity, in early 1868 the government set up a new "national deliberative assembly" (kōgisho) with an upper house made up of court nobles, daimyo, and their highest retainers, and a lower house made up of representatives from each domain. Intended to reassure the domains rather than to establish representative government, the new assembly provided the kind of federal conciliar structure proposed by Tosa leaders in 1867, and it had considerable power. The upper house, for example, was given the responsibility of establishing a constitution, enacting new laws, exercising supreme judicial power, and concluding treaties.

Ruling through the domains was a temporary but unsatisfactory expedient. Administrative practice varied widely from domain to domain, creating enormous confusion. In some domains, officials ignored the decrees promulgated by the new government, while in others they launched sweeping reforms that ran ahead of the government. But the main difficulty was that political loyalties remained fragmented as long as the domains were intact. To strengthen the country, it was essential to shift political loyalties toward the new central government, which otherwise would remain fragmented and weak. As Kido Takayoshi noted, "A single rod, even though a stout one, may be broken by a young child, but if ten rods, though all are weak, are made into a bundle, they cannot be broken even by a full-grown man."[4]

The centralization of power began after months of persistent negotiation, with the return of domain land and population registers to the emperor in early 1869. This halfway measure, more symbolic than practical, was to demonstrate that the realm belonged to the emperor and that all its people were his subjects. In principle at least, the domains were allowed to retain their powers to raise taxes and so forth, but the daimyo, who were appointed as local governors, were treated as "servants of the emperor." Other measures aimed at administrative rationalization and centralization soon followed: elaborate status distinctions within the samurai class were replaced by the establishment of just two ranks (*shizoku* and *sotsu*); the stipends of samurai retainers were reduced; all remaining fiefs were made public land; and uniform procedures for tax collection and the like were established. Finally, more than three years after the Restoration, in August 1871 the Meiji emperor assembled the former daimyo to announce the abolition of the domains and the creation of new prefectures.

The abolition of the domains, seen by some as a "second Restoration," had an immediate impact on the provinces. The daimyo were ordered to move from their castle towns to Tokyo and the symbols of domain authority were literally dismantled. Castle moats were filled in, daimyo mansions levelled, and other structures sold for their stone, wood, and copper. The old domain boundaries vanished as the government divided the country into seventy-two new prefectures (later reduced to forty-six). In place of the daimyo, new prefectural governors, many of them former low-ranking samurai from Chōshū, Satsuma, and their allies, moved into the old domain offices. As agents of the new imperial government with no local connections, they often rode roughshod over the local populations, who resented them as "outsiders" with little concern or sensitivity toward their sentiments.

To the foreigners the abolition of the domains seemed a radical, even revolutionary event. The British minister, Harry Parkes, concluded that the government had succeeded by an act of Providence. But it was political realities not the hand of God that brought about this "bloodless revolution." Many domains, deeply in debt as the result of both long-standing obligations and expenses incurred during the post-Restoration civil war, were anxious to shift their financial burden to the new government. During a debate in the *kōgisho* in the early summer of 1869, nearly half the domain representatives expressed support for a more centralized administrative system, and several domains surrendered their domain registers even before the government ordered them to. For its part, the government eased the transition by guaranteeing stipends for the old local political elite. Samurai retainers received only a third of their former stipends, but the daimyo, who were guaranteed incomes equal to 10 percent of their domain tax revenues, did rather well.

Although the abolition of the domains was a major step toward consolidating national consciousness among the former samurai, the idea of Japan as a single nation was still a distant abstraction for much of the country's population. Slowly but deliberately, however, the leadership reinvented the emperor as a focus for popular political loyalty. Traditionally, the emperor had been a mysterious and remote figure, living isolated—"above the clouds," in the phrase of the times—in the imperial palace compound at Kyoto, where he was seen by few but a narrow circle of court aristocrats. His existence was hardly known to the people outside the region around the old capital at Kyoto. Within the new imperial government, a small cadre of officials under the influence of nativist ideas hoped to restore "unity of ceremony and rule" (*saisei itchi*) by turning the emperor into the high priest of a national cult based on Shinto practices. The newly formed ministry of ceremonies (*jingikan*), which embarked on a campaign to purify the country of Buddhist influence, revived public rituals that celebrated the divine origins of the imperial family.

Top government leaders like Ōkubo Toshimichi did not want to revive the ancient monarchy so much as create a highly visible modern one around whom the people could rally. When the emperor first arrived in his new capital at Tokyo in 1868, he travelled hidden from the public gaze in a curtained palan-

Portrait photograph of the new Emperor Meiji in military uniform (circa 1872).

quin, but by the early 1870s he could be seen astride a white horse reviewing military parades or touring the streets in a horse-drawn carriage. To serve as a role model for his subjects, in public he wore a dashing Western-style uniform, replete with gold braid, buttons, epaulets, and a European sabre at his waist, instead of traditional court costume. (The empress, on the other hand, wore traditional court clothes much longer, a reminder that the new reforms affected women less than men.) In a radical departure from historical precedent, the emperor also embarked on a series of imperial progresses through the country, visiting famous shrines and temples or historical sites, observing local public works projects, meeting with local officials and other luminaries, and bestowing gifts and awards on deserving subjects. Festive crowds lined the roads hoping to catch a glimpse of the emperor's progress, and local innkeepers were proud to boast that "the emperor had slept here." (While some spectators had no idea who the emperor was, others thought him a potent "living god" with magical powers stronger than the local *kami*.)

To bolster a sense of patriotism, the government quickly adopted the symbols of the nation state deployed in the West. In early 1870, the "rising sun" flag, with a red disk against a white background, originally adopted by the bakufu for all Japanese ships, was declared to be the national flag. From 1873 onward, the government also declared new national holidays, beginning with one to celebrate the emperor's birthday and another to commemorate the accession to power of the first emperor Jimmu. Devising a national anthem took more time. An English music teacher in Japan set to music a tenth-century Japanese poem (*Kimigayo* or "My Lord's Reign") the same year, but the imperial household ministry was reluctant to adopt a national anthem written by a foreigner. Several years later it adopted a different score written by a Japanese composer. The new anthem, based on Western-style music, was first performed on the emperor's birthday in 1880. Eventually it became a kind of non-official national anthem, sung in the schools and performed on other public events.

TAX REFORM, CONSCRIPTION, AND EDUCATION

With the successful abolition of the domains, the top leaders of the new government felt confident enough to embark on a mission around the world in 1871. Led by Iwakura Tomomi, the mission was originally intended to open treaty revision negotiations, but its members quickly discovered that the Western governments were reluctant to do so. Instead, they spent a year and a half traveling across the United States and Europe, visiting factories and arsenals, government ministries and military academies, museums and schools, public parks and private schools. Received by curious but friendly crowds wherever they went, the mission members were often stunned by the great discrepancies between their own society and the ones they visited. Few of them had been abroad before, and the experience was an eye-opening one.

The West proved more diverse than many mission members had expected. The United States, Great Britain, and France—the three countries where they stayed longest—represented the most advanced face of the West, but Russia and Italy appeared more backward, perhaps not so very far ahead of Japan itself. But it was the newly established German Empire, formed by the unification of a large number of small principalities, whose historical experience seemed closest to Japan's, and it was the advice of the German Chancellor Otto von Bismarck, the architect of the German state, that seemed most pertinent to their own situation. On their way back through Asia, the mission members saw first hand how differently the "civilized" Westerners acted in their colonial territories than they did at home—and this stiffened their resolve not to be treated like the "barbarian" or "semi-civilized" peoples. While Japan still had a great distance to cover in catching up with the Westerners, the mission members returned optimistic that the task was not impossible. After all, the Western countries had acquired their preponderant wealth and power only two or three generations before.

As the Iwakura mission made its leisurely tour of the globe, the pace of reform accelerated at home. Before the mission departed, a caretaker government put under the leadership of Saigō Takamori promised to abstain from major changes, but the urgent problems facing the imperial government called for quick solutions. Reform-minded younger officials, many of them "Western experts" who had studied Western institutions and knew how they worked, were eager to accelerate change. Gaining influence at the expense of more conservative former loyalist elements, they pushed forward a set of sweeping reforms intended to build a "rich country and strong army" (*fukoku kyōhei*).

The most urgent problem was how to keep the government afloat financially. During its early days, the new regime lived from hand to mouth. To wage its military campaigns against the bakufu forces and the disgruntled domains in the northeast, it borrowed money from privileged Osaka merchant houses like the Mitsui, the Konoike, and the Shimada as well as other official purveyors and merchants with close ties to the bakufu. Once the new government gained control over the former bakufu domains and the territories of the defeated northeastern domains, it could tax their inhabitants as well, but this meant running the whole country with revenues from only part of it. To make ends meet, the government began printing paper currency, but since the general population had little confidence in the government's credit, it depreciated in value rapidly.

These short-term expedients were no substitute for a stable long-term flow of revenue. Kanda Takahira, a young "Western expert," suggested turning all cultivated land over to the peasantry and taxing them as its owners. More conservative officials, however, wanted the government to buy up all the land in the country and resell it to the former samurai. Before his departure on the Iwakura mission, Ōkubo Toshimichi devised a land tax plan intended to bring in revenues roughly equivalent to those of the bakufu and the domains. Based on private ownership of land, it proposed a national survey to determine the extent and value of all the cultivated land, whose owners would be obliged to pay taxes directly to the national government. In 1873, Ōkubo's plan became the basis for a new land tax law.

The new law overcame a basic weakness in the Tokugawa tax system: since the value of the rice collected for taxes fluctuated as its price rose and fell, it was difficult if not impossible to make accurate budget projections. The new system assessed taxes on the value of the land rather than on the size of the harvest, collected them in cash rather than in rice, and levied them on individual landowners rather than on village communities. Those who received land certificates giving them title to land were required to pay taxes equal to 3 percent of its value. In the mid-1870s, a national cadastral survey was carried out by local farmers and village officials working under the supervision of government experts to determine who owned what fields. While the surveys were usually fair, they rode roughshod over many variations in local customs and practices, creating unrest in many areas.

The caretaker government also moved forward on plans for a new military force. Although the abolition of the domains was accomplished with little violence, and fear of foreign invasion had ebbed, government leaders worried about local unrest. In the immediate post-Restoration years, peasant disturbances had flared up on the territories taken over from the bakufu, and disgruntled samurai attacked government officials to protest the sudden changes sweeping the country. In 1870, an imperial guard force, recruited from the rump of the Restoration army, was given responsibility for preserving domestic order, but its ranks were filled with former samurai loyalists who were reluctant to submit to Western-style military drills and discipline—and who cosseted grievances of their own against the new regime. Some government leaders, who had discovered in the 1860s that commoner militia forces were capable of holding their own in battle, proposed a conscript army open to former samurai and commoner alike. Conservatives, who thought that arming ordinary people was ridiculous, if not dangerous, insisted instead on a volunteer army drawn from the former samurai class.

Yamagata Aritomo, who had returned from a tour of Europe convinced that the military systems in France and Prussia served to educate and mobilize the population behind the government, was the most forceful advocate of conscription. A conscript army, he argued, could become a "great civil and military university" where recruits would not only learn military skills but would be exposed to the ways of "civilization." In January 1873, the government promulgated a conscription law requiring every young male regardless of social rank to spend three years on active service followed by four in the reserves. In principle, the whole male population was obliged to serve, but exemptions were made for government officials, students, adopted sons, household heads, physicians, and the physically disabled. For the substantial sum of ¥270 a potential recruit could also buy his way out of military service. The new conscription system seriously undermined the position of the former samurai class. Indeed, the conscription edict pointedly attacked the samurai for "having lived a life of idleness" at the expense of others. "Neither the samurai nor the common people will have the status they were accustomed to in the past," it proclaimed, "nor will there be any distinction in the service they render to their country, for they will all be alike as subjects of the Empire."[5]

The new conscript army did not get off to an auspicious start. Many young commoners, and even many youths from former samurai households, who were less than enthusiastic about spending three years in military service, took advantage of the exemption clauses or bought their way out of service. Even in the mid-1870s the government barely managed to draft 14,000 to 15,000 men a year. Recruitment was not made any easier by the fact that most officers and noncoms in the new conscript army were former samurai, who often treated commoners under their command with contempt and brutality. Nor were conscripts moved by intense patriotism or attachment to the government. Most were second or third sons of peasant families too poor to buy an exemption or to get married. As one dissident general complained, the new army was made up of "grimy peasants."[6] Yet many of these "grimy peasants" became the first members of their communities to enter the world of modernity, not only learning how to sleep in beds and use indoor plumbing but how to submit to new disciplines of time and authority. As Yamagata had hoped, the new conscript army did indeed become a "university" for much of the population.

The caretaker government also put the finishing touches on a new educational system. Inspired in large part by the example of the United States, where elementary education reached most children, the new school system aimed at spreading the practical knowledge and practical arts needed to build national strength. The education regulations of 1872, which mandated universal compulsory elementary schooling, made clear that a single class or gender would no longer monopolize access to education. "In no village shall there be a house without learning," it proudly proclaimed, "and in no house an individual without learning."[7] Schools were open to girls and boys alike. Officials hoped that education would produce "free and independent individuals" able to advance their own position in life while serving the nation. Following advice from American experts, the new ministry of education drew up plans for an elaborate three-tiered structure of eight universities, 256 middle schools, and 54,000 elementary schools.

It was easier to issue a boldly conceived educational decree than to put the new system into practice. By 1875, more than 25,000 elementary schools, nearly half of them converted from existing *terakoya* or commoner schools, had been established, but the system faced problems. First, the central government's finances were too fragile to support such an ambitious and elaborate structure. Since top budget priority went to training technicians and experts, the burden of paying for the elementary system, the construction of new schools, and the hiring of teachers was left to local communities, whose resources were quite limited. Second, it was not easy to find teachers to teach new subjects like world geography or even able to comprehend arithmetic textbooks using Arabic numerals instead of Chinese numerals. Finally, it was almost as difficult to recruit school pupils as army conscripts. Many families refused to send their children to school because of the economic burden it posed. Poorer peasant households could not afford to pay school fees, and they needed their children to do light work in the fields or to take care of younger siblings. Attendance rates remained low, rising from about 23 percent in 1873 to no more than 27 percent in 1877.

THE END OF THE SAMURAI CLASS

Debates over basic reform revealed a fundamental cleft in the government's ranks. Infighting among the ministries grew worse, regional rivalries intensified, and wrangling over the direction of reform continued. Younger officials knowledgeable about the West wanted to move ahead rapidly, dismantling old laws and institutions as fast as possible, even if it meant trampling on the privileges and prerogatives of the old samurai elite. To them, it was clear that unless the government did so the country would remain as weak as it had been when Perry sailed into Uraga Bay. On the other hand, more conservative leaders, including Saigō Takamori, the leader of the caretaker government, were reluctant to undermine the samurai elite or shift society away from an agrarian base. Frustrated at the pace of change, Saigō returned to Kagoshima for several months in 1872, leaving the government in Tokyo rudderless.

Tension inside the government came to a head over the question of whether or not to send an expedition to "chastise Korea." The Korean court had repeatedly rebuffed its requests to shift to Western-style diplomatic exchange. In 1873, relations deteriorated further when Korean officials at Pusan, accusing the Japanese of "lawless" behavior and "shameless" imitation of the Western barbarians, threatened to cut off all contacts. To rebuke the Koreans for these "insults," and to force them to accept a new diplomatic relationship, Saigō Takamori, with the backing of Itagaki Taisuke, Gotō Shōjirō, and Etō Shimpei, proposed to lead an armed expedition to the peninsula. The hidden agenda behind his proposal was to pacify former samurai, especially from the old domains of Satsuma and Chōshū, who were upset by the decline of their class. By offering an opportunity for military glory abroad, supporters of the "chastise Korea" expedition hoped to deflect this discontent.

On returning from their tour of the "civilized" world in mid-1873 members of the Iwakura mission expressed strong opposition to a foreign adventure that would dissipate financial and military resources and might provoke foreign intervention into the bargain. The government's priorities, argued Ōkubo Toshimichi, should be to put the government finances on a sound basis, build up its military strength, and lay the foundations for a new political economy. In the end, opponents of the Korean expedition succeeded in having the emperor reverse the caretaker government's decision. But this reversal shattered the uneasy harmony that had held the Restoration coalition together. The leaders who favored the expedition, Saigō and Itagaki, left the government immediately, ceding a dominant role within the government to Ōkubo. In his push for further institutional reform, he was supported by Itō Hirobumi, Ōkuma Shigenobu, Yamagata Aritomo, and other young reformist officials, who were to dominate Japanese politics for a generation.

Their most vexing challenge was how to deal with the former samurai class, whose *raison d'être* had been undercut by the conscription law. Even though government stipends to the samurai had been scaled down, the class remained an enormous burden to the government, gobbling up as much of its budget as all other administrative expenses combined. It was clear that entitlements on this grand scale could not continue indefinitely. After Saigō resigned, the government made stipends taxable, taking from the samurai with one hand what it gave with the other. Few doubted that it was only a matter of time before the former samurai were stripped of all their privileges, privileges that remained a glaring anachronism in a country aspiring to join the ranks of the "civilized" countries.

Adopting a proposal of Ōkuma Shigenobu, in 1874–1875 the government offered to commute samurai stipends into interest-bearing bonds. The hope was that energetic samurai would use these negotiable bonds as capital to invest in land and industry or to set up small business ventures of their own. Only a few former samurai, perhaps a fifth of the class, took advantage of the offer; the majority were reluctant to relinquish their guaranteed incomes, however paltry. Fearful that its finances were on the verge of collapse, the government decreed a mandatory commutation program in late 1876. In effect, this was a forced buy-out of the class, paid for by government bonds that would only come due in the future. To complete the disestablishment of the samurai, the government also denied the right to wear a sword—a privilege that for centuries had set the samurai apart from the commoners—to anyone but military officers, policemen, and other appropriate officials.

For many samurai households, commutation of the stipends spelled financial ruin. Interest income from the bonds amounted to only half the monetary value of their former pensions. Perhaps 80 to 85 percent of them found themselves with annual incomes of less than ¥66 (and many as little as ¥9-10) at a time when the price of one *koku* of rice (approximately enough to feed one person for one year) was ¥5-6. Even relatively well-off middle and upper samurai families were pushed to the edge of subsistence as prices rose in the late 1870s. As the purchasing value of their fixed income fell, many sold their bonds for cash just to make ends meet. To cushion the devastating social impact of the change, the government devised programs to convert the former samurai into farmers by selling or leasing them uncultivated government-owned land in northeast Honshu and in the newly opened northern island of Hokkaido. Since samurai were unaccustomed to manual labor or thought it beneath their dignity, these programs were not very successful. Low-cost government loans to invest in agriculture or manufacturing found more takers. Some samurai enterprises such as the tea cultivation companies organized by former bakufu retainers in the Shizuoka prefecture were highly successful, but many more were poorly managed and quickly went broke. By 1889, 80 percent of the samurai loans had gone into default.

The former samurai nevertheless had survival skills that allowed them to weather the loss of financial and social privilege. Nearly all samurai were literate and trained for public service. Compared to the rest of the population, they were highly educated. Not surprisingly, many found employment in the lower echelons of the burgeoning government structure. Some took jobs as school teachers, while others served as minor civilian functionaries, policemen, court bailiffs, or officers and noncoms in the new conscript army. By the early 1880s, 65 percent of all officials in the central and prefectural governments were former samurai; and so were 41 percent of all school teachers. Even former samurai unable to find new occupations themselves sent their sons off to Tokyo to acquire the knowledge and skills required by the new society. Indeed, the recruitment of a new educated elite drew heavily from the ranks of the old elite.

THE NEW POLITICAL ECONOMY

In the early years after the Restoration, the new government had been unsure how to manage the economy. To revive trade and production, it followed the example of the bakufu and the domains—managing trade with the help of privileged merchants. After banning the old domain monopolies, the Tokyo government set up a new system of official "exchange companies" to take over the work of private money changers, and official "trading companies" to take over the role of urban wholesale merchants. These official companies, financed with freshly printed government currency, were run by the merchants they were intended to replace, so this venture in government-managed trade quickly proved a failure. As government currency depreciated, the companies slipped into financial difficulty, and their merchant managers were poorly equipped to save them. As Shibusawa Eiichi later recalled, "They bowed and scraped the moment they saw a government official, they were uneducated, devoid of initiative, and utterly uninterested in new ideas of innovation."[8] But the real cause of failure lay in economic realities. Western merchants in the treaty ports were reluctant to deal with a government monopoly over foreign trade, and the domestic economy had long since grown too large and complex for internal trade to be controlled by official monopolies.

It was not long before the government's priority shifted from reviving trade to building an economy that could match the West. It was clear that the country's strength could no longer rest on an agricultural base. As Kanda Takahira wrote, "The nations that depend on business are always rich while those that depend on agriculture are always poor. Therefore, the eastern countries are always poor and the western ones always rich."[9] Any lingering doubts about the importance of developing trade and industry were dispelled by the experience of the Iwakura mission. As Ōkubo observed of his travels in England, "There is nowhere we have not been. And everywhere we go, there is nothing growing in the ground, just coal and iron. . . . Factories have increased to an unheard-of extent, so that black smoke rises to the sky from every possible kind."[10] (Although "black smoke" conjures up images of pollution today, for the Meiji leaders it signified the source of Britain's enormous wealth and strength.)

From the outset there was consensus, springing from the anti-foreign sentiments of the 1850s and 1860s, that the country should not rely on foreign loans to build up the economy. Indebtedness to foreign countries, it was feared, could open the way to subtle forms of foreign domination. In any case, it soon became apparent that foreign capitalists, who viewed the new and unstable regime as a risky venture, were willing to lend money to the Japanese only at a high cost. For example, when the new government tried to negotiate a loan with a British bank to pay off the huge debts the bakufu had incurred with the French, it demanded a high interest rate of 15 percent and asked that the loan be secured against the revenues of the Yokohama customs house. Faced with what it regarded as outrageous terms, the government decided to put an end to all foreign borrowing. It was safer and cheaper for Japan to pull up its economy by the bootstraps.

The government had fallen heir to the arsenals, ship yards, iron foundries, and other enterprises acquired by the bakufu and the domains in the 1860s, but building a modern economy required much more than military production. To catch up with the advanced industrial countries meant that the Japanese had to learn new ways of mining gold, silver, and copper; they had to learn how to manufacture bricks, glass, and cement for new Western-style buildings; they had to find ways to increase the production of export products like silk and silk yarn; and they had to learn how to manufacture the cotton yarn and other imported manufactures flooding in from the West. In the early 1870s, the government embarked on an effort to "increase production and encourage industry" by introducing foreign technology. It was the only entity in the country with enough capital, international contacts, and motive to do so. "Our people are particularly lacking in daring," lamented Ōkubo. "To encourage them to overcome this weakness and to study industry and overcome its difficulties is a responsibility that government must assume."[11]

Indeed, for nearly a decade the government was the principal (though not sole) entrepreneur, manager, and financier of modern manufacturing enterprises. In some ways, its activities harked back to domain attempts to boost local products such as indigo or cotton yarn. But the resources required were more vast in scale, and the technological rupture much greater. In 1870, a new ministry of industry, established at the suggestion of a British engineer, began laying railway lines, developing modern mines, stringing telegraph lines, and building lighthouses along the coast. The ministry also imported manufacturing facilities to produce glass, cement, woolen cloth, silk yarn, and other modern goods. Neither Western governments nor Western manufacturers imposed any restrictions on the flow of technology to Japan. Indeed, the foreigners were delighted to sell the machinery, construction materials, and even hand tools used in these enterprises to the Japanese. What was good for Japanese economic development was good for Western business enterprises too.

Although the Japanese were reluctant to depend on foreign capital, they had no qualms about relying on foreign engineers, technicians, and workmen. During the 1870s, more than 3000 "honorable hired foreigners" (*oyatoi gaikokujin*) were put on the government payroll at enormous salaries, and another 2500 were hired by private organizations. Not all these foreign "experts" remained sober all the time, and many were barely qualified for their jobs. (For example, Henry Brunton, a civil engineer rejected by Indian colonial authorities as too young and inexperienced for employment there, was hired by the Japanese to build lighthouses but ended up supervising a host of projects, from telegraph lines to a water and sewer system in Yokohama.) The government hoped that the foreign experts could train the Japanese to take over their tasks in the long run. Once the technical or managerial skills were mastered, the hired foreigners were sent home, and their Japanese apprentices taught their "new knowledge" to others. To train Japanese scientists and engineers, in 1871 the ministry of industry also founded an engineering school staffed by foreign teachers, who taught basic mathematics, geometry, physics, chemistry, architecture, engineering, or other technical specialties needed by a modern industrial economy.

Hundreds of promising young men (and a handful of young women) also went to study abroad on government scholarships. In contrast to many developing countries, no "brain drain" resulted. Occasionally, a student might switch from one field to another, but nearly all those who studied in Europe and the United States returned home to serve as engineers, professors, officials, or managers in government or private enterprises. To be sure, few had an opportunity to stay abroad since Westerners had little interest in hiring "Orientals" as technical experts. But the strong sense of obligation students felt toward their country was more important. The majority, who came from former samurai families and had been trained for public service, would have found it unthinkable not to return to Japan after the government had given them such an important opportunity.

Building a new political economy also required institutions to channel private investment into modern enterprises. Merchant houses, who preferred to put their capital in traditional activities such as commerce or money-lending, were reluctant to invest in railroad, factories, or other new ventures. For example, in 1869, when the government tried to induce Osaka merchants to invest in a Kyoto-Osaka railroad line, the project failed for lack of interest, even though the government guaranteed a return of 7 percent on invested capital plus half the profits. To encourage greater boldness, the government authorized the organization of joint stock companies, widely used in the West to finance new ventures. By selling shares or stocks, an enterprise could gather a far larger pool of capital than a traditional merchant house or wealthy individual could. Not everyone understood the idea, however, and many new companies often failed owing to the unscrupulousness or incompetence of their promoters.

With few exceptions, traditional merchant houses had difficulty in weathering the transition to the new economic order. Not only did they lack the skills and "new knowledge" needed to run modern ventures, many were hard hit by the changes of the early 1870s. Although the government promised to take over the old debts of the daimyo and the bakufu, it cancelled loans made before 1843 and paid the rest off very slowly. According to one estimate, the market values of such loans dropped by 80 percent, driving many former Osaka, Edo and provincial merchants into bankruptcy. Only a few with good official connections, such as the Mitsui, survived. The main beneficiaries of the new political economy were freewheeling entrepreneurs, promoters, and profiteers, who built their fortunes during the unsettled conditions of the 1860s and 1870s. Some, like Ōkura Kihachirō, made their money in the burgeoning silk and tea trade at Yokohama, supplying arms to the contending political forces in the 1860s, or speculating in currency. Others, like Iwasaki Yatarō, were "political merchants" who traded on inside government connections to build profitable modern enterprises. Iwasaki, a former samurai from Tosa, used personal ties with top officials to acquire a fleet of government-owned merchant vessels and form a private shipping firm that became the foundation of the Mitsubishi interests. And Shibusawa Eiichi, the "Johnny Appleseed" of the business world, who founded more than 500 companies during his career, had been a government official himself. All of these entrepreneurs benefitted from government favoritism, but they succeeded mainly by their willingness to take advantage of new economic opportunities.

Not all historians agree that the role of the government in "increasing industry and promoting production" was either positive or important. Some have pointed out that the Meiji government's investment in industry was small compared with that of contemporary European governments and that imported government enterprises were inefficient and unprofitable. Others have argued that by promoting mechanized industry so quickly, the government made it difficult for a strong private enterprise sector to emerge without government assistance. And still others point out that the importation of foreign technology and the subsidies dispensed to new entrepreneurs were financed by taxing a rural population that enjoyed few immediate benefits from the new political economy. While it is difficult to deny that the government spent only a small portion of its budget on promoting modern industry or that its economic policies often proved unsuccessful or that the mass of the people experienced few short-term gains, it is equally difficult to deny that government played a central role in building the infrastructure for a modern economy, in the diffusion of new technology, and in the reallocation of national human resources. Indeed, few non-Western governments negotiated the transition to economic modernity as agilely as the Meiji government did.

"CIVILIZATION AND ENLIGHTENMENT"

The headlong plunge in reform during the early 1870s was cheered on by a new intelligentsia: scholars, officials and journalists who had been trained in Dutch Studies or studied in the West. In contrast to the Dutch Studies scholars, who had focussed on Western science and technology, this new intelligentsia was more interested in Western laws, institutions, and society, and sought to diffuse knowledge about the West through popular writings and translations. A hunger for books about the West grew rapidly. Fukuzawa Yukichi's *Conditions in the West (Seiyō jijō)*, an encyclopedic compendium describing everything from Western tax systems to lunatic asylums, sold 150,000 copies in its first edition (1866), and Nishi Amane found ready readers for his *Links of All Sciences (Hyakugaku renkan)*, a summary of the whole corpus of Western scholarly knowledge, from history and theology through mathematics and physics. Another best seller was Nakamura Masanao's translation of Samuel Smiles' *Self-help*, a Victorian paean to the virtues of ambition and hard work, that attracted readers eager to learn how the Westerners had become more advanced than the Japanese. Few aspects of Western culture, secular or sacred, did not excite public curiosity. Fukuzawa even wrote an illustrated guide book instructing readers how to wear Western-style clothes, sleep in beds, and eat with knives and forks.

The most important role played by this Western-oriented intelligentsia was to introduce a new vision of historical change. Rather quickly they absorbed the contemporary Western belief in the possibility, and indeed the inevitability, of human progress. In this view, history was marching upward and onward toward an eventual state of human perfection, and all human societies were ranked by how far they had advanced on this march. The dynamic countries of the West represented "civilization," the most advanced stage of human development, while China, India, and pre-Restoration Japan were "semi-civilized" and the rest of the world was "savage" or "barbarian." The "civilized countries" (*bunmeikoku*) of the world were seen as superior not only economically and militarily but morally as well. Yet "civilization" was not the monopoly of the West. As Fukuzawa noted in one of his essays, it was no more possible to stop the spread of civilization than to stop an epidemic of measles.

Coming from a Confucian intellectual tradition that linked learning with statecraft, the new Western-oriented intelligentsia hoped to build national "wealth and strength" by hurrying Japan along the path toward "civilization." They thought Japan was weak not simply because its technology was backward but because its people were mired in "superstition, irrationality, ignorance, and backwardness." To overcome its cultural deficiencies, the country had to undergo a cultural or intellectual revolution by acquiring the "spirit of civilization." As Fukuzawa put it,

> Schools, industries, armies, and navies are all the mere external forms of civilization. They are not difficult to produce; all that is needed is the money to pay for them. Yet there remains something immaterial, something that cannot be seen or heard, bought or sold, lent or borrowed [that] pervades the whole nation and [whose] influence is so strong that without it none of the . . . external forms would be of the slightest use. This supremely important thing is . . . the spirit of civilization. [12]

In 1873, Fukuzawa, Nakamura Masanao, and several other Westernized intellectuals organized the Meirokusha, an association to spread the "new knowledge" from the West and to promote the "enlightenment" of the Japanese public. It held regular discussion meetings, as Western scholarly associations did, and it published a journal carrying essays written by its members.

The Meirokusha intellectuals launched an iconoclastic attack on "backward" and "uncivilized" customs, ideas, and behavior in Japan. One of their main targets was the ethical ideas propagated by Buddhism and Confucianism. As Nishi Amane pointed out, these traditional belief systems stressed negative virtues—gentleness, weakness, modesty, deference, frugality, self-abnegation, and obedience—that weakened the country by suppressing the normal human instincts and desires. Only by actively seeking health, knowledge, and wealth as the "civilized" peoples did could the country become strong. At the same time, the Meirokusha intellectuals directed withering criticism toward Confucianism with its emphasis on hierarchical values in family, marriage, and politics. Confucian ethics seemed not only inhumane but ridiculously impractical. (Spoofing the traditional story of the filial son who dowsed himself with rice wine and slept naked by his parents' bed to keep the mosquitoes from biting them, Fukuzawa suggested that it would have been simpler to buy mosquito netting.) Inspired by the utilitarian, rationalistic, and empirical outlook the Meirokusha intellectuals found in the "civilized countries," they denounced traditional morality and learning as unscientific and unprogressive.

If the new intellectuals were certain about what was wrong with traditional culture, they were in less agreement about what constituted the "spirit of civilization." Nakamura Masanao, for example, found it in Christianity.

"The industry, patience, and perseverance displayed in (Western) arts, inventions, and machinery," he wrote, "all have their origin in the faith, hope, and charity of their religion."[13] For him, Western strength and wealth were "the outward leaf and blossom" of Christianity, a sentiment that Western missionaries applauded. But most enlightenment intellectuals felt rather that the spirit of civilization lay in the secular values of the West: materialism, scientific rationality, and personal individualism. "If we would look for the origins of Western civilization," wrote Fukuzawa, "it comes down to one thing: doubt." In countries like Japan people never questioned the principle underlying nature and society but relied on uncritical acceptance of authority; they lacked a spirit of personal independence, initiative, and responsibility. "To defend our country against the foreigners," said Fukuzawa, "we must fill the whole country with the spirit of independence, so that noble and humble, high and low, clever and stupid alike will make the fate of the country their own responsibility and will play their part as citizens."[14] Fundamentally, the values propagated by the enlightenment thinkers were those of the liberal, middle-class, capitalist nations of Western Europe and North America.

In their infatuation with the ways of the "civilized" world, the Meirokusha intellectuals often advocated ideas deemed quite radical at the time. Nowhere were their ideas more radical than on questions of gender and family. In a long diatribe against the morality embodied in the *Greater Learning for Women (Onna Daigaku)*, Fukuzawa argued that women should not be treated as inferior human beings, nor should their lives be stunted like dwarf trees. Attacking the practice of concubinage as barbarous, he argued that monogamy was the only proper kind of marriage and that a man who kept several mistresses was "no better than a bird or beast." Indeed, marriage ought to be a contract between equal partners, and wives ought to have rights equal to their husbands. And to ensure greater equality with men, women ought to be given full property rights and educated in "new knowledge." (Radical though these ideas were for the time, neither Fukuzawa nor other Meirokusha intellectuals considered the possibility that women might become involved in politics or that they might pursue professions outside the home.)

For ordinary Japanese, "civilization" was represented less by the values of the West than by its material culture. A popular craze for Western goods and fashions swept through the country, even in remote provincial cities, where men began to let their forelocks grow, donned ill-fitting shoes and jackets, and watched Western-style government office buildings rise where once castles had stood. As Nishi Amane remarked in 1874, the opening of Japan was like "the overturning of a bottle"—Western clothing, architecture, food, fashion, even haircuts spilled out into Japan in indiscriminate, often bizarre, ways.[15] Kanagaki Robun, a popular writer, satirized the fad for Western things in a series of humorous works. In his *Aguranabe (Around The Stew Pot)*, he described a typical Westernized dandy with long flowing cologne-scented hair, calico underwear peeping from under his kimono, a gingham umbrella at his side, and a cheap Western pocket watch ostentatiously consulted from time to time. As the "beef eater" gobbled down a plate of beef (long proscribed by Buddhist practice), he waxed eloquent about how fortunate it was that "even people like ourselves can now eat beef, thanks to the fact Japan is becoming a truly civilized country."[16] Those "savages" who still refused to do so, he told his neighbor, should be forced to read Fukuzawa's essays on the advantages of eating beef.

ENDNOTES

1. The text of the Charter Oath may be found in Ryusaku Tsunoda et al., *Sources of Japanese Tradition* (New York: Columbia University Press, 1958), 643–644.

2. Michio Umegaki, *After the Restoration: The Beginning of Japan's Modern State* (New York: New York University Press, 1988), 109.

3. The journalist was J. R. Black. See his book *Young Japan, Yokohama and Yedo, A Narrative of the Settlement and the City from the Signing of the Treaties in 1858 to the Close of the Year 1879,* 2 vols. (London: Trubner and Co., 1880–1881).

4. Quoted in Joseph Pittau, *Political Thought in Early Meiji Japan, 1868–1889* (Cambridge, Mass.: Harvard University Press, 1967), 33.

5. Ibid., 23.

6. Quoted in Ienaga Saburō and Inoue Kiyoshi, *Kindai Nihon no sōten,* vol. 1 (Tokyo: Mainichi shimbunsha, 1967), 177.

7. The edict on the school system is quoted in Joseph Pittau, *Political Thought in Early Meiji Japan, 1868–1889* (Cambridge, Mass.: Harvard University Press, 1967), 24–25.

8. Shibusawa Eiichi, *The Autobiography of Shibusawa Eiichi From Peasant to Entrepreneur,* trans. Teruko Craig (Tokyo: University of Tokyo Press, 1994), 137.

9. Ienaga Saburō and Inoue Kiyoshi, *Kindai Nihon no sōten,* vol. 1 (Tokyo: Mainichi shimbunsha, 1967), 186.

10. Ōkubo's comments on the need to industrialize may be found in *Meiji Japan through Contemporary Sources,* vol. 3 (Tokyo: The Centre for East Asian Cultural Studies, 1970), 18–23.

11. Quoted in Thomas C. Smith, *Political Change and Industrial Development in Japan: Government Enterprise, 1868–1880* (Stanford, Cal.: Stanford University Press, 1955), 40–41.

12. Quoted in Carmen Blacker, *The Japanese Enlightenment: A Study of the Writings of Fukuzawa Yukichi* (Cambridge: Cambridge University Press, 1964), 31.

13. Nakamura Masanao is quoted in ibid., p. 29.

14. Ibid.

15. See Thomas R. H. Havens, *Nishi Amane and Modern Japanese Thought* (Princeton, N.J.: Princeton University Press, 1970), 78–85.

16. See Donald Keene, *Modern Japanese Literature* (New York: Grove Press, 1956), 31–33.

6

Protest and Dissent

Despite their initial caution, the leaders of the new imperial government had wrought a major social revolution. To be sure, they were social revolutionaries in spite of themselves. They had dismantled the old society less from ideological fervor than from a pragmatic realization that its customs and institutions were unsuited to a competitive modern world. Their revolutionary decisions nonetheless unleashed waves of turmoil and confusion. Many post-Restoration reforms were slow to take hold, but by the mid-1870s, the shock of change had spread to the farthest reaches of the country, upsetting many elements in the population. Disgruntled members of the Restoration coalition had left the government, nursing grudges against their former comrades; the centralization of power had created a reservoir of discontent in provincial and rural communities; and the ruthless firmness of the government in carrying out its reform policies had spawned resentment of "official tyranny." The post-Restoration decade was a troubled one, marked not only by a breakthrough to modernity but by vocal and often violent opposition to the government.

PEASANT RIOTS AND SAMURAI REBELLIONS

In the early 1870s, the most conspicuous opposition was nostalgic, conservative, and counterrevolutionary. Not surprisingly, it often came from the peasant population, whose folkways and traditions were suddenly disrupted by government policies. Peasant disturbances, common during the final century of Tokugawa rule, reached a new peak in the post-Restoration years. During the first Meiji decade, several hundred disturbances were recorded, a much higher rate of frequency than even during the Tempō period. In 1869 alone, there were 110 incidents. Many disturbances were not very different from those earlier in the century, when poor and middle peasants turned against rich peasants and village officials. Angered by crop failures, rising prices, dishonest officials, or hoarding by rich peasants, they demanded reduced rents or lower taxes. To be sure, the immediate causes of these disturbances were the unsettled conditions created by civil war, but at the heart of these intra-village conflicts were the long-term effects of proto-industrialization and commercialization on the countryside. When agricultural conditions improved in the early 1870s, however, the number and frequency of these traditional peasant disturbances declined markedly.

Gradually another pattern of peasant disturbances became more pronounced—disorders sparked by the government's reforms. In territories formerly under bakufu control conflicts were touched off when officials from the imperial government changed village boundaries or overzealous tax collectors squeezed the peasants more than their predecessors had. There were protests over larger changes as well. When the domains were abolished in 1871, peasants in Hiroshima, Okayama, Fukuyama, and elsewhere protested the replacement of their daimyos by new centrally appointed prefectural governors. The government onslaught on "backward" or "ignorant" customs, which constituted the warp and woof of the commoners' lives, set off protests as well. The abolition of class distinctions, the emancipation of the *eta* (a pariah class traditionally regarded as polluted), the destruction of Buddhist temples as part of the campaign to establish Shintō as the state religion, the legalization of beef-eating, and even the outlawing of traditional male coiffures were unwanted intrusions into the lives of ordinary folk. When the Western solar calendar was officially substituted for the traditional lunar calendar in 1873, many peasant farmers, whose yearly cycle of work and festivals was tied to the old calendar, felt their world had been turned topsy-turvy by "Jesus Christ's New Year."

Less surprising perhaps was opposition by commoners to new burdens imposed upon them by modernizing reforms. Peasants often rioted when they discovered that the new elementary school system was going to gobble up their taxes and take their children away from work on the family plot. The new conscription law excited even greater suspicion and bewilderment. To arouse popular patriotism, the government referred to conscription as a "blood tax." Some peasants took the phrase quite literally. Rumors spread that young men recruited for military service were to be mutilated for some dire purpose or that their blood was to be sold to foreign countries. Alarmed villagers attacked army recruiters or refused to send their sons off as conscripts. The new tax laws, although phased in slowly, were another source of peasant discontent. Although the peasants' tax burden remained the same in theory, the new land tax had to be paid year in and year out, regardless of whether the harvest was good or bad. The system was much more rigid than the old one, in which domain authorities had often decreed tax reductions in years of bad harvests. As the land was surveyed to determine the value of individual plots, allegations of unfair assessment often sparked anger at the government. For those who bore the burden most directly, the tax reform made the costs of modernization quite clear. Since unarmed peasants were no match for government police and troops, local authorities usually had little difficulty in putting their protests down.

Local village unrest neither worried the government a great deal nor did it have much of an impact on the country as a whole. Far more alarming was anti-government sentiment among the former samurai class. Anti-foreign samurai activists, who had expected the fall of the Tokugawa to signal the final expulsion of the foreigners, were sorely disappointed when it did not. The domain of Chōshū, for example, was beset by turmoil in the wake of the Restoration. In late 1869, a group of anti-foreign samurai assassinated War Minister Ōmura Masajirō, a former Chōshū leader, for advocating the recruitment of commoners into a conscript army. In their eyes, he had besmirched the honor of the "sacred land" by shamelessly imitating the ways of the foreigners. When Chōshū militia units were disbanded in 1869–1870, more than 2000 local samurai attacked local government offices, setting off disorders that lasted for several months. Indeed, some rebels who managed to escape capture joined other disgruntled samurai in northern Kyushu and continued their resistance.

As the pace of change accelerated, discontent deepened. One resentful ex-samurai memorialized the emperor as follows in 1874:

> In the reforms . . . introduced since the Revolution, has the method been in accord with that of a well-governed country? Or have things been managed as in a country of disorder? . . . If the latter has been our practice let it at once be reformed, and let us return to the institutions of our ancestors. What need have we to imitate the customs of foreign countries 10,000 *ri* [leagues] away?[1]

Such feelings grew more widespread during the middle of the 1870s as the status of the former samurai class eroded steadily under the impact of government reforms.

The defection of top government leaders in 1873, after the failure of the Korean invasion plan, provided leadership for this diffuse discontent. Etō Shimpei, a former minister of justice, left the government convinced that the failure to chastise Korea would be seen as a sign of national weakness. In early 1874, he agreed to launch an armed uprising against the government with the backing of rebellious former samurai in Hizen (now called Saga), who were disappointed at losing the opportunity to gain glory in a Korean expedition. A rebel force of several thousand men attacked the local government army garrison, but they were quickly suppressed by a vastly superior expeditionary force dispatched by the Tokyo government. Although Etō managed to escape to Tosa, he was captured, tried and quickly executed by the authorities, who were upset that such a prominent former official had taken up arms against them.

No doubt personal jealousy or rivalry lay behind some samurai discontent, but so did resentment at the undermining of the old samurai class. Maebara Issei, a former student of Yoshida Shōin who held high office in the ministry of war, grew increasingly distressed at the government's callous indifference toward the former samurai. When the last vestiges of samurai privilege were abolished in 1876, he launched his own rebellion in Hagi, the former Chōshū castle town. "What on earth have one million samurai done wrong?" he demanded. "If the government rides herd on the samurai with this attitude in mind, then for certain it will foment great troubles in the realm."[2] Although dissident samurai groups in Fukuoka, Kumamoto, and other parts of Kyushu had sought to join his uprising, hasty and inadequate preparations doomed all to failure. The former samurai rebels, like the loyalist radicals of the early 1860s, were bands of like-minded men who had no plans to mobilize broad support or even to act in careful concert with fellow malcontents elsewhere. Divided and dispersed, they were easily crushed by the better-organized central government.

The most serious revolt of all came a few months later in February 1877, when an army of 15,000 former samurai under the leadership of Saigō Takamori set out from Kagoshima to overthrow the imperial government at Tokyo. Provincial loyalties and localist sentiments remained strong in the former domain of Satsuma (renamed Kagoshima prefecture). Even after the Restoration, the Kagoshima government retained considerable autonomy, refusing to forward tax revenues to Tokyo and continuing to observe the old lunar calendar. Although the province remained a citadel of all the government

An 1877 woodblock print of Saigō Takamori rallying his troops against a bombardment by imperial naval forces during the Satsuma Rebellion. Note that while his troops are depicted in samurai fighting garb, an idealized Saigō wears a Western-style general's uniform.

wanted to demolish—traditional learning, samurai privilege, and local autonomy—powerful patrons like Saigō and Ōkubo protected it against retaliation. When Saigō left the government accompanied by a contingent of Satsuma men from the Imperial Guard, he became a rallying point for antigovernment malcontents in Kagoshima. Using his government pension, he financed the establishment of several "private academies" to provide local samurai training in military arts and classical Confucian learning. These academies, more paramilitary than educational in character, soon became recruiting grounds for anti-government elements.

The government in Tokyo, watching support for Saigō grow, feared that rebellious sentiments in Hagi might spread to Kagoshima, and in early 1877 decided to confiscate arms and munitions at the arsenal there. Suspecting that the government was also planning to assassinate Saigō, members of the private academies rose in revolt. The rebel plan was quite simple: they hoped to march all the way to the capital, gathering supporters in Kumamoto and other regions along the way where anti-government sentiment was strong. Their ultimate goal was to overthrow the new government. The rebel advance ground to a halt at Kumamoto, however, when, instead of forging ahead, the rebel commanders decided to lay siege to Kumamoto Castle, where the local government garrison had fortified itself. The delay allowed time for the government to dispatch a large force of new conscript army recruits to put the rebellion down. Within a few weeks, the government counterattack turned the rebel forces back from Kumamoto, and the dwindling Kagoshima army was finally surrounded in September. Saigō, refusing to surrender, committed traditional suicide (*seppuku*), passing into popular mythology as an embodiment of the samurai spirit. (A statue of the bulky Saigō, with his loyal dog at his side, remains a favorite tourist attraction at Ueno Park in Tokyo even today.)

The Satsuma Rebellion, a bloody civil war that cost more deaths and casualties than the campaigns against the bakufu in 1868–1869, was the last serious internal threat to the new government. Its failure taught both the government and its critics important lessons. First, it demonstrated how few former samurai really wished to return to the old days. Although the Kagoshima rebels had hoped their bold initiative would spark a wave of response among other resentful samurai, the legion of sympathizers they hoped for never materialized. Complaining about the government was one thing, but open sedition was another. Second, the government victory demonstrated the effectiveness of the new conscript army. Although commoners proved no better as individual fighting men than their opponents, the government army was vastly superior in number, much better equipped, and much better supported than Saigō's forces. Its success proved that military modernization was more important than samurai "spirit." Finally, the failure of the rebellion demonstrated the impossibility of dislodging the government or reversing reform by force. While reactionary elements continued to use violence, they turned to assassination rather than rebellion. Indeed, Ōkubo Toshimichi, who had emerged as the key figure in the government in the late 1870s, was cut down by six former Satsuma men in May 1878, less than a year after this old comrade-in-arms, Saigō, had taken his own life. But the defeat of the Kagoshima forces foreclosed the possibility of counterrevolution.

"LIBERTY AND POPULAR RIGHTS"

In contrast to the peasant riots and samurai rebellions in the early and mid-1870s, a more peaceful form of political protest relying on political agitation, local organization, journalistic attacks, and popular petitions gathered strength in the late 1870s. This was the "popular rights movement," begun by Itagaki Taisuke, Gotō Shōjirō, and several other former officials from Tosa shortly after resigning from the government over the Korea question. Unlike Saigō, who returned to his province, they issued a public manifesto in early 1874 urging radical political reforms to end the "tyranny" of the narrow inner circle of officials dominating the government. Under the influence of ideas disseminated by translated Western political works, such as J. S. Mill's *On Liberty*, they petitioned for the establishment of a national council chamber elected by the "people." Broadening the base of political decisions, they said, would "arouse in our people the spirit of enterprise and . . . enable them to comprehend the duty of participating in the burdens of the empire."[3] Not surprisingly the government, which had retreated from its early experiment with a representative body (*kōgisho*), rejected the petition. Instead of resorting to violence, Itagaki and his followers returned to Kōchi (formerly Tosa), where they organized the Risshisha, a political association that adopted the untraditional tactics of mobilizing public opinion. By spreading the doctrines of "natural rights" or "inherent human rights" the Risshisha sought broad support for a national assembly.

In its initial stages, the popular rights movement was neither particularly democratic nor even very popular. It was recruited and led by former samurai, mainly from Tosa. Indeed, one purpose of the Risshisha was to help local samurai adjust to their new economic and social circumstances. Although the movement attempted to rouse a new kind of political consciousness, its members often found it difficult to shed their older attitudes. Few ex-samurai had much confidence in the wisdom of the common people or in their readiness to govern themselves. When they spoke of the "people," what they had in mind were the traditional elites: the ex-samurai class, village leaders, and the well-to-do peasants who had dominated their communities in pre-Restoration times. Despite their talk of "public opinion," many advocates of popular rights also had a strong penchant for violence. Ueki Emori, one of the movement's leading propagandists, proclaimed that liberty had to be bought with "fresh blood" and that the "people" had a right to revolt against a tyrannical government.[4] Some of Itagaki's followers, who were convinced that the imperial government should be resisted by force, urged him to join Saigō's revolt in 1877.

Although the government rejected the 1874 petition, the growing agitation in Tosa had its effect. Worried that Itagaki might make common cause with other disaffected samurai, the government leaders made conciliatory gestures. In early 1875, Ōkubo Toshimichi lured Itagaki Taisuke back into the government with a promise to make gradual steps toward establishing a national assembly. In a number of prefectures, Tokyo-appointed governors, hoping to rally local public sentiment behind them, had already organized publicly elected prefectural assemblies. When the government refused to establish assemblies in every prefecture, however, it became clear to Itagaki that Ōkubo had a very different timetable from his own, and he left the government once again.

The character of the popular rights movement changed after the suppression of the Kagoshima rebellion. Hot-heads who had urged Itagaki to join forces with Saigō were arrested for seditious activities, confirming that violent resistance was a dead end. Even more important, the movement broadened its social base by gathering into its ranks well-to-do peasant landlord-entrepreneurs, government officials, journalists, school teachers, poor peasants, and even common laborers and porters. This development took place against the background of relative prosperity in the countryside. In the late 1870s, rising rice prices and declining currency values produced windfall profits for the rural landowning classes. In Tokugawa times, when taxes were collected as part of the harvest, landholders had to share their prosperity with the government. But now that taxes were assessed in fixed money payments, inflation reduced the value of taxes and increased the economic value of the harvest. The result was a rise in land prices, a rash of land speculation, and the burgeoning of new local businesses and enterprises. Good times had arrived in the countryside, and the new rural prosperity convinced the well-to-do rural elite that they had a stake in national politics, especially in how the government spent their taxes.

The nationwide establishment of prefectural assemblies in 1878, which had been intended to win over the prosperous rural elite elements, accelerated their politicization. The right to vote for assembly representatives was restricted to local men of property who bore the heaviest tax burden. Far from being friendly to the government at Tokyo, however, many members of this class were quite hostile toward its development policies. As the reform program continued, a strong populist mood spread in the provinces. The government seemed to be drawing off the wealth of the rural areas without giving anything in return. Many prefectural officials, who were concerned mainly with building up the central government and enforcing its writs, were arrogant and insensitive toward local interests. This volatile combination of circumstances often led to clashes between prefectural officials and prefectural assemblies, which became training schools for opposition politics.

The spread of new ideas, especially the writings of the "enlightenment" intellectuals, also made converts to the broadening popular rights movement. By the late 1870s, translations of works by J. S. Mill, Montesquieu, Rousseau, and other Western political philosophers had found readers even in remote provincial towns. Anti-government newspapers attacked traditional political submissiveness to authority and linked political protest to the spirit of self-help and independence. "[Nature] endows men with freedom," wrote Ueki in 1879. "If people do not take this natural endowment, it is both a great sin against nature and a great disgrace to themselves. Disgrace does not merely reside in taking things which should not be taken, but in not taking things *which should be taken!*"[5] The message was clear: the people should assume greater control over the government, which professed to govern for them.

As popular rights leaders and journalists called for "a constitution based on a contract with the people," the meaning of *people* broadened in concept as well as in fact. By the late 1870s, more than six hundred local political associations (*seisha*) had sprung up. About half were organized in the six provinces around Tokyo, but they could be found throughout the country. These associations, recruited mainly from the better educated rural elite, debated current policy issues and discussed exciting new ideas like "popular sovereignty." Their members even produced draft constitutions, often including provisions for broad popular representation or the protection of civil rights from government interference.

In the fall of 1877, the Aikokusha, a new organization started by Itagaki, took advantage of the rising popular political interest to mobilize public support for a national assembly. Local newspapers were founded to voice the movement's demands, and ardent agitators were dispatched all over the country to give speeches at temples, schools, shrines, or wherever they could draw a crowd. In 1880, representatives from the local political associations met to organize a League for the Establishment of a National Assembly, with a central headquarters in Tokyo. The country was divided into twelve districts for political agitation, and activists gathered more than fifty-five petitions demanding a representative assembly and a constitution. It was the first time in Japan's history that pressure-group tactics were systematically organized on a national scale.

The popular rights movement took place against a background of indifference or confusion among the mass of the rural population, but that it took place at all was a radical departure from traditional politics. Although well-to-do peasants had concerned themselves with political events beyond the village or domain boundaries before the Restoration, they rarely became involved in them. The emergence of the popular rights movement, a national organization that cut across political provincialism, represented not only a broadened political consciousness but the awakening of a new nationalist sentiment. The popular rights movement criticized the government, but its members shared the goal of creating a strong and unified Japan able to stand up to the foreigners. In the long run, this shared goal was to override short-term political disagreements.

TOWARD CONSTITUTIONAL GOVERNMENT

The authorities in Tokyo put the popular rights movement in a different perspective, however. In Tokugawa Japan, there had been no conception of a loyal opposition; failure to obey constituted authorities, like all acts of insubordination, was regarded not only as a threat to incumbent officials but to the very regime itself. Opposition was equated with disloyalty, and those who formed factions outside the government were thought to be pursuing selfish ends rather than the public good. Not surprisingly, high government officials, who viewed the popular rights movement against the background of earlier violent anti-government outbreaks, were filled with apprehension. As Yamagata Aritomo noted in a letter to Itō Hirobumi in 1879, "Every day we wait, the evil poison will spread more and more over the provinces, penetrate into the minds of the young, and inevitably produce unfathomable evils."[6] To blot up the "evil poison," the government was quick to resort to the tactics of repression. A series of laws, beginning with libel and slander laws promulgated in 1875, gave the government powers to censor the press, disband political rallies, and clamp down on political agitation of all kinds. Police supervision of the movement was so intense that some anti-government newspapers employed "jail editors," nominally in charge of the paper, but in fact hired to suffer imprisonment if the paper infringed the libel laws. The government's repressive tactics, however, were far less harsh than those of the traditional regime, which had usually punished dissent with severity, even with execution.

Although government leaders were alarmed by talk of natural rights or popular sovereignty, they did not oppose the idea of either a national constitution or a national assembly. Constitutionalism appealed to the government leaders because it was a practice of the "civilized" countries. All of the advanced Western powers were constitutional nations, and the establishment of a constitutional order would signal Japan's progress to the outside world, perhaps even persuade the foreigners to revise the treaties. The Western example also demonstrated that constitutional government was compatible with internal order and might even enhance it. As Kido Takayoshi had noted on his return from the Iwakura mission, a constitutional system could buttress national power by setting "the weal of the entire country on a firm basis."[7] On Ōkubo Toshimichi's initiative, a government bureau had been set up to investigate the drafting of a constitution in 1875. By the late 1870s the main question for most government leaders was not *whether* to establish a constitution and national assembly but *what kind* should be established and *when*. It was on these latter questions that they differed with the opposition.

The issue, as Iwakura Tomomi noted, was whether Japan should follow the English model of parliamentary government and responsible cabinets or the German model of a strong monarchy, strong cabinet, and a weak national assembly. In response to an imperial request for their opinions, in 1880–1881 a majority of the government's leaders expressed preference for the German model. Not only had Germany emerged as the leading continental European power in the 1870s, but like Japan it was a newly unified nation with a strong monarchical tradition and was woven together from a welter of smaller principalities. Ōkuma Shigenobu, however, stood apart from this consensus by proposing the immediate adoption of an English-style system: a national assembly should be established by 1883; the cabinet should be made responsible to the national assembly; and political parties should control the government. His memorial, written with the help of Fukuzawa Yukichi's students, was startling in its radicalism. Other top government leaders, who resented his growing political influence, closed ranks against Ōkuma and forced him to resign from office. Like the earlier split over the Korean question, his departure narrowed the government's inner circle to a small number of men from Satsuma and Chōshū.

The crisis of 1881 forced the oligarchs to defuse the public clamor for popular rights. To mollify the popular rights movement and its supporters, the emperor announced his intention to establish both a constitution and a national assembly by 1890. From the outset, the government had a clear notion of what kind of constitution it wanted. Iwakura Tomomi laid out a plan for a constitution to be granted by the emperor to the people with no constitutional convention nor any other opportunity for popular consultation. Not only was the constitution to be a "gift" of the emperor but the power to command the country's military forces and to appoint cabinet ministers was to be placed in his hands as well. To be sure, a national assembly was to be created but its powers were to quite limited, with no rights to control the cabinet nor even to initiate legislation. In short, what the oligarchs contemplated was not a constitutionally limited monarch but a constitutionally limited national assembly.

Even as the emperor announced his intention to establish a constitutional system, his edict also warned that "those who may advocate sudden and violent changes . . . disturbing the peace of the realm" would fall under imperial displeasure.[8] Opposition was to be tolerated, but just barely. The popular rights movement continued undaunted, however, though it aspired to greater respectability and better organization than during its early years. In late 1881, the followers of Itagaki formed the Jiyūtō (Liberal Party) under his leadership, and in early 1882 the Kaishintō (Progressive Party) formed around Ōkuma and a number of junior officials who left the government with him. Although they styled themselves as "political parties," both organizations really functioned as pressure groups engaged in a polemical war with the government. The Kaishintō, which drew its support from urban intellectuals, journalists, and businessmen, called for a moderate British-style constitutional system along the lines that Ōkuma had proposed. The Jiyūtō, on the other hand, took a more radical position, committing itself to the notion of popular sovereignty, a national constitutional convention, and greater decentralization of government. To combat its critics, the government organized a party of its own, the Teiseitō (Imperial Party), made up of pro-government journalists who attacked the other two parties in a heated newspaper debate over the locus and character of national sovereignty.

Confrontation between the popular rights organizations and the government also occurred at the local level. In 1882, for example, the governor of Fukushima prefecture, Mishima Michitsune, a veteran of the anti-bakufu movement, announced his intention to smash the local popular rights movement. In response, the local Jiyūtō branch, incensed at his arrogance, rejected his budgets and his plan to double local taxes to build a new road system. When local peasants resisted Mishima's orders to work on road construction, he had them arrested, and when local Jiyūtō leaders criticized his actions, he had them thrown in jail. The confrontation showed that the government, with all its legal power and police force, was a formidable opponent. In the end, Mishima managed to break the power if not the spirit of the local popular rights movement.

As political initiative on the constitution shifted into the hands of the government, the popular rights movement lost its momentum. Its leaders, aware of how futile it was to pressure a government so little inclined to heed them, lost enthusiasm, and the parties' rank and file showed signs of fracture. The well-to-do landowners who dominated the local assemblies came to realize that they could use their limited powers to extract concessions from the government rather than to fight it. Gradually, the acrimonious clashes in sessions of the prefectural assembly gave way to political horse-trading. In return for supporting the prefectural governor, assembly members bargained to lighten their tax burdens or to secure tax money for roads, bridges, irrigation systems, and riparian works in their districts. The landlords, whose support had been so critical in the early phases of the popular rights movement, were learning the advantages of conservatism.

The movement was also weakened by the deflationary fiscal policy adopted by the government in the early 1880s. Economic conditions in the countryside worsened, creating unrest that exploded here and there into political violence. The Kaishintō, drawing support from among educated and well-to-do elements in Tokyo, was not much affected by these developments, but the Jiyūtō found itself divided by internal disputes. In 1884, impoverished peasants in the Chichibu region west of Tokyo rose in revolt when local moneylenders refused a moratorium on their debts. Although the origins of the disturbance were entirely local, some rebels claimed that they were followers of Itagaki and proclaimed themselves "warriors of the Jiyūtō." Anxious to dissociate themselves from any hint of sedition, the Jiyūtō leadership decided to disband the party in late 1884, leaving its more radical members despairing and disillusioned.

Despite its ultimate collapse, the popular rights movement played an important historical role. It both forced the government's hand in agreeing to a constitutional system and legitimized a new kind of political dissent. Even within the constraints imposed by repressive legislation, the movement had battled the government in the public arena, attempting to mobilize popular support and change public opinion through pamphlets, newspapers and other publications, or by confrontational tactics in the local assemblies. The movement thus established a robust tradition of peaceful opposition to the state, very different from the peasant risings of the late Tokugawa period or the samurai violence of the 1870s. It shaped a new political culture in which the government had to tolerate some degree of dissent. Although its leaders were excluded from power, memories of the movement lived on. In the 1890s, many of its veterans became professional party politicians, who struggled against the oligarchic government in the new Imperial Diet. Charges of official tyranny originally raised by the movement also lingered, haunting the oligarchs as they constructed new constitutional order.

CONSERVATIVE COUNTERCURRENTS

Not everyone was comfortable with the eruption of overt but peaceful opposition to the government in the 1870s. On the contrary, the unsettled political atmosphere made many educated Japanese nostalgic for the orderliness of pre-Restoration Japan. Although they had no quarrel with the government's goals of centralization, military self-strengthening, and industrialization, they were disturbed by the influx of radical new ideas, often with government encouragement. The spread of popular rights ideas—natural rights, the legitimacy of rebellion and protest, and equality of people—seemed to undermine respect for constituted authority. Aware that it was not possible to turn back the clock completely, these conservatives still felt that national wealth and power would be served by revitalizing traditional ethical attitudes. Yearning for a return to the public virtues of discipline, obedience, and order, conservative intellectuals called for a return to the values and morality of the old society.

To a degree, the turn toward conservatism was a reaction against the influx and uncritical acceptance of Western culture in the early 1870s. Nowhere was this more evident than in the newly established school system. As Motoda Nagazane, the emperor's personal advisor, complained in 1878, "Efforts are being made to convert Japanese into facsimiles of Europeans and Americans." In a long memorial on the educational system, he severely criticized the use of Western-inspired textbooks in government schools and argued that the new government educational system spread idle theories that made students into troublemakers and malcontents. Instruction in the schools, he said, should be founded upon "the Imperial ancestral precepts, benevolence, duty, loyalty, and filial piety" and Confucianism should be revived as the cornerstone of ethical instruction.[9] These sentiments were shared by Nishimura Shigeki, a prominent "enlightenment" intellectual of the early 1870s, who called for a selective revival of Confucian morality, especially the values of loyalty and filial piety. While Confucian metaphysics could not stand under the scrutiny of Western science, he said, Confucian ethical values were still useful in mobilizing the country spiritually and restoring social stability.

The call for a revival of Confucian-style moral education was just one side of the conservative reaction. The other, and perhaps more important side, was the discovery that there was more to Western "civilization" than the Anglo-American liberalism translated by the enlightenment intellectuals and propagated by the popular rights movement. Indeed, many former "enlightenment" intellectuals shifted their views as they discovered alternative ideas. Katō Hiroyuki, a member of the Meirokusha, who had been an early advocate of the natural rights theory, found himself drawn to German political thought after translating the work of the German legal theorist J. C. Bluntschli. Whereas the popular rights propagandists who espoused "popular sovereignty" had placed the people above the state, Bluntschli argued that the state should answer to no power but itself. By the early 1880s, Katō had disavowed the idea that people were endowed by nature with human rights and concluded that such rights were won instead by political struggle. Adopting a position close to the government's, he declared that Prussian-style constitutionalism was more congenial to national self-strengthening than British-style parliamentarianism, and he argued that the country should be less concerned with the people's rights than with its "national rights" as a sovereign state.

The introduction of Social Darwinism also fed the conservative reaction. Its view of history as a struggle for the "survival of the fittest" challenged the optimistic notion of progress as the upward and onward march of human reason and morality. As Katō Hiroyuki wrote in his *New Theory of Human Rights (Jinken shinsetsu)*, "the great law of nature is that the universe is a great arena of combat . . . [where] every organism competes for its own survival and growth, with one organism always being the winner, and another always being the loser."[10] Human progress, in other words, was the result of a brutal struggle in which the strong triumphed over the weak by force. Such a view made sense of Western intrusions in Asia and the rest of the world, and it fit well with the country's pursuit of national wealth and strength. As the popular rights movement lost momentum, many intellectuals came to feel that it was more important to preserve the country's independence in the "international struggle for survival" than to theorize about "liberty" and "rights."

Even Fukuzawa Yukichi, whose works had helped spread ideas about progress, equality, and the "spirit of independence," took a turn toward conservatism. Although he continued to believe that individual initiative and emancipation were necessary to national strength, he was no longer so sure that the country required a liberal political system. In 1882, he remarked,

> The one object of my life is to extend Japan's national power. Compared with the considerations of the country's strength, the matter of internal government and into whose hands it falls is of no importance at all. Even if the government be autocratic in name and form, I shall be satisfied if it is strong enough to strengthen the country.[11]

Although he admired the Western nations as the vanguard of "civilization," and wished Japan to join their ranks, his zeal for reform and change was muted by a growing pessimism. Like many of his contemporaries, he was overcome by a new caution about the future and a new wave of Western expansionism.

The change in the country's mood was most visible to those who had been absent from it. Tsuda Umeko, who had been sent to the United States with Iwakura mission as a young girl, was surprised at the Japan to which she returned in 1882. "A few years ago everything foreign was liked, and the cry was progress," she wrote to an American friend. "Now Japanese things are being put ahead, and everything foreign is not approved of. . . ."[12] Conservative ideas were not only reinforcing a move toward statism, they encouraged a renewed appreciation for traditional ways of thinking, which was displacing intellectual infatuation with "civilization and enlightenment." As the government moved to consolidate its earlier reforms in the 1880s, these intellectual trends accelerated.

ENDNOTES

1. Quoted in *Meiji Japan Through Contemporary Sources,* vol. 2 (Tokyo: The Centre for East Asian Cultural Studies, 1970), 168.

2. *Meiji ishin,* (Tokyo: Yomiuri shimbunsha, 1968), 240.

3. The text of this memorial may be found in *Meiji Japan Through Contemporary Sources,* vol. 2 (Tokyo: The Centre for East Asian Cultural Studies, 1970), 134–141.

4. Quoted in Ienaga Saburō and Inoue Kiyoshi, *Kindai Nihon no sōten,* vol. 1 (Tokyo: Mainichi shimbunsha, 1967), 131–141.

5. A discussion of Ueki's views may be found in Nobutaka Ike, *The Beginnings of Political Democracy in Japan* (Baltimore: Johns Hopkins Press, 1950), 129–137.

6. Quoted in George Akita, *Foundations of Constitutional Government in Modern Japan,* 1868–1900 (Cambridge, Mass.: Harvard University Press, 1967), 25.

7. Kido's memorial may be found in *Meiji Japan Through Contemporary Sources,* vol. 2 (Tokyo: The Centre for East Asian Cultural Studies, 1970), 99–110.

8. Ibid., 69–70.

9. Motoda is quoted by Donald Shively in David S. Nivison and Arthur F. Wright, eds. *Confucianism in Action* (Stanford, Cal.: Stanford University Press, 1959), 327.

10. For a slightly different translation see Kosaka Masaaki, *Japanese Thought in the Meiji Era,* trans. David Abosch (Tokyo: Pan-Pacific Press, 1958), 155–156.

11. Quoted in Carmen Blacker, *The Japanese Enlightenment: A Study of the Writings of Fukugawa Yukichi* (Cambridge: Cambridge University Press, 1964), 134.

12. Yoshiko Furuki et al. (eds.), *The Attic Letters: Ume Tsuda's Correspondence to Her American Mother* (New York: Weatherhill, 1991, 18.

7

The Turn Toward Stability

In contrast to the confusion, uncertainty, and experimentation of the post-Restoration years, Japan entered a period of retrenchment, conservatism, and stability in the early 1880s. The change in atmosphere resulted in large measure from consolidation of the nation's leadership. In place of the loose and volatile coalition of daimyo, court nobles, and samurai who had come to power in 1868 there had emerged a tightly knit oligarchy, purged of dissenters, confident in its control of the state, and possessed of a much clearer vision of what the new Japan should be. Its members, all former Satsuma and Chōshū men, were less interested in radical innovation than in consolidating gains already made. The oligarchs had grown concerned that the country had moved too far in too short a time, perhaps without forethought. Many of their reforms had brought unanticipated destabilizing consequences that might impede the goal of "national wealth and strength." Although they did not fear popular revolution, they worried about the effects on the general population of both popular rights ideas and enlightenment thought. To maintain political stability without sacrificing progress toward equality with the West, they built an institutional and constitutional structure that was to last for the next two generations.

RETRENCHMENT AND DEFLATION

Perhaps the most pressing problem faced by the government in 1880, aside from the rising demand for a constitution and national assembly, was the prospect of imminent financial crisis. Despite the institution of the land tax system and the commutation of samurai stipends, the government wallowed in red ink during most of the 1870s. Interest payments on samurai bonds ate up a large portion of the government's revenues and the suppression of the Satsuma rebellion in 1877 and 1878, though very profitable politically, had been enormously expensive. Inflation doubled the price of rice between 1877 and 1880, bringing rural prosperity but reducing the real value of government tax revenues. To make matters worse, Japan was buying much more abroad than it sold. Gold and silver bullion were flowing out of the country, increasing inflationary pressures and undermining the government's financial position even further. By 1880, only about 5 percent of government currency was backed by metal, and public confidence in the government's credit was plummeting. As the dimensions of the financial crisis grew, it caused much anxiety in official circles.

Before his ouster from the government, Ōkuma Shigenobu had proposed floating a large loan in London to tide over the crisis, but Iwakura Tomomi averred that he would rather sell Kyushu and Shikoku to the foreigners than to borrow from them.[1] Given this determination not to rely on foreign help, the only alternative was to pursue a policy of government retrenchment proposed by Matsukata Masayoshi, a former Satsuma samurai who became minister of finance in 1881. A student of Western financial orthodoxy, Matsukata believed that the only way to establish the government's credit and fiscal reliability was to balance the budget, keep expenditures within the limits of revenues, and establish a sound currency backed by metal specie. Under his guidance, all government-owned factories except for strategic arsenals and shipyards were sold to private investors. A tight clamp was put on new spending; new consumer taxes were levied on tobacco and sake; and the money supply was decreased by 20 percent between 1881 and 1885. Some central government expenditures were shifted to prefectural governments, and local taxes were raised to pay for them. Belt tightening caused a rapid drop in prices between 1881 and 1885, including a 50 percent drop in the rice price. This sudden deflation gave the government a fiscal windfall similar to the one landlords had enjoyed a few years before.

To foster economic confidence and stability, Matsukata gave priority to organizing a sound banking system. A national bank system established in 1876 proved a disaster. Not only were many banks poorly managed, but they issued bank notes with an abandon that exacerbated inflation. In 1885, the government established the Bank of Japan, a central government bank authorized to issue specie-backed bank notes. One of its functions was to redeem unsound private and government paper notes in circulation. By soaking up this inflated paper currency the government was able to create sound money trusted by both business and the general public. Eventually, the Bank of Japan became the center of a system of specialized semi-government banks (such as the Yokohama Specie Bank, the Hypothec Bank, and the Agricultural and Industrial Bank) that promoted investment in industry, agriculture, and foreign trade. Financed in part by government capital and operating under close official supervision, these financial institutions played a key role in later economic development.

The main positive effect of Matsukata's policies was to smooth the way for private investment in the modern sector of the economy. With inflation checked, the government's financial confidence restored, and new sources of capital available, astute entrepreneurs were encouraged to launch new ventures. Businessmen and merchants could turn for capital to the government-connected banks without having to rely entirely on their own resources. A sound currency brought down interest rates after 1885, lowering the cost of borrowing investment capital. By the late 1880s, with these new inducements to launch new ventures, the infant modern manufacturing sector enjoyed a modest boom, especially in railroad construction, silk reeling, and cotton spinning. Private railroad track expanded from 63 to 898 miles between 1883 and 1890, and the number of cotton spindles in operation doubled between 1886 and 1890.

If the "Matsukata deflation" made businessmen and investors happy, it was enormously unpopular with the rural population. The drop in rice prices brought farm incomes tumbling down. Local weather conditions also led to a series of bad harvests between 1881 and 1884, and many peasant farmers found themselves driven to the wall. Large landholders tried to tide themselves over by collecting rents ruthlessly, calling in loans, and foreclosing mortgages. Many economically marginal peasant households went down the path to debt, foreclosure, and tenancy. As a result, between 1883 and 1891 the number of landholding cultivator households dropped from 39 percent to 33 percent of the total farm population, and the number of landholders paying sufficient taxes to qualify for suffrage in prefectural assemblies dropped by one third. Hardship in the countryside, especially among the poorer peasants, was the price paid for economic stability.

THE BUREAUCRATIC STATE

While Matsukata was setting government finances aright, other leaders were at work shaping a new bureaucratic state structure, designed to be managed by "men of talent" free from popular interference or control. Shaped by their Confucian education, the Meiji leaders took a paternalistic view of government. They thought that officials should protect the lives and livelihood of the people without empowering them to make decisions by themselves. Indeed, the consensus among the Meiji leadership was the people were not yet "enlightened" enough for political responsibility and that those who sought to represent them were often either irresponsible extremists or ambitious opportunists. Their ideal was a polity run by "wise and able" officials who put public duty ahead of private gain or personal ambition. As their knowledge of the West deepened, the oligarchs discovered that this ideal was neither

archaic nor nostalgic but followed by the new German Empire, whose statesmen and statecraft had made a strong impression on the Iwakura mission.

The oligarchs centered the state structure on the monarchy, but they felt
that the imperial institution itself needed strengthening. Despite his frequent
progresses through the country in the 1870s, the emperor remained a remote
and little-known figure to much of the populace. (One foreign resident noted
with distress in 1880 that people hung out flags on the emperor's birthday
only when prompted to by the police.) Equally important, the imperial family remained impecunious. To ensure its financial independence and give it
the wherewithal to maintain its public pomp, the government transferred
government-owned land, especially forest land confiscated from the bakufu,
to the imperial family. It also diverted large amounts of cash, private company stocks, and government bank bonds into the imperial household treasury. By 1889, the imperial family held 3,650,000 *chō* of land (as opposed to
600 *chō* in 1880) and ¥8, 600,000 in stocks, an amount roughly equal to 10
percent of the government's budget that year. This enormous fortune was administered by the Imperial Household Ministry, an independent body created
in 1885 and staffed by officials appointed by the emperor. The imperial court
was thus converted into a self-contained fiscal and administrative citadel, immune from outside political leverage but malleable to the purposes of the
government. For example, although the imperial household treasury was intended to support the imperial family and its charitable enterprises, the government often tapped it as a slush fund for political purposes.

To provide "living ramparts" for the monarchy, the oligarchs created a
new aristocratic class. The new imperial government had been solicitous of
the old daimyo and court noble families in the years after the Restoration,
establishing a special Peers' School (*Gakushūin*) for the education of their
offspring in 1877. By identifying the old elite with the newly refurbished imperial institution, they hoped to accelerate the erosion of old local loyalties.
In July 1884, peerage titles were granted to former court noble families, the
heads of former daimyo houses (including the Tokugawa family), and also to
"mature statesmen, men of merit, and erudite scholars." With the new titles
came grants of stocks and cash stipends. Not surprisingly, peerage ranks
were bestowed on oligarchs themselves, who had risen from humble samurai
backgrounds, and even on dissident leaders such as Itagaki Taisuke, Gotō
Shojirō, and Ōkuma Shigenobu, who had helped build the post-Restoration
regime. Having done so much good for Japan, the oligarchs clearly felt that
they should do well for themselves too.

Since both the imperial throne and the new peerage were set apart from the
administration of state affairs, their political roles were largely symbolic. The
task of making national policy was put in the hands of the cabinet, a new central decision-making body created in 1885 to replace the old and rather unwieldy grand council, which had functioned as the highest executive body. The
cabinet was headed by a prime minister appointed by the emperor and legally
responsible to him. It consisted of nine other ministers (foreign affairs, home

affairs, justice, finance, army, navy, education, agriculture and commerce, and transportation). The prime minister was initially granted the right to appoint and supervise his ministers, but these strong executive powers were curtailed by the constitution promulgated in 1889. Not surprisingly, the first cabinet, headed by Itō Hirobumi, was dominated by the oligarchs and their lieutenants, who maintained a monopoly over key ministerial posts into the 1890s.

To execute the cabinet's laws and policies, the civil bureaucracy was reorganized. In the hectic early years of Meiji the ranks of officialdom had been recruited rather haphazardly. Fellow provincials, personal followers, and promising young men were pulled into the government as need required. Since officials enjoyed the status privileges of the former samurai class, the government had no trouble finding office-seekers, but many proved to be inept, corrupt, or incompetent. In the early 1870s, the government set up official academies, often attached to particular government ministries, to train specialists to work for the burgeoning state. By the late 1880s, after some experimentation, it was decided to recruit officials by civil service examination. In 1887, regulations divided the new civil service into "higher civil officials" who occupied key executive positions in government ministries and "ordinary civil officials" who took care of routine paper work and detail. All were to be selected by examination.

To ensure recruitment of the brightest and best into the higher civil service, the government turned the new Imperial University in Tokyo (founded in 1886) into a training ground for fledgling officials. Indeed, by the 1890s graduates of the university's Faculty of Law dominated the middling ranks of the bureaucracy and were on their way to monopolizing its upper echelons as well. By linking access to official posts to educational qualifications, the oligarchs hoped to keep the civil bureaucracy free from partisan politics. To protect the highest echelons of the bureaucracy against outside political pressure, all but the highest posts (bureau chief and vice minister) were closed to patronage appointments. Officials were not to be subordinated to a national parliament nor to popularly elected politicians. To have allowed that, Itō Hirobumi noted, would have been tantamount to shifting power from the monarch into the hands of the people.

Higher civil officials regarded themselves neither as "public servants" nor as "silent servants" but as "slaves of the emperor." In theory, they were held to a higher standard than ordinary imperial subjects. Regulations governing official behavior stressed the importance of ethical qualities—integrity, probity, dignity, fairness, loyalty and industriousness—as much as technical or intellectual competence. As one ranking Meiji bureaucrat put it, "the official takes on an obligation of obedience that is immensely heavier than that of an ordinary subject."[2] Like the emperor, higher civil officials were supposed to be "above politics," able to take a long view of the country's interests, and devoted to the "national good" (*kokuze*) rather than partisan advantage or sectional interests. In the view of the Meiji leadership, high officials should neither pander to an electorate nor be swayed by the political passions of the moment. The notion that the official was uniquely equipped to serve the nation nurtured a bureaucratic élan steeped in elitism, dedication, and arrogance, but in fact, it was no easier to keep the civil bureaucracy out of politics than it was to keep the emperor above politics.

The prestige traditionally attached to official position persisted—so much so that high officials were often addressed as "Your Excellency, Mr. Official (*kannin-sama*)." The material rewards of bureaucratic service were also high. According to an 1884 government report, officials enjoyed the highest living standards in the country, second only to Buddhist priests. Not only were they paid handsome salaries to deter them from accepting bribes, but they enjoyed the privilege of regular holidays and vacations during the summer. Many high government officials settled in houses or villas once owned by bakufu direct retainers in the bucolic Yamanote ("mountainside") section of Tokyo. Since most rose up the same educational ladder, from preparatory higher schools into the national university, "old school cliques" (*gakubatsu*) provided networks for mutual collaboration or mutual advancement within the bureaucracy. Such cliques led to favoritism when classmates promoted each other's march up the ranks, but it also allowed high officials to cut across red tape and get things done through consultations outside official channels.

Parallel to the civil bureaucracy, a new military hierarchy, headed by a high command independent of civilian control, also took shape in the 1880s. In the wake of the Satsuma rebellion, army leaders like Yamagata Aritomo had decided to separate the command structure from military administration. In 1878 an army general staff, modeled on the German high command, was given full responsibility for strategic planning and full control over the deployment of military forces. These organizational principles were later reiterated in the general staff regulations of 1889. The army and navy chiefs of staff, like the prime minister, were appointed directly by the emperor and responsible to him alone, giving the high commands the same right of direct access to the throne as the prime minister. The military bureaucracy and the officer corps were free from cabinet control, and the chief of staff had the power to send troops into the field unchecked by any authority but the emperor. (The war minister, on the other hand, was not in control of the army, but merely its representative in the cabinet.)

The intent behind the separation of the military high command from civilian policy-making was to keep decisions on defense and strategy in the hands of professional military men. Like the civil bureaucracy, the officer corps was supposed to be technical and professional in character, not political. During the 1870s, when discontent was widespread in the former samurai class, army leaders were particularly anxious to protect the army from subversion by the anti-government agitation. In 1882, the Imperial Precepts for Soldiers and Sailors enjoined military men not to "be led astray . . . by popular opinions nor meddle in politics, but with single heart fulfill your essential duty of loyalty."[3] In fact, however, keeping the army out of politics was easier said than done. On questions that directly affected the interests of the army and navy, such as foreign policy or budget-making, their leaders had no compunction about making their wishes known. When challenged by other political forces, however, they could conveniently retreat behind their "right of direct access to the throne." As long as a unified oligarchy controlled both the military and civil hierarchies, disputes between them could be resolved informally, but the independence of the military gave it considerable political influence in the long run.

During the 1880s, the central government also extended firmer control over local communities. In the decade and a half after the Restoration, town and village assemblies raised local taxes, and town mayors or village chiefs were publicly elected by a local albeit highly restricted electorate. If not quite as independent as Tokugawa villages, local communities still had much say in managing their own affairs. Beginning in 1884, this local autonomy was gradually stripped away in the name of administrative centralization and

Itō Hirobumi, the principal author of the Meiji constitution. He served as prime minister five times between 1885 and 1901.

convenience. Village heads and town mayors were appointed instead of elected; town assemblies were headed by an appointed mayor; and the central government assumed greater power over the expenditures of local tax revenues. Towns and villages became the bottom rung of an administrative ladder that ran up through the prefectural governors to the Home Minister. The end of traditional self-government meant that local leaders had to turn to Tokyo for favors. The merging of many older natural communities into newly created village administrative units also diminished their importance as political entities. Local self-government was created from above, placing the mass of the rural population under direct control while shutting out all but the more aggressive and well-to-do from political participation.

THE MEIJI CONSTITUTION

Unlike the American constitution, the Meiji constitution did not create new institutions; it merely consolidated those already in existence. By the late 1880s, all the main elements of the new constitutional order, with the exception of the promised national assembly, had been put in place. This was no accident. The oligarchs had set up a firm base for a bureaucratic state structure before venturing into the uncertain waters of constitutional politics. The drafting of a constitution did not begin until the summer of 1887 under the personal direction of Itō Hirobumi. Since the constitution was to be the "gift" of the emperor to his subjects, there was no need to submit it to a constitutional convention nor to provide any sort of popular consent. Indeed, its provisions were unknown to the public until its final promulgation by the emperor on February 11, 1889. The only group to review the draft constitution was the privy council, whose twelve members nearly all belonged to the oligarchic inner circle and who conducted their deliberations in such elaborate secrecy that they turned in their documents at the end of each meeting.

Since even the popular right opposition embraced the idea that the "emperor and people should rule together" (*kunmin dōchi*), the new constitution concentrated most of the powers of state in the emperor's hands. Its preamble proclaimed that the emperor had inherited "the right of sovereignty of the State" from his ancestors, and other provisions gave him the right to appoint all the top officials of state, as well as the power to legislate, to convoke a national diet, to alter the organization of the bureaucracy, to declare war and make peace, to conclude treaties, to confer ranks and honors, and so forth. Very few political leaders, least of all the oligarchs themselves, expected that the emperor would act as a personal monarch, making decisions all by himself. Having overthrown what they regarded as a despotic regime, the oligarchs were not anxious to create a new one. It was clearly understood that the emperor would not exercise any of his constitutional powers on his own personal initiative. As Itō Hirobumi noted in 1888,

> The spirit behind the establishment of constitutional government is first to impose restrictions on the powers of the monarch, and second to secure the rights of subjects. . . . In whatever country, when you do not protect the rights of subjects and do not limit the power of the monarch, you have a despotic government, in which the rights of the ruler have become as unlimited as the duties of the subjects.[4]

The emperor might have been the keystone of the state, but he was firmly held in place by the pillars of constitutional law.

The imperial throne, in Itō's view, was to be the "pivot of the country." Its main function was not to make important decisions but to provide the moral cement for state and society that religion did in Western countries. Although the constitution established the principle of imperial sovereignty, the powers of the emperor were woven into a complicated fabric of constitutional checks and balances. The emperor could appoint and remove ministers at will, but his decrees had to be countersigned by them to take effect; the prime minister had no appointive control over his ministers, but he could suspend or reprimand them; the cabinet was granted considerable executive powers, but had to share them with the privy council, the imperial household ministry, and the military high command. Far from creating an absolutist system, the constitutional framework created space for political conflict and competition.

The main new institution under the constitution was the Imperial Diet, an elective national assembly. Some Meiji leaders, who regarded the Diet as a peripheral body, thought that it should merely be a sounding board for the cabinet, empowered to debate legislation but not to enact it. But Itō Hirobumi insisted that consent of the governed was an essential element of constitutional government, particularly on fiscal matters, so the constitution gave the Diet the power to debate and approve the annual budget, to enact legislation of its own, to confirm or reject imperial ordinances issued when the Diet was out of session, and to petition or memorialize the throne. Given the oligarchs' distrust of political opposition, these were considerable concessions.

Every effort was made to assure that the Diet would act moderately, however. To check the "rash impulses" of popularly elected representatives, the constitution provided that a House of Peers, made up from the newly created aristocracy, approve the budget and other legislation. The Diet session was limited to three months a year, hardly enough time to dominate the business of government, and the House of Representatives could be dissolved at the order of the emperor. To ensure that only sound, stable, and respectable social elements were elected to the lower house, suffrage was limited to those who paid over fifteen yen in direct national taxes. This excluded all but 400,000 (or about 1 percent) of the population in 1890. Similar restrictions were placed on Diet candidates as well. Since balloting was open, not secret, it is clear that the oligarchs expected that official surveillance would block "extremist" or "radical" elements from being elected.

Public reaction to the constitution was highly favorable. As one local newspaper put it, ". . . where there is a nation there is necessarily a constitution, and without a constitution there is no nation worthy of the name."[5] To be sure, critics like Ōkuma, Itagaki, and other former popular rights leaders found the constitution wanting in certain ways, but they were no less proud than the oligarchs that Japan had become the first Asian nation to adopt a constitutional system. Not only was the document the capstone of the long effort to achieve parity with the Western powers, its promulgation signaled the beginning of a new political era. The oligarchs occupied the political high ground but their wall of political exclusiveness could be breached more easily. The promulgation of the constitution made clear that the "people" (*kokumin*), however indirectly, were now part of the political process.

EDUCATION AND IDEOLOGY

To make sure that the "people" did not veer off in unpredictable or undesirable directions, the government adopted an ideological program to ensure their political docility. The spread of liberal and radical doctrines by the popular rights movement had prompted rethinking of educational goals. While the school curriculum continued to stress basic literacy and other practical skills, emphasis on the development of independent and self-reliant citizens was supplanted by a new concern to restore the social discipline and order of the old Japan. Government leaders abandoned the facile liberal notion that education could make people free for the more traditional notion that education could make them obedient. In 1881, the ministry of education admonished teachers not to engage in "stubborn or extreme talk" about politics and religion, and forbade both teachers and students to attend political meetings or join political associations. In a move to purge the schools of anti-government sentiments, the governor of Kōchi prefecture, heart of the popular rights movement, fired all teachers suspected of being political activists in the movement. The ministry of education also asserted greater control over the curriculum, curbing schools from choosing their own textbooks. In 1883, it issued a list of authorized textbooks, eliminating works regarded as politically dangerous.

If the authorities were averse to having the schools radicalize the young, they had no qualms about turning them to their own political purposes—the inculcation of political values such as obedience to authority, patriotism, loyalty to the emperor, and filial piety. Conservative scholars like Nishimura Shigeki and Motoda Nagazane, who advocated Confucian ideas as the best moral guide for the young, exercised considerable influence over educational policy in the early 1880s. Reviving the habit of submissiveness as civic virtues, primary-school ethics primers admonished pupils to bow low before the emperor, to treat government officials with respect, and to refrain from insulting policemen "who protect us all and help us at times of hardship and disaster."[6] In the late 1880s, Minister of Education Mori Arinori introduced regimentation, quasi-military exercises, and student uniforms in government teacher-training schools. Summing up the government's educational policy, he noted, "What is to be done is not for the sake of the pupils, but for the sake of country."[7]

The Imperial Rescript on Education promulgated in 1890, provided a basic statement of the social, political, and moral values the government wished to encourage. The document was drafted after a long debate between those who wanted to make Confucianism the official faith of the country and those, including Itō Hirobumi, who opposed establishing an official orthodoxy, on the grounds that morality was a matter of private conscience. The result was an uneasy compromise. On the one hand, the rescript lauded the Confucian virtues of loyalty (*chū*), filial piety (*kō*), affection between siblings, harmony between husband and wife, and friendship among comrades. But the rest of the document stressed practical personal values such as the importance of study and modern nationalist values such as obedience to the constitution, respect for the law of the land, and willingness to make sacrifices for the nation. Most of these would have seemed unexceptionable to educators in Western countries, whose governments also used the school system to inculcate politically acceptable values.

The Imperial Rescript, however, soon became a talisman of reverence for the emperor as an embodiment of the state. Copies of the rescript were dispatched to every school, where the document was solemnly intoned like a Buddhist sutra at school ceremonies on national holidays. Few children understood the difficult and archaic language of the document, but as they listened to its recitation with heads bowed in respect they knew it dealt with grave and important matters. The emperor's "august photograph," placed in every school, also came to be revered as a sacred object. Indeed, stories circulated about school principals who committed suicide after failing to rescue the portrait from a fire or stumbling in their recitation of the Imperial Rescript. By the turn of the century, the emperor had become a much more familiar figure to school children than he had been for their parents, who grew up barely aware of his existence. But the school rituals turned him into a distant figure wrapped in a mantle of sacredness at the pinnacle of society. Textbooks depicted Japan as a vast hierarchy stretching from the emperor to the family below, weaving everyone into a web of unlimited obligation to all above them.

By the late 1890s, the schools not only taught school children to be "imperial subjects" but tried to build their patriotism by inculcating them with the belief that the Japanese nation and the Japanese people were unique. Ethics, reading, and history courses taught that Japan possessed a special national polity (*kokutai*) that made it different from all the other countries in the world. This concept, familiar since the early nineteenth century, was given new meaning by Inoue Tetsujirō and Hozumi Yatsuka, both professors at the Imperial University, who identified it with the belief that the Japanese people had enjoyed the imperial rule "in an unbroken line for generations." In numerous tracts and textbooks, they attributed this remarkable continuity to the sacred origins of the imperial household, whose divine ancestors had

Illustrations from a late Meiji primary school ethics primer showing the virtues of punctuality (upper right), persistence (lower right), good manners (upper left), and orderliness (lower left).

"deeply and firmly implanted virtue" both in the monarch and in the common people. Hozumi argued that natural and spontaneous unity knitted the emperor and the subjects together in a "family state." In a very literal way, he described the people of Japan as the "emperor's children." Filial piety, or respect for one's parents, became a paradigm for loyalty to the monarch, the state, and superiors in general; and the concept of political loyalty was reinforced by respect for the family head. Indeed, Hozumi seemed to equate the nation with race. "Our family state is a racial group," he wrote in 1897. "Our race consists of blood relatives from the same womb. The family is a small state; the state is a large family. The origin of that which links the two, and the power than unites them in the same blood relationship is belief in ancestor worship."[8]

Some historians have suggested that the school system attempted to turn the traditional samurai ethic into a new national ethic for everyone. To be sure, textbooks were filled with stories about the bravery of historical heroes like Kusunoki Masashige, the medieval general who sacrificed himself for the imperial house. But children were also given inspiring commoner role models such as Toyotomi Hideyoshi, the humble sandal bearer who rose to unify the country, or Ninomiya Sontoku, the "peasant philosopher" who became an advisor to his daimyo. Textbook illustrations, for example, showed Ninomiya as a boy taking care of his younger brothers, repairing his family's decrepit dwelling, or intently reading a book as he carried a load of firewood home on his back. The government hoped to promote the mundane virtues of hard work, thrift, personal achievement, cooperation with others, and affection for family that would prepare young people as workers in the burgeoning economy and inoculate them against the social strains that were bound to accompany industrialization. Hierarchy, cooperation, and diligence in one's work were blended into a civic orthodoxy that owed as much to traditional commoner values as to the samurai ethic.

RECONSTRUCTING THE FAMILY

In its attempts to stabilize Japanese society, the government intruded into the world of the family. In early encounters with the West, Japanese leaders and intellectuals were often struck by how different Western family and marriage relations were from their own. Members of the Iwakura mission were surprised at the uxoriousness of Western men, especially American men, who seemed to wait on their wives hand and foot, a complete inversion of the way things were done at home. In debates over how to bring Japanese gender practices in line with those of the "civilized countries," many enlightenment intellectuals urged greater equality in marriage. Mori Arinori, for example, proposed that marriage contracts give husband and wife equal rights to sue for divorce. (His own unfortunate first marriage ended in divorce when his wife had an affair with a foreigner.)

The most widely accepted redefinition of women's social roles was proposed by Nakamura Masanao, the translator of Samuel Smiles. In an essay on "creating good mothers," he argued that since women's nature was to nurture, they could strengthen the moral foundations of society by educating their children as sound citizens and by influencing their husbands against immoral behavior. The woman's proper role, he said, was to act as a "good wife and a wise mother" (*ryōsai kenbo*). By the 1880s, this view dominated elite discourse on women and the family. It implied, on the one hand, that the woman's influence ought to dominate the home, but it also suggested that the cultivation of the woman's moral sense was of great importance to society. While these ideas might not seem particularly radical to contemporary Americans, they represented a break with an older gender ideology that defined women by their capacity to produce or reproduce. The idea that a woman should be more than a hard worker or a "borrowed womb" embodied a new notion of domesticity that centered on the home rather than the family lineage.

While the government often paid only lip service to this new idea, it did give priority to raising the educational level of women. From the outset, compulsory elementary education was extended to girls as well as boys. Female literacy had been on the rise by the end of the Tokugawa period, but the official commitment to basic female education signified that the government thought that women and girls were as important "human capital" as men and boys. School attendance rates for the girls at first lagged behind those for boys, but by the turn of the century the rate had risen to 60 percent for girls as opposed to 85 percent for boys. By 1910, nearly all children of both sexes were acquiring basic numeracy and literacy in the country's elementary schools. But there was little question that the education of women was intended primarily to prepare them to serve as patriotic wives and mothers. As Minister of Education Mori Arinori noted in 1887:

> In the process of educating girls and women, we must put across the idea of serving and helping their country. The models for women are a mother nurturing her child; a mother teaching her child; her son coming of age and being conscripted to go to war and leaving his mother with a good-bye; a son fighting bravely on the battlefield; and a mother receiving a telegram informing of her son's death in the war.[9]

In practical terms, the elementary curriculum placed special emphasis on training girls in the skills needed to manage a household—etiquette, child care, sewing and home economics.

Most parents discouraged their daughters from continuing their education beyond the elementary level, and very few girls did so. The development of advanced educational institutions for women was left to private initiatives by foreign missionaries who founded academies for girls in Tokyo, Kobe, Sendai, and other parts of the country. Only in 1900 did the government order each prefectural government to establish at least one four-year high school for girls. Women were also excluded from the government institutions of higher learning, including Tokyo Imperial University, which was reserved for men only. Young women who sought a college education had to attend private institutions like the Women's English College founded by Tsuda Umeko to help women learn skills for an independent career. As the demand for school teachers grew with rising school enrollments, however, the government also opened teacher training schools for women.

While the government supported new domestic roles for women, it wanted to keep them out of politics. Women had played little or no formal role in traditional domain or village government, which had been the exclusive preserve of men. In the 1880s, however, a few adventurous women participated in the popular rights movement. Kishida Toshiko, the learned daughter of a Kyoto merchant family who had lectured the Empress Meiji on Confucian classics, established herself as a champion of women's rights. In 1883, she was arrested for a fiery public speech attacking the traditional hierarchical marriage system. Such subversive thoughts were tolerated when expressed by "enlightenment" intellectuals like Fukuzawa and Mori, but they were infinitely more threatening when uttered by a woman. Just before the opening of the first Imperial Diet in 1890, the cabinet promulgated a law (reaffirmed in

1900) that barred women from attending political meetings or joining political parties. The rationale was that women as wives and mothers had a higher duty to the country than politics; it was important that they stand apart from political bickering, competition, and backbiting and exert their moral influence in the home instead.

The lives of women and their families were also affected by the drafting of a new civil law code, which reshaped the legal framework of family relations. In hopes of creating a modern legal system that meshed with prevailing Japanese customs, the government carried out nationwide surveys during the 1880s to find out what "standard" marriage, family, and inheritance practices were. The investigation revealed wide local variations in practice, so in 1888 the ministry of justice decided to base family law on the customs of the samurai rather than on those of the commoners or peasants. The samurai household, a strongly patriarchal unit dedicated to preserving the family lineage over the generations, put enormous power in the hands of its male head. So did the legal code finally promulgated in 1898. The household head, normally the husband and father, was given the authority to approve or veto nearly all the basic life decisions of the household members, including such matters as the selection of marriage partners, choice of residence, and ownership of property. For example, until the age of twenty-five in the case of women, and thirty in the case of men, adult children had to secure parental permission before they could get married.

The new legal code also reinforced the notion of domesticity embodied in the ideal of the "good wife and wise mother." Only monogamous marriages were recognized, and concubines (though common) enjoyed no legal status. But marriage continued to be arranged by parents or relatives, and the bride was thought to join her husband's family rather than starting a new one. Under the new legal code, the right to divorce, once a largely male prerogative, was extended to wives, but the legal balance of power still tipped in the husband's favor. A woman could divorce her husband on grounds of cruel treatment, desertion, imprisonment, or other serious misconduct, but not on grounds of adultery. Since a divorced wife received neither custody of her children nor any financial settlement—and risked public opprobrium as well—the incentives to avoid divorce were considerable. On the other hand, husbands often found it easy to bully or intimidate wives into signing divorce agreements.

Despite the efforts of the government to impose the samurai family model on the rest of the population, the emerging gender system embraced both traditional and modern elements. Since it gave men a clear preponderance of legal power over women both in public affairs and in the family, relations between men and women were still asymmetrical, but they were asymmetrical in a new way. The ideal of "good wife and wise mother" validated the importance of women to the nation as well as to the household, and it enlarged their sphere of empowerment in the home. The new gender system was slow to spread. It caught hold in the cities, especially among the better educated and wealthier classes, who often came from samurai or merchant back-grounds. But the new gender ideology and family institutions met with resistance in many rural areas where local customs persisted. In some parts of the country, for example, older practices, including succession to the family headship by the eldest daughter, survived well after the turn of the century. It was one thing to impose a new set of laws on the country, quite another to change deeply rooted social habits. (And strong-minded wives and hen-pecked husbands were probably no less common than they ever had been.)

ENDNOTES

1. Iwakura's views are cited in Thomas C. Smith, *Political Change and Industrial Development in Japan: Government Enterprise 1868–1880* (Stanford, Cal.: Stanford University Press, 1955), 97–98.

2. Yui Masaomi and Obinata Sumio, *Kindai Nihon shisō taikei*, vol. 3 *Kanryō* (Tokyo: Iwanami shoten, 1990), 162.

3. The text of the Imperial Precepts for Soldiers and Sailors may be found in Ryusaku Tsunoda et al. *Sources of Japanese Tradition* (New York: Columbia University Press, 1958), 705–707.

4. The quote from Itō may be found in *Meiji Japan through Contemporary Sources*, vol. 2 (Tokyo: The Centre for East Asian Cultural Studies, 1970), 121–123.

5. Quoted in Carol Gluck, *Japan's Modern Myths: Ideology in the Late Meiji Period* (Princeton, N.J.: Princeton University Press, 1985), 49.

6. Quoted in Ienaga Saburō and Inoue Kiyoshi, *Kindai Nihon no sōten*, vol. 1 (Tokyo: Mainichi shimbunsha, 1967), 381.

7. Mori is quoted in Herbert Passin, *Society and Education in Japan* (New York: Columbia University Press, 1965), 81.

8. Quoted in Sepp Linhart, "The Family as a Constitutive Element of Japanese Civilization," in Tadao Uemsao et al. (eds.), *Japanese Civilization in the Modern World: Life and Society*, vol. 16 (Senri Ethnological Studies, 1984), 53.

9. Quoted in Kumiko Fujimura-Fanselow and Atsuko Kamada (eds.). *Japanese Women: New Feminist Perspectives on the Past, Present and Future* (New York: The Feminist Press, 1995), 96.

8

The Rise of Imperialism

In the decade following the Restoration, the Japanese found themselves relatively free from foreign pressure. The last venture in Western gunboat diplomacy came in 1865 when a joint foreign fleet arrived in Osaka Bay to force the opening of the port of Hyōgō (later Kobe) and imperial recognition of a new commercial treaty. Once the foreign powers secured the rights they sought, however, they ceased bothering the Japanese with further demands. No foreign interventions threatened the existence of the new imperial regime nor did disputes with the foreigners prove difficult to resolve by negotiation. The fall of the bakufu also drained off the wrath of domestic xenophobes. The Meiji leaders did not bear the stigma of having given in to the foreigners, nor of having sold out the country's interests. On the contrary, they had strong credentials as anti-foreign activists themselves. This clean slate helps to account for the survival of the Meiji government in its early years.

POST-RESTORATION DIPLOMACY

The country's relations with the outside world were never far from the minds of its new leaders, however. In the immediate post-Restoration years, they wrestled with conflicting impulses. On the one hand, the new government took every care not to offend the Western powers, whose vastly superior military strength had been amply demonstrated. Public notices warned the population against anti-foreign violence, and every effort was made to accommodate the foreigners' sensibilities by banning public nudity, mixed bathing, and urination in the streets. On the one hand, as veterans of the anti-foreign movements of the 1860s, the Meiji leaders were determined to overcome the humiliation of the "unequal treaties" signed with the Western nations. "It is an extremely disgraceful situation," wrote Iwakura Tomomi, "when . . . foreign troops are billeted on our shores and when resident Westerners are able to appeal to their officials when they have violated our country's laws."[1] Many officials, especially in the newly established foreign office, urged decisive action, even military action, to restore the "national honor" forfeited by the bakufu in its concessions to the foreigners.

Renegotiating the treaties was the obvious way to retrieve "national honor," but such negotiations proved more difficult than anticipated. It was clear from Western treatises on international law that large and small countries had equal rights and settled their differences by negotiated agreements as well as by force. The Iwakura mission departed for the West in 1871 with hopes of opening negotiations for treaty revision, but they still had much to learn about how Westerners conducted diplomacy. Since the mission arrived in Washington without any documents authorizing them to negotiate, two members had to return home to fetch them before the Americans would deal with the treaty question. It soon became clear, however, that the Americans and other Westerners were reluctant to make concessions on the treaties unless the Japanese carried out major legal and constitutional reforms. After the mission returned home, the foreign ministry continued negotiations with the British and others to regain control over tariffs, but its overtures were persistently rebuffed.

Neither was the government very successful in retrieving the "national honor" by asserting Japan's diplomatic superiority over its Asian neighbors. In 1870, a Japanese mission was dispatched to Beijing with a proposal that would have imposed on the Qing court an "unequal treaty" modelled on Western treaties with China. The Chinese did not take the proposal seriously, however. The mission returned home in 1871 with a treaty of friendship that placed China and Japan on an equal footing, providing for the exchange of diplomatic representatives, low tariff rates, and extraterritorial privileges for the citizens of both countries. As we have already seen, the government was even less successful in persuading the Korean court to abandon its traditional relations through Tsushima and adopt "civilized" Western diplomatic practices. Indeed, it was Korean stubbornness that persuaded leaders like Ōkubo Toshimichi and Iwakura Tomomi to abandon "hasty ventures" abroad while consolidating the program of reform at home.

During the mid-1870s, however, the government began a slow but steady shift toward a more assertive foreign policy, albeit one constrained by a feeling that the Western powers were constantly peering over their shoulders. For one thing, the new imperial regime expanded political sovereignty over territories never fully under Japanese control. On the northern frontier in Ezo, an area inhabited by Ainu tribes that had long traded with the Japanese but had never been fully assimilated into Japanese culture, the government embarked on a crash colonization program. To forestall Russian encroachments, the bakufu had already placed Ezo under its control after 1854, and the following year it signed a treaty dividing the Kurile Islands with the Russians, but the new imperial government set up a colonial office to develop the sparsely settled northern island, which it renamed Hokkaidō. To encourage settlement, the government poured money into clearing the land, building roads and rail lines, staking out new towns and cities, and opening coal mines. The first emigrants to Hokkaidō were military colonists (*tondenhei*), mainly former samurai from northeast Honshu lured by offers of official assistance. Gradually, adventurous peasants and commoners seeking new economic opportunities arrived in growing numbers too. To secure diplomatic recognition of the new northern border, in 1875 the government signed a treaty with the Russians, who recognized Japanese sovereignty over the Kurile Islands in return for abandonment of Japanese claims on the island of Sakhalin.

To the south, where there were no European powers to contend with, the government was more willing to use saber-rattling to extend its territorial boundaries. In the spring of 1874, partly as a sop to the "chastise Korea" party, the government dispatched a military expedition under the leadership of Saigō Tsugumichi (Takamori's brother) to punish Taiwanese aborigines for attacks on fishermen from the Ryukyu Islands. While Ryukyu islanders were closer to the Japanese in language and culture than the Ainu, they had maintained a quasi-independent position during Tokugawa times, when their ruler acted both as a vassal of Satsuma and a tributary of the Qing court. The Qing government, which claimed suzerainty over Taiwan, agreed to pay an indemnity to the families of the fishermen, thereby establishing its own claims on Taiwan but also tacitly recognizing Japanese claims over the Ryukyus. In 1879, the islands were incorporated into Japan as the new prefecture of Okinawa, and the Ryukyu ruler was pensioned off as the daimyo had been several years earlier.

As the government gained confidence in its ability to manipulate international law to advance its own interests, it turned attention once again to its unresolved differences with Korea. In more-or-less conscious imitation, the government decided to "open" Korea just as the Americans had "opened" Japan. Using an attack on the crew of a Japanese surveying vessel as a pretext, the government dispatched a gunboat expedition to Korea in 1876 to demand the establishment of normal diplomatic and trade relations. Unwilling to risk war, the Korean court finally agreed to negotiations. Ironically, the Japanese imposed on the Koreans the same kind of unequal treaty system that they sought to shed themselves. The Treaty of Kangwha, signed in January 1876, recognized Korea as an independent sovereignty and provided for the exchange of diplomatic representatives between Japan and Korea, but it also opened the ports of Pusan, Wonsan, and In'chŏn and gave the Japanese extraterritorial rights.

THE EXPANSIONIST IMPULSE

During the 1870s, foreign policy issues took second place to domestic reforms, but by the early 1880s a new wave of Western aggressiveness (sometimes called the "new imperialism") loomed on the horizon. With the achievement of an international balance of power on the European continent, the advance of industrialization, and the spreading use of steam vessels and telegraphic communication, the European powers found themselves in a new position to extend their power over the less developed regions of the world, from sub-Saharan Africa to the southwestern Pacific. The result was a new and intense competition for colonies, naval bases, and spheres of influence outside of Europe. As this "new imperialism" accelerated, it intruded into East Asia. While the Russians and British struggled for influence in Central Asia on the western borders of China, the French penetrated the Indochina peninsula, Germany began to show an increased interest in China and the South Pacific, and the United States developed strong interests in Hawaii. Although these developments were motivated primarily by rivalries among the Westerners, to many Japanese they seemed to represent a clear and present danger to "the peace of the Orient."

The "new imperialism" provoked vociferous demands from both right and left in the early 1880s for a more positive and aggressive foreign policy. The popular rights press, under the influence of Social Darwinist ideas, argued that international relations were governed by a struggle for the survival of the fittest, and their editorials urged the government not only to guarantee popular rights but to assert "national rights" as well. Indeed, once the government agreed to establish a constitutional order, it was easier for the anti-government opposition to attack it on foreign policy issues than on domestic political questions. In any case, critics focussed both on the government's failure to revise the unequal treaties and its restraint toward China and Korea. Talk of expansion also appealed to the rump of the conservative opposition, particularly in Kyushu, traditionally the gateway to the Asian continent. In 1881, a group of former samurai from Fukuoka, many of them former supporters of Saigō Takamori, formed the *Genyōsha,* a chauvinist society dedicated to defending the honor of the nation, promoting reverence to the emperor, and lobbying for a more aggressive foreign policy.

Criticism of the government's foreign policy was both opportunistic and idealistic. It was obvious to critics that the failure of the Chinese and the Koreans to undertake reform left them prey to conquest and dismemberment by the Western powers. One popular rights activist, after a trip to China in 1884, argued that since the Westerners were about to make a feast of a "narrow-minded and obstinate" China, Japan should be a "guest at the table" too.[2] On the other hand, liberal critics argued that Japan's new national strength brought with it a responsibility to help its neighbors "civilize" themselves. It was not so long since the Japanese had been as vulnerable as the Chinese and the Koreans. Fukuzawa Yukichi, for example, urged military and cultural protection for China and Korea to defend them from Western powers while introducing them to Western civilization. Impelled by similar sentiments, Ōi Kentarō, a popular rights radical who styled himself a "Japanese Lafayette," even mounted a plot to overthrow the reactionary elements in the Korean court and establish a reform government there.

The Meiji leaders were not entirely unsympathetic with their critics' goals. It was clear that the "civilized" countries were bent on extending their dominion over the rest of the world, and that everywhere in Asia weak countries were falling under Western control. While no longer afraid of direct Western aggression against Japan, the Meiji leaders were deeply concerned about the fate of neighboring countries. In 1887, Foreign Minister Inoue Kaoru lamented that the "continents of Asia and Africa are about to become the cockpit of conflict among the Europeans."[3] What concerned him most was that once independent countries like Persia (Iran), Siam (Thailand), and Korea might soon become the object of the Western colonial advance, a turn of events that would bode ill for the security of Japan. If Korea or China were to come under the thrall of the Westerners, Japan would become increasingly vulnerable to foreign military and diplomatic pressure.

Strategic doctrines associated with "new imperialism" made their way to Japan by the early 1890s. The acquisition of colonies, naval bases, and spheres of influence, once far beyond the imagination of the Japanese political elite, now seemed as necessary to maintain national independence as a strong army and navy. Yamagata Aritomo, for example, argued it was necessary to maintain national independence by protecting not simply Japan's home islands ("a line of sovereignty") but also an outer perimeter of adjacent territory ("a line of interest").[4] There was little danger that the foreigners would encroach on Japan's "line of sovereignty," but it was quite likely that they would seek a foothold within the country's "line of interest." In Yamagata's view, Japan had to assure it own ascendancy in these adjacent territories in order to "maintain peace in the Orient." His ideas reflected a growing consensus that national security required that Japan dominate the East Asian region lest it fall prey to the Western imperialists.

Apprehension over the instability in the region prompted a steady buildup of Japan's military and naval forces. In 1880, military spending had amounted to only 19 percent of the government budget, but by 1890 it had risen to 31 percent. While the original mission of the Japanese army had been to maintain domestic order and quell disturbances such as the Satsuma rebellion, it was now preparing itself to fight wars overseas. Within the army general staff, it had become an axiom that the security of Japan required keeping Korea, "a dagger pointed at the heart of Japan," independent from control by any other power. Indeed, in 1887 the army began preparing contingency plans for a war with China to secure the independence of Korea, and in the early 1890s it began staging large-scale maneuvers in preparation for operations on the continent. The navy, in the meantime, expanded its fleet to include warships that could fight on the high seas and transport ships to carry troops across the Korean straits. Under the influence of the doctrines of the American Admiral Mahan, an advocate of naval expansion, naval leaders argued that control over neighboring seas backed by a strong navy and merchant marine was essential to national security.

The Meiji leaders were also aware that international political competition was inextricably linked with international economic competition. Not only did

European leaders argue that colonial expansion brought economic benefits to the home country, they often used trade, loans, and investment as an entering wedge for political penetration. While Japan's modern industries were still in their infancy in the 1890s, just beginning to find capital and markets at home, the Meiji leaders knew that political expansion required economic expansion as well. After the opening of Korea in 1876, for example, the government had encouraged private businessmen like Shibusawa Eiichi and Ōkura Kichachirō to start up trading operations at the newly opened port of Pusan, and it did its best to defend the interests of Japanese traders on the peninsula. Only about one quarter of Japan's trade went to Asia by the late 1880s, but expanding that trade was critical to the spread of Japanese influence in the region. The "line of interest" might be strategic in its goals, but it required economic underpinnings.

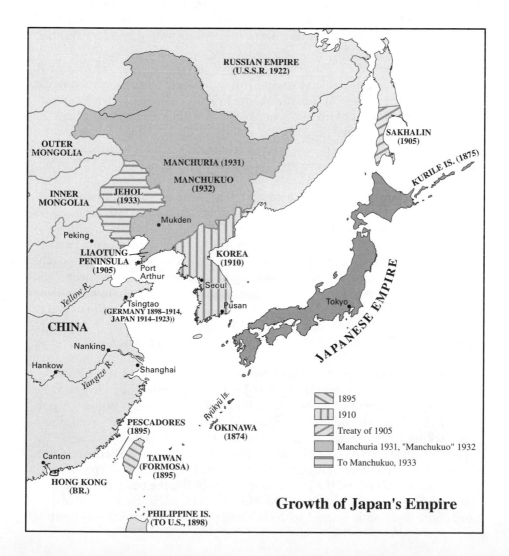

Growth of Japan's Empire

KOREA AND THE SINO-JAPANESE WAR

The strategic anxieties and economic ambitions of the Japanese leadership focussed on the Korean peninsula, where Japanese influence had grown after the "opening" of Korea in 1876. By the early 1880s, Japanese merchants in the treaty ports of Pusan, Wonsan, and In'chŏn dominated Korea's external trade, selling Western cotton goods and sundries in exchange for rice and other foodstuffs. With encouragement from the Japanese government, some members of the Korean elite looked to Japan as a model for reform in their own country. In 1880, a group of Korean officials was invited to Japan to tour factories, arsenals, schools, government ministries, post offices, museums, military camps, and other examples of Japan's progress toward "civilization." Far from seeing their neighbor as a potential aggressor, an "enlightenment" faction at the Korean court urged closer ties with Japan, and in 1881 the Korean king invited Japanese army officers to train a modern military force.

Just as the arrival of Perry had provoked an anti-foreign movement in Japan, the sudden influx of Japanese bearing ideas and new goods roused a conservative opposition in Korea. Many Korean scholars and officials regarded the Japanese as "Oriental renegades" who had betrayed their heritage by shamelessly imitating the Western countries. In July 1882, a mutiny of disgruntled Korean soldiers, angered over unpaid wages, provided the conservatives an opportunity to recoup their position. The mutineers killed their Japanese military advisor, set fire to the Japanese legation, and forced the Japanese minister to flee the capital. The Korean king's father, a virulent opponent of opening the country to foreign influences, assumed power as regent (*Taewŏn'gun*). But a more serious consequence of the mutiny was the arrival of 5,000 troops dispatched by the Qing government to "assist" the Korean court in putting down the rising. The Chinese ousted the Taewŏn'gun, returning power to Min clan, the family of the queen, and promptly re-established tributary relations with Seoul. To undercut Japanese influence, Chinese advisors or pro-Chinese foreign advisors were installed in every government department, and the Chinese encouraged the Koreans to trade with the Westerners in order to reduce Japanese influence.

In the face of the Chinese intrusion, the Japanese could do little more than demand an indemnity and an apology from the Korean court. In 1884, however, the "enlightenment" faction led by pro-Japanese officials, Kim Ok-kyun and Pak Yŏng-hyo, attempted a countercoup to oust the Chinese. While the government in Tokyo provided no support for the plotters, they enjoyed financial backing from private Japanese sources and unofficial collusion by the Japanese minister to Korea. The coup, aimed at instituting a Meiji-style program of reform, was quickly put down with the help of Chinese troops, who forced the reformers and the Japanese minister to flee the country. Rumors of war with Korea spread in Japan. The Meiji leaders, pursuing a policy of caution, chose diplomatic detente with the Qing government, which was fighting the French in Indochina and was not anxious to start hostilities with Japan as well. In 1885, Itō Hirobumi and Li Hongzhang (Li Hung-chang), who dominated Chinese foreign policy, negotiated the Tianjin (Tientsin) Convention, which provided for a withdrawal of both Chinese and Japanese troops and military advisors from Korea and committed both governments to give prior notice in the event that grave disturbances required a new dispatch of troops.

The pro-Chinese faction remained in control of the Korean court, however. The Chinese representative in Korea, Yuan Shikai (Yüan Shih-kai), attempted to turn Korea into a modern style protectorate, subservient to Chinese interests and dependent on Chinese aid. Japan's political influence declined and so did her trade. Had China been strong, Japanese leaders might not have been concerned about Chinese domination of Korea, but the defeat of Qing armies at the hands of the French in Indochina during the mid-1880s revealed China's continuing weakness. A backward and weak Korea under the control of an equally backward and weak China seemed easy prey for one of the Western powers. There was little doubt that the Russians, anxious to have a warm-water port in Korea, harbored ambitions on the peninsula. When the Russians announced plans for a trans-Siberian railroad linking their Pacific maritime eastern provinces with European Russia, Japanese leaders grew even more alarmed.

By the early 1890s, "the independence of Korea" had become a fixed goal for the Japanese government. The term, however, was an ambiguous one. For the Japanese army, it meant a Korea free from Chinese rule and firmly under Japanese political domination. For Diet politicians and journalists, it meant a Korea free of "despotic" government and open to guidance by a "progressive" Japan dedicated to freeing the Korean people from the thrall of ignorance and backwardness. For the Meiji oligarchs, it meant both. In their eyes internal reform within Korea was inextricably linked with establishing a dominant Japanese political influence there. Only if the Chinese were ousted would it be possible for the Koreans to undertake the self-strengthening reforms needed to guarantee a Korean independence that was as vital to Japanese national security as to the freedom of the Korean populace.

The stage for a final clash between Japan and China was set by the outbreak of a peasant rebellion in the southern part of the peninsula. The rising was led by the Tonghaks, a religious sect that promised sweeping social changes and embraced strong anti-foreign sentiments. The Korean court had been able to suppress the Tonghaks temporarily in 1893, but by the spring of 1894 a revived Tonghak force, meeting little or no effective resistance, was marching toward the capital at Seoul. The Japanese feared that if the rebels succeeded in overthrowing the court, Korea would plunge into an anarchy that would invite foreign intervention. When the Chinese dispatched a force of 4,000 troops to help suppress the Tonghaks, the Japanese government countered by sending a larger force of its own under the provisions of the Tianjin convention.

The army leadership, confident in the army's ability to rout the Chinese, wanted a preventive war to drive China out of the Korean peninsula and establish paramount Japanese influence. Civilian leaders like Prime Minister Itō Hirobumi and Foreign Minister Mutsu Mumemitsu, who did not wish to provoke the Western powers, were more cautious. They preferred to maintain a balance of power with the Chinese, perhaps even persuading them to embark on a joint reform of the Korean court. Only when the Chinese, refusing to take the "dwarf barbarians" seriously, rejected Japanese proposals for mutual withdrawal of troops and a joint reform effort, did the Itō cabinet finally decide for war. In late July 1894, Japanese troops seized the royal palace, forcing the Korean king to sign an agreement authorizing the Japanese to expel the Chinese, and on August 1 Japan formally declared war on the Qing government.

The Sino-Japanese War of 1894–1895 was vindication of all the government's efforts to build up national wealth and strength. Most foreign observers, including the Chinese themselves, were certain that the tiny Japanese island kingdom was no match for the great Chinese empire. Not only was the Chinese army vastly superior to the Japanese in manpower, the Chinese navy boasted twice as many modern warships as the Japanese. But the Chinese leadership was divided by factional rivalries, and their military preparedness had been weakened by a bureaucracy riddled with corruption and incompetence. Naval development funds, for example, had been diverted to constructing a great stone paddle boat for the pleasure gardens of the dowager empress. In September 1894, the Japanese navy quickly established control of the Yellow Sea, decisively defeating the Chinese northern fleet in a five-hour battle, and highly disciplined and well equipped Japanese army troops swept the motley Qing army out of the peninsula. By October, Japanese expeditionary forces landed on the Liaodong (Liaotung) Peninsula to confront the Chinese on their own territory. As one Japanese journalist ungraciously noted, the war proved the Qing empire was not a "sleeping giant" but a "sleeping pig."

Within a few months of the war's outbreak, the Ch'ing court was ready to make peace. The terms exacted by the Japanese in the Treaty of Shimonoseki signed in April 1895 paved the way toward the establishment of an overseas empire. Not only did the Ch'ing government recognize the independence of Korea, it ceded Taiwan and the Pescadores Islands to Japan, which provided the Japanese protection on their southern flanks, and it gave Japan territorial control over the Liaodong Peninsula, which commanded sea approaches to the Chinese capital. To defray the costs of the war, the Chinese agreed to pay an indemnity of ¥364 million, an amount half again as large as Japan's actual war expenditures, and they also agreed to a commercial treaty that gave Japan the same extraterritorial rights and most favored status that the Western countries enjoyed in China. In short, not only did Japan manage to turn a profit on the war, it also acquired a foothold on the Asia continent that was to expand steadily over the next generation.

THE RUSSO-JAPANESE WAR

Although the Americans and the English reacted favorably to the emergence of Japan as a new power in East Asia, the continental Europeans were not so ready to admit the Japanese to the imperialist club. Indeed, much alarmed at the Japanese victory, they sought to curb the Japanese gains. In May 1895, Russia, backed by France and Germany, advised Japan to relinquish its new rights over the Liaodong Peninsula. Since war with the Europeans or unsuccessful mediation were the only likely alternatives, the Itō cabinet gave in peacefully. This "Triple Intervention," which robbed Japan of territory the public thought had been fairly won on the battlefield, was a serious blow to the national pride. To add insult to injury the Russians secured a ninety-nine-year lease on the Liaodong Peninsula in 1898, making obvious why they had wanted Japan to return it to China. Anti-Russian sentiment gathered force in the late 1890s. Aroused by a determination to "suffer privation to achieve revenge" (*gashin shōtan*), the cabinet launched a crash program of naval and military expansion in preparation for a possible war. In 1896, the Diet authorized a six-division increase in the army and a naval construction program to add four new battleships, sixteen cruisers, and twenty-three destroyers to the Japanese fleet. Not surprisingly, Russia replaced China as the chief hypothetical enemy in strategic plans.

The war of 1894–1895 had made Korea independent of Chinese suzerainty, but it also opened the way for Russia to extend its influence there. Political bungling by the Japanese had a good deal to do with this new turn of events. During the war, Japanese diplomats working with the Korean "enlightenment" faction had forced a massive program of political and social reform on the Korea court. Regulations establishing legal equality for all classes, instituting modern legal procedures, prohibiting of slavery and child marriage, and the like were promulgated pell-mell. The reform program reflected Japanese exasperation at the backwardness and corruption of the Korean ruling class, but the radical character of the reforms, to say nothing of their Japanese sponsorship, provoked elite resentment and popular opposition.

Encouraged by the sight of Japan's buckling under Russian pressure in the Triple Intervention, conservative Korean officials, including members of the queen's clan, intrigued against pro-Japanese reformers who controlled the Korean cabinet. The Tokyo government dispatched a blunt and simple-minded general, Miura Gorō, to deal with the situation as minister to Seoul. Working with Japanese chauvinist activists on his own initiative, Miura arranged the murder of Queen Min, who was thought to be the center of the anti-Japanese faction. When the Korean reformers ordered that all Korean men cut off their topknots, worn as a mark of filial piety, open rebellion broke out in the provinces. Anti-Japanese "righteous armies" were organized to oust the Japanese and their Korean allies. Taking advantage of the confusion, in early February 1896 the Korean king fled for protection to the Russian legation, where he remained for the next year.

The escape of the king brought Japanese supremacy in Seoul to a sudden end. A new conservative regime in Seoul was backed by the Russians, who planted their own military and financial advisers with the Korean government. But the Russians were as inept as the Japanese at handling their Korean clients, and after failing to ingratiate themselves with the Korean court, they finally struck a bargain with the Japanese. In March 1898, the two powers signed an agreement that made Korea into a joint protectorate and committed both sides not to assist Korea in military or financial matters without prior consultation and agreement. The Russians, who were concentrating on building their influence in Manchuria, also agreed to recognize that Japan had paramount economic interests in Korea. The diplomatic detente gave the Japanese a new opportunity to secure a firmer economic foothold on the peninsula. A consortium of Japanese business interests secured rights to build railroad lines linking Seoul with the major ports of Pusan and In'chŏn, and the Japanese minister worked to arrange Japanese bank loans to shore up the finances of the Korean government. But the strategic anxieties of the Japanese leaders remained unassuaged.

In 1899–1900, the outbreak of the Boxer Rebellion, a peasant rebellion in northern China that climaxed with a rebel siege of the foreign legations at Beijing, created new anxieties. Not only did the Qing court seem on the verge of collapse, but the Russians, who sent a large expeditionary force into southern Manchuria during the rebellion, kept their troops there after the rebellion had been suppressed. Taking advantage of Chinese weakness, the Russians put pressure on the Qing government to sign an agreement making Manchuria a Russian protectorate. These Russian territorial ambitions alarmed the Japanese leaders, who worried that Japan's "line of advantage" was under threat. If Manchuria came under Russia's control, then its troops would be poised on Korea's northern border. From Japan's strategic standpoint, this was an intolerable situation.

The oligarchs preferred to negotiate with the Russians than deal with them by by force, but they disagreed about what diplomatic strategy to adopt. Itō Hirobumi proposed to offer recognition of Russian paramount interest in Manchuria in return for Russian recognition of Japan's paramount interest in Korea. This policy of "trading Manchuria for Korea" (*Man-Kan kōkan*) was imperialist diplomacy in the classic fashion. Other oligarchic leaders, including Yamagata Aritomo and his protege, Prime Minister Katsura Tarō, who did not trust the Russians, proposed to outflank them by an alliance with the British, their chief rivals in Asia. In early 1902, the British agreed to an alliance with Japan that committed each country to come to the defense of the other if it engaged in war with more than one opponent. In effect, the Anglo-Japanese alliance warned Russia's allies against becoming involved if Russia went to war with Japan. With its diplomatic flanks secured, the Katsura government opened negotiations with St. Petersburg to settle differences over Korea and Manchuria, but it soon became clear that the Russians did not take the Japanese overtures seriously. Goaded by an anti-

Russian hue and cry for war and frustrated by the unresponsiveness of the Russians, the Katsura cabinet decided for war in early 1904.

Although the army leadership had been relatively confident it could beat China in 1895, war with Russia was more of a gamble. Not only was the vast expanse of Russia's territory intimidating, but the Russian government commanded an enormous military garrisoned in European Russia. If its superior manpower were brought to bear on the fighting, Japan would almost surely face defeat. On the other hand, the Japanese enjoyed certain advantages of their own: the ability to launch a surprise attack on the Russians, proximity to the scene of the fighting, and a temporary superiority in the number of troops immediately available for combat. Japanese strategic plans capitalized on these advantages by aiming at a short, limited war. The goal was to win a series of decisive early victories that would bring the Russians to the negotiating table.

The war went according to plan at first. An initial battle on the Korea-Manchuria border in May 1905 gave Japan a morale-boosting victory over Russian forces. Indeed, news of the Japanese victory was electrifying in the rest of Asia, since it was the first time that an Asian army had defeated a Western one in modern times. The Japanese soon made successful amphibious landings on the Liaodong Peninsula, where the bulk of the Russian garrison forces were concentrated, but the Japanese offensive lost momentum when General Nogi Maresuke, commander of the expeditionary force, embarked on a long and bloody siege of the major Russian military base at Port Arthur. In January 1905, after nearly half a year of bloody assaults that cost the Japanese 56,000 casualties, Port Arthur finally fell when the Japanese captured the high ground overlooking the city. But the retreating Russian army slipped through Japanese lines to set up new defensive positions in central Manchuria, where reinforcements were pouring in from European Russia.

By the spring of 1905, the strains of war were beginning to tell in Japan. Manpower reserves had dwindled; munitions were in short supply; and war costs put a heavy financial strain on the government, which had already borrowed heavily in the New York and London money markets. After the Japanese land offensive bogged down near Mukden in central Manchuria, it was clear that the Russians were not likely to sue for peace short of a Japanese assault on Moscow. This was obviously an impossibility. In late May 1905, however, a Japanese fleet under Admiral Tōgō Heihachirō won a decisive naval victory in the Straits of Tsushima, where his fleet all but destroyed a vast but incredibly inept Russian fleet that had sailed around Africa from the Baltic Sea to support the Russian land effort. While the Japanese lost only three torpedo boats, the Russians lost six battleships, six cruisers, five destroyers, and more than a dozen other vessels. Facing what promised to be a military stalemate, both sides agreed to accept the good offices of Theodore Roosevelt as broker for peace negotiations.

The Treaty of Portsmouth, concluded in September 1905, consolidated Japanese influence on the Asian continent. Not only did the Russians recognize Japan's paramount political, military, and economic interests in Korea,

Comparison of Japanese and Russian Strength

	Japan	Russia
Troops mobilized	1,088,996	2,000,000
Size of fleet	258,000 tons 6 battleships/6 cruisers	510,000 tons 12 battleships/10 cruisers
War expenditure	¥1.5 billion	¥2.1 billion
Dead/missing in action	c. 118,000	c. 115,000
Prisoners of war	c. 2,000	c. 79,500

Source: Ian Nish, *Origins of the Russo-Japanese War* (New York: Longman, 1985).

they ceded to Japan the southern half of Sakhalin, their leasehold on the Liaodong Peninsula (called the Kwantung Peninsula in Japanese), and the South Manchurian Railway line between Port Arthur and Mukden. To secure a dominant position in Korea, in late 1905 Itō Hirobumi negotiated a treaty with the Korean court that established a Japanese protectorate. The Japanese government assumed control over Korea's diplomatic relations with the outside world, and Japanese advisors were dispatched to shore up the Korean government's finances and to reform its institutional structure. In the wake of the war, Japanese settlers, hopeful of taking advantage of new opportunities, flooded into the peninsula, consolidating the Japanese economic presence.

In contrast to the Triple Intervention, which had deprived Japan of the full fruits of its victory over China in 1895, the Western powers gave full recognition to Japan's new international position. The United States agreed to recognize Japan's "paramount interests" in Korea, and the French and British soon followed suit. The attitude of the Western nations reflected general admiration for the stunning performance of the Japanese military and naval forces at the time of war, and it ratified their acquiescence in accepting Japan as a diplomatic equal. In 1894 the British and the other Western countries had finally agreed to end the "unequal treaties." Extra-territorial privileges of foreign residents had been phased out beginning in 1899, and all the treaty powers had agreed to restore tariff autonomy to Japan by 1910. With the country's full sovereignty restored, the Japanese leaders now saw themselves as full-fledged members of the imperialist club.

IMPERIALISM AND POPULAR NATIONALISM

The waging of two foreign wars that touched the lives of ordinary Japanese in so many ways forged powerful new bonds linking the mass of the population with the nation state and its fate. In 1894–1895 nearly a quarter million men had been mobilized, and in 1904–1905 more than a million were. The two wars made clear that being a "child of the emperor" involved more than paying taxes or obeying the law. Families and neighbors at home participated in the war along with the soldiers at the front. Local communities subscribed to war bonds, local villagers gathered food and other gifts for troops at the front, and peasant families pitched to help neighbors whose menfolk had been mobilized. In school classrooms teachers taught their pupils that Japan's cause was "righteous," and students marched off to local shrines to pray for the safe return of the troops. In more frivolous fashion, urban housewives celebrated the fall of Port Arthur in 1905 with hairdos modeled on the peak from which Japanese guns bombarded the Russian positions, and every conceivable kind of consumer good, from combs and fans to cakes and confections, was plastered with the rising sun flag and other patriotic symbols.

The Sino-Japanese War also demonstrated to the public that the emperor was not only a constitutional monarch but the country's paramount military leader. Shortly after the Sino-Japanese war broke out, the Meiji emperor moved to the imperial headquarters at Hiroshima. The press reported his deep involvement in daily operations. Rising early in the morning to don his uniform as commander-in-chief, he spent the day in austere quarters, perusing dispatches, approving orders, and sharing the simple meals of his troops. When the war ended, the emperor made a triumphal return to Tokyo, parading through a victory arch in the midst of the city. Perhaps because a victorious outcome seemed less certain in 1904, the imperial profile was lower during the war with Russia, but the Meiji empress played a highly visible role, visiting the wounded in hospitals, helping to roll bandages and providing a model for patriotic women.

The popular press, long a vehicle for the views of the political opposition, supported both wars with enthusiasm. Newspaper editors seeking to build broad audiences stirred public patriotism in any way they could–running dispatches from the front, staging competitions for the composition of war songs, featuring vivid illustrations of military victories, and publishing dramatic serial novels celebrating the heroism and courage of the Japanese troops. Newspaper reports made their way into popular culture. By the turn of the century, for example, every school child knew the story of the heroic bugler, Kiguchi Kōhei, who died with his bugle at his lips summoning his comrades to charge; and after the Russo-Japanese War, thousands of homes also displayed portraits of Lt. Hirose Takeo, who died during the siege of Port Arthur while trying to rescue a friend who had once saved him from death. The public avidly devoured colorful woodblock prints that depicted the effortless bravery of Japanese soldiers, their faces fixed with stern determination as they routed Russian troops, or showed helpless Russian warships sinking into the Korean straits under withering Japanese fire.

Military victory, first over China, then over Russia, fed a surge of new national pride. Among the elite, there was a widespread feeling that Japan had truly joined the ranks of the "civilized" nations as a result of its triumphs on the battlefield. As Ōkuma Shigenobu put it, Japan was no longer a "Japan for itself alone," absorbed in its own domestic concerns, it had become a "Japan for the world."[5] War changed popular attitudes toward Japan's Asian neighbors too. During the Sino-Japanese War newspaper reports, cartoons and popular prints portrayed the Chinese and Koreans as bumbling, stupid, or cowardly adversaries. Returning soldiers brought home first-hand tales about life on the Asian continent. Many were astounded at the pervasive backwardness and dirt, strange smells and odd customs, peculiar food and shabby dwellings they encountered. Journalists also reported on the "spiritual backwardness" of the Chinese and the Koreans, who seemed to lack any sense of patriotism, public spiritedness, or hard work. Traditional images of China as the land of civilization were displaced by more negative ones, and ordinary Japanese began to refer to the Chinese as *chankoro* ("Chinks") or *tombi* ("pigtails"). Some serious-minded scholars, anxious to dissociate the Japanese from their fellow Asians, speculated that the Japanese "race" was more closely related to the "Aryans" or "Turanians" who had conquered much of the Eurasian continent than to the "Mongolians" who inhabited Korea and China.

By the time of the Russo-Japanese War, the mass of the population may have become more imperialistic than their leaders. Indeed, on the eve of the Russo-Japanese war, most newspaper editorials urged far more militant policies than the oligarchic leadership did. The disparity between popular chauvinism and official caution became dramatically evident when the terms of the Portsmouth Treaty were made public in September 1905. The failure of the government to secure greater concessions from the Russians, especially an indemnity to defray war costs, infuriated many. Aware of the steady victories against the Russians, yet ignorant of how hard pressed the government had been in the last months of the war, the public was angered by the leniency of the treaty. An antitreaty movement erupted throughout the country, reaching its high point in a major riot at Hibiya Park in Tokyo. To be sure, wartime tax increases and inflation contributed to popular discontent but it was not popular hardship alone that incited the rioting crowds. Rather it was betrayed expectations.

Even after the antitreaty movement subsided a vast reservoir of popular nationalism and imperialist sentiment remained. Public memories of wartime sacrifice lived on, and so did a belief in the invincibility of the Japanese army. Every village had its monument to the fallen war dead; veterans of Manchurian campaigns spun tales for village youth; and schoolbooks celebrated the glorious victories of General Nogi and Admiral Tōgō. Among the educated elite the idea that Japan had a national mission or national destiny to pursue on the world stage became commonplace. For some, like Okakura Kakuzō, the nation's mission was defined in purely cultural terms. Japan, he said, could become a spokesman for the "spiritual East" to the "materialist West."[6] For others, the national mission meant Japan should work for a "harmonization of East and West" in culture, ideas and politics. But for most the victory of 1905 meant Japan was in a position as never before to protect the "backward" nations of Asia and help them toward independence and self-government. For better or worse, many now felt that Japan could rightly aspire to a role of leadership in Asia, a sentiment that was to animate the popular imagination for the next generation.

ENDNOTES

1. *Nihon gaikō bunsho,* vol. 1, pt. 1 (Tokyo, 1936), 422.

2. Sugita Teiichi's views are quoted in *The Emergence of Imperial Japan: Self-Defense or Calculated Aggression,* ed. Marlene Mayo (Lexington, Mass.: D. C. Heath, 1970), 6.

3. Quoted in Peter Duus, *The Abacus and the Sword: The Japanese Penetration of Korea, 1895–1910* (Berkeley: University of California Press, 1995), 17.

4. Yamagata's views are summarized by Marius B. Jansen in "Modernization and Foreign Policy in Meiji Japan" in *Political Development in Modern Japan,* ed. Robert E. Ward, (Princeton, N.J.: Princeton University Press, 1968), 182.

5. Ōkuma is quoted in *Kindai Nihon shisōshi kōza: Sekai no naka no Nihon,* ed. Takeuchi Yoshimi (Tokyo: Chikuma Shobo, 1961), 140.

6. Okakura's views are outlined in *Japanese Thought in the Meiji Era,* ed. Kosaka Masaaki (Tokyo: Pan-Pacific Press, 1958), 217–224.

9

The Beginning of Industrialization

Turning points are hard to discern in social and economic history, but sometime between 1895 and 1905 Japan achieved self-sustained modern economic growth. The happy statistics of rising factory production veered upward sharply; railroad and telegraph lines crisscrossed the country in tightening grids; factory chimneys pierced the sky on the outskirts of Tokyo and Osaka; and the screech of the morning whistle shattered the calm even in provincial towns and cities. By the turn of the century, Japan was in the midst of an industrial revolution that would establish it as the first modern industrial economy outside the West. The groundwork for this economic change had been laid down by government policies in the 1870s and 1880s, but no less important was the diffusion of new social values and ideas—a belief in the possibility of endless material progress, a recognition of the legitimacy of private profit, and a commitment to punctuality, efficiency, and industriousness—values and ideas that were needed to sustain industrial growth driven by private initiative.

THE CHANGING COUNTRYSIDE

The economic resilience of the countryside, where nearly two-thirds of the working population was to be found at the turn of the century, eased the transition to economic modernity. The agricultural sector, already flourishing during the Tokugawa period, continued to grow steadily after the Restoration. Although the population rose from 33.1 million in 1872 to 41 million in 1892, and to 52.1 million in 1912, agricultural growth protected

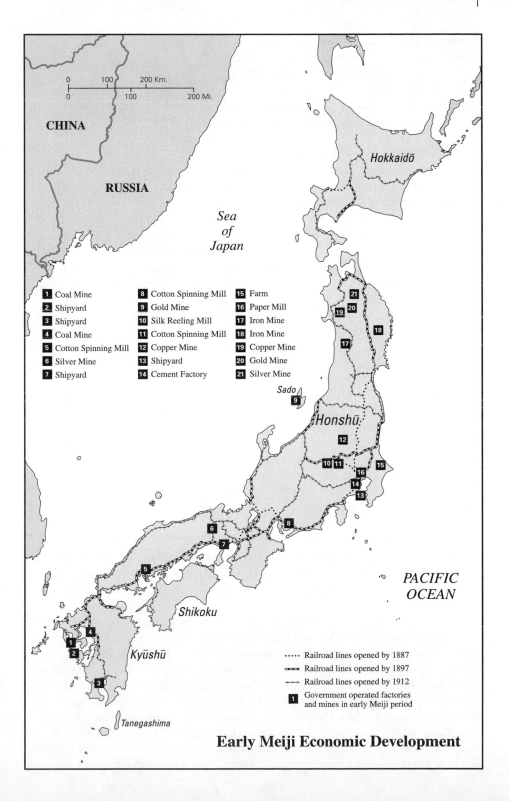

CHINA

RUSSIA

Sea
of
Japan

Hokkaidō

1	Coal Mine	8	Cotton Spinning Mill	15	Farm
2	Shipyard	9	Gold Mine	16	Paper Mill
3	Shipyard	10	Silk Reeling Mill	17	Iron Mine
4	Coal Mine	11	Cotton Spinning Mill	18	Iron Mine
5	Cotton Spinning Mill	12	Copper Mine	19	Copper Mine
6	Silver Mine	13	Shipyard	20	Gold Mine
7	Shipyard	14	Cement Factory	21	Silver Mine

Sado

Honshū

PACIFIC
OCEAN

Shikoku

Kyūshū

..... Railroad lines opened by 1887

Railroad lines opened by 1897

+++ Railroad lines opened by 1912

Tanegashima

1 Government operated factories
and mines in early Meiji period

Early Meiji Economic Development

Japan against a race with famine, so common in many countries during the initial stages of modern development. Economic historians do not agree on just how fast agriculture grew after 1868: some say as little as one percent a year, others as high as 2.4 percent. All are agreed, however, that the production of food grew faster than population (about one-half percent per year on average), making it possible to feed more and more of the increasing population with enough left over to support the government's modernization efforts and private investment in the modern sector.

The agricultural sector contributed to the economic transition in other ways as well. During the 1850s, a blight had killed off silkworms in France and Italy, creating a sudden rise in European demand for raw silk and silkworm eggs from Japan, and American demand for Japanese tea expanded after the Civil War as a fad for tea drinking swept the country. These agricultural exports earned Japan the precious foreign exchange it needed to buy raw materials and machinery overseas to fuel the industrial engine at home. Without these exports, the economy might have faced a persistent foreign deficit, long-term inflation, and social instability—nearly all of which it avoided. At the same time, more and more farmers shifted to production for external as well as domestic markets. This brought prosperity to many sections of the countryside, increasing the buying power of the rural population and boosting domestic consumer demand. While farmers suffered during years of crop failures or crop gluts, average rural household income was on the rise.

Agricultural growth did not result from a major social reorganization of production. Land holdings remained small and fragmented, and the main work unit continued to be the peasant household. Neither did Japanese farmers boost output by importing foreign farming techniques. In the 1870s, English and American agricultural experts had urged that Japanese peasants turn themselves into Western-style dirt farmers by raising cabbages, potatoes, and corn, or hitching horses to the family plow. Here and there, a few enterprising well-to-do peasants planted apple orchards or grazed cows on lands difficult to turn into rice paddies, but only in the newly colonized Hokkaidō, where silos, barns, corn fields, and grazing cattle became part of the landscape, was Western-style agriculture adopted even on a modest scale. Elsewhere, peasants continued to raise rice, a crop better suited than Western cereals to sustain a population as dense as Japan's on so limited a land base.

Agricultural improvement instead came from the diffusion of superior traditional techniques—higher-yielding strains of rice, more intensive use of fertilizer, and improved irrigation. All these techniques had been known during the Tokugawa period, but barriers to communication and population movement had hindered their spread outside the areas where they originated. When experiments with foreign-style agriculture failed, the government shifted to a policy of making the best existing traditional agricultural methods more widely available. In the late 1870s, government-sponsored local farmers' meetings and agricultural fairs allowed seasoned, successful farmers to show their fellows how to increase crop yields. Their advice found a ready audience in a rural population long accustomed to agricultural improvement and production for the market. The most enthusiastic innovators were usually the larger well-to-do landowners, who were literate enough to read government manuals and other treatises on farming, and who were able to take risks in experimenting with new techniques.

Although increased agricultural surpluses contributed to aggregate rural prosperity, village social structure remained stable. In most villages, a handful of well-to-do households dominated a much larger number of households with middling or small land holdings. If anything, agricultural growth had the effect of accelerating the concentration of land ownership. The tenancy rate climbed faster than it had during Tokugawa times. According to some estimates, only about 30 percent of the land was farmed by full-time or part-time tenants in the early 1870s, but by 1908 the proportion had risen to 45 percent. Acquisitive peasants, through direct purchase or foreclosure of mortgages, accumulated land from their less fortunate or less foresighted neighbors, who often found themselves tenants on land they had once owned. Peasants who lost their land were often reluctant to leave their ancestral villages. It was easier to remain in the communities where they had been born, with all their emotional ties, than to risk the uncertainties of city life. The existence of a surplus rural population ensured a ready supply of tenants and kept rents high. Under these circumstances, tenancy made more economic sense than large-scale farms worked by hired hands. The increase in tenancy was not really checked until the 1920s, when falling rice prices and land values made landlordism less and less profitable.

The terms "tenants" and "landlords" conjure up visions of rapacious exploitation, rank-renting, and dispossession of inefficient farmers, but this misrepresents the general situation. Although tenants usually held their land at the will of the landlord, village custom and opinion served as a powerful check against arbitrary dispossession. The landlord and his tenants were neighbors in the same village, and the tie between them usually rested on informal understandings rather than on legal contracts enforceable in a court of law. The most general pattern was sharecropping, where the landlord collected a portion of the harvest in kind rather than a money rent: in bad years the landlord and the tenant shared the loss, and in good years shared the gain. In many villages, the landlord was expected to take care of his tenants in other ways, such as arranging marriages for their offspring, finding jobs for their sons, or inviting them to annual banquets at the New Year. These non-economic ties softened the tenancy relationship.

Landlords, by and large, were farmers themselves, cultivating plots of their own. Few if any large-scale capitalist landowners like the landed aristocracy in Victorian England or plantation owners in the pre–Civil War American South were to be found in Japan. To be sure, there were some absentee landlords: sons of well-to-do households who moved away after inheriting their patrimony or city dwellers who bought land as an investment. But more typical were resident landlords, farmers who owned more land than their families could work themselves or villagers with other sources of income—such as village officials, school teachers, doctors, priests, or shopkeepers—who rented out land they had inherited or had purchased for investment. The majority of the landlord class lived a modest life more comfortable but not radically different from their tenants.

A minority of the village landlords were affluent "gentlemen farmers" (*inaka shinshi*) with substantially greater means and leisure than their neighbors. These men dominated village society, making the biggest contributions to local shrines or temples, managing village affairs, or serving as local assembly members. Since only large landlords paid enough taxes to vote, it was they who had the most interest in national politics as well. While they often sent their sons, particularly their younger sons off to the city to study, big landlords rarely had more than an elementary or middle school education. Like their fellow villagers, their outlook was provincial and parochial. As pillars of village society, the landlords stood behind traditional values such as harmony, cooperation, conformity, and respect for authority. Fairly typical was a large landlord who made his tenants pledge to "preserve our station in life, show humility and proper respect for others, be industrious and frugal, and so live up to the deeds of our ancestors and bring their work to fruition."[1] In other words, the large landlords constituted a bulwark of social and political conservatism.

While agricultural growth brought an overall increase in rural prosperity, its benefits were not distributed equally. In many parts of the country, pockets of poverty persisted. Nagatsuka Takeshi, the scion of a landlord family, vividly described the lot of the landless peasant in his 1910 novel *The Soil*:

> Kanji's fields yielded a pitifully small harvest that fall. It was not that the weather had been bad or that the soil itself was poor. He had got his crops in late and had not applied much fertilizer. No matter how much energy he expended the results were bound to be disappointing. It was the same for all poor farmers. They spent long hours in their fields doing all they could to raise enough food. Then after the harvest they had to part with most of what they had produced. Their crops were theirs only for as long as they stood rooted in the soil. Once the farmers had paid the rents they owed they were lucky to have enough left over to sustain them through the winter. . . . To poor farmers the winter had always been and would always be a time of suffering. They knew nothing else. [2]

Life was probably not so grim for the majority of the rural population, but a substantial minority faced this dreary hand-to-mouth existence.

THE INDUSTRIAL REVOLUTION

Impressive though agricultural growth was, the manufacturing sector grew much more rapidly. In 1910, agricultural production was half again as large as it had been in 1885, but manufacturing had more than quadrupled, more than doubling between 1890 and 1900, and doubling again by 1914. In

1894, there were only 1400 factories employing more than ten workers, but by 1902 their number exceeded 7000. To be sure, small-scale mills and workshops, employing fewer than thirty workers, accounted for much of this growth. As in the past, small workshop production was an important source of by-employment and income for both peasant families in the countryside and for poorer families in the city. In this respect, Japan was no different from most other economies in the early stages of industrialization, including Great Britain, where large-scale factories did not become common for a generation or two after the invention of the steam engine.

Despite the radical institutional transformation of the country, most ordinary Japanese continued to consume traditional goods. They wore homespun tunics or handmade kimonos instead of frock-coats and bustles; they ate with wooden chopsticks instead of knives and forks; and they lived in wooden houses with straw mat floors instead of brick cottages with wooden floors. Traditional crafts from carpentry to mat-making continued to flourish, and with the expansion of population effective demand for their total output grew as well. But the Meiji thirst for "foreign goods" also provided new opportunities for proto-industrial enterprises. Umbrellas, kerosene lamps, clocks, buttons, iron pots, and the like could be made as easily in small workshops as in large factories by substituting manpower for machinery and capital investment. Matches, for example, could be dipped and packaged with the same painstaking hand labor that earlier had gone into making paper fans and lanterns. By the turn of the century, the slums of Tokyo and Osaka were filled with small back alley workplaces where poor families struggled to make ends meet producing "handmade" Western goods.

Modern economic growth, however, was driven by the expansion of mechanized production. Small-scale workshops employed most workers in the manufacturing sector, but by 1914 large-scale factories driven by new power sources accounted for more than half of manufacturing output. The earliest mechanized factories had relied on wheel wheels or water turbines. In a country with cheap and abundant water resources like Japan, water power had great advantages over steam, especially for small mill and workshop owners with limited capital. But water power was fast becoming an outdated technology in the advanced Western economies, and modern manufacturing firms soon switched to steam. The foundations of a modern textile industry, for example, were laid in 1882 when Shibusawa Eiichi founded the Osaka Spinning Company, one of the first successful private manufacturing firms. Instead of relying on water power, he decided to power the company's 10,000-spindle mill with a steam engine. By the turn of the century more than 80 percent of all cotton mills were steam-powered. Domestic production of stationary steam engines was well established, and in 1904 production of steam turbines began as well.

It was in the steam-powered mechanized industries—cotton spinning, mining, shipbuilding, and railroads—that output grew fastest, quality improved most significantly, and that production costs dropped most rapidly. The effects rippled through the rest of the economy. For example, the growth of the cotton spinning industry created demands for fuel, stimulating the production of coal; its need for raw cotton imports, and eventually its pursuit of overseas markets, prompted the growth of a shipbuilding industry and merchant marine; the wages paid to its managers and workers, many of them girls and young women from poor rural households, created effective demand for a wide variety of ordinary consumer goods; and its need to compete with foreign firms forced innovation in production techniques, especially in the mixing of raw cotton before spinning. Most important of all, industries such as mechanized cotton spinning demonstrated that investment in modern enterprises was not only safe but highly profitable; and the success of ventures like the Osaka Spinning Company induced other entrepreneurs to follow its example.

Once in motion, industrial growth was largely a bootstrap process. Successful manufacturers, large and small, channeled profits and surpluses back into expanded industrial production, raising productivity and continual technological innovation. In contrast to China and other Asian neighbors, where foreign capital played a large role in the development of a modern economic sector, in Japan most investment came from domestic sources. Capital was mobilized through joint stock companies, private banks, or specialized government banks. Foreign loans did not begin on any large scale until 1900, and even then the government rather than private industry was the biggest borrower. The domestic market, including the government, also provided the principal demand for modern manufactured goods. While the value of exports had risen to 13 percent of the GNP by 1913, foreign trade grew because Japan was producing more industrial goods not because it needed exports to sustain growth. To be sure, fluctuations in foreign demand had important short-run effects on the business atmosphere, influencing the cycle of boom and recession in certain industries, but the fundamental force behind Japanese industrial growth continued to be internal demand.

It would be a mistake, however, to assume that the industrial revolution marked an immediate transformation in the whole economy. According to one estimate private factory output still accounted for less than 6 percent of the total national product, and even if the government factories are included, the proportion was probably under 10 percent. Large manufacturing plants, moreover, remained fairly small in size. For example, the Ōji Paper Mill, which produced one-third of all the country's Western-style paper, employed a labor force of only 363 workers. Even by 1909, only a little over a thousand factories in Japan employed more than one hundred workers and only fifty-eight had as many as a thousand. Industrial capitalism had made headway mainly in the cities, but the rest of the society remained predominantly agricultural.

ENTREPRENEURSHIP AND CAPITAL

Much of the entrepreneurial energy that drove industrial expansion came from the government. Even after selling off factories and mines in the 1880s, the government operated a wide range of modern enterprises such as arsenals and shipyards, telegraph and telephone systems, and railroad lines; and it also controlled a substantial amount of capital through a system of quasi-official banks. In 1897, government-owned and operated enterprises accounted for nearly 30 percent of all paid-in capital and capital reserves in mining, manufacturing, and transportation. In a sense, government enterprises were "public firms" or "national firms," valued as much for their contribution to political and military strength as to economic growth and development. And both the central government and local governments continued to invest in key fixed-capital assets—such as roads, bridges, harbors, dams, and irrigation systems—that were essential to economic growth.

Government played a key role in the development of heavy industry, especially iron and steel, a strategic industry whose development required huge sums of capital. In the late 1880s, more than 80 percent of all the country's iron and steel came from abroad, and the main private domestic producer, the Kamaishi Iron and Steel Works, relied on a technology well behind the most advanced steel makers in the West. Using part of the Sino-Japanese War indemnity settlement for capital, the government announced plans in 1897 to build a huge modern steel works in northern Kyushu, using coal from local mines and iron ore imported from China. When the plant opened in 1901, it was plagued with technical problems, not the least of which was adapting German equipment to local raw materials. Once these issues were resolved, the Yawata Iron and Steel Works produced more than three quarters of the total domestic output. Building the mill had required ¥40 million, an investment well beyond the resources of any private entrepreneur, and the operation broke even only after ten years. No private firm would have been willing to sustain losses over such a long period.

Even larger was the government's investment in a national railroad system, an enterprise that affected everything from national defense to economic growth. Several successful private railway companies had gotten their start in the 1880s with considerable technical assistance from the government, which built public lines as well. In 1891, when the government proposed to nationalize the private lines, some politicians and businessmen objected, arguing that the government would run them for political or strategic purposes. It was clear, however, that only the government could command the huge sums necessary for long-term railroad development. After a railroad nationalization law finally passed the Diet in 1906, the government bought 2800 miles of railroad line from seventeen private companies at a cost of ¥456 million, a staggering sum equal to nearly half the regular national budget. While some private railway owners objected, the consensus was that government ownership would ensure uniform national rates and encourage long-term planning.

By contrast, private initiative and private capital provided the main entrepreneurial energy behind the growth of light industry. By the late 1880s, for example, a small but significant group of private entrepreneurs had emerged in the cotton-spinning industry. Unlike the early Meiji business leaders, a disproportionately large number of whom were former samurai, the major-ity of these entrepreneurs came from a broader social base. A study of 55 cot-ton-spinning mills established between 1885 and 1896 shows that more than two-thirds were financed and managed by provincial merchants, well-to-do landlords, or other local notables. Since modern manufacturing depended on imported technology, none of these mill owners were "inventor" entrepre-neurs like Henry Ford or Thomas Edison, but they had enough book learning to study new production methods and often made slight improvements to suit local conditions. Coming from backgrounds in commerce or traditional proto-industrial production, these new entrepreneurs also knew how to mar-ket their goods and how to bargain for raw materials.

Whatever their social origin, the early industrial entrepreneurs shared am-bition, hard work, good luck, and a willingness to venture into activities no one had contemplated before, whether it was building a cement plant or set-ting up a trading office in London. They were very different in style from tra-ditional merchants, who were rentier capitalists more interested in a safe and steady return on capital. As Fukuzawa Yukichi put it, a rich man might be a "man of property" (*shisanka*) but he was not a "capitalist" (*shihonka*) unless he increased the national wealth while pursuing his own profit. The new en-trepreneurs scrambled to find financial backers wherever they could, draw-ing on their own savings or turning to friends, neighbors, and kin for money, but by the 1890s their main vehicle for raising capital was the privately owned joint stock company. In the Western economies, the joint stock com-pany had become the principal way to organize business ventures because it limited the financial liability of investors when a venture failed. In Japan, its main purpose was to pool large amounts of capital. By selling shares, a group of investors could start up a technologically advanced enterprise that was be-yond the financial capacity of any of them as individuals.

The real take-off of private joint stock companies after Matsukata's re-trenchment policies had taken hold in the mid-1880s. The stabilization of the national currency, coupled with a drop in interest rates, created a financial environment in which speculation was no longer attractive and cheap credit made it easy to borrow money for productive enterprises. The success of early private ventures like the Osaka Spinning Company demonstrated that holding shares in a company could be as safe and profitable as more tradi-tional investment. By the late 1880s, a "company boom" had begun. Private merchants, landlords, businessmen, and other holders of capital poured money into company shares, and the number of joint stock companies chartered by the government leapt from 2038 in 1887 to 4296 in 1890. More often than not investors were attracted less by the thrill of participating in an exciting new venture than by the high returns promised by company promoters, espe-cially in the textile industry. By 1898, about 650,000 individuals—a little over 1 percent of the population—held stocks or company shares, a broad stratum considering the relative novelty of the joint stock company. It became common for rural landlords to buy stock instead of land as a long-term investment and for ordinary city merchants to put their money in modern ventures like cotton spinning.

Since investors expected relatively risk-free returns, companies were often forced to pay high dividends, even when they made little or no profit. To escape this dilemma, many companies built up company reserves, plowing profits back into the firm rather than relying solely on new issues of stock to finance expansion. For working capital, manufacturing companies turned more and more to private banks, and even set up new banks of their own or acquired control over existing ones to finance their operations. These banks, known as "organ banks," maintained long-term relations with a particular company, and their managers were often willing to make high-risk loans to keep affiliated companies from going under. To promote industrial growth, the government also established the Industrial Bank in 1902 to provide long-term loans to modern enterprises, to promote the inflow of foreign capital, and to develop a market for company and government bonds. Most of the bank's domestic loans went to heavy industry—shipbuilding, steel, chemicals, and machine tools—but even so it was relatively unimportant as a source of capital when compared with direct private investment in company stocks and shares.

BUSINESS AND POLITICS

By the mid-1890s, the enormous wealth of the new entrepreneurial class had attracted public attention. In 1901, one newspaper reported that there were only 440 individual Japanese with personal fortunes over ¥500,000, and the overwhelming majority—about three-quarters of them—were bankers, merchants, financiers, manufacturers, and company officials. The two richest men in the country were probably Iwasaki Hisaya and Iwasaki Yanosuke, heirs of the formidable founder of the Mitsubishi interests. With wealth came social honors. After the Sino-Japanese War, Mitsui Hachiroemon, head of the Mitsui interests, was given a peerage rank in recognition of his firm's services to the country, and other business leaders, like Shibusawa Eiichi, soon joined him. Times had clearly changed since the days when profit-making was scorned and merchants were ranked at the bottom of the social hierarchy.

Meiji business leaders did not consider themselves as heirs of the old merchant class. Despite their profit-making activities, they preferred to think that they were "serving the nation." In the 1870s, for example, Shibusawa Eiichi had coined a new term, *jitsugyōka* or "man of affairs," to distinguish the new entrepreneurs from the old merchant class. What set them apart, he said, was that they were working for "national profit" not mere personal gain. As one pioneer in foreign trade grandly proclaimed, "I state positively that the secret to success in business is the determination to work for the sake of society and mankind as well as for the future of the nation, even if it means sacrificing oneself."[3] When businessmen were in a particularly fervent mood of self-congratulation, they likened themselves to modern-day samurai, rallying stockholders instead of vassals, and plunging into the fray of the market armed with abacus and balance sheet instead of spear and sword.

Few Meiji business leaders were committed to the Western liberal doctrines of laissez-faire economics championed in the 1870s by the Meirokusha intellectuals. While the journalist Taguchi Ukichi, the translator of Adam Smith, supported the "moral principle" of free trade in his *Tōkyō keizai zasshi (Tokyo Economic Magazine)*, the doctrine received little support from the business community. By the late 1880s, the ideas of the German economist Friedrich List, an ardent supporter of protectionism, who argued that government should protect domestic trade and industry too weak to compete with foreign competition, were much more persuasive. Free trade, free competition, and laissez-faire government seemed luxuries that only advanced countries like Great Britain could afford. When government intervention in the economy promised advantages for the country and for themselves, businessmen eagerly supported it.

The growing economic importance of the business community boosted their political influence as well. At the time of the Sino-Japanese War, for example, the government mobilized leading bankers and business men to raise war loans, and cabinet ministers continued to consult with large private banking interests—Yasuda, Mitsui, Mitsubishi, Sumitomo, and Daiichi—to underwrite public bond issues. On the eve of the Russo-Japanese War, Premier Katsura summoned leaders of the financial community to his official residence, urging them to give their wholehearted political and financial support to the conflict with Russia. During the postwar years, it became a regular practice for the finance minister to brief business leaders on the annual budget. Since officials often seemed to feel that what was good for business was good for the country, businessmen regarded the government as an ally rather than as an adversary.

As their political influence grew, business leaders lobbied actively for government subsidies, tariff reductions, and other economic benefits, and they also opposed higher business and income taxes or the regulation of working conditions and hours. Since the existing voting laws were biased in favor of rural landowners and landlords, in the late 1890s the business community called for lower tax qualifications on the suffrage so that more urban merchants and small businessmen could vote and urged the establishment of independent urban electoral districts. After the Russo-Japanese War, the National League of Chambers of Commerce mounted a national campaign to oppose expanding armament expenditure, to eliminate consumer taxes, and to balance the budget. While attempts to form a businessman's party in the Diet did not succeed, more and more businessmen stood for election.

Close political ties among businessmen, officials, and politicians rested on a tradition of government-merchant cooperation stretching back to Tokugawa times—"special favors for special services," as one historian has put it.[4] At the crassest level, this meant bribery of government officials or Diet members.

In the famous "sugar scandal case" of 1909, executives of the faltering Japan Sugar Refining Company paid ¥600,000 to Diet members (twenty-three of whom were later convicted) to vote for nationalization of the sugar industry, and in 1913 several civil bureaucrats and ranking naval officers were caught accepting large bribes from the Siemens interests in Germany. No doubt many similar cases never came to light. Most large business firms were able to prosper without corrupting officials or politicians, but they did try to maintain a political atmosphere congenial to business interests.

THE NEW INDUSTRIAL WORKING CLASS

The expanding manufacturing sector needed a new wage labor force to work its factories and machines. The practice of working for wages was well established before the Restoration, and in most economically advanced areas villagers supplemented their incomes by proto-industrial employment—cotton spinning, silk reeling, or textile weaving. Taking temporary work outside of the village was also common, both for men who worked in sake breweries or as construction workers during the winter months and for young women who went off to nearby market towns or castle towns to work as maids before marriage. The factory system, however, with its larger scale of production, more complex division of labor, and machine technology, required new kinds of managers, workers, and work organization.

The government, which invested heavily in the education of bright young men to replace "hired foreigners," played the largest role in creating a new technical and managerial elite. By the 1880s, graduates of the government's engineering college were being recruited by private entrepreneurs to build and manage new cotton-spinning mills, mines, shipyards, and railroad lines. Often they were jacks-of-all-trades, planning new factories, buying new equipment, setting up production schedules, and even repairing broken machinery. Given the scarcity of technical and managerial talent, they enjoyed high salaries and considerable independence. A few even worked for more than one company at a time. The number of lower-level technicians, trained in government vocational schools and institutes, increased as well, though often their level of competence was limited.

Recruiting factory workers was more complex, with wide variations from industry to industry. The early government arsenals, shipyards, and factories hired traditional craftsmen such as carpenters, smiths, cabinet-makers, coopers, and the like. Once they had mastered imported technology under the tutelage of "hired foreigners," it was easy for these skilled workmen to find jobs. Since their new knowledge was in high demand, they could afford to be quite independent. Like the traditional journeymen who migrated from city to city in search of work after completing their apprenticeships, they changed jobs often, and their work habits were independent as well. Skilled workers usually kept their own hours, arriving late or finishing early as it suited them.

They often failed to show up at all after pay day, when they splurged on sake or trips to the brothel quarters.

Early factories were less integrated plants under unified management than assemblages of small workshops, each manned by a separate gang of workers. Workers clustered around experienced craftsmen, usually called *oyakata*, who treated them as their own apprentices or journeymen: training them, paying their wages, and often providing them with room and board as well. The *oyakata* was a subcontractor who provided the factory with the services of his work gang for a fixed price and deeply resented any management interference in his relations with them. This meant that workers owed their loyalty to the *oyakata* rather than the company. Indirect control over workers was often unavoidable given the lack of experienced school-trained lower-level technicians or engineers, but factory and mill owners were eager to curb the independence of their skilled workers.

By the turn of the century, the *oyakata*'s authority was weakened by the introduction of new and more complex technologies. Manufacturing firms gained tighter control over skilled workers by replacing the *oyakata* with foremen and school-trained technicians. Most workers continued to do on-the-job training, performing menial tasks while waiting for moments of guidance from experienced workers, but some large companies set up vocational programs to train workers and lower-level technicians. To build company loyalty, admission to this training was limited to offspring or kin of company employees. By introducing new rules and regulations governing the work place, company managers also assumed direct responsibility for worker discipline. Company managers had no compunctions about reaching into the private lives of workers to ensure that they remained productive. Fines and other punishments were imposed for drunkenness, gambling, or absenteeism, and workers were required to put part of their wages into compulsory savings programs.

A few large companies began to offer promotions, semi-annual raises, or long-term contracts to skilled workers with good work records. These positive incentives, intended to prevent such workers from seeking employment elsewhere, were justified by ideas of industrial paternalism. Many business leaders described their enterprises as families bound by personal ties. As the Tokyo Chamber of Commerce noted in 1898, "In our country, relations between employers and employees are just like those within a family . . . they are enveloped in a mist of affectionate feeling."[5] No doubt many skilled workers enjoying the benefits of paternalistic policies repaid their employers with loyalty and hard work. Less dewy-eyed businessmen were well aware that workers produced more when employers took care of them. In any case, company paternalism in heavy industry produced a "labor aristocracy" set off from the vast majority of workers who did not enjoy the same job benefits or security.

Most workers in the manufacturing sector were female factory hands in spinning mills. Indeed, by the turn of the century perhaps 80 percent of the workers in the cotton and silk industries, the largest employer of factory labor, were girls and women. Since spinning and weaving had been traditional women's work, done after evening chores or in the winter months, it is not surprising that spinning and reeling-mill owners decided to rely mainly on female labor. At first, mills recruited local women, but as the industry expanded rapidly in the 1890s, they relentlessly raided their competitors for experienced operatives. Some companies faced worker turnover of 100 to 120 percent per year. To strengthen their hand against the workers, mill owners signed agreements not to hire each other's workers, but more often than not these broke down when companies found themselves short-handed.

By the late 1890s, mill owners sought workers farther afield. Cheap, docile, unskilled young women could be found in almost inexhaustible supply in the countryside. From the mill owners' point of view, girls raised far from urban centers made better workers, not only because they were more likely to be hard-working but because their families needed extra income. Indeed, many cotton and silk-reeling companies located their mills in provincial towns close to this source of inexpensive labor. Others sent recruiting agents to lure peasant girls with glowing promises of good food, high wages, and an exciting life in the city, and to win over their reluctant parents with presents and loans. Such tactics were most successful in poor areas beset by hostile climate

A woodblock print showing female operatives at the government operated Tomioka Silk Reeling Mill ca. 1872. Although later silk reeling mills recruited farm girls as workers, most of the operatives in the Tomioka mill were daughters of former samurai families.

or low farm yields, such as Niigata prefecture, which became known as a recruiting ground not only for mill operatives but for prostitutes as well.

Working conditions in the textile mills were often harsh and dangerous. To get maximum use out of their investment, mill owners ran machinery constantly, requiring female operatives to work day and night on twelve-hour shifts (at a time when eight to ten hours was normal in England and the United States). Rest periods were limited, and only brief times were allowed for meals. Tired workers often injured themselves on machinery, and high humidity and heavy air pollution in the cotton and silk mills made them susceptible to tuberculosis and other respiratory diseases. Living conditions were often no better. While some factory owners provided decent quarters, others put their workers in contract boarding houses run by petty gangsters or usurious money lenders. Even "free lodging" in company dormitories often meant crowded quarters, sharing mattresses with workers on other shifts, and barely edible food rations. To keep the female workers from fleeing these conditions, company dormitories were often prison-like structures, surrounded by high fences and guarded at the gates. To make matters worse, wages were low and often sequestered to pay off loans to parents.

In many mills, managers and foremen enforced discipline by punishing workers harshly for laziness, carelessness or petty theft. In 1906 one worker reported the abusive treatment she had witnessed to government investigators:

Q: Do you get scolded?

A: We are taken to a room next to the office and are reprimanded there. We are also beaten. And, until we show a change of heart, we are kept there in the dark for several days.

Q: Are you fed?

A: No.

Q: Are there other forms of punishment?

A: If anyone steals something she is stripped naked and marched around the factory with a flag attached to her shoulders. They then take her to the dining hall and report her misdeed to everybody.[6]

It is little wonder that many female workers found work in the mills like being in a prison without chains. Since most were still in their teens and expected to return to their villages one day, however, they were not entirely without hope. Indeed, the most common form of protest against working conditions was simply to escape from the mill. Some estimates suggest that perhaps half the female textile workers fled their jobs in the first six months. Those who stayed on the job often expressed their discontent in song or banter, and although they did not organize unions, they sometimes resorted to strikes and sabotage.

A labor movement hardly existed in Japan before 1914. Since skilled male workers worked under the protection of their *oyakata* or enjoyed a strong bargaining position as independent artisans, they felt little need for collective action. In 1897, Takano Fusatarō, who returned to Japan after several years in California, tried to organize an iron workers' union on the model of the American Federation of Labor, and a year later locomotive engineers employed by the Japan Railway Company did the same. The issues that bothered skilled workers often had more to do with status than with wages and working conditions. When locomotive engineers struck in 1898, for example, their main complaint was that they were required to kneel on the floor when receiving instructions from an assistant station master seated on a chair. After the Russo-Japanese War, when the economy was hit by recession, strikes occurred more frequently, even in government-owned arsenals, but worker organization was spontaneous and temporary.

Skilled male workers more often took collective action to help fellow workers and their families through crises such as prolonged illness or death. Needless to say, there was no system of worker disability or accident insurance, nor any laws regulating safety conditions in the workplace. Informal mutual aid was common in many large factories, where workers passed the hat to collect money when one of their fellows was injured or killed in an accident on the job. As in most societies during the early stages of industrialization, life in the factory was precarious. Yet the skilled worker's lot was probably no worse than that of the poor peasant or tenant farmer—and probably better in most respects. The flow of younger sons and daughters of farm families from the vast rural reservoir of cheap labor continued, giving the mill and factory owners the ultimate advantage in a labor market that worked almost entirely in their favor.

The rest of the industrial work force was made up of semi-skilled or unskilled workers employed in small workshops or tiny factories in the crowded slums of Tokyo and Osaka. Some were little better than day laborers, working irregularly, hired and fired at will by employers in temporary need of their services, and barely able to scrape together a living. In the early 1900s, the journalist Yokoyama Gennosuke described the poverty of their lives in his *Nihon no kasō shakai (Japan's Lower Classes)*. Even those who worked steadily were paid much less generously than workers in large modern mills or factories and enjoyed lower living standards. When the economy was in a slump, wage differences between workers in small-scale and larger-scale enterprises also widened. The families of poorer workers lived in unsanitary conditions in jerry-built hovels or slum tenements, often plagued by alcoholism, infidelity, and other symptoms of social stress. In the eyes of many elite observers, they appeared ruthlessly exploited, living lives little better than those of primitive savages.

Many academics, journalists, and politicians feared that if the economy industrialized at an accelerated rate, an emerging gap between rich and poor would create class conflict. In Europe, industrialization had been accompanied by labor unrest, unruly workers, and eventually socialist ideas. In their view, since socialism called for the destruction of the state and an end to the system of private property, it threatened the very foundations of society. They worried that a widening gap between the rich and the poor, and especially the emergence of a new working class, would spark class conflict. The Association for the Study of Social Policy, formed by a group of concerned professors, urged the timely adoption of government policies to forestall the problems the Westerners had suffered. As they declared in 1900, "We oppose laissez-faire. The reason for this is that the extreme exercise of self-interest and uncontrolled free competition would result in an excessive gulf between rich and poor. We also oppose socialism. The reason for this is that the destruction of the existing economic structure and the abolition of capitalists would be harmful to the progress of the national destiny."[7] The association proposed to work for "social harmony" within the existing economic system through individual actions and public policies.

INDUSTRIALIZATION AND THE WORLD MARKET

As the industrial revolution accelerated, trade with the outside world grew rapidly. By the early 1900s, foreign trade amounted to perhaps 20 percent of the GNP and was climbing rapidly. Indeed, the volume of Japan's foreign trade was growing faster than that of Great Britain, the United States, or Germany. Until the 1890s, Japan had been known primarily as an exporter of agricultural goods (tea), raw materials (raw silk), and craft goods, but by the turn of the century machine-made products like cotton and silk yarn accounted for a larger and larger share of its exports. As industrialization changed Japan's comparative advantage in the world market, its pattern of trade looked less and less like that of a colonial or undeveloped country and more and more like that of an industrial one. Heartened by these changes, business and political leaders began to talk about building Japan as a "commercial and industrial power."

By 1900, the future of the Asian market seemed particularly promising to many Japanese businessmen and officials. It was clear that Japan, which could just produce enough food to feed itself, would never compete with grain-exporting countries like the United States, Canada, and Russia. Neither could its manufactured goods, however cheap, make inroads in the Western markets. Trade with the Western countries was likely to continue as it had, with the Japanese relying on the West for machinery, producer goods, and industrial raw materials. But Japanese manufactured goods could compete in Asia, especially in China, with its hundreds of millions of customers. Proximity to the

China market meant low transportation costs for Japanese goods; and a shared cultural background made it easy for Japanese traders and businessmen to understand Chinese needs and tastes. In return for Japanese manufacturing goods, China could provide Japan with the raw materials and food resources it needed. As one official noted, "If one looks at the whole world today, there is no place for Japan to secure commercial and industrial profits but Asia."[8]

Expansion into Asian markets was inextricably linked with Japan's emergence as an imperialist power. As one business journal put it, the country was engaged in a "great economic war" with the other industrialized powers; it was fighting not just for territory but for a larger share of the Asian market. As a result of the peace settlement in 1895, Japan became a full-fledged participant in the "unequal treaty" system in China, enjoying the same special rights and privileges as the Western powers. Sensing a new opportunity, domestic cotton manufacturers stepped up shipments to the continent, and by 1897 the country's exports of cotton yarn exceeded its imports. Territorial and political expansion brought tighter economic links with the new colonial possession of Taiwan, the protectorate in Korea, and the territorial enclave in southern Manchuria. Capital from quasi-governmental firms like the South Manchuria Railway and the Oriental Development Company, and from some private firms as well, flowed into the building of railroad lines and other infrastructure in the country's new Asian sphere of influence.

Expanding foreign trade required new institutions. The Yokohama Specie Bank, set up by the government in 1880 to provide credit to merchants dealing overseas, opened branches in New York, London, and other major overseas cities in the early 1890s. To encourage a flow of information about foreign markets, commercial officers were placed in overseas embassies, legations and consulates; and to entice foreign customers Japanese goods were displayed at international exhibitions and local trade fairs in China and other parts of Asia. But private enterprise, particularly general trading companies, a peculiarly Japanese business institution, played a key role in expanding trade too. The Mitsui Trading Company, for example, established worldwide networks of branch offices in Asia, Europe, and North America, and by 1910–1913 it alone handled about one-fifth of the country's exports. Not only did trading companies gather economic intelligence, they negotiated long-term contracts that brought down the costs of raw materials and organized domestic producers to penetrate overseas markets.

The expansion of foreign trade created new economic opportunities, but it also made the country more dependent on the outside world. As imports and exports grew, so did the economy's sensitivity to ups and downs in the world market. Where once the size of the harvest determined the country's prosperity, shifts in overseas demand were now just as likely to do so. Although the industrial revolution brought national wealth once unimaginable to most Japanese, it also stripped away the comforting cocoon of self-sufficiency that the policy of isolation had provided. Increasingly, household income, company profits, and even the level of domestic consumption became hostage to political and economic events beyond the country's borders. Industrialization, like so many other aspects of the country's modernization, vanquished old problems only to create new ones.

ENDNOTES

1. Quote is from Ronald P. Dore, *Land Reform in Japan* (London: Oxford University Press), 51.

2. Nagatsuka Takeshi, *The Soil: A Portrait of Rural Life in Meiji Japan*, trans. Ann Waswo (London and New York: Routledge, 1989), 47–48.

3. Quoted in Byron K. Marshall, *Capitalism and Nationalism in Prewar Japan* (Stanford, Cal.: Stanford University Press, 1967), 36.

4. See Arthur Tiedemann, "Big Business and Politics in Prewar Japan," in *Dilemmas of Growth in Prewar Japan,* ed. James W. Morley (Princeton, N.J.: Princeton University Press, 1971), 267–316.

5. Quoted in Byron K. Marshall, *Capitalism and Nationalism in Prewar Japan* (Stanford, Cal.: Stanford University Press, 1967), 57–58.

6. Quoted in Mikiso Hane, *Peasants, Rebels and Outcasts: The Underside of Modern Japan* (New York: Pantheon, 1982), 186. For an excellent treatment of female textile workers, see Patricia E. Tsurumi, *Factory Girls: Women in the Thread Mills of Meiji Japan* (Princeton, N.J.: Princeton University Press, 1990).

7. Tessa Morris-Suzuki, *A History of Japanese Economic Thought* (London and New York: Routledge, 1989), 64–65.

8. Ramon Myers and Mark R. Peattie (eds.), *The Japanese Colonial Empire, 1895–1945* (Princeton, N.J.: Princeton University Press, 1984), 136.

III

Political Change, Crisis and War, 1905-1945

10

The Rise of Party Government

lthough the constitution of 1889 established a political framework, it
was ambiguous in many respects, and nowhere was it more ambiguous than on the question of selecting who would run the government.
At first, this presented no problem since the oligarchs, nearly all in their early
fifties, were still capable of providing firm and vigorous leadership. Elevated
to the extraconstitutional status of *genrō* or "elder statesmen," their opinions
carried decisive weight on cabinet appointments and major policy questions.
But by the late 1890s, there was rising impatience with continued oligarchic
rule. Many thought that the Meiji leaders had outlived their usefulness and
should step aside to make way for younger leaders. It was not so clear who
would take their place, however. A group of ranking younger bureaucrats,
protégés and lieutenants of the oligarchs, who had helped in building up the
new political and social order in the 1870s and 1880s, aspired to succeed
them, and so did opposition party politicians in the Diet. Both groups felt
that they had legitimate claims to power, but the oligarchs favored their protégés. The result was two decades of experimentation, maneuver, and struggle that ultimately brought the political parties to power.

THE STRUGGLE AGAINST
CLIQUE GOVERNMENT

The early years of constitutional government were marked by almost constant
clashes between the cabinet and the lower house of the Diet. From the outset,
the oligarchs made clear that they did not intend to share power with their

old foes or with the popularly elected representatives. All the oligarchs, including Itō Hirobumi, the author of the constitution, stood behind the principle of "transcendental cabinets" (*chōzen naikaku*), by which they meant nonpartisan cabinets "above politics" answerable only to the emperor. As genrō, it was easy for them to ensure that control of the cabinet did not slip from their hands. Until 1901, all the prime ministers were oligarchs, and so were most of the other key ministers. The only junior figures admitted to the cabinet were men like Katsura Tarō or Saionji Kimmochi, who enjoyed the personal trust of the oligarchic leaders. In popular parlance, this cozy political cronyism was known as *hanbatsu seiji* or "clique government."

Opposition to "clique government" found its most ardent expression in the newly opened House of Representatives. There was enormous competition during the first election in 1890, with an average of three to six hopeful candidates standing in each constituency. Since a Diet seat was an official post (and therefore a mark of high status), many sought office simply for prestige. (As one candidate freely admitted, "Were I to receive only one vote . . . I should want this for my family tree."[1]) But the election also returned many activists of the popular rights movement who were determined to oust the oligarchs from power. When the first Diet session convened, new political parties—called "popular parties" (*mintō*)—organized themselves around former anti-government leaders, Ōkuma Shigenobu and Itagaki Taisuke. With memories of official harassment still fresh, the popular parties were determined to fight for "constitutional government." By this, they meant cabinets controlled by the lower house of the Diet.

Not surprisingly, during the early Diet sessions the parties chose the tactics of head-on confrontation with the government. The party politicians discovered quickly that they had considerable political leverage despite all the constitutional restrictions placed on the Diet. For one thing, the lower house offered a forum where politicians were able to attack oligarchic leadership free from police harassment and unhindered by press or libel laws. (Indeed, so outspoken were some Diet members that Prime Minister Yamagata Aritomo had dyspepsia attacks whenever obliged to address the lower house.) The parties were also able to use the Diet's right of appeal to the emperor to pass resolutions impeaching government ministers. Although these had no legal force, they were profoundly embarrassing. Most important of all, the constitution gave the Diet some power over the national budget. While the cabinet could rely on the previous annual budget if a new one was not approved, steadily rising government expenditures, especially increases in the military budget, left the cabinet vulnerable to pressure. During the first years of the Diet, bitter fights over the budget were chronic, and the government was forced to give in to the parties or dissolve the House of Representatives and call new elections.

The oligarchs were divided on how best to deal with the recalcitrant Diet. Yamagata Aritomo, chief of the anti-party hardliners, favored firm resistance to party demands and the use of state power to destroy their electoral base. In the election of 1892, Home Minister Shinagawa Yajirō ordered prefectural governors to use every means at their disposal to defeat anti-government candidates. Open police interference and deployment of pro-government strong-arm men (*sōshi*) were widespread. The campaign left twenty-five dead and 388 wounded in its wake. Nevertheless, the anti-government parties retained a Diet majority. The futility of electoral interference was clear to Itō Hirobumi, who thought that transcendental cabinets were politically impractical and that positive efforts should be made to educate the people for responsible participation in politics. He proposed instead to form a "national party" of Diet members loyal to the emperor and sympathetic to the oligarchs.

A similar split divided the anti-government parties in the Diet. Moderate party leaders urged a shift from the tactics of confrontation to the tactics of compromise. Attacks on the oligarchs might satisfy a taste for political revenge, but they were not likely to bring about constitutional government in the long run. As Kōno Hironaka, a prominent party leader, put it, it was better to outflank the oligarchs than to charge headlong against their ranks. The war with China in 1894–1895 brought a temporary truce between the government and the parties, who buried their differences at a time of national crisis. Once the war was over, an attempt was made to resolve party-oligarchic conflict by political compromise. After the Triple Intervention, the Jiyutō, led by Itagaki Taisuke, agreed to support the Itō cabinet by voting for increased military appropriations. A series of party-oligarchic alliances followed in the late 1890s.

These party-cabinet alliances have been characterized as a sell-out by the popular parties, but it would be equally accurate to describe them as a sell-out by the oligarchs. Both sides had to make concessions. If the parties gave up their forthright opposition to clique government, the oligarchs were forced to abandon the idea of "transcendental cabinets." Using their new political leverage, the parties succeeded in shaping many national policies, securing appointment of party leaders as cabinet ministers, and opening the upper ranks of the bureaucracy to party appointments. Distasteful as this was to members of Yamagata's faction, it was the only way to keep government from coming to a standstill. Indeed, the parties had become so indispensable to the political process that in 1898 the genrō decided to turn the cabinet over to Ōkuma and Itagaki, whose followers banded together to form the Kenseitō, a party commanding an absolute majority in the Diet.

This experiment in constitutional government proved short-lived. The coalition soon fell to squabbling among themselves, jealously competing for official posts and unable to agree on basic policies. When high officials in several ministries refused to cooperate with party-linked ministers, the cabinet collapsed. Yamagata, wooing one faction of the Kenseitō with the offer of another party-oligarchic alliance, took power again in 1899. He moved to blunt party influence by issuing ordinances protecting both the civil bureaucracy and the military high command from outside political influence. All posts in the civil bureaucracy, from vice minister on down, were closed to patronage appointment (and therefore party influence). The war and navy ministers were required to be generals or admirals on active service, giving the military services veto power over the formation of cabinets. To make sure his work was not undone, Yamagata also enlarged the powers of the Privy Council (of which he soon became president) to include approval of any further changes in civil service and military personnel regulations.

In contrast to Yamagata's determination to curb the parties, Itō Hirobumi regarded their expanding influence as an inevitable and even desirable trend. In 1900, he organized the Seiyūkai, a national party of the kind he had proposed in the early 1890s. As he told a friend, with its backing him in the Diet he would rely no longer on "mercenaries" in the Diet but on a "standing army" of his own, loyal to his leadership and ready to support his policies. The new party proved less manageable than Itō had hoped. Its members were delighted to have such a prestigious leader, but they were not inclined to follow his dictates docilely. Faced with internal party opposition, Itō resigned its presidency, turning over the reins of leadership to his protégé Saionji Kimmochi, a member of the court nobility who dabbled in the popular rights movement. Although Itō's departure shook the Seiyūkai temporarily, the party soon emerged as the central force in Diet politics.

THE EXPANSION OF PARTY POWER

The expansion of Seiyūkai influence rested on its success in converting temporary party-cabinet alliances into a perennial alliance with whatever government was in power. Hara Takashi, an astute ex-official who had risen rapidly in party ranks, master-minded this political strategy. Although a newcomer to politics, Hara was no less committed to achieving constitutional government than the veterans of the popular rights movement. He realized, however, that behind-the-scenes maneuvering was more important than heroic confrontations on the Diet floor. After Itō resigned as prime minister in 1901, the oligarchs turned responsibility over to Katsura Tarō, a lieutenant of Yamagata Aritomo, who managed to get through his first several Diets by striking bargains with shifting party coalitions. On the eve of the Russo-Japanese War, Katsura wanted to ensure passage of wartime budget increases. In December 1904, Hara promised him the Seiyūkai's support in return for a promise to resign in favor of Saionji, the Seiyūkai president, at the war's end. This bargain turned the Seiyūkai into a semi-permanent government party as the prime ministership passed back and forth between Katsura and Saionji for the next several years.

The inclusion of Seiyūkai leaders in every cabinet between 1906 and 1912 opened the way for greater party influence over the bureaucratic structure. When Hara became Home Minister, he worked assiduously to win over high civil service officials in his ministry. The task was facilitated by the emergence of a generation of younger officials who had worked their way to top bureaucratic positions without oligarchic patronage. Hara also used his powers to promote and transfer prefectural governors to create a body of loyal followers among them as well. Since these officials supervised national elections, controlled local official appointments, and made decisions affecting the local economy, they were crucial to building an electoral base. A prefecture run by a pro-Seiyūkai governor was more likely to return a pro-Seiyūkai majority at election time, and its prefectural assembly was more likely to be dominated by Seiyūkai partisans.

Some historians have argued that Hara and his party paid too much attention to striking bargains with the oligarchs and too little cultivating popular support. But the Seiyūkai would not have succeeded without rice roots support. Indeed, one of Hara's principal goals was to build an absolute Seiyūkai majority in the Diet. Since the right to vote was restricted by tax qualification, this did not require mass support or mass political organizations but rather winning over the moderately affluent elements who made up the majority of the voters—large landlords, prosperous peasant farmers, provincial entrepreneurs, urban property owners, and, of course, business leaders—by catering to their interests and aspirations.

Local politicians first learned the art of political horse-trading and log-rolling in the prefectural assemblies of the 1880s. By the time the Diet opened, they were well aware that promoting local economic interests was the best way to build electoral support. Under the slogan of "Relieving the people's burden" (*minryoku kyūyō*), the Jiyūtō appealed to the landlords and other well-to-do rural constituents by opposing land tax increases, urging a shift of the tax burden to urban elements, and pressing for budget cut-backs. By the late 1890s, party pressure had reduced the land tax from 60 percent of government revenues in 1890 to around 35 percent. The difference was made up by increased personal, business, customs, and consumption taxes. Vocal objection by business interests, the need to strike compromises with the oligarchs, and growing military expenditure forced a retreat from these policies, but the politicians had learned the usefulness of economic issues in winning votes.

After the Russo-Japanese War, the Seiyūkai relied heavily on pork barrel tactics to expand its electoral base. In 1905, the party proclaimed a "positive policy" to divert tax money from military to civilian purposes, especially for local economic development. To secure support from local landlords and businessmen, the party promised to expand government spending on local railroad construction, new roads and schools, bridges and telegraph lines, local harbor development, and expansion of irrigation works. Wakatsuki Reijirō, a leading Finance Ministry official, complained, "We are not building railroad lines where they must be built, but we are building them through little mountain villages with small populations. Here no one supports the Seiyūkai, so we don't build railroad lines, and there they do support the Seiyūkai, so we construct them. That's how the railroads are being used for the expansion of party power."[2] By the 1910s, few Diet members, in the Seiyūkai or not, were reluctant to pander to local demands for pork barrel projects.

The Seiyūkai sought the support of the business community too. "If you do not have the confidence of the businessmen you cannot manage state affairs smoothly," noted one prominent party leader.[3] When the Seiyūkai was founded, leading industrialists like Shibusawa Eiichi as well as leaders of local Chambers of Commerce were invited to join. Businessmen were an important source of political funds. Party leaders like Hara received contributions from large entrepreneurs and business concerns, and politicians were often given sinecures as company directors. The price of expanding party power through linkages with special interest groups was a decline in the crusading zeal, the obstreperous tactics, and the rhetorical heroics that characterized the popular parties of the early Diets. But the Seiyūkai and other party leaders felt that there was no other way to build a base for party rule. As Hara once told a fellow politician, "If you don't give men official position or money, they won't be moved." Such a view smacked of political cynicism but it rested on the recognition that this was the only practical way to build power in the entrepreneurial society that the oligarchs had created.

THE ESTABLISHMENT OF PARTY RULE

Had the Seiyūkai continued to dominate the Diet unchallenged, the achievement of "constitutional government" might have been achieved sooner, but the expansion of its power aroused the hostility of politicians who found themselves sinking into impotence as the Seiyūkai piled up majorities. Some were indignant at the party's willingness to strike bargains with clique government leaders, but others were moved by the more palpable disappointment that they might be missing out on a good thing. The result was a series of party merger movements aimed at creating a second party to compete with the Seiyūkai for votes, funds, and influence.

The anti-Seiyūkai merger movements were unable to achieve their goal until the army precipitated a political crisis in 1912–1913 by toppling the second Saionji cabinet for refusing to expand the army with new divisions. The War Minister resigned under orders from the army high command, who refused to provide a replacement. Public indignation at military intrusion into politics was exacerbated when the genrō nominated Katsura to serve as prime minister again. Despite his long-standing accommodation with Hara, Katsura remained a potent symbol of "clique government." In December 1912, a coalition of journalists, politicians, and businessmen organized a nationwide "movement to protect constitutional government" to protest his return. Its slogans were "overthrow clique government" and "establish constitutional government." To weather the crisis, Katsura decided to organize the anti-Seiyūkai forces into a political party of his own, the Dōshikai. The scheme failed when the Seiyūkai cast their lot with the popular movement, forcing Katsura to step down after three months in office.

The fall of Katsura did not bring about the establishment of party rule, as many had hoped. Pursuing the tactics of compromise, the Seiyūkai backed a new prime minister, Yamamoto Gonnohyōe, who was neither a party man nor a Diet member but a ranking admiral nominated by the genrō. The 1912–1913 crisis had altered the political landscape in significant ways, however. For one thing, it showed how weak clique government had become and how easily a political party could determine the fate of a cabinet. Indeed, the Seiyūkai used its return to power to open key bureaucratic posts to party patronage and to end the requirement that service ministers be general officers on active duty. Equally important, Katsura's new political party survived under the leadership of Katō Takaaki, an ex-diplomat. Although the party's program at first was not radically different from the Seiyūkai's, it provided an alternative political base for cabinet support. In 1914, the oligarchs, hopeful of breaking the Seiyūkai majority, encouraged his successor, Ōkuma Shigenobu, to rely on the Dōshikai. In the 1915 elections, the Seiyūkai, challenged by the same combination of government pressure and money power it had used against its opposition, suffered heavy losses.

If the genrō had hoped Katō Takaaki and his party would be more docile than the Seiyūkai, their hopes were shattered. Katō, an ardent Anglophile who admired stable middle-class British parliamentary democracy, was not inclined to heed the genrō's advice or cater to their whims. In 1916, the oligarchs decided to revert to clique government, nominating Terauchi Masatake, another Yamagata protégé, to head a new government. Yamagata, still deeply distrustful of political parties, saw them as private cabals more concerned with partisan interests than with the national good. These sentiments, justified or not, collided with political reality. Even loyal followers like Terauchi were impatient at the continued oligarchic interference in government decisions, and the lower echelons of the civil service could no longer be manipulated by the oligarchs from behind the scenes. Many high officials, convinced that the political parties represented the wave of the future, were eager to climb aboard the party bandwagon in hopes of securing ministerial posts through party patronage.

Under these circumstances the genrō were finally forced to accept "normal constitutional government." When riots protesting inflated rice prices brought an end to the Terauchi cabinet in 1918, the genrō nominated Hara Takashi as his successor. The immediate reasons were threefold: first, none of the oligarch's immediate protégés were willing to take the job; second, Hara led the majority party in the Diet; and third, if a party prime minister were not appointed, the two major parties might join hands to oppose a nonparty cabinet. The decision, however, was not intended to establish a precedent nor did it signal that the genrō had relinquished their influence. Indeed, Yamagata privately hoped that the Seiyūkai leadership would make a botch of things so that the country could return to bureaucratic cabinets.

The Hara cabinet, often called the "first party cabinet," did its best to solidify the Seiyūkai's absolute majority. In 1920, the Diet passed an electoral reform bill that lowered the tax qualification to ¥3, a change that doubled the size of the electorate. Most of the new voters were small landlords likely to vote for the Seiyūkai. The law also introduced the small electoral district and redrew electoral district boundaries to the party's advantage. To lure voters, the Hara cabinet continued its "positive policy" of spending on local infrastructure, higher education, and national defense. Hara was also careful to strike an alliance with powerful factions in the House of Peers, and to cultivate close relations with the military leadership, especially Chief of Staff Tanaka Giichi. The bureaucracy continued to become increasingly partisan, as the party recruited prefectural governors and opened high positions in the overseas colonial bureaucracies to political appointments. Had Hara not been assassinated by a right wing youth in late 1921, he might well have succeeded in establishing a long term political hegemony for his party.

"NORMAL CONSTITUTIONAL GOVERNMENT"

The death of Hara delayed the routinization of party cabinets. In an attempt to restore "transcendental government," the genrō nominated three non-party prime ministers between 1922 and 1924. This detour from the "path of normal constitutional government" proved only temporary. For one thing, the death of the last surviving Meiji oligarchs (Yamagata in 1922 and Matsukata in 1923) left Saionji Kimmochi, a man willing to adjust to the "trends of the times," as the sole genrō. But even more important, the frustration of the political parties at their exclusion from power led them to join hands to force a return to party rule. When "a cabinet of peers" under Count Kiyoura Kīyotaka was nominated in 1924, the leaders of three main parties—the Kenseikai, the Seiyūkai, and the Kakushin Club—organized a new "movement to protect constitutional government." Although it was neither popular nor generated as much public enthusiasm as the 1912–1913 movement had, the coalition parties won a collective majority in the 1924 election. Saionji had little choice but to nominate Katō Takaaki, the Kenseikai president, to head a coalition cabinet.

With the appointment of the Katō cabinet, "the era of normal constitutional government" began. Down until 1932, the cabinet passed back and forth between the two major parties, the Seiyūkai and the Kenseikai (reorganized and renamed the Minseitō in 1927), whose presidents served as prime ministers. With Saionji's blessing, the party controlling a majority or plurality in the lower house automatically took power. It seemed that the main path to political influence now lay through the portals of the Diet. Not only did more and more senior officials seek election to the Diet, but nearly all the party prime ministers in the 1920s were former top bureaucrats. In 1924, even Tanaka Giichi, a former Chief of Staff and a close protégé of Yamagata, accepted the presidency of the Seiyūkai. The general public also realized that the balance of power had tipped in favor of the parties. When a local school principal wanted extra funds from the Ministry of Education or a town mayor needed a government subsidy to cover a tax deficit, he turned to a local party leader or Diet member to intercede on his behalf with the bureaucracy.

To the general public, the arrival of party rule seemed to bring with it an escalation in political corruption. Bribery of voters became widespread. Party candidates, using their own funds or those supplied by the party leadership, distributed money to voters through networks of local politicians, members of the prefectural and village assemblies; or they hired local "election brokers" who made a profession of vote buying. More dramatic were frequent political scandals involving the bribery of Diet members, party officials, or bureaucrats by local businessmen, promoters, or special interests seeking political favors. Often the corruption revolved around local construction or public works projects financed by government money. In 1926, for example, it was revealed that prominent politicians in both parties had received bribes from real estate companies in Osaka who sought to relocate a brothel district to their property. One of the accused alleged that he had done so under orders from Prime Minister Wakatsuki Reijirō when he had served as home minister. By the late 1920s, the major parties were routinely trading charges of corruption, a political tactic that eroded public confidence in party rule.

The party cabinets also found that they had to strike compromises with other centers of power such as the Privy Council, the House of Peers, and the military high commands. All these institutions were able to obstruct or delay party policies, as earlier the parties had obstructed or delayed the programs of nonparty cabinets. The parties might have circumvented them by constitutional revision or legislative reform but both were difficult in practice. In 1925, for example, when Prime Minister Katō attempted slight alterations in the powers and composition of the House of Peers, the upper house held the cabinet's entire legislative program hostage until the proposed reform was watered down considerably. Rather than changing the institutional structure, party leaders tried instead to find allies among the nonparty power centers or to play one nonparty faction off against another. With the oligarchs no longer on the scene to dominate contending political forces, such maneuvering was unavoidable. Party cabinets rested on pragmatic political working arrangements. As long as party cabinets were capable of handling the nation's problems, there was no reason to abandon party rule. Only a major national crisis was likely to shake it.

DEMOCRACY, RADICALISM, AND DISSENT

The final triumph of the political parties was not greeted by undiluted public enthusiasm. On the contrary, many regarded party cabinets as a triumph neither for popular government nor for good government. Indeed, complaints about the abuse of party power and about party corruption had been grist for journalistic mills since the turn of the century. By the 1920s, the press routinely referred to the parties not as "popular parties" (*mintō*) but as "established parties" (*kisei seitō*), who seemed more interested in raising funds, buying votes, and behind-the-scenes maneuvering than in representing the people. Disillusionment spread among middle-class intellectuals who felt that the parties had forsaken their role as advocates of the people. As one reform-minded Diet member noted in 1923, "It is a grave fact for the future of parliamentary government in our country that we can discern a trend toward loss of confidence in parliamentary politics . . . even among the educated classes who believe in constitutional government."[4]

Disillusion with the political parties burgeoned into a demand for basic political change. Yoshino Sakuzō, a professor in the Law Faculty at Tokyo Imperial University, who called for democratization of both national policy and the political process, gave it voice. For too long, he said, popular interests had been sacrificed to the pursuit of national power or the gain of vested private interests, and the time had come for greater popular control over government and greater government responsiveness to popular needs and demands. The appeal of Yoshino's ideas lay in his argument that democracy, or *minponshugi* (literally, "people-as-the-base-ism"), was compatible with both the Meiji constitutional structure and the doctrine of imperial sovereignty. Other middle-class intellectuals, inspired by the slogans of Wilsonian democracy, joined Yoshino in his plea for democratic reform.

The call for "democracy" gained momentum in 1918 when the country was shaken by massive rice riots, sparked by sharply inflated rice prices and rumors of rice hoarding. The riots began with a small incident involving a few fishermen's wives in Toyama prefecture, but disturbances soon spread along the main routes in central and western Japan to major cities like Osaka. For nearly two weeks crowds of ordinary people—farmers, workers, fishermen, shop clerks, and housewives—took to the streets, gathering at public rallies to attack the government, breaking into the warehouses of rice merchants, and protesting the rapid inflation. The government estimated that over 700,000 persons participated in 36 cities, 129 towns, and 145 villages. Press coverage of the disturbances, which was generally sympathetic to the rioters, may have contributed to the rapid spread of disorder. The rioting subsided as quickly as it had broken out, but many drew the conclusion that ordinary Japanese were discontent with their lot and no longer willing to accept it docilely. As one leading newspaper pointed out, "The people are not asking, `What will become of the country?'; they have risen to cry out, `What will become of us?'"[5]

If the rice riots accelerated a call for democratic reform, so too did the victory of the Western democracies in World War One. The collapse of the German Empire, the model so admired by the Meiji oligarchs, signalled the defeat of militarism, authoritarianism, and state autocracy in the outside world. The subsequent establishment of constitutional republics in Germany, Austria, and Hungary, as well as in Tsarist Russia, suggested that the wave of the future lay with government based on popular consent. Not surprisingly, the gospel of democratic reform spread quickly, stirring the imagination not only of middle-class intellectuals but of university students, educated workers, and women as well. Small political associations and study groups sprang up all over the country, just as they had earlier in the 1870s. Students at Tokyo Imperial University, the chief recruiting ground for the business, bureaucratic, and intellectual professions, organized the Shinjinkai (New Man Society), a radical student group that proclaimed "democracy," "emancipation," and "reconstruction" as their goals, and students at other major private and national universities soon followed suit. In the heady political atmosphere, a women's rights movement also emerged under the leadership of Ichikawa Fusae, a former school teacher and journalist, who joined hands with Hiratsuka Raichō to found the New Women's Association (*Shin fujin kyōkai*), which was dedicated to improving the legal and social position of women.

At first, advocates of "democracy" focused on electoral reform. From early 1919, rallies and demonstrations supporting universal manhood suffrage were staged in Tokyo and other major cities. If the vote were extended to all adult males, the suffragists argued, the Diet would become less dependent on special interests, less able to rely on vote-buying, and more responsive to popular needs and aspirations. Unlike the rice rioters, whose often diffuse goals varied from region to region, the universal manhood suffrage movement was marked by a high degree of political consciousness, disciplined organization, and direct peaceful appeals to the political authorities. Blue-coated laborers crowded into the Diet building to buttonhole legislators, and demonstrators delivered petitions for suffrage reform to political party headquarters. This new mode of political action, presaged by the "movement for constitutional government" in 1912–1913, did not repudiate party rule but attempted to influence it. Its rhetoric, however, demanded extending political rights beyond the propertied elements to the propertyless classes, who were no less affected by government decisions than the affluent.

The major political parties reacted to the suffrage movement in different ways. The Kenseikai, together with a number of smaller Diet factions, hesitantly introduced a universal suffrage bill in the 1920 Diet. The Seiyūkai majority, on the other hand, feared the effects of an expanded electorate not only on its own power but on long-term political stability. As if to confirm the most pessimistic appraisals of party politicians, the Seiyūkai voted the bill down; and a surge of public indignation of the sort once reserved for the leaders of "clique government" was now directed against the Seiyūkai. The defeat of the suffrage bill, coupled with signs of growing and more vocal labor unrest, led to the radicalization of the democratic reform movement. Interest in simple political reform waned, and more sweeping solutions were proposed for the country's political and social ills.

By the early 1920s, the call for "democracy" was overwhelmed by radical voices from the left, who laid the blame for the nation's problems on the capitalist social and economic system rather than on the political structure. At the turn of the century, a small socialist movement had already made headway among a limited circle of intellectuals, journalists, and students. After the Russo-Japanese War, however, the movement split between those who wanted to rely on parliamentary tactics and those, like the anarchist Kōtoku Shūsui, who advocated extraparliamentary methods such as general strikes.

When several socialist leaders, including Kōtoku, were arrested, tried and executed in 1910 for an alleged plot on the life of the Meiji emperor, social radicalism fell on its "winter years," but the Russian Revolution of 1917–1918 gave radical ideas a new lease on life. Inspiring reports of socialist reconstruction under the Bolshevik regime emboldened the Meiji socialists to speak out again, but more important these developments induced new converts, especially students, to join their ranks. Sakai Toshihiko, an old socialist leader who saw the country on the verge of a new age, wrote in 1919, "I have a sense that we will for the first time step into a world of our own."6

The emergence of a new and militant left wing was buoyed by a conviction that capitalism was on the brink of final collapse. The "trend of the times" was toward liberation, emancipation, and equality, it seemed, and the country was poised on the verge of radical political and social change. But there was considerable disagreement about how change would take place. While those swept up in the "socialist fever" all agreed that power, wealth, and privilege should be more equitably distributed in Japanese society, they were divided over whether or not to rely on legislative action, economic cooperatives, worker agitation, general strikes, or even revolutionary violence. During the early 1920s, lively debates over goals and tactics filled university campuses, intellectual journals, and even the popular press. Gradually, the new left wing sorted itself out into factions advocating a variety of "isms"—guild socialism, anarcho-syndicalism, Marxism, and even national socialism.

The activities of the left alarmed government officials, police authorities, and conservative politicians. The staging of the country's first May Day demonstration in 1920, followed by the formation of a Socialist League and the organization of a clandestine Communist Party with Soviet help in 1922 were profoundly threatening to social stability and social order. The police seized every opportunity to contain the left by force. Policemen lined the routes of public demonstrations, broke up rallies and meetings, and arrested violators of the laws that restricted free speech. Police harassment and surveillance of dissident groups became routine. In the chaos created by the Tokyo earthquake of 1923, zealous military policemen killed several leading radical intellectuals and labor leaders in cold blood. But some political leaders argued that it would be better to provide "proper guidance for popular thought" by passing universal manhood suffrage. Extending the vote, they said, would curtail the spread of "dangerous thoughts" by providing an outlet for popular grievances and discontent.

The passage of a universal manhood suffrage law under the Katō Takaaki cabinet in 1925 marked an important political turning point for the left. On the one hand, it encouraged many left wing leaders to return to the path of moderate parliamentary action. Optimistic that the newly enfranchised masses would seek new leaders, they organized a "proletarian party" movement, aimed at capturing the new voters. Their original goal was a single unified mass party, but ideological sectarianism and personal factionalism frustrated efforts to create one. During the late 1920s, the number of "proletarian parties" proliferated. A Labor-Farmer Party, formed by moderate social democrats committed to parliamentary action, called for improvements in popular living standards and protection for the rights of workers and tenant farmers. It was soon taken over by radical Marxist ideologues who advocated the overthrow of "government by the capitalists and big landlords." A faction of moderates who defected from the party formed a firmly anticommunist Social Democratic Party, which drew support from large labor organizations; others organized the Japan Labor-Farmer Party, another moderate group that called for tenant rights, reduced public utility rates, and other modest social programs. Beside the legal left wing, a small but active Japanese Communist Party, supplied with guidance and funds from the Soviet Union, set out to revolutionize the working class in preparation for "proletarian revolution" in Japan.

In the meantime, the judicial bureaucracy busily set up new machinery to control radicalism. From 1919 onward, alarmist elements in the parties and the bureaucracy allied to support repressive legislation that would check the spread of "dangerous thoughts" at home and curb the intrusion of "subversive elements" from outside. Hoping to counter the possible dire effects of universal suffrage and the resumption of diplomatic relations with the Soviet Union, in 1925 the Diet also passed a Peace Preservation Law by a nearly unanimous vote. The new law outlawed political organizations advocating changes in the *kokutai* or attacking the system of private property. The law was first used to crack down on student Marxist study groups in elite higher schools and universities, but in May 1928 it was invoked to round up the clandestine Communist movement. The home ministry also established a new Special Higher Police to control "dangerous thoughts," to study methods used abroad to counter Communist activities, and to investigate those suspected of political crimes.

Although the party governments cracked down on the Communists and extreme Marxist groups, they tolerated the more moderate left. Conservative politicians realized that the new proletarian parties constituted no immediate political challenge to the social order or to their own political power. During the first universal suffrage election in 1928, for example, the left wing won only five percent of the popular vote and only eight seats in the Diet. Split into small factions, lacking financial resources or political experience, and distrusted by the rural population, the proletarian parties were simply unable to compete with the "established parties." Left wing candidates continued to make gains in the early 1930s, but the Diet remained in firm control of the Seiyūkai and the Minseitō, who continued to run up overwhelming electoral majorities.

The political parties did not emerge unscathed from their encounter with the left, however. Distrust of Diet politics deepened among the intellectual community as the notions of class struggle, radical reform, and the identification of party rule with "bourgeois domination" became conventional wisdom. Declining confidence in the parties was accelerated not only by reports of political scandals but by the outbreak of fistfights, brawls, and other unseemly antics on the floor of the Diet. The press subjected the professional politicians to ridicule, and political cartoons underlined their venality. In 1926, the *Asahi shimbun*, a major newspaper catering to a middle-class audience, even suggested that Diet members were like prostitutes running after customers.[7] The processes of parliamentary democracy were neither as orderly nor dignified as the educated classes expected them to be.

This middle-class disaffection was all the more ominous since the parties were also under attack from right-wing conservatives who argued that competition for power and pursuit of special interests ran counter to "traditional" values of selflessness, harmony, and loyalty. One right-wing ideologue fumed that the electoral process itself was being basically un-Japanese:

> The candidate must speak of himself as if he were the best person in the world and has to beg votes from people as a beggar would do or otherwise he has to buy votes like a mean merchant. Is this really a thing for a gentleman to do? . . . Thoughtful Japanese would prefer not to join in politics, and the Diet becomes a gathering place for scoundrels.[8]

Although most of the electorate continued to vote for the "established parties," these sentiments were widely shared. Politicians simply did not command popular respect commensurate with their political influence and authority. As a result "normal constitutional government" rested on a moral base as fragile as its institutional base, vulnerable to the shock of some new crisis. That crisis was to come in the early 1930s when economic collapse coupled with a new spurt of overseas expansion brought an end to political ascendancy of the political parties.

ENDNOTES

1. The anonymous candidate is quoted in R. H. P. Mason, *Japan's First General Election: 1890* (Cambridge: Cambridge University Press, 1969), 127.

2. Wakatsuki is quoted in Ōshima Fujitarō, *Kokutetsu* (Tokyo: Iwanami shoten, Tokyo, 1961), 50–51.

3. Hoshi Tōru quoted in Masumi Junnosuke, *Nihon seitōshiron*, vol. 2, (Tokyo: Tokyo daigaku shuppan kai, 1966), 225.

4. Quoted in Peter Duus, *Party Rivalry and Political Change in Taishō Japan* (Cambridge, Mass.: Harvard University Press, 1968), 24.

5. Ibid., 111.

6. Quoted in Peter Duus (ed.), *The Cambridge History of Japan, vol. 6, The Twentieth Century* (Cambridge and New York: Cambridge University Press, 1988), 689.

7. Quoted in Nobuya Bamba, *Japanese Diplomacy in a Dilemma* (Vancouver: University of British Columbia Press, 1972), 70, n. 48.

8. Quoted in ibid., 76.

11

Economic Growth and Social Change

By the 1920s, the modern sector of the economy was reaching maturity. Output and technology were advancing on every front, but especially in heavy industry. Between 1912 and 1932, real national income per capita more than doubled, and living standards rose as well. Economic growth, though visible everywhere, was most evident in urban areas. The city of Tokyo, still an exotic place to foreign visitors at the turn of the century, had taken on the look of a modern metropolis, its downtown streets clogged with trolleys and lined with modern office buildings; and Osaka, once the commercial capital of the country, was ringed with industrial suburbs. Despite growth, however, the economy suffered from significant structural problems. As foreign trade grew, fluctuations in the world market, which had had relatively little impact on the Meiji economy, brought a cycle of boom and bust over which the Japanese had little control. It was also clear that the benefits of industrialization were not evenly distributed within society. While some prospered complacently, others found themselves facing new insecurities and hardship. In the late 1920s, when the country plunged into a major depression, these inequities generated a sense of deep social crisis.

BOOM, BUST, AND STAGNATION

In the wake of the Russo-Japanese War, the economy had been saddled with a large public debt, rising prices, a fall-off in exports, and a steadily unfavorable balance of trade. The outbreak of World War I, however, reversed the country's economic fortunes dramatically. Save for the occupation of the

German concession on the Shandong (Shantung) peninsula in China and the capture of German island colonies in the Southwest Pacific, the Japanese devoted little energy and few resources to military operations. More important, the war created new opportunities for Japanese trade. Great Britain and its allies turned to Japan for supplies of munitions and other manufactures. The fighting in Europe also compelled Western business to withdraw from the markets of India, the Dutch East Indies, and China. To fill the slack in supply, Japanese exports of cotton yarn, textiles, and other manufactures moved in to replace European-made products. And in China, Japanese cotton-spinning firms invested in mills in the treaty ports of Shanghai, Qingdao (Tsingtao) and Tianjing (Tientsin) to meet the demand there.

The result was a tremendous wartime boom. Between 1914 and 1919, the GNP rose by more than a third, and the output of the mining and manufacturing sectors by nearly a half. The biggest advance came in textiles and other light industries producing for the export trade, but growth was marked in other areas too. The merchant marine fleet doubled in size to handle the expanded volume of trade; heavy industry grew to meet the demand for producer capital goods like iron, steel, coal, and heavy machinery; the development of hydro-electric power spawned the growth of the electrical goods industry; and finally, rising employment and wages created new domestic demand for consumer goods and foodstuffs. The business community, swept up in a mood of exhilarating optimism, expanded plant and hired new workers as never before. Profits rolled in so easily that some companies declared annual dividends of 100 percent on their stock. Much of the profit was fictitious, however, since rapid wartime inflation devoured its value.

With the end of the war came harder times, as the Americans and the Europeans moved to recapture their pre-war dominance in the Asian market. The upward surge of Japanese exports was checked, and once again the country faced chronic foreign trade deficits. The slowdown was exacerbated by the high price of Japanese goods, severely inflated by the boom, and Japanese export staples, such as cotton textiles, were low value-added relative to the raw materials, semi-manufactures, and advanced technology Japan continued to import from the West. By 1920, a postwar recession was in full swing, and growth continued to lag. During the rest of the decade, the GNP expanded at only half the rate of the war years. The collapse of the boom left once optimistic business firms overcapitalized and saddled with heavy debt. To finance wartime industrial expansion, many firms had borrowed heavily at inflated wartime prices. When prices fell after the onset of the recession, they found themselves facing reduced profits too. To aggravate the situation, many firms, still operating under a boom psychology, continued to pay stock holders high dividends, even though profits were falling or non-existent. Banks, holding company stocks as collateral for loans, continued to lend money to risky business clients out of fear that their collapse would bring down the bank as well. Unfortunately, many bank loans went to pay dividends and interest rather than to retire old debts or to build new productive capacity. In 1920 and again in 1922, banking crises weeded out the shakiest firms, but many survived by taking on new debt.

The great Kantō earthquake of 1923 brought new strains to the economy. The tremor, which struck just as housewives in the Tokyo-Yokohama area were lighting their wood and charcoal stoves for the noon meal, did less damage than the fires that spread rapidly in its wake. In Tokyo 71 percent of the population lost their homes, and in Yokohama 85 percent did. More than 100,000 persons were reported dead or missing, and more than 50,000 were injured. Since the Kantō region was the country's major commercial, industrial, and financial center, the earthquake wrought serious damage to the country's economic infrastructure. The cabinet declared a moratorium on debts and extended new credits to business as a relief measure. A "reconstruction boom" in 1924–1925 provided the business world a temporary respite, but much government credit was simply used to buoy up debt-ridden and overextended companies. The financial instability of the business community persisted.

By the mid-1920s, business and political leaders were increasingly concerned about the fundamental health of the economy. Prices remained high; foreign trade deficits continued to grow; and foreign exchange reserves dwindled. In hindsight, some economic historians have suggested that the government might have spurred general prosperity and faster growth by a deflationary tight money policy that would have brought prices down and made Japanese goods more competitive in the world market. Unlike the tough-minded Matsukata Masayoshi in the early 1880s, however, the party leaders of the 1920s vacillated and temporized, failing to reach agreement about the best course of action. Fiscal policy swung from one pole to another with each change in cabinet. The Kenseikai-Minseitō, dominated by former finance ministry officials, stood for retrenchment, balanced budgets, and fiscal conservatism, while the Seiyūkai continued to advocate a "positive policy" of government spending. Even party leaders committed to retrenchment and budget-cutting were careful not to tread on the toes of political supporters. The rank and file in both parties objected to any budget cuts that threatened pork barrel funds, and overextended business supporters objected to tight money policy. This deadlock made the economy particularly vulnerable to the collapse of the world market after 1929.

THE DUAL STRUCTURE

Although the overall condition of the economy was fragile, large-scale enterprises in technological advanced industries enjoyed continuing gains in profits, wages, and productivity. Indeed, the 1920s saw a growing concentration of power over markets, resources, and capital in the hands of such large firms. To some extent, every modern economy tends toward oligopoly—the domination of markets by a limited number of firms—but in Japan the political climate also encouraged this trend. To remain competitive with foreign firms, which had a head start in technology, experience, and capital accumulation, the political consensus was that it made sense to strengthen domestic capitalism by tolerating, and indeed nurturing, cartels, trusts, and other forms of business concentration. Government officials and political leaders saw little advantage in encouraging cutthroat competition at home.

By the 1920s, large business conglomerates known as *zaibatsu* (financial combines), a term invented by the press on the eve of World War I, were growing in economic importance. These business empires, founded by aggressive pioneering entrepreneurs like Iwasaki Yatarō, had gotten their start in the 1870s and 1880s with direct or indirect help from the Meiji leadership. By the time of the Russo-Japanese War the larger and more powerful zaibatsu—the Mitsubishi, the Mitsui, and the Sumitomo—had developed into complex conglomerate structures with growing clout in the marketplace. The large zaibatsu usually centered on a bank and a general trading company, but included a cluster of manufacturing enterprises, shipping companies and service firms like insurance and real estate as well. Smaller zaibatsu such as the Yasuda interests specialized in banking or the Furukawa in copper mining occupied an oligopolistic position in a particular industry. The wartime boom allowed all the zaibatsu to build up large capital reserves that enabled them to weather the economic slowdown of the postwar period.

During the 1920s, the zaibatsu grew by organizing new firms and investing in new industries on the technological frontier, such as chemicals and electrical goods, which had promise of future growth. But the zaibatsu also deployed the tactics of corporate takeover. The process was usually gradual: a zaibatsu bank or a zaibatsu-related firm would buy stock in an independent firm, then advance it loans; as the zaibatsu increased its stake in the firm, it asserted more and more financial control, and even manipulated resource supplies; and in the end the once-independent firm found itself hemmed in by zaibatsu management and woven into the total fabric of the zaibatsu complex. Through such a process, for example, the Mitsui Holding Company, boosted its assets from around ¥50,000,000 on the eve of World War I to ¥300,000,000 by the late 1920s. Its control extended over a network of direct affiliates and subsidiary firms with assets nearing 15 percent of the total of all business firms.

The pyramidal structure of the zaibatsu placed enormous wealth in the hands of zaibatsu owner families and enormous economic power in the hands of their managers. Top zaibatsu management aimed at expanding the profitability of the whole zaibatsu. Affiliates were even forced to sell their products at a loss to other affiliates or to buy supplies from them at inflated prices that were to the zaibatsu's overall interest. To consolidate their control over affiliates, top zaibatsu managers felt free to intervene in the appointment and promotion of their executives. In the long run, the concentration of decision-making and financial power paid off in stability and security for these large firms. Since zaibatsu affiliates could fall back on the resources of the whole conglomerate during an economic slowdown, they had greater survival power than ordinary firms. Their employees were better protected against economic fluctuations too. And since the decisions of zaibatsu managers could have a major impact on the economy, top political and bureaucratic leaders were careful to listen to their views.

The emergence of corporate giants did not spell an end to small-scale enterprises. In the 1920s, big business existed side by side with a vast number of small and medium-sized firms, creating what economists call a "dual structure" in the modern sector. In part, small enterprises survived by adapting to new technology. By shifting to the use of electrical power, which had become available by the 1920s, they could substitute machinery for hand tools and muscle power. Small enterprises also fulfilled important economic functions. Since the Meiji period, they had not only dominated the production of processed foodstuffs, housing, clothing, and daily consumer goods, but played an important role in the production of export commodities—silk yarn, cotton cloth, ceramic goods, and "cheap Japanese gimcracks" marketed abroad by zaibatsu-affiliated general trading companies. Small enterprises also served more and more as suppliers or subcontractors for large companies, undertaking some production operations (such as making or assembling parts) more cheaply than the larger factories could. Given their aggregate importance to the economy, it is not surprising to find that in 1930 about 55 percent of the total urban working force were employed in small-scale workshops (under five employees).

In comparison to zaibatsu affiliates and other large firms, these small enterprises or workshops were insecure, beset by chronic uncertainty over the future, frequent bankruptcy, and little economic influence. Typically, their

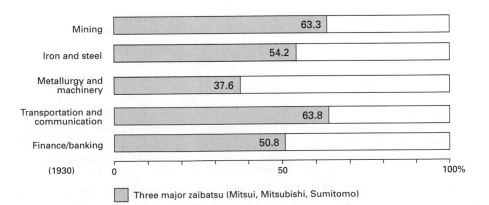

Zaibatsu Share of Major Industries in 1930

Source: Sakamoto Shōzō and Fukuda Toyohiko, *Shinsen Nihonshi zuhyō*, Tokyo: Daiichi gakusha, 1985, p. 149.

owners were capital-poor, operating with little extra cash or savings to spare, and often forced to borrow from small local banks. Subcontractors for large firms were vulnerable to sudden changes in demand, and the canceling of an order could mean bankruptcy. Competing intensely with one another in the scramble for business, small firms and workshops had to cut both profits and wages to an absolute minimum. Economic uncertainty affected not only their owners but also their workers, who received lower wages, worked less regular hours, and enjoyed far less security than those in large factories and concerns. Indeed, with a steady stream of workers clamoring for employment in the small enterprises, the wage gap with large firms continued to widen.

Government policy, however, by and large ignored the problems of the small enterprises or their workers. While party cabinets encouraged big firms to merge, form cartels, and strengthen their position in the market; and while the Diet continued to vote for subsidies and tax relief to industries like shipbuilding, iron and steel, petroleum, air transport, and chemical dyestuffs, small firms were largely left to fend for themselves. In 1925, the Diet authorized the establishment of export guilds to encourage small businesses to cooperate in marketing their products abroad, but little or nothing was done to help subcontractors, small retail shops competing with big city department stores, and producers of traditional consumption goods. Government intervention in the economy, which was skewed toward helping large-scale capital-intensive production, consolidated the "dual structure" and even accelerated its development.

URBAN LABOR UNREST

The lagging economic growth of the 1920s also took place against a background of urban labor unrest. The wartime boom created a sudden demand for labor, especially skilled male workers in the expanding heavy industry sector. By 1919, the factory labor force was twice as large as it had been ten years before, and a majority of new entrants into the labor market were men. From all over the country job-seekers poured into the cities. Farm youths fresh from primary school or a stint in the military service had little difficulty finding work. Employers competed intensely for workers, who shifted easily from job to job. Under these circumstances, wages rose. In 1919, an official report lamented the inconstancy and prodigality of workers under boom conditions: "Habits of hard work and parsimonious saving are going out of fashion, and wasteful behavior rules the day. Workers simply go out for money without knowing where they are going or what they are going to do."[1]

The sudden expansion of the working force laid the foundations for rising labor militancy. Between 1914 and 1918, the number of strikes and other labor disputes leaped from 50 to 417. Many disputes were touched off by wartime inflation. Wages rose, but they did not keep pace with rising prices and rising profits. As the gap grew, disgruntled workers took their grievances to factory managers. Deeper social changes lay behind the new militancy as well. For one thing, workers were better educated then they had been during the Meiji period and better able to read newspapers, to form their own opinions, and to compare their lot in life with that of their bosses. Many had served in the army as well. The reorganization of the workplace, with foremen replacing the *oyakata* and management assuming more direct control over discipline on the factory floor, also made many workers feel that their status was being diminished. While economic issues were at the forefront of most disputes, an undercurrent of social resentment was at work too.

The formation of a national labor movement was spearheaded by the Yūaikai (Friendship Society), organized in 1912 by Suzuki Bunji, a graduate of Tokyo Imperial University influenced by the Christian "Social Gospel," with financial help from businessmen like Shibusawa Eiichi. Aimed at uplifting the workers through mutual aid, education, and self-improvement, the Yūaikai adopted an ideology stressing the common interests between workers and employers, but as labor tensions mounted, it took a role in mediating disputes or helping workers bargain with their bosses. Inspired by the American Federation of Labor and its leader Samuel Gompers, the organization became increasingly activist as the war boom continued. By 1919, its leadership, which now included many young leftist intellectuals, decided to reorganize as the Japan Federation of Labor and to campaign actively for an eight-hour day, the right to form unions, and expansion of the right to vote. Many younger workers were organizers themselves, and the ranks of the federation were swelled by the formation of new local branches.

The onset of the postwar recession intensified labor militancy. With the collapse of the boom came a rash of lay-offs and wage cuts. In 1919, the number of labor disputes skyrocketed to 2388, five times as many as the year before. By 1921, about three hundred labor unions, many of them affiliated with the Japan Federation of Labor, had been organized. Picketing, sabotage, and work stoppages became common, and violence flared when management called in the police for support. With the workers better organized, and radical doctrines like "Bolshevism" or anarcho-syndicalism spreading among the union leaders, strikes lasted longer and grew more bitter. In 1920, disgruntled workers demanding better working conditions at the government-owned Yawata Steel Works shut down its huge blast furnaces for the first time since they had been lit twenty years before, and the following year 30,000 shipyard workers in the Kobe-Osaka area struck for nearly two months. Although the number of strikes dropped off in the mid-1920s, the union movement continued to gather strength as dedicated organizers urged workers to pursue their interests through collective action.

The rise of unions, labor unrest, and industrial disputes disturbed officials and political leaders, who felt that labor strife threatened social stability and undermined the country's competitive position. Some were shocked at the workers' "selfish individualism," while others worried that strikes hindered production or brought higher labor costs. Conservative politicians were disposed to meet labor unrest with confrontation or suppression. Prime Minister Hara privately fulminated against "faint-hearted capitalists" who gave in to worker demands; and his cabinet mobilized police and even army troops to combat striking workers. Home ministry officials often gave covert support to strike-breaking organizations such as the Kokusuikai (National Essence Association), and the authorities encouraged employers to fire striking workers or refuse to reinstate them. Police officers interfered with worker meetings, halted speeches that smacked even faintly of radicalism, and arrested labor organizers on the flimsiest of pretexts.

But some political leaders and officials thought that a conciliatory policy toward labor made more sense. Kenseikai-Minseitō leaders, working with reform-minded officials in the home ministry, argued that the best way to restore social peace was to abandon a laissez-faire attitude toward labor. In 1911, the Diet had already passed a factory law that curtailed child labor, shortened the working day for women, and obligated factory owners to support disabled workers and their families. Although hardly radical, it established a precedent for further legislation. During the mid-1920s, the Diet produced a steady trickle of social welfare laws designed to improve the lot of the working class—a labor exchange law, a national health insurance law, a minimum age law, and additions to the original factory law. Less successful were attempts to pass a comprehensive law regulating labor unions and their

Female workers on strike at the textile factory ca. 1935.

activities. In 1926, the Katō cabinet repealed an official ban on strikes and set up machinery for the voluntary arbitration of labor disputes, but its attempt to legalize labor unions was unsuccessful, as was another attempt in 1931. The main opposition came from large manufacturing firms represented by the Japan Industrial Club and the Japan Economic Federation, who worked with conservative allies in the parties, the house of peers, and the judicial bureaucracy to thwart any effort to legalize unions or collective bargaining.

Employers, especially large manufacturing firms, were well aware of the need to respond to labor unrest, but they wished to do so on their own terms. Trained, skilled workers remained a valuable commodity, and employers were anxious to keep them contented with their jobs. To maintain their loyalty, many companies offered skilled workers annual wage increases, shortened working hours, improved working conditions, and amenities such as low-cost company housing or company-paid excursions. "Regular workers" were kept on the payroll even in slack times and were assured of higher wages the longer they stayed with the company. To forestall the organization of unions, some firms also instituted work councils, which afforded opportunities, albeit limited, for consultation between labor and management. By adopting paternalistic policies, employers hoped to show that unions and work stoppages were not the only way for workers to improve their situation.

Company paternalism probably did more to inhibit the growth of working class consciousness than repressive official policies, but paternalism itself was a response to labor militancy. Even if unions could not force employers to make concessions, their mere existence made managers more conciliatory. In large companies, where workers were better organized, managers were more likely to adopt paternalistic policies. Even so, the beneficiaries of company paternalism, who constituted a privileged "labor aristocracy," remained a minority within the labor force. Female textile operatives, workers in small-scale firms, day laborers, and temporary workers were left at the mercy of the labor market, protected neither by government legislation nor company paternalism. Unable to organize themselves into unions, these less advantaged workers could only return to the countryside in times of distress. But when urban prosperity faded in the late 1920s, they found conditions no better there.

THE AILING COUNTRYSIDE

Although the agricultural sector had contributed to overall economic growth in the Meiji period, by the 1920s the countryside was falling behind rapidly. To be sure, war brought prosperity to the countryside as it did to the rest of the country, and most farm families found themselves better off than they had ever been before. The price of rice and silk worm cocoons skyrocketed, bringing in new cash income and stimulating production. Since even marginal land could be farmed at a profit, it was brought into cultivation, and advances were made in farming techniques (better threshing machines, mechanized irrigation pumps, and chemical fertilizers.) The wartime boom also created opportunities for by-employment, and many farm household members took temporary jobs in industry during the off-season. Like the rest of the population, farm households found their new prosperity eaten away by wartime inflation, but on the whole their living standards rose noticeably. Many peasant farmers could now buy food, clothing, and even incidentals they once had been unable to afford.

The postwar economic reversal affected the rural economy no less than the urban. A lingering agricultural depression set in after 1920. The industrial sector was less and less able to absorb surplus rural labor, and workers turned out of jobs in the cities drifted back to their native villages, putting strain on farm household budgets. The farm population, however, suffered less from such hidden unemployment than from a long-term drop in the price of agricultural goods. Although rice prices had shot up steeply during the war, after the rice riots of 1918 the government increased rice imports from Korea and Taiwan to cover shortfalls in domestic food production. Since the colonial standard of living was much lower than in Japan, colonial rice was much cheaper, and the government regulated its inflow to make sure that it remained cheaper. This rice policy helped urban consumers, but it deepened economic troubles among the rural population.

Interestingly, the onset of agrarian depression checked the growth of tenancy. Throughout the 1920s, there was a slow but steady increase in the number of small- and medium-size owner-farmers, who had made the most gains during the war years. It was they rather than non-cultivating landlords who worked most assiduously at reclaiming new land, constructing new drainage and irrigation works, and improving farming techniques. By contrast, as rice prices declined, landlords found themselves faced with declining profits. Rental receipts dropped and land prices leveled off. Other investments, including company stocks, were more attractive to many landlords, especially those whose ties with their tenants and their land had weakened by their move out of the village.

Tenancy disputes also made landlordism less attractive. As tenant farmers followed the lead of their city cousins, popular unrest that unsettled the cities in the postwar years spread to the countryside. Better educated young farmers read about urban strikes and demonstrations in the newspapers or heard about them from younger brothers or cousins who had moved to the city. From the end of World War I, the number of tenancy unions grew, from 173 in 1917 to more than 4500 in 1927. Their total membership reached a peak of 365,000. The majority of tenant unions were to be found in central Japan, where agricultural improvement had been pursued most vigorously and rice yields were highest. Disputes were also more common where absentee landlordism had eroded community ties. When relations between landlords and tenants became purely economic, unmitigated by landlord largesse or community leadership, tenants were more likely to develop a sense of rights.

Radical activists, lecturing on manhood suffrage or the labor movement, tried to raise tenant consciousness, and in 1922 several reformers organized the Japanese Farmers' Union with the goals of fundamental land reform. As one of its leaders proclaimed, "Like the peasants of Russia we must fight until we have land and freedom."[2] But this grandiose goal proved elusive early on, since most tenants had more limited goals and grievances. During the mid-1920s, as farm household incomes dropped, most tenant disputes were fought over the demand for rent reduction. The politicians were not entirely unresponsive to the situation. To reduce tension in the countryside, the Diet passed a tenancy dispute-arbitration law in 1924, and two years later instituted a program of low-interest loans to tenants wishing to buy the land they farmed.

Although the tenancy system was weakening, the situation of the farm population deteriorated in the late 1920s as bumper crops depressed the rice price even further. Many farm households tried to make ends meet by cash cropping, especially by raising silkworms. According to one estimate, by 1929 nearly 40 percent of all farm households depended on sericulture for extra income. The production of raw silk was three times what it had been in 1914, and not surprisingly, the price of raw silk had dropped as a result. Even more important, however, was a decline in demand overseas. With the development of rayon and other artificial fibers, exports to the United States, the main market for Japanese raw silk, dropped steadily. The net effect was to make life increasingly difficult for the country's 5.5 million farm families, who still accounted for about half the population.

The government increased subsidies to agriculture in the late 1920s, but this policy had very little effect. The fundamental problem was the farmers' lack of leverage in the marketplace. Small-scale farmers were powerless as individuals to control prices, and their lack of collective effort exacerbated their vulnerability. When the price of rice or silk dropped, most peasants worked even harder to produce more to maintain their incomes instead of cutting production to force prices back up. The effect, of course, was to aggravate the price decline further, and the vicious cycle continued. Lacking any collective political organization, the farm population remained socially powerless. The "problem of the villages" grew even more serious by the end of the 1920s.

URBANIZATION AND MIDDLE-CLASS LIFE

While farmers grappled with the long-term agricultural depression, a burgeoning "new middle class"—company managers, middle echelon bureaucrats, academics and teachers, journalists and professionals—enjoyed relative prosperity in the cities. The system of higher education, constructed to produce a "society of talent" (as Fukuzawa Yukichi put it), gave shape to a new technical and managerial elite. Since the 1890s, bright and ambitious young men, inspired by textbook stories of heroes like Napoleon, Benjamin Franklin, and Toyotomi Hideyoshi, who had risen from humble origins through hard work, diligence, and devotion to the public good, scrambled up the educational ladder in pursuit of personal success. By the turn of the century, national and private institutions of higher learning were attracting young men (though not young women) from every social class, including landlords, shop-keepers, and even poorer peasant farmers and fishermen. While status and patronage still played a role in determining social opportunity, so did the ability of parents to provide their children with higher education.

As one scholar described him, the typical candidate for middle class status was

> the lad from the country inspired by articles in the magazines on "How to Live in Tokyo on 6.50 Yen a Month," making his way through the university on a diet of rice, dried fish, and bean curd . . . sustained through it all by hopes of glittering rewards to follow, of honor in his native village, or the gratifying glow of virtue fulfilled in which he would kneel at [his ancestors' shrine] and tell them that he had made—or restored—the family fortune.[3]

The ambitions of such young men were fed by magazines like *Seikō* ("Success"), founded in 1902 for the "man of character who helps and respects himself, lives by his own enterprise and his toil, and creates his own fate by the exercise of his own abilities." Its pages were filled with inspirational stories about hard-working students who had risen to the heights of social success and offered practical advice on study and career building. Publishers also found a ready market for guidebooks on how to live in the city on a small budget, how to pass university examinations, how to qualify for civil service or other specialized jobs, and how to get government scholarships.

By the time of World War I, opportunities for dramatic personal success had declined. No one expected to be an Iwasaki or an Itō anymore, and as more and more young men graduated from middle school and entered higher education, competition for middle-class status stiffened. But at the same time, the expanding economy created new white collar jobs in business that provided an alternative to employment in local government or the national civil service. Salaries in business gradually drew abreast of government salaries, and so did other benefits. Promising university students found themselves courted by private firms, who often helped them defray university expenses—and in extreme cases offered the class valedictorian the hand of the boss's daughter. Life as a company employee was attractive not only for its high social prestige but for its relative economic security. The employment pattern of the new middle class followed the model of the civil service. Once a fresh university graduate found a post, he was usually assured of life-time employment, and salaries depended on seniority as much as on proficiency or achievement. Companies offered other benefits such as semi-annual bonuses, housing and family allowances, or free medical care. New middle-class households, whether in business or government service, were relieved of the insecurity that plagued small entrepreneurs and even landlords, who remained at the mercy of fire, flood, and the market.

By the early 1920s, the white collar worker—or "salary man" (a term coined at the end of World War I)—was a ubiquitous figure in the urban landscape. Perhaps 1.5 million (or about 5.5 percent of the gainfully employed) occupied white collar positions in private companies or government offices, and their lifestyle was marked by new patterns of work, consumption, and amusement. Most visible were new downtown business districts and new commuter suburbs, especially in the great metropolitan areas. In Tokyo, for example, a large central railroad station was completed in 1913, and the nearby Marunouchi section became a major business hub, filled with major banks, insurance companies, and industrial concerns. New technologies (the telephone, the electric tramway, and the high-rise office building) created the possibility of a more dispersed city. During the 1920s, new private electric rail lines promoted the growth of suburban residential areas, especially after the 1923 earthquake destroyed housing in the central city. The older downtown neighborhoods, where commoners had lived in Tokugawa times, remained an area of small-scale shops and workplaces, but the heart of the city shifted to the bustling business section crowded with salary men and office workers during the day and the amusement areas they frequented in their after hours.

White collar workers, middle managers, and middle-class professionals were often first-generation migrants to the city who saw their lives as a great improvement over the crude ways of the countryside. "An educated child," went a popular saying, "turns up his nose at the privy back home." The new middle class had an avid taste for the "modern" and the "cultured." Its upper echelons pursued the symbols of respectability and success: Western business suits and patent leather shoes, shopping trips to the Mitsukoshi Department Store, and weekly visits to the Imperial Theater (modeled on the Paris Opera). For more modest middle-class households, a "cultured life" (*bunka-teki seikatsu*) meant living in a house with at least one Western-style room, a kitchen with a floor, and an inside toilet; riding in trams or taxis rather than rickshaws; dining at Western-style restaurants that served exotic dishes like "curry rice" or "omelet rice"; and wearing Western suits and frocks to work. And middle-class children marched off to school in brass-buttoned Western-style school tunics or middy blouses instead of homemade kimonos.

With a voracious appetite for self-improvement, the new middle class, self-consciously pursued a life style marked by "scientific" rationality, efficiency, and functionality. By the 1920s, new magazines, filled with articles on everything from child-rearing through cooking to tips on how to master

English, advised middle-class readers how to lead a "cultured life" (*bun-kateki seikatsu*) and guided them through their life crises. Publishing companies also found an almost limitless market for books that appealed to the culture-thirsty middle class, and the number of retail bookstores jumped from 3000 in 1914 to 10,000 in 1927. The Iwanami publishing company bombarded the highbrow middle class with translations of European philosophy and recent works on Japanese thought, but other publishers found it more profitable to publish inexpensive works of fiction or multi-volume "complete works" of famous authors, often prized as much for their appearance in the parlor as for their content.

With the spread of literacy, the reach of the mass media grew rapidly. By 1920, there were 1100 newspapers with a combined circulation of six to seven million. According to one estimate, nearly half of the country's eleven million households subscribed to a daily paper. Large metropolitan dailies like the *Yomiuri shinbun*, which dominated the newspaper business, attracted readers by sponsoring airplane shows and baseball teams. New magazines appeared almost weekly. Intellectual journals like *Chūō Kōron* and *Kaizō* were crammed with political analyses by men like Yoshino Sakuzō and fiction by writers like Tanizaki Junichirō. A wider audience turned to monthlies like *Kingu (King)* magazine, which fed them a diet of lively features, patriotic essays, and action-packaged light fiction. In downtown movie palaces, the urban public could watch the latest Chaplin comedy or thrill to rousing samurai films like *The Last Days of the Bakufu*. Government-operated radio stations began regular broadcasts in 1925, and by 1928 about 500,000 households owned wireless receivers.

By the 1920s, an urban middle-class women's culture also took shape. The idea of domesticity encouraged most middle-class women to work as full-time housewives, but as more and more women graduated from middle school or college many found opportunities for white-collar employment as teachers or clerical workers. Both groups provided an audience for new women's magazines like *Seitō* (Blue Stocking), *Fujin kōron* (Women's Review), and *Shufu no tomo* (The Housewife's Friend) that dealt with women's issues. By the late 1920s, these publications reached hundreds of thousands. *Fujin kōron* published feminist debates about whether women should devote their energies to home or work, or how best to improve the lot of ordinary working women; while *Shufu no tomo* carried articles that dealt with domestic problems like child-rearing, marital relations, home management, and family thrift. Newspapers also carried advice columns for women that told them how to handle philandering husbands and obnoxious mothers-in-law.

After the feminist leader Ichikawa Fusae persuaded the government in 1922 to repeal regulations prohibiting women from attending public meetings or joining political organizations, many middle-class women plunged into movements to expand women's rights. The Women's Suffrage League was organized to secure for women the right to vote or run for public office, and in the 1928 election, women speakers participated in election campaigns for the first time—albeit in support of male candidates. The League also encouraged its members, particularly housewives, to become involved in local community affairs, to protect themselves as consumers, and to debate problems that affected their lives as wives and mothers. While efforts to pass a woman's suffrage bill failed in 1930 middle-class women drawn into the movement found a growing scope for community, charitable, and other activities outside the home.

Urban life also had a frivolous side that journalists characterized as "erotic," "grotesque," and nonsensical" (*ero-guro-nansensu*). It was symbolized by the Japanese version of "flaming youth"—the pleasure-seeking *mobo* and *moga* (short for *modan boi* and *modan garu,* "modern boy" and "modern girl"), who frequented the new dance halls, "milk parlors," and cafes that popped up in Tokyo and Osaka and flaunted convention by smoking cigarettes, drinking beer, and dancing check to cheek. The dizzy pace of these privileged young people unsettled their staider parents who feared that the "modern disease" had infected their offspring. But others worried that life in the cities was becoming more hedonistic, materialistic, and individualistic. The importation of musical reviews, the tango and the fox trot, and other "degenerate" influences from abroad alarmed conservative defenders of the country's "moral purity."

While economic opportunity drew rural youth to urban areas, the cultural gap between city and country was growing. Hardworking farmers resented the frivolity of city dwellers whose lives seemed so much easier and more carefree than their own. The materialism, hedonism, and individualism of urban culture threatened cherished traditional values like frugality, hard work, harmony, and decorum. This cultural gap, which was as important in fomenting rural discontent as the imbalance between the rural and modern sectors of the economy, did not seek expression through left-wing political activism. The rhetoric of class struggle, so popular among urban intellectuals and reformers, fell on deaf ears in the countryside. Rural discontent, though it may have sprung from economic inequities, instead sought an outlet in a renewed commitment to the purity of the "Japanese spirit" and "the Japanese way of life." This discontent was soon to find catharsis in a mounting enthusiasm for expansion abroad and restoration of national solidarity.

ENDNOTES

1. Quoted in Koji Taira, *Economic Development and the Labor Market in Japan* (New York: Columbia University Press, 1970), 132.

2. Quoted in Ienaga Saburō and Inoue Kiyoshi, *Kindai Nihon no sōten,* vol. 3 (Tokyo: Mainichi shimbunsha, 1967), 149.

3. Quoted in Ronald P. Dore, *Aspects of Social Change in Modern Japan* (Princeton, N.J.: Princeton University Press, 1967), 120–121.

12

The Empire Between the Wars

The Japanese victory over Russia, which overturned the idea of Western invincibility, kindled hopes among Asian nationalists that their colonial yoke could soon be cast off. "Japan's example has given heart to the rest of Asia," wrote the Indian poet Rabindranath Tagore. "We have seen the life and strength are there in us, only the dead crust has to be removed."[1] Revolutionary anti-imperialist nationalism spread quickly among students from China and other parts of Asia who flocked to Tokyo to learn the secrets of Japan's success. These young Asian nationalists saw Japan as a potential liberator, an idea shared by their Japanese supporters and sympathizers. Indeed, some Japanese journalists, inspired by a vision of Pan-Asian unity, even spoke of their country's mission to defend their Asian brothers as "the yellow man's burden." But this grand dream was dashed by the realities of international power politics. While mouthing Pan-Asianist slogans, the Japanese government had little choice but to cooperate with the very Western colonialist powers against whom Asian nationalist movements were struggling. It was simply not possible for Japan to be imperialist and anti-colonialist at the same time.

THE CONTINENTAL COMMITMENT

Although both the Sino-Japanese and Russo-Japanese Wars had been fought to allay strategic concerns, the acquisition of new colonial territories (Taiwan, southern Sakhalin, and eventually Korea) and a new territorial enclave in China (the Kwantung territories and the South Manchuria Railway zone) only magnified them. As they were drawn more and more deeply into the imperialist game, Japan's leaders had to worry about defending not only the country's sovereign borders but its colonial perimeter as well. The rumble of the guns had barely stilled in 1905 before army and navy leaders called for a military buildup in anticipation of a Russian war of revenge. The two services had rather different strategic priorities, however. Within the army, the "Chōshū generals" surrounding Yamagata Aritomo wanted Japan to become a "continental state" and pushed for an aggressive strategy that would use Korea as a base in potential conflicts with Russia or even China. The navy, on the other hand, was more worried about the United States, which had emerged as a Pacific power after its acquisition of the Hawaiian and the Philippine Islands. The debate was resolved in 1907 with the establishment of a new national defense plan that envisaged Russia, the United States, and France (Russia's principal ally) as the country's chief hypothetical enemies and projected an expansion of the army to twenty-five divisions and an increase of naval strength by eight battleships and eight heavy cruisers.

While the generals and admirals argued about how to defend Japan's new sphere of influence, Japanese emigrants were busily populating it. The emergence of Japan as an imperialist power set in motion the first Japanese overseas diaspora in historic times. In 1895, only about 42,000 Japanese had lived abroad, mainly in the continental United States or the Hawaiian islands where they worked as field hands in the sugar plantations, but by 1910 their ranks had swelled to 400,000, with nearly three-quarters living in the colonial territories of Taiwan and Korea, the leasehold on the Kwantung peninsula, and the treaty ports in China. The shift of migration toward the Asian continent was a reaction in part to barriers rising against them elsewhere. Discrimination against Japanese immigrants to California become an irritant in relations with the United States in 1906 when the San Francisco school board excluded the children of Japanese immigrants from regular public schools, and the Japanese government responded by agreeing to restrict emigration to America. At the same time, Foreign Minister Komura announced a policy of concentrating overseas migration to Korea and Manchuria, to build Japanese economic and political influence as well as reduce further tension with the Americans.

The Japanese government did very little to encourage migration to the continent. The efforts it did make, such as a plan to send hundreds of thousands of agricultural settlers to Korea under the auspices of the Oriental Development Company, ended in failure. Few peasant farmers were willing to settle abroad, and it was costly to send those who were. The typical Japanese migrant was not a farmer-settler but a member of the lower middle class. What drew Japanese to the continent was the lure of easy economic success. The colonial regimes in Taiwan, Korea, and the Kwantung territories created jobs for policemen, mailmen, technicians, clerks, and other petty functionaries, and the growth of colonial trade opened up opportunities for shop keepers, small traders, company employees, restaurant owners, and others engaged in small-scale commerce. The rewards of migration were social as well as economic. Everywhere they settled, except perhaps in the treaty ports of China, the Japanese emigrants were a privileged class, enjoying higher living standards, higher wages, and better access to schools, hospitals, and other social amenities than the indigenous population.

The flow of Japanese migrants to the continent was sustained by the expanding economic ties. The colonies of Taiwan and Korea, where the Japanese enjoyed near-monopolies over foreign trade, provided secure markets for Japanese manufactured goods and an important source of food supplies, especially rice from Korea and sugar from Taiwan. But China, with its vast population and undeveloped natural resources, was the country's main trading partner in Asia. As one aggressive young Japanese businessman noted in 1900, "China is a broad and boundless country, whose demand increases day by day, month by month, year by year . . . practically without limit."[2] Indeed, by 1910 total Sino-Japanese commodity trade was about five times that of Korea and Taiwan combined, and within a few years China (especially the northern provinces and Manchuria) had became Japan's chief source of coal, iron ore, and raw cotton. Growing economic dependence on China, where Japan's presence was more vulnerable than in the colonies, made the Japanese increasingly sensitive to market conditions there as well as to its political stability.

Not only was trade with Asia expanding but so was investment. In China, for example, Japanese investment at the turn of the century had been negligible, perhaps around $1 million, but by 1913 it had reached $220 million and was growing by leaps and bounds. The flow of capital was concentrated in Manchuria, where the South Manchuria Railway Company, a semi-governmental corporation established in 1906, was the main engine of economic penetration. Zaibatsu trading companies and affiliates moved into Manchuria once the Japanese political presence had stabilized, and government banks underwrote private enterprises to make them more competitive with Western business interests there. After the outbreak of World War I, Japanese cotton spinning firms invested in mills in the Chinese treaty ports, especially Shanghai, to take advantage of cheap Chinese labor and gain a larger share of the Chinese market.

This web of economic ties reinforced the political and strategic ties linking Japan to its colonies and its informal empire in China. By the early 1910s, defense and maintenance of the empire, supported by a broad consensus at home, had become a basic axiom of Japanese foreign policy. No domestic anti-imperialist movement opposed the possession of colonies, nor did more than a handful of dissenters question the desirability of the continental commitment. The Pan-Asianist idea that Japan was the natural leader of the Asian peoples took deep hold of the public imagination. In the colonies of Taiwan and Korea, the Japanese saw their task as "civilizing" the indigenous inhabitants. The long-term goal was to lift them out of backwardness and turn them into full-fledged "children of the emperor" through a policy of "assimilation" (*dōka*). The Koreans and the Taiwanese were often referred to as "younger brothers" in need of protection by their Japanese "elder brothers," terms that underlined a Japanese sense of superiority. Although respect for Chinese traditional culture, the source of Japan's own higher culture, remained strong, a similar tone of condescension crept into attitudes toward contemporary China.

It was increasingly common for political leaders, diplomats, and officials to speak about a "special relationship" with China. This rhetoric implied that Japan's historical, cultural, and ethnic links with China were older and deeper than those of the Western countries. It also reflected a conviction that events in China were more likely to affect Japan politically, militarily, and economically. Vast distances separated the Westerners from East Asia, but the Japanese lived next door to the continent. In many ways, this concept of a "special relationship" with China was not unlike the view that the United States had a special relationship with its southern neighbors in the Western hemisphere. Indeed, when American officials complained about Japan's actions on the continent, Japanese leaders often replied that they were merely pursuing an "Asian Monroe Doctrine." What they meant was that the Japanese enjoyed a position of natural dominance in East Asia, just as the Americans did in Mexico, Cuba, Nicaragua, and other parts of Latin America.

While there was consensus that Japan should occupy a dominant position in East Asia, the Japanese political elite was divided by disagreements on the question of how to achieve and maintain Japanese leadership. On one side were "multi-lateralists" who thought Japan ought to cooperate with the other imperialist powers rather than go it alone. Ready to accept the rules of the imperialist game already laid down by the Westerners, they supported the "Open Door" principles that no single power should upset the status quo in China by grabbing territory or establishing exclusive spheres of economic influence. In dealing with China, the multi-lateralists were willing to cooperate with the Western powers, presenting a united front in defense of common interests, such as the maintenance of the "unequal treaty" system. Confident of Japan's ability to hold its own in international politics, but aware of the country's financial and technological dependence on the West, multi-lateralists favored the diplomatic caution that had characterized early Meiji foreign policy.

After the Russo-Japanese War, the Katsura cabinet and its successors, followed such a policy, pursuing a diplomatic offensive to consolidate Japan's hold over its new sphere of influence. The Japanese took care not to offend the other imperialist powers, especially Great Britain and the United States, who had helped finance the war through loans to Japan. In 1906, when both countries complained that Japanese occupation forces restricted their business activities in Manchuria, the Saionji cabinet agreed to a troop withdrawal and established a colonial administration in the Kwantung Peninsula. Through a series of bilateral diplomatic agreements, the Japanese secured recognition of their new position in Korea and China from the British, Americans, and French, and in 1907 they concluded a secret agreement with the

Russians to divide southern and northern Manchuria into separate spheres of influence.

Others called for a more independent policy in Asia. Instead of constantly following the Westerners' diplomatic lead in China and elsewhere, they argued, Japan should pursue its own special interests even at the risk of upsetting the other powers. Patriotic societies like the Genyōsha and the Amur River Society (Kokuryūkai) expressed this view most stridently in public, but in private so did army leaders who wanted to expand their territorial and military advantage on the continent, especially in Korea and Manchuria. The army high command, for example, urged the annexation of Korea in 1910 most strongly, and it backed negotiations to expand Japanese economic rights in Manchuria. The tug of war between this approach to East Asia and the multi-lateralist approach was to bedevil foreign policy decision-making until 1931.

THE CHINA PROBLEM

The outbreak of revolution in China in October 1911 complicated Japan's continental policy. After overthrowing the Qing dynasty, a coalition of nationalist revolutionaries under the nominal leadership of Sun Yat-sen (Sun I-xian) announced the establishment of a new Chinese republic. The Qing dynasty, which guaranteed Japan's treaty rights and its foothold in Manchuria, had been easy to deal with, but its fall from power introduced new uncertainties. The republican revolutionaries were determined to build a strong "New China" able to put an end to the country's humiliating subjugation to the imperialist powers. Far from rescuing China from its plight, however, the revolution plunged the country into political chaos. Real power lay in the hands of Yuan Shikai (Yüan Shih-kai), a strong man in command of the most modern fighting force in China, who quickly became president of the new republic. When conflict broke out between Yüan and the revolutionaries, the country entered a period of civil strife and political instability.

The Japanese response to the new political uncertainties in China was confused and indecisive. When the revolution broke out in 1911, army leaders hoped to detach Manchuria from the rest of China, genrō like Yamagata favored intervention on the side of the Qing, and supporters of Sun Yat-sen favored aid to the revolutionaries. All hoped the revolution would produce a China friendly to Japan. The Saionji cabinet, waiting to see how the other imperialist powers reacted, decided not to intervene in the revolution at all. Rather it chose the path of caution. It soon became clear that the Western powers, Great Britain in particular, did not care who governed China as long as a stable regime recognized the imperialist rights and privileges granted by the Qing government. In 1913, an international banking consortium was formed to provide Yuan's government with a loan of £25,000,000. Despite an antipathy toward Yuan, who had thwarted the Japanese in Korea during the 1880s, the Japanese government decided to cooperate in shoring up his regime.

The outbreak of World War I, which diverted Western attention from Asia, prompted an abrupt about-face shift in China policy. The genrō, the military high command, and many civilian politicians saw the war as an opportunity to advance the country's interests without consulting the other powers. In 1914, the Ōkuma cabinet decided to enter the war on the side of Great Britain and its allies, and Japanese expeditionary forces quickly seized Germany's island colonies in the Southwest Pacific and the German concessions on the Shandong (Shantung) peninsula in China. But more ambitious schemes were in the air.

In early 1915, the Ōkuma cabinet presented Yuan Shikai with the so-called Twenty-One Demands, a draft treaty settling several issues pending between the two countries. The first fourteen demands (Group I–IV) asked China to confirm Japan's position in Shandong, extend Japanese leaseholds and grant new economic rights in Manchuria, place the Daye (Tayeh) iron mines under monopoly control of a Sino-Japanese joint venture, and guarantee that no leaseholds be given to any other power in Fujian (Fukien), the province opposite Taiwan. The last set of demands or "requests" (Group V), included as the result of army pressure, would have made China into a quasi-protectorate by placing Japanese advisors in key government agencies, requiring China to purchase arms from Japan, and granting broader residence rights and other privileges to Japanese nationals. Although Yuan eventually agreed to the first set of demands, he skillfully used Western, especially American, indignation at Japan's unilateral actions to avoid accepting Group V.

Despite the hostile Western reaction, the Japanese continued to fish in China's troubled political waters. After Yuan died in 1916, the country was plunged into a prolonged struggle among regional warlord cliques, all fighting for control over the vestigial central government at Beijing. Japanese army general staff officers hoped to detach Manchuria and Mongolia from China by backing independence movements launched by local warlords, but these attempts ended in failure. In 1917, the Terauchi government cabinet, returning to a policy of backing a strong man, advanced a loan of ¥45,000,000 to Yuan's successor, Duan Qirui (Tuan Ch'i-jui), ostensibly for the development of railroads and repair of flood damage, but in fact to subsidize military campaigns against rival warlords. This blatant interference in Chinese politics outraged young Chinese nationalist intellectuals, who saw the Japanese linking themselves to the most reactionary forces in the country. Anti-Japanese sentiments, fed by deep suspicions about Japanese motives toward China, finally exploded on May 4, 1919, when thousands of Chinese students, merchants, and workers staged demonstrations all over China to protest the decision of the Versailles Peace Conference to leave Japan in control of the Shandong territories. Boycotts against Japanese goods spread throughout the treaty ports on the China coast.

The outbreak of the Bolshevik Revolution in 1917 had an equally unsettling impact on Japanese foreign policy. Hoping to capitalize on political disorder in Russia, the army general staff proposed a military expedition to occupy the trans-Siberian railway line as far west as Lake Baikal. The project was supported by Foreign Minister Motono and Home Minister Gotō Shimpei, who hoped to set up a pro-Japanese puppet regime in eastern Siberia and a Japanese sphere of influence in Mongolia and Northern Manchuria. The leaders of both major political parties, Hara Takashi and Katō Takaaki opposed the scheme—and so did Yamagata Aritomo, who feared it might provoke the United States. When Japanese troops were sent to Siberia in August 1918, they went as part of an Allied expedition to rescue Czech forces stranded by the revolution. But the army leadership, using its discretion in planning operations, mobilized a force far larger than the Americans and its allies and kept them in Siberia after other forces withdrew in 1920. Although the expedition accomplished little, it cost Japan dearly in lives (3500 dead) and money (¥700 million), deepened Western suspicions about Japanese ambitions on the continent, and soured relations with the new Soviet Union.

The genrō had been in command of foreign policy decisions down through the Russo-Japanese War, but these postwar swings in continental policy signaled a breakdown in their influence. In 1914, Foreign Minister Katō Takaaki refused to ask their counsel when Japan entered the war against Germany. The genrō retaliated by forcing Katō out of office, but they never really regained the initiative. Just as domestic politics was complicated by the emergence of the political parties, foreign policy decision-making became a contest among a welter of forces—the cabinet, the foreign office, the military services, and the party politicians as well as the surviving genrō themselves. The army, which enjoyed a constitutional autonomy from the cabinet, often acted quite independently, while the civilian government steered in one direction and then in another as power changed hands. As Yoshino Sakuzō noted in 1920, "Japan has two representatives in China, the consuls representing the Foreign Office and the men who are over there in large numbers representing the General Staff. When the consuls point to the right, the men representing the General Staff point to the left. And so the Chinese are saying, 'What is Japan doing, anyway?'" [2] It was little wonder that both the Chinese and the Westerners accused Japan of a duplicitous "dual diplomacy."

THE WASHINGTON CONFERENCE SYSTEM

The party cabinets of the early 1920s, reacting against the aggressive unilateralism of wartime policy, returned to cooperation with the Western powers in China. Playing the lone wolf on the continent had undermined Western confidence and provoked Chinese hostility without significantly improving Japanese interests. By contrast, the tremendous wartime expansion of trade and investment in China demonstrated that "economic diplomacy" could be as advantageous to Japan as military posturing and political intrigue. Expanding Japanese political influence through peaceful penetration of overseas markets attracted the support of party leaders as well as the business community. At the Versailles Peace Conference, the Western powers seemed to accept the Wilsonian ideal of a postwar world order based on the principles of national self-determination, international peace, and collective security. To be sure, the Westerners showed no readiness to give up their colonial possessions, and even divided among themselves as "mandates" territory once under the control of the defeated Germans, Austrians, and Turks, but at least they were willing to preserve a peaceful international status quo through multi-lateral international agreements.

Convinced that Japan's best interests lay in following the Western lead, the Hara cabinet agreed to participate in the Washington Conference, convened in 1921–1922 to work out a new international order in East Asia. The participating powers (the United States, Great Britain, France, Italy, and Japan) reaffirmed the "Open Door" principles of maintaining the territorial integrity of China and recognizing commercial equality for all nations there. Declaring resolve to work for the establishment of a stable government in China, the powers also signaled their willingness to discuss ending the "unequal treaty" system through the abolition of extraterritoriality and the restoration of tariff autonomy. To demonstrate its good intentions, the Japanese delegation unilaterally agreed with the Chinese to give up control over the Shandong territories and to relinquish certain rights wrested from China during the Twenty-One Demands. On the surface at least, it appeared that Japan, like the other powers, was turning over a new leaf in China.

The Washington conference also produced a naval arms limitations agreement intended to halt an incipient arms race between Japan and the United States. In 1916, on the eve of its entry into World War I, the American government embarked on a naval construction program to build a fleet second to none in the world. In 1920, the Hara cabinet approved a long-projected plan to expand the Japanese fleet by eight battleships and eight cruisers. The Five Power Treaty signed in Washington established a 10:10:6:3.5:3.5 ratio for the tonnage of capital ships in the British, American, Japanese, French and Italian navies. The Japanese agreed to a lower ratio when the Americans and the British promised to build no new fortifications in the Pacific west of the American naval base at Pearl Harbor or east of the British base at Singapore. In effect, this meant that the Japanese fleet would be equal in size to the combined Pacific fleets of the Anglo-American powers, guaranteeing enough naval strength to defend the Japanese home islands and colonial possessions against attack. The Washington Conference established a naval balance of power, allowing Japan supremacy in the Western Pacific, and it made possible a reduction in the country's naval budget.

Within the Washington Conference agreements, the Japanese attempted to build cordial political and economic ties with China. The main advocate of this policy was Shidehara Kijūrō, who served as foreign minister during the

Kenseikai-Minseitō cabinets (1924–1927 and 1929–1931). No less committed to maintenance of empire than anyone else, Shidehara's priority was to
protect and expand Japan's overseas trade by pursuing "peaceful coexistence
and coprosperity" with China. Emphatically rejecting needless saber-rattling
or bellicose gestures, he tried to pursue a strict policy of non-intervention in
China's domestic troubles. When the British suggested a joint show of foreign force in response to anti-imperialist demonstrations, such as the May 30
movement in 1925, Shidehara refused. Rather than antagonize the Chinese,
he expressed sympathy toward rising nationalist sentiment. On the other
hand, Shidehara was reluctant to make any concessions to Chinese nationalism that worked to Japan's economic disadvantage. In 1925, Shidehara stubbornly resisted the return of tariff autonomy to the Chinese for fear that a
rise in tariffs might make Japanese goods, especially textiles, less competitive, and he also opposed Chinese efforts in the late 1920s to build railway
lines that competed with the South Manchurian Railway Company.

Whatever its merits, Shidehara's diplomacy did not reflect political consensus. Critics condemned it as a "weak policy" that sacrificed national security
and national honor to an unrealistic pursuit of harmony with the Anglo-
American powers, who often treated the Japanese with condescension or
even contempt. Not only did the "Anglo-American imperialists" pursue their
interests with scant regard for "international cooperation," their domestic
policies were blatantly racist. When Japan proposed the insertion of a "racial
equality" clause in the Versailles Peace Treaty, the British and the Americans,
under pressure from the Australians, turned them down. Japanese immigrants were barred from "White Australia," and they faced rising discrimination in the United States as well. In 1924, the American Congress, turning a
deaf ear to Japanese diplomatic protests, passed a new immigration bill,
which all but halted Japanese immigration to the United States. The law was
seen as a national affront not only by rabidly chauvinistic patriotic societies,
who staged popular protest demonstrations, but even by admirers of American culture and democracy. It became difficult to see American "friendship"
toward Japan as anything more than expedient.

Even more controversial was Shidehara's apparent indifference to the growing militancy of Chinese nationalism. Boycotts against Japanese goods had
erupted periodically after the May 4th incident, and Japanese cotton mills in
Shanghai became the object of prolonged and sometimes violent strikes by
Chinese workers. To make matters worse, in 1924 the Guomindang (Kuo-
mintang), which re-organized itself with help from the Soviet Union, admitted members of the Chinese Communist Party into its ranks and announced a
policy of "revolutionary diplomacy" to end imperialist rights and privileges.
In the summer of 1926, Guomindang armies under the leadership of Chiang
Kai-shek (Jiang Jieshi) launched an expedition against local warlord regimes
in central and north China to bring the country under the party's centralized
leadership. While Shidehara regarded reunification as inevitable and perhaps
even to Japan's long-term advantage, many military leaders, politicians, and

even businessmen feared that confrontation between Chinese nationalism and Japanese treaty rights was inevitable.

In 1927, Premier Tanaka Giichi, who was sympathetic to these sentiments, announced a new "positive policy" toward China. His policy, which assumed that economic expansion and cooperation with the Anglo-American powers were essential to an effective China policy, did not represent a 180-degree shift away from Shidehara diplomacy, but it differed in two important respects. First, when the Guomindong's northern expedition threatened Japanese residents in north China, the Tanaka cabinet twice dispatched Japanese troops to protect them; second and perhaps more important, Tanaka's policy viewed Japan's interests in Manchuria as fundamentally distinct from its interests in the rest of China. Even if the Guomindang established itself as the legitimate government of China, he wanted to keep Manchuria beyond its jurisdiction. While maintaining relatively friendly relations with the new Guomindang government at Nanjing (Nanking), Tanaka supported Zhang Zuolin (Chang Tso-lin), the regional war lord in Manchuria, who had long-standing ties to the Japanese military, as a foil to the nationalists. Whether this policy would have been any more successful than Shidehara's in the long run is difficult to say, since it was soon nullified by actions by the Japanese military.

ARMY DISCONTENT AND THE MANCHURIAN INCIDENT

The political fortunes of the Japanese army were in decline during the early years of party cabinets. Not only was militarism in bad repute at the end of World War I, the army had brought unpopularity upon itself by its costly and ultimately futile expedition in Siberia. Prime Minister Hara suggested that it might be time to abolish the general staff, while finance ministry officials and business leaders called for a reduction in military spending. With Russia weakened by revolution and China swept by civil war, the strategic threat on the continent had receded. Since the navy agreed to arms limitations at Washington, it seemed time to reduce the army budget as well. In 1922, the cabinet of Admiral Katō Tomosaburō, the head of the Japanese delegation to the Washington conference, began to cut military spending. The policy continued under the coalition cabinet of Katō Takaaki, which reduced the army by four divisions, or about 35,000 men, including several thousand officers. Military and naval spending, which had taken 39 percent of the national budget in 1919, dropped to around 16 percent between 1923 and 1931.

While retrenchment put a lid on increases in military spending, the army leadership seized it as an opportunity to modernize the army as a tactical force, able to use military technology that had developed on the battlefields of World War I. In the mid-1920s, War Minister Ugaki Kazushige used the savings achieved by manpower cuts to build a mechanized army that relied on motor transportation and new weapons such as tanks, machine guns, long-range artillery, and airplanes. To strengthen the civilian constituency for the army and to provide employment for cashiered officers, Ugaki also introduced military training into the middle schools and organized local army reserve associations among factory workers as well as rural villagers. By the late 1920s, as a result of Ugaki's modernization program, the army was not only better equipped, it was more closely linked with the mass of the population.

Military modernization was the work of a new generation of army leaders who embraced the new strategic doctrine of "total war." The fighting in Europe during World War I made it clear that modern wars were won on the home front as well as on the battle front. Without a total mobilization of the civilian population and more crucially, a strong and autonomous industrial base, victory would be difficult. General Ugaki and his gifted lieutenant, Nagata Tetsuzan, believed that the temporary peace of the 1920s should be used to prepare the country, internally and externally, for a global conflict that was sure to come in the long run. The army general staff began preparing national defense mobilization plans that contemplated building up military-related industries and stockpiling strategic materials.

The new strategic doctrine intensified army interest in Manchuria, the three northeastern provinces of China, which occupied a critical geopolitical position as a buffer separating China from the Soviet Union. The region was rich with industrial raw materials such as iron ore, coal, and oil shale, and its vast expanses of uncultivated land were open to development. If Japan wanted to create a self-supplying, self-sufficient economic sphere in preparation for total war it would need these resources to fuel the heavy industrial sector at home; and if Japan wanted to relieve "excess population" at home, it would have to send Japanese emigrants to this new frontier where they could cultivate land and grow crops to augment the nation's food supply. These views found support as well among the Japanese community settled in the Kwantung territory and in the South Manchuria Railway zone.

As Guomindang armies moved north, ever closer to Manchuria, officers in the Kwantung army, the Japanese garrison force in the region, concluded the time had come for decisive action. They hoped to keep Manchuria out of Chinese hands, but unlike the politicians at home they were willing to use military force to do so. In June 1928, Kwantung army conspirators engineered the assassination of the Manchurian warlord Zhang Zuolin by blowing up his personal railroad car as it passed through Shenyang (Mukden). The Kwantung army claimed the Chinese were responsible for Zhang's death in hope of provoking a Japanese occupation of Manchuria, but an appalled Prime Minister Tanaka, who knew that Japanese officers were responsible, refused to take advantage of the assassination. The plot was covered up, however, and the plotters received only light punishment by the army authorities. Far from strengthening Japan's position in Manchuria, the incident pushed the assassinated warlord's son and successor, Zhang Xueliang (Chang Hsueh-liang), into closer ties with the Guomindong.

A sense of alarm within the army deepened as the country's persistent economic troubles finally reached crisis proportions in 1929. The Hamaguchi government, which had decided to shake up the economy by a thoroughgoing deflationary policy, launched a program of severe budget cutbacks, "rationalization" of heavy industry, and a return to the gold standard to increase foreign confidence in Japan. While the government anticipated that a drop in prices and employment would result from this policy, it did not foresee the crash of the New York stock market in October. As the effects of the crash rippled through the world economy, the world market on which the Japanese economy had become so dependent, shrank dramatically. The unfortunate convergence of domestic retrenchment and world depression immediately plunged Japan into hard times. Large manufacturers cut production, reduced wages, and laid off workers in large numbers. The number of strikes spiked upward. The impact of the depression on small-scale enterprise and on the rural population was even more serious. A sharp drop in employment in the textile industry flooded the villages with returning workers; the rice price index (1926 = 100) dropped to 67.7 by late 1930, and 49.2 in late 1931; silk prices fell equally drastically; and a serious crop failure in northeastern Japan cut the harvest to 50 to 70 percent below normal. The condition of much of the population was summed up by the comment of one wholesale dealer in Kyoto: "We have grown accustomed to falling prices. We sell an item of ¥100 at ¥80 so that we can eat. . . . We are nothing but a group of hungry demons."[3]

Neither the Hamaguchi government nor its predecessors were totally responsible for this economic disaster, but they did little to alleviate its consequences. Although civilian bureaucrats bailed out failing business firms with easy credit or encouraged manufacturers to increase productivity by "rationalizing" their work forces, they did little to relieve the hardships of the peasant, the working man, or the small entrepreneur. Not surprisingly, blame for social distress and economic chaos fell on the country's civilian leadership. At the same time, civilian intrusion on the constitutional prerogatives of the naval high command riled elements in the military who were already alarmed at the dimensions of the economic crisis.

In 1929, as a token of commitment to international peace and cooperation, the Tanaka cabinet had signed the Kellogg-Briand Pact, a grandly idealistic agreement that renounced war as an instrument of national policy and committed signatories to resolving disputes by peaceful means. This upset military leaders, but to make matters worse, the Hamaguchi cabinet agreed to new naval arms limitations at the London Naval Conference of 1930. Rejecting the advice of the navy general staff, the Japanese delegation accepted a 10:10:6 ratio with Great Britain and the United States in light cruiser strength and parity in the tonnage of submarines. While the agreement did not seriously diminish Japanese naval strength, the naval high command was

Children chewing on *daikon* radishes to fill their stomachs during a crop failure in Iwate prefecture in northeastern Honshu in 1934.

incensed that the cabinet had ignored its advice. The naval chief of staff charged that the civilian cabinet had violated its right of direct access to the throne, and for purely partisan reasons the opposition party, the Seiyūkai, took up the cry in the Diet. Prime Minister Hamaguchi counter-argued that the cabinet had the right to conclude treaties after consulting the military authorities in proper fashion, and after a bitter struggle, he secured Privy Council approval.

Angered by the government's political victory and concerned about the deteriorating situation in Manchuria, field grade officers in the Kwantung army, working in concert with members of the general staff, had already begun tactical planning for a military seizure of the region. The economic crisis linked these plans with schemes for a military coup d'état at home. In March 1931, hoping to bring about "national reconstruction," a group of staff officers in Tokyo plotted an army revolt to replace civilian political leadership with a military dictatorship under the leadership of General Ugaki to deal with the domestic crisis and threats to national security. Ultimately, the plan was thwarted by the opposition from the top army leadership, including Ugaki, who refused to become involved, but the incident was hushed up and the conspirators went unpunished.

Plans for the Manchurian takeover moved ahead, however. On the evening of September 18, 1931, officers from the Kwantung army garrison at

Shenyang dynamited a few feet of the South Manchuria Railway on the outskirts of the city. Claiming that the explosion was the work of Chinese saboteurs, the Kwantung army declared a state of emergency. Japanese troops seized control of Shenyang, and within a few weeks the Kwantung army, with the tacit consent of the general staff and strengthened by the dispatch of a division from the army in Korea, had occupied most of south Manchuria as a "defensive measure." In Tokyo, the Wakatsuki cabinet, with Shidehara as foreign minister, struggled to contain the hostilities but was powerless to reverse the *fait accompli*. The war minister, as well as members of the general staff, kept assuring the civilian leaders that military action in Manchuria would be limited in scope. By the time it became clear that this was not the case, it was too late for the government to act without loss of face.

Not only were many civilian politicians, including Home Minister Adachi Kenzō, sympathetic to an aggressive policy in Manchuria but the press praised the Kwantung Army's decisiveness. Even if the cabinet had not been divided against itself, the Kwantung army was determined to push ahead. As one officer remarked to the Japanese consul at Shenyang, if the civilian government objected to its policies, the Kwantung army was prepared to secede from Japan. Perhaps decisive international action might have blocked Japanese military expansion in Manchuria, but no foreign power, including the Chinese, did more than make outraged statements. The Guomindong government in Nanjing did not even send troops to the Manchurian border in a show of force. Instead, it encouraged a new round of boycotts against Japanese goods and appealed to the Western powers to put diplomatic pressure on Japan. The American government toyed with the idea of economic sanctions against Japan, but it was unable to persuade the British or any other country to go along. In the final analysis, the Kwantung army takeover of Manchuria faced no serious challenge either at home or abroad. Its success, however, marked the triumph of a unilateralist foreign policy that was to alter Japan's relations with the outside world radically and to lead eventually to "total war."

ENDNOTES

1. Tagore is quoted in D. MacKenzie Brown, *The Nationalist Movement: Indian Political Thought from Ranade to Bhave* (Berkeley: University of California Press, 1970), 9.

2. Yoshino is quoted in *What Japan Thinks,* ed. Karl Kiyoshi Kawakami (New York: Macmillan, 1921), 88.

3. Quoted in Takahashi Kamekichi, *Taishō Shōwa zaikai hendōshi* (Tokyo: Tōyō keizai shimpōsha, 1954), 1179–1180.

13

Militarism and War

The Manchurian incident not only overturned a decade of cooperative diplomacy, it changed the direction of domestic politics. In its wake came a deepening sense of national crisis that brought a retreat from the relative political and intellectual freedom of the 1920s and a wave of political terrorism that ended party rule. As Japanese aggression on the continent accelerated, observers at home and abroad (and many historians since) discerned a "rise of fascism" that seemed to parallel developments in Italy and Germany. While fascist ideas found support in Japan, nothing like a popular fascist movement ever came close to displacing the entrenched political elite or overturning the social status quo from below. Instead, the country was reorganized from above into a "national defense state" devoted to preparation for war. The growing external crisis created a sense that Japan's very survival depended on doing so. It would probably be accurate to speak of a "rise of militarism" during the 1930s, but it was a militarism in the broadest sense, confined not simply to the military services but infiltrating every corner of society and often finding its most enthusiastic support among civilians.

THE SHIFT TO THE RIGHT

News of the Manchurian incident heartened a population plunged into anxiety and uncertainty over the future by the onset of the depression. The major urban newspapers, competing for circulation, dispatched special correspondents and photography teams to the continent to report on the triumphant advance of the Kwantung Army, and government-operated NHK radio broadcasts updated the public with regular news programs and occasional news flashes from the front. The image of Manchuria as a new economic "lifeline" rich in land, resources, and opportunity probably kindled as much public enthusiasm as the military's triumphs in the field. Most Japanese, after all, were facing hard times. Collapsing farm income, rising debt, and food shortages created widespread rural desperation, and in the cities blue collar workers and university graduates alike faced unemployment. It is little wonder that many held high hopes that "defense of the lifeline" would improve their own lot in life.

The crisis in Manchuria provided fertile ground for a resurgence of chauvinistic nationalism and a reflorescence of traditionalistic values. Conservative politicians and officials, with enthusiastic backing from the army, mobilized the school system to orchestrate a revival of "Japanese spirit" centering on devotion to the emperor and the *kokutai*. While the schools had always promoted patriotism, nationalism in the classroom intensified during the early 1930s. Elementary instruction put new stress on the idea of the emperor as a "living god" and the country as a "divine land," and school yard rituals honoring the "imperial photograph" became more elaborate. Textbooks included stories of anonymous heroes ready to sacrifice their lives for the country, like the "three human torpedoes," a trio of infantrymen who blew themselves up in an attack on an enemy position during fighting in China in 1932. And teachers, who represented to their pupils the authority of the state, often imposed strict classroom discipline, punishing lazy, inattentive, or impertinent students with slaps or shakings— just as army noncoms disciplined recruits.

Official efforts to revive the "Japanese spirit" were applauded by conservative right-wing groups, who feared that the country had been brought to the brink of social and moral collapse by the spread of "materialism," "hedonism," "individualism," and other corrupting ideas from the outside world. Many such groups had been active in the 1920s. For example, the *Kokuhonsha* (National Foundation Society), an "educational" association founded in 1924 by Hiranuma Kiichirō, a conservative judicial official, was organized to fight "dangerous thoughts" like democracy and combat the "decline of traditional morality." Its membership, which included leading politicians, prominent businessmen, high level officials, and even ranking generals and admirals, broadened in the early 1930s as it mounted campaigns to revive the "uniquely Japanese" virtues of loyalty to the emperor, filial piety, self-sacrifice, and duty to the state.

Local branches of the Imperial Reservists Association (*Teikoku zaigō gunjinkai*), organized in 1910 with support from the army high command, played an active role in propagating military and patriotic values at the rice roots level. Its membership, made up of ordinary farmers, workers, and shopkeepers, saw itself as a bulwark against social unrest and left-wing radicalism. In 1918, for example, local reservists joined police and other authorities to put down the rice rioters in many places, and in the succeeding decade they sometimes helped to break up strikes. (In 1923, when rumors spread that Korean immigrants were poisoning wells and spreading confusion in the wake of the Kanto earthquake, local reservists participated in massacres that killed several thousand Koreans.) As the public mood shifted to the right after 1931, the reservist associations became more active politically and more vigilant in ferreting out radicals.

By the early 1930s, right-wing conservatives aggressively defended the *kokutai* by attacking those who showed disloyalty or disrespect toward the imperial throne. In 1934–1935, for example, under the prodding of a right-wing academic, the local reservist associations took the lead in assailing the constitutional theories of Minobe Tatsukichi, a professor in the Law Faculty at Tokyo Imperial University, who argued that the emperor was an "organ of state" just like the Diet or the military or the judiciary. Although most academics, intellectuals, and ranking civil service officials regarded this theory as common sense, a coalition of right-wing organizations attacked it as an affront to the imperial throne. Insisting on "clarification of the *kokutai*," they called for official repudiation of the theory. Under heavy political pressure, Minobe was forced to resign from the House of Peers to which he had been appointed in 1932. This success emboldened more intense persecution of "un-Japanese" views, even moderately liberal ones, during the next few years.

If the conservative right wing was devoted to maintaining the status quo, the radical right wanted to change it. Between 1932 and 1936, membership in patriotic associations, national socialist political parties, chauvinist religious sects, and crank right-wing study groups rose from 300,000 to over 600,000. The authorities did little to check their growth. The radical right wing was enormously complex, fragmented into many small groups centering on a charismatic leader and his teachings. Often they were more like cults than political organizations. Fragmentation made it difficult for the radical right-wing groups to coalesce into a mass movement, but this did not lessen their effectiveness in creating an atmosphere of political fear and intimidation. While the Special Higher Police were relentless and ruthless in their surveillance and control of the left wing, the resonance of right-wing ideas with official ideology made the authorities less inclined to deal harshly with the right. Indeed, the police were often quite sympathetic to their goals.

The radical right shared with conservative right-wingers an anti-foreign outlook and hoped to cleanse Japan of "corrupting" foreign cultural and intellectual influences. But they also harbored a powerful antipathy toward the entrenched economic and political elite. While appalled by left-wing radicalism and doctrines of class conflict, they laid the blame for the spread of social unrest on business leaders, whose exploitation of workers and indifference toward their distress had encouraged the spread of radicalism. In their view, bankers, financiers, and other big business leaders were so intent on pursuing profit that they neglected their duty to state and society. At the same time, the radical right were also indignant at the incompetence, corruption, and partisan selfishness of civilian political leaders, who pandered to special in-terests while callously neglecting the nation's fundamental problems. They feared that as the entrenched elites went their self-serving ways, the country was going to rack and ruin. Government officials summarized the views of one right-wing activist group as follows:

> The political parties, the zaibatsu and a small privileged group attached to the rul-ing classes . . . pursue their own egotistic interests and desires, to the neglect of na-tional defence and to the confusion of government. As a result national dignity is lost abroad, while at home the morale of the people collapses; the villages are ex-hausted, and medium and small industry and commerce have been driven to the wall.[1]

Interestingly, many left-wing activists, sympathetic to this kind of radical so-cial critique, formed alliances with right-wing elements or even "converted" to the right themselves.

The right-wing radicals, however, were divided not only organizationally but in their vision of Japan's future. Some, like Gondō Seikyō, were agrarian romantics violently hostile to the "Prussian" statism adopted by the Meiji leaders. Their model of the good society was the village community, a reservoir of traditional values and a bulwark of social order. They hoped to revive the countryside through decentralization of political power, local economic self-sufficiency, and a general redress of the imbalance between city and country. But for others, it was the state not the village community that needed strength-ening. Kita Ikki, an influential national socialist thinker, preached a highly cen-tralized form of state socialism aimed at mobilizing the energies and strength of the nation by tight authoritarian controls over all aspects of society, politics, and the economy. His goal was a holistic society, free from class conflict and united under direct imperial rule, capable of liberating Japan's "700 million brothers in Asia" from the bonds of colonial rule. Kita's state-socialist ideas gained currency among disgruntled army officers convinced of the need to pre-pare for "total war" as well as among reform-minded civilian activists who rejected left-wing ideas. Many right-wing tracts blended both agrarian roman-ticism and nationalist socialism in glassy-eyed rhetoric.

For all their talk about popular economic distress, the radical right was more concerned with national strength than with social justice. Perhaps that was one reason why the radical right never attempted to organize popular mass movements but opted instead for terrorist tactics. Their penchant for violent action was fostered by a mystique of personal heroism and a lust for self-glorification, paradoxically fed by the idea of selfless personal devotion to nation and emperor. But it also reflected a feeling that terrorism was more likely to produce change than was the tedious job of organizing mass sup-port. The lackluster efforts of the proletarian parties demonstrated that the entrenched political parties held a firm grip on the electorate and that the mass of rural population still responded to the influence of local political bosses. With the entrenched elite in firm control of the police, the courts, and other instruments of state power, illegal tactics were the best way to fight them. For right-wing radicals, assassination or political coups offered the best hope of bringing about "national reconstruction."

POLITICAL TERROR AND ARMY RADICALISM

A surge of terrorist activity that one foreign journalist called "government by assassination" began in November 1930, when a young right-wing fanatic gunned down Premier Hamaguchi to protest the London Naval Treaty. Terrorism escalated with mid-level army officers' plans for coups d'état, first in March 1931, as a prelude to the Manchurian incident, and then again in October. These plots aborted largely because prominent army leaders like General Ugaki refused to go along, but they succeeded in setting the stage for bolder action by the so-called young officers movement, a loose group of junior army and navy officers, many of whom were familiar with left-wing as well as radical right-wing ideas. Appalled at the poor physical condition of many rural recruits, the young officers were angered at the widespread hardship in the countryside. But they were also alarmed by the crisis created by the Manchurian incident. Fearing that Japan was facing its greatest test since the *bakumatsu* period, they called for a "Shōwa Restoration" to rescue the emperor from his circle of "evil advisors." Indeed, they saw themselves as heirs to the loyalist movement of the 1850s and 1860s, ready to rescue the country from a corrupt and incompetent leadership in the face of "threat from without" and "troubles within."

By adopting terrorist "direct action," the young officers hoped to bring down the existing regime. While they were not always clear about what might follow, they hoped that terrorism would pave the way for a military takeover of the government. "We thought about destruction first," one radical officer later confessed. "We never considered taking on the duty of construction. We foresaw, however, that once the destruction was accomplished someone would take charge of the construction for us."[2] In early 1932, a group of naval officers struck an alliance with Inoue Nisshō, leader of the Blood Pledge Corps (Ketsumeidan), a right-wing civilian group, to launch a "Shōwa Restoration" by assassinating prominent business and political leaders. They succeeded in murdering Inoue Junnosuke, a former finance minister whose fiscal policies had intensified the impact of the world depression, and Dan Takuma, director of the Mitsui zaibatsu. Backed by other radical rightist groups, the plotters mounted a major terrorist attack against the government on May 15, when a band of assassins barged into Prime Minister Inukai Tsuyoshi's official residence and cut him down with a submachine gun. Associated gangs attacked the headquarters of the Seiyūkai and the Mitsubishi Bank and disabled several power stations in Tokyo. After surrendering to the military police, the conspirators were tried in military courts in 1933.

Under pressure from the military, newspaper coverage of the trial stressed the selfless patriotism of the radical young officers and their civilian allies. War Minister Araki Sadao publicly praised them as "pure and naive young men" who had acted not for fame or personal gain but out of "the sincere belief that they were [acting] for the benefit of Imperial Japan."[3] These views by no means represented the rest of the political elite. Prince Saionji, the last surviving genrō, felt that the parties had lost credibility in domestic and foreign policy, but he was appalled by the military insubordination in Manchuria and the spread of political terrorism. Acting on the advice of the *jūshin* ("senior officials"), an informal group of court officials and former cabinet ministers, Saionji decided the best course of action would be to replace party cabinets with nonpartisan "national unity" cabinets based on coalitions among political party leaders, ranking civilian bureaucrats, and the military services. Two such cabinets, led by retired admirals, the first under Saitō Makoto, and the second under Okada Keisuke, governed Japan for the next four years.

While the army had a significantly larger voice in both "national unity" cabinets, the army high command was rent by factional fighting. On one side ranged the generals of the Imperial Way Faction (*Kōdōha*), led by War Minister Araki, who made himself popular with the radical young officers by his sombre pronouncements about the efficacy of the "Japanese spirit" in solving the country's ills. Placing relatively little importance on long-term economic planning and national mobilization, the Imperial Way generals thought traditional infantry tactics and "spiritual mobilization" were sufficient preparation for war. Opposing them was a powerful faction in the General Staff, who were upset by the war minister's indulgence of the radical officers, disliked his spouting of right-wing rhetoric, and feared that the Imperial Way generals did not understand modern warfare. Behind the scenes, the anti-Imperial Way generals undermined the influence of General Araki and engineered his resignation as war minister. In August 1935, a radical officer struck back by assassinating Nagata Tetsuzan, a central figure in the anti-Imperial Way faction, in his war ministry office.

Frustrated by the failure of earlier military plots, radical young officers made a last desperate effort to bring about a "Shōwa Restoration" in early 1936. On February 26, elements in the First Division at Tokyo led by radical young officers staged a major military insurrection. Nearly fifteen hundred troops seized the government nerve center in Tokyo, while assassination bands set out to murder the prime minister, key cabinet ministers, key imperial court officials, several ranking army leaders, and Prince Saionji, the last genrō. The rebels announced their intention to begin national renovation by removing "traitors and evil-doers surrounding the Throne." The army's leaders, some of whom sensed an opportunity to take over the government, initially took little action to put down this unprecedented insurrection. But the emperor was aghast at this major breach of army discipline, and the navy, incensed by assassination attempts on senior admirals like Prime Minister Okada, former Prime Minister Saitō, and Grand Chamberlain Suzuki, moved warships into Tokyo Bay with their guns trained on the rebel positions. The insurrection quickly collapsed, the troops returned to their barracks, and the leaders of the rebellion (as well as Kita Ikki) were summarily executed by army firing squads.

Although the radical officers failed to achieve their goal, the terrorism of the early 1930s had a significant political impact. Civilian politicians and bureaucrats were severely shaken by the officer plots. Tainted by failure to control public discontent, the political parties declined sharply in influence. In the face of right-wing terrorism the parties found it increasingly difficult to recruit business or bureaucratic support. Fewer party politicians were invited to join cabinets after 1932, and fewer ambitious high officials showed an interest in joining the political parties. In the wake of the May 15th incident, the zaibatsu— first Mitsui, then Mitsubishi— gradually withdrew financial support from the parties, and in late 1932 the Saitō government ended the patronage power of the parties by trimming the power of the home minister to appoint prefectural governors and local police officials. Party politicians continued to lobby for local interests, but it was clear that they could do little to reverse their decline. Having risen to power through compromise, the parties now found themselves squeezed by those who sought to compromise with the army instead.

After the February 26 incident, the army leadership attempted to restore discipline and put an end to factionalism within its ranks. A clean-up campaign weeded out radical junior officers and forced their high-ranking sympathizers into inactive status. To exclude the purged generals from cabinet posts, the government restored the requirement that the war minister be on active status, which gave the army the same veto power over the formation of cabinets that it had enjoyed until 1913. Quite apart from this leverage, the army spoke with a new authority born of the deepening military commitment in China. With the future direction of Japan's continental policies still unresolved, military opinion was bound to carry greater weight. Indeed, as many observed, the army was gradually becoming the driving force in politics.

THE CHINA QUAGMIRE

Although the Kwantung Army would have preferred to turn Manchuria into a Japanese colony, the government in Tokyo decided to pay lip service to the principle of "national self-determination." In 1932, the "independent state" of Manchukuo headed by Puyi (P'u-yi), the last emperor of the Qing dynasty, was established under Japanese military auspices. But the Western powers paid little attention to this gesture. Not only did they refuse to give diplomatic recognition to Manchukuo, the League of Nations condemned Japan as an aggressor. In February 1933, the Tokyo government responded by having Matsuoka Yōsuke, the Japanese delegate to the League Assembly, dramatically walk out in protest, and a month later announced its decision to withdraw from the League altogether. Criticism from abroad only bolstered commitment to continental expansion and created an anti-Western mood. Unfurling the banner of Pan-Asianism, government leaders spoke of Japan as a champion of "Asia for the Asians," committed to defending the region against political and military interference from the outside.

This confident rhetoric masked enormous confusion and uncertainty at the high echelons in Tokyo. Aside from support for the maintenance of Manchukuo in the face of Western hostility, no clear consensus existed on national goals. When fighting broke out between Chinese and Japanese forces at Shanghai in January 1932, for example, some army leaders urged expansion of military operations into other parts of China, but they found little support for the idea. The finance ministry objected that new military operations would place an unbearable strain on the economy; the navy high command, as well as the foreign ministry, feared that it would provoke hostilities with the British and the Americans; and the Imperial Way generals thought it would deflect energies from preparation for conflict with the Soviet Union. This lack of consensus, complicated by army factional struggles and a rapid overturn of cabinets, kept the Tokyo government from making any precipitous foreign policy moves.

By contrast, the Kwantung Army, backed by sympathizers in the army high command, continued to nibble away at Chinese territory, making national policy by default. Claiming the military necessity of defending Manchukuo's borders, Kwantung Army forces moved into Rehe (Jehol) in the winter of 1933. In April, the Japanese signed the Tanggu (Tangku) truce agreement with the Chinese government, which extended the Japanese area of occupation to the Great Wall and established a demilitarized zone in north China around Peking. On the move again in 1935, the Kwantung Army used military pressure and negotiation to expel Guomindang troops from Hebei (Hopei) province as well. Encouraged by their successes, in the fall of 1935 local Japanese commanders, hoping to create a buffer zone between Manchukuo and the rest of China, encouraged local Guomindang generals to launch "independence movements." The goal of this "North China autonomy movement" was to keep the Chinese divided and weak while linking the resources of north China to the Manchurian economy.

This creeping aggression met with little Chinese resistance. Chiang Kai-shek (Jiang Jie-shi), well aware of Japanese military superiority, focused his energies on building a stable central regime at Nanjing. The Guomindang's main preoccupation in the early 1930s was to eradicate Chinese Communist bases in south China. Extermination campaigns against the Communists left no leeway for military confrontation with the Japanese. But when the Communists fled to Yan'an (Yenan) in north China in 1934–1935, mounting student protests against Japanese aggression coupled with pressures from his generals pushed Chiang toward a reversal of priorities. In December 1936, after Chiang was forcibly detained in Xi'an (Sian) by Zhang Xue-liang (Chang Hsueh-liang), former warlord in Manchuria, he finally agreed to cooperate with the Communists in an anti-Japanese united front. This shift in policy, and the intensification of anti-Japanese nationalism that it reflected, substantially increased the likelihood of a major Sino-Japanese confrontation.

The leaders of the Japanese army, who were anxious to consolidate the Japanese position in north China, in the meantime pressed for more money and resources, but senior civilian bureaucrats, party leaders, and businessmen, who resented the army's growing influence, tried to thwart further army domination of the state apparatus. In late 1936, the Diet opposed massive increases in the military budget proposed by the army-backed Hirota cabinet. When army leaders publicly questioned the patriotism of the political parties, a Seiyūkai Diet member offered to commit ritual suicide if the war minister could substantiate the charge—and challenged him to do likewise if he could not. The *jūshin* attempted to patch over this acrimonious and mutual distrust by recommending Prince Konoe Fumimaro, a protégé of Saionji, to the prime ministership. Personally aloof, but well connected in all political camps and known as a critic of "Anglo-American imperialism," Konoe seemed to be the only political figure able to bring the national leadership together. Backed by a "national unity" cabinet in June 1937, he was eager to build a "national defense state" in preparation for a wider conflict on the continent.

When war finally came, it caught the newly formed Konoe cabinet almost by surprise. On July 7, 1937, a minor skirmish occurred at Marco Polo Bridge (Luguoqiao) near Beijing between Chinese troops and Japanese troops stationed under a 1900 agreement. The local commanders succeeded in arranging a truce, but the Nanjing government sent new troops into the area to demonstrate its determination to stand up to the Japanese. The Konoe government, no less concerned to make a show of strength, replied in kind with the dispatch of forces from Japan. When Chinese bombers attacked the Japanese settlement in Shanghai in August 1937, a full-scale undeclared war was underway in north China. The better-armed and better-trained Japanese forces quickly advanced southward into the Yangzi (Yangtze) Valley. Exultant Japanese field commanders, meeting little effective resistance, sent back reports of victory after victory and confidently predicted that Chiang could be defeated in six months. By mid-December, Japanese forces entered the Guomindang capital at Nanjing, where they embarked on a rampage of killing, raping, and looting that lasted several weeks. According to one postwar estimate, Japanese troops raped 20,000 women, young and old, killed 42,000 civilians, including women and children, within the city, and killed another 100,000 civilians and prisoners of war in the vicinity. While these

Wire service photograph showing a Japanese sentry standing guard on the wall of a captured Chinese city in 1938.

massive atrocities were later blamed on a breakdown in army discipline, it is clear that officers not only permitted but supervised much of the slaughter.

Although the army high command had neither long-range plans for operations in China nor extensive stockpiles of equipment and material when the fighting began, it reassured Prime Minister Konoe that each upcoming campaign would smash Chinese resistance. The government enthusiastically authorized new operations. Some general staff officers, including Ishihara Kanji, one of the planners of the Manchurian incident, opposed this reckless expansion into south China. Skeptical of the view that China would collapse under a series of punishing blows, they feared that Japan was not prepared economically and industrially for a full-scale war and that Japanese forces would be swallowed up in the vast territorial expanse of China. If operations in China were not quickly brought to an end, they argued, it would be difficult to prepare for a possible clash with the Soviet Union, which they saw as the chief enemy. Rather than continuing to fight Chiang's armies, Ishihara urged that no further military advances be made, that the status quo be maintained in north China, and that peace negotiations be opened with the Guomindang.

Early military successes in China, especially the fall of Nanjing in December 1937, only made the Konoe government more inflexible. In January 1938, after an unsuccessful diplomatic attempt to secure Chinese recognition of

Manchukuo and the demilitarization of north China, Prime Minister Konoe burned his diplomatic bridges by announcing unwillingness to negotiate further with Chiang and expressing hopes for the emergence of a new regime "friendly" to Japan. In effect, this announcement committed Japan to military subjugation of Chinese resistance. The decision proved disastrous. The Guomindang government, adopted a scorched earth policy, burning towns and cities and destroying Yellow River dikes to impede the Japanese advance with flood water. Chiang Kai-shek, hoping to defeat the Japanese by a war of attrition, retreated to the interior city of Chongqing (Chungking) beyond the easy reach of Japanese land forces. While the Japanese continued to win battles, capturing the great industrial-commercial complex at Wuhan in October 1938, they lacked the manpower, material, and financial resources to defeat the Chinese decisively. By the end of the year Japan had dispatched twenty-three divisions (700,000 men) to the front in China. Another nine divisions were committed to the occupation of Manchukuo and Korea, leaving only one division in reserve at home. With manpower resources stretched to the limit, the military effort in China slowly bogged down.

By the summer of 1939, the worst fears of Ishiwara and other general staff officers had come true. After two years of hard fighting, the momentum of the Japanese offensive operations had nearly come to a halt. The Japanese controlled the main coastal cities, the area around Beijing, the Wuhan industrial complex, and most major railway lines. Every day, Japanese bombers harassed the new Guomindang capital at Chongqing, but Japanese land forces were unable to mount an offensive through daunting Yangzi River gorges. In Japanese-occupied territory local guerrilla movements, sometimes led by Guomindang elements, and sometimes by Communists, waged underground warfare against Japanese forces. And to make matters worse, in mid-1938 and again in the spring of 1939 clashes with Soviet troops on the borders of Manchukuo, which cost the Japanese nearly 20,000 casualties, renewed anxieties over the possibility of war with the Soviet Union. Despite earlier heady confidence, the Japanese forces on the continent had reached a military stalemate from which there was no simple escape.

These dismaying realities did not blunt enthusiasm at home for the war, as official pronouncements portrayed a struggle to "liberate" China from the thrall of "Anglo-American imperialism." In November 1938, Prime Minister Konoe announced his government's vision of a "New Order in East Asia," based on "cooperation" among Japan, Manchukuo, and China, whose peoples shared a common interest as "have-not nations" excluded from their rightful place in the world by the Western powers. In Konoe's rhetoric, the unexpected war was transformed into a struggle to end Western domination in China, and the Japanese invaders were depicted as allies of the Chinese people in their struggle against Chiang Kai-shek, the "running dog" of the Western powers. The army's exploitative economic policies in China, its brutality toward Chinese civilians, and its ruthless pacification campaigns against

Chinese guerrillas belied this vision of a harmonious "new order." But the Japanese civilian population, who were ignorant of these realities, stood behind what seemed to be their country's high moral goals and supported the heroic sacrifices of its fighting men. As in 1894 and 1905, war renewed a sense of national purpose.

ECONOMIC RECOVERY

The outbreak of the China War accelerated plans for massive economic mobilization. The country was already well on the road to economic recovery. The groundwork had been laid during the early 1930s by the policies of Finance Minister Takahashi Korekiyo, a "premature Keynesian" who believed that active public spending was needed to stimulate the economy. His approach to reviving the economy was straightforward: first, a de facto devaluation of the yen reduced the price of Japanese goods, making them more competitive in the world market; second, cutting the interest rate nearly in half stimulated private investment in the economy; and finally, government spending was increased on military procurements as well as on public works projects, particularly in the rural areas, to put cash in the hands of the farm population. By 1936, Japan was enjoying a mild prosperity. An expanding military budget, which swelled from ¥450 million in 1931 to ¥1.4 billion in 1937, created new jobs, promised new profits for both large-scale industry and small-scale entrepreneurs, and guaranteed a market for food produced by the farm population. It was not difficult for ordinary working people to associate foreign adventure with good times. Even though Japanese troops were dying, the civilian population had yet to suffer the adverse consequences of war.

During the early 1930s, however, the depression had eroded public confidence in a market economy. Demands for increased government intervention and control over the economy gained wide currency. The strongest support for economic reorganization came from the army, which wanted to create a "national defense state" based on central planning, state control over industrial production, and perhaps nationalization of key industries. Staff officers argued that an economy based on pursuit of private profit could not mobilize resources efficiently and that uncontrolled capitalism undermined the country's social and economic woes. As a 1936 army pamphlet put it, "We fear that the intensification of free competition will foment . . . [the] concept of class conflict."[4] A country riven by social divisions would be unable to defend itself against a hostile outside world, and an economy left in the hands of the capitalists would remain strategically weak.

Civilian officials, intellectuals, and politicians favored a controlled economy for quite different reasons. For one thing, many doubted that the world economy would ever return to the free trade structure that had prevailed down through the 1920s. Tariff and trade barriers were rising everywhere, as the advanced industrialized economies attempted to protect themselves—and their colonial possessions—from outside competition. In a world of closed economic blocs, the survival of Japan seemed to require not only privileged access to the markets and resources of Asia but increased government economic management. Some economists, very much under the influence of Marxist theory, also suggested that basic structural changes in the economy were undermining its vitality. Under a free enterprise system, they argued, monopolistic firms like the zaibatsu could accumulate enormous profits without technological innovation or increased efficiency. Unless the government intervened, the economy was headed toward stagnation.

By the mid-1930s, "renovationist bureaucrats," taking advantage of growing support for economic controls, pushed for the adoption of an "industrial policy" that targeted certain industries for government support. Not surprisingly, nearly all were "high tech" industries crucial to military mobilization: automobiles, machine tools, synthetic oils, aluminum and light metals, and organic chemicals. The government offered leading firms in these industries tax breaks, subsidies, compensation for business losses, and other benefits in return for increased government controls. Targeted firms were required to submit annual plans to government officials, and they had to give priority to government interests. The automobile industry, for example, was ordered to manufacture trucks and military vehicles rather than private automobiles and to sell most of its output to the government. This "industrial policy" program encouraged the emergence of the so-called new zaibatsu, large industrial conglomerates in technologically advanced industries founded by entrepreneurs with technical backgrounds who catered heavily to the needs of the military effort.

The best known "new zaibatsu" was the Japan Industrial Company (or Nissan, as it later became known). The conglomerate was started by Aikawa Yoshitsuke, an engineering graduate of Tokyo Imperial University, who had studied in the United States. After taking over a mining company that had been run by his brother-in-law, Kuhara Fusanosuke, who entered politics, Aikawa turned it into a holding company that bought dozens of faltering companies during the early 1930s and dispatched experienced management teams to straighten them out. Taking advantage of the government's policy of encouraging domestic automotive production, he founded the Nissan Motor Company, which manufactured a small passenger car, the Datsun, but concentrated mainly on military contracts. In 1937, Aikawa moved his operations to Manchukuo, where he set up the Manchuria Heavy Industry Company, a conglomerate to develop the chemical and heavy industry sector there.

The army's drive to build a "national defense state" met with considerable political opposition. Although the Diet readily approved an increased military budget, party leaders, who were suspicious of army influence, opposed plans to impose massive administrative controls over the economy. Entrenched bureaucrats feared that new economic machinery might undercut the powers of existing ministries, and old-line big business leaders opposed any government constraints on profits or business decisions. But the Konoe cabinet, capitalizing on the sense of urgency created by the outbreak of war in China, proposed a plan for centralized economic controls. In late 1937, a new Cabinet Planning Agency (Kikakuin), staffed with "renovationist bureaucrats" intent on eliminating the "inefficiencies" of a market economy, drafted an economic mobilization law giving the government regulatory powers over everything from foreign trade to labor organization.

The left-wing parties, who saw the draft bill as a first step toward social reconstruction, supported it, but to big business leaders it smacked of state socialism. The moderate conservative party leaders attacked it as unconstitutional. Under heavy army pressure, the Diet finally passed a National Mobilization Law, but only after the Konoe cabinet had diluted the army's plans for a "national defense state" in significant ways. Economic regulations were to be screened by a council representing not only the military but also political parties, businessmen, and the bureaucracy. Proposed provisions for government regulation of private profits were struck from the law. Controls over foreign exchange, the import of raw materials, and the manufacture of consumer goods were soon phased in, but big business firms maintained their freedom to make basic business decisions.

The business community was more cooperative with government plans to curb labor unrest during the national emergency. In order to promote "industrial harmony" and the "unity of labor and capital," in 1938 the government established factory councils that encouraged employer and worker representatives to avoid strikes and other confrontations in the workplace. In the summer of 1940, despite strong protests from labor activists, all unions and other worker organizations were dissolved. In their place, officially sponsored Industrial State Service Associations (*Sampō*) were gradually established in all large factories, mills, and plants. The ostensible purpose of these associations was to promote the idea of "the enterprise as a family." By reducing status distinctions, managers and workers were treated as "equal" members of the firm. But it was clear that the associations aimed increasing output and restoring managerial control rather than protecting worker welfare. Indeed, workers were organized into military-style units, marched off to the workplace in orderly ranks, and compelled to attend fire drills, air raid drills, and study groups on the "Japanese spirit."

THE "NEW ORDER" MOVEMENT

Intensification of hostilities in China spurred political schemes to create a totalitarian-style structure in Japan like those in Fascist Italy or Nazi Germany, where dictators backed by a popularly based mass movement created a fa-cade of national political unity. No such structure had emerged sponta-neously in Japan, nor was it likely to. For one thing, the public cult of imperial loyalty, designed by the Meiji leadership to build popular support for the new constitutional state, thwarted the emergence of a charismatic popular leader. The reigning emperor, Hirohito, was wrapped in an aura of sacredness that the Meiji emperor had never enjoyed, and patriotic indoctri-nation had made the notion of "dying for the emperor" commonplace to a population whose grandfathers had hardly known who the emperor was. Mounted on his white horse in full military regalia, the emperor was no longer a symbol of "civilization and enlightenment" but of an exclusivist na-tionalism. No charismatic political leader could hope to compete for popu-larity with the imperial throne. Neither was there a strong social base for a fascist mass movement. In contrast to the highly urbanized societies in Eu-rope, where feelings of rootlessness or abandonment propelled many recruits into such movements, most Japanese still lived in small rural villages or ur-ban neighborhoods, where family, kinship, and community networks re-mained strong. Even in the depths of the depression, they could rely on these networks for psychological and material support.

The engineering of a totalitarian structure from above was in part a re-sponse to the army's demands for a "national defense state" and in part a re-sponse to the instability that plagued national leadership despite the public's near unanimity behind the war effort. To rally all-out public support for the war effort in China, in 1937 the Konoe cabinet launched a "National Spiri-tual Mobilization Movement," but it did little more than propagate well-worn patriotic slogans and mount public campaigns to promote savings or to conserve gas and electricity. In the meantime, political in-fighting among the political elites persisted. During the three years after the Marco Polo Bridge incident, the country went through four prime ministers and five cabinets. To end this instability, Prince Konoe, who had juggled the conflicting demands of the military, the civilian bureaucracy, and the parties during his two years as prime minister, called for a "new political order" to restore harmony among the national leadership and mobilize the people behind them as he prepared to assume office again in June 1940.

The creation of a "new political order," however, was confounded by competing conceptions of what it should be. Leaders of the Seiyūkai and the Minseitō, the two main political parties, wanted to merge into a strong uni-fied party with an absolute Diet majority. Their goal was to resist army pres-sure and regain lost political clout. Radical civilian politicians, whether members of the proletarian parties or the radical right, looked to European fascist models. Their vision of a "new political order" was a national mass party built from the bottom up and resting on local popular organizations. Army leaders, disgusted with the disruptive and "unpatriotic" tactics of party politicians, also wanted a one-party state that would mobilize the popular support for the war effort and facilitate the creation of a "national defense state." Finally, home ministry officials, long resentful of party influence over local leaders, wanted to strengthen their control over local village, town, and city communities. In sum, everyone proposed a "new political order" that would enhance their own influence.

What finally emerged from the debate was the Imperial Rule Assistance Association (IRAA), a national organization set up in the fall of 1940 to provide a popular base for the Konoe cabinet. It was loosely conceived on the model of a totalitarian "one party state," but from the beginning the army, the parties, and civil bureaucrats competed for control. Conservative elements, fearing that the IRAA would infringe imperial prerogatives, attacked it as an unconstitutional "bakufu-like structure" that stood between the emperor and the people, and right-wing groups called it a "lair for communists." By early 1941, Konoe, tired of the political squabbling, abandoned any attempt at fundamental political reform and permitted a bureaucratic takeover of the "new political order." Far from resembling a totalitarian mass party, the IRAA became an unwieldy sprawling national organization that meshed with the existing bureaucratic structure.

The basic function of the IRAA was to increase popular identification with the state and expedite the downward flow of official orders. The prime minister served as its ex officio president and prefectural governors headed its local branches. Ordinary Japanese participated either as members of a functional or professional association (for example, the Patriotic Women's Association, the Imperial Rule Assistance Youth League, the Agriculturalists' Patriotic Association, or the Writers' Patriotic Association) or as members of local neighborhood associations (*tonarigumi*). These neighborhood associations, set up in 1938 to by-pass local political party machines, were groups of ten or so households that participated in the distribution of ration cards, campaigns to gather scrap, and other mundane activities. In the final analysis, the IRAA did little more than serve as an arm of the home ministry.

The failure to establish a totalitarian structure demonstrated how difficult it was to dislodge the existing political elite. The leaders who presided over Japan's slow descent into militarism represented no radical break from those who had led the country since the turn of the century. They were an uneasy coalition of the brightest and the best in the civil bureaucracy, the military hierarchy, the political parties, and the business world, who had risen through the regular channels of elite recruitment and regarded themselves as servants of the nation. No radical right-wing violence was able to dislodge them, nor did any popular fascist movement loosen their grip on politics. Rallying the population behind the emperor, and hiding behind a facade of "national unity," this entrenched elite not only tightened state power over the population but clung to an expansionist policy that ultimately led to national disaster.

ENDNOTES

1. Quoted in Masao Maruyama, *Thought and Behaviour in Modern Japan* (New York: Oxford University Press, 1963), 45.

2. Quoted in Takahashi Masae, *Shōwa no gunbatsu* (Tokyo: Chūō kōron sha, 1969), 163–164.

3. General Araki is quoted in Ben-Ami Shillony, *Revolt in Japan: The Young Officers and the February 26, 1936 Incident* (Princeton, N.J.: Princeton University Press, 1973), 36.

4. *Kokubō no hongi*, 1936, 52.

14

The Pacific War

Just as the defense of Manchukuo became a basic axiom of national policy after 1931, victory in China was a goal no longer questioned in public after 1938. The war on the continent had generated policy commitments that could not be gracefully repudiated. Battlefield victories shaped strategic planning; strategic planning shaped foreign policy; and foreign policy dictated domestic reform. To be sure, the cabinets of the late 1930s could have extracted Japan from the mainland by withdrawing unilaterally or by softening its demands to the Chiang government. But to propose either course of action bordered on treason. In February 1940, when a Minseitō member, Saitō Takao, suggested on the floor of the Diet that Japan simply did not have the capacity to defeat the Chinese he was expelled from his seat by an overwhelming majority vote. Far from contemplating withdrawal or a negotiated peace in China, army and navy planners were proposing an expansion of the war into Southeast Asia to crush Chinese resistance once and for all.

THE ROAD TO PEARL HARBOR

The idea of a move south gained momentum after the outbreak of war in Europe. Early German victories, culminating in the fall of France in June 1940, opened intoxicating new perspectives for the Japanese military. With France and Holland under Nazi control and England besieged by the German air force, an Axis victory in Europe seemed imminent. The European colonies in South and Southeast Asia, which lay weak and unprotected, were a tempting target for the Japanese. In late summer, the Konoe cabinet announced its intention to create a "Greater East Asia Co-Prosperity Sphere," a regional bloc

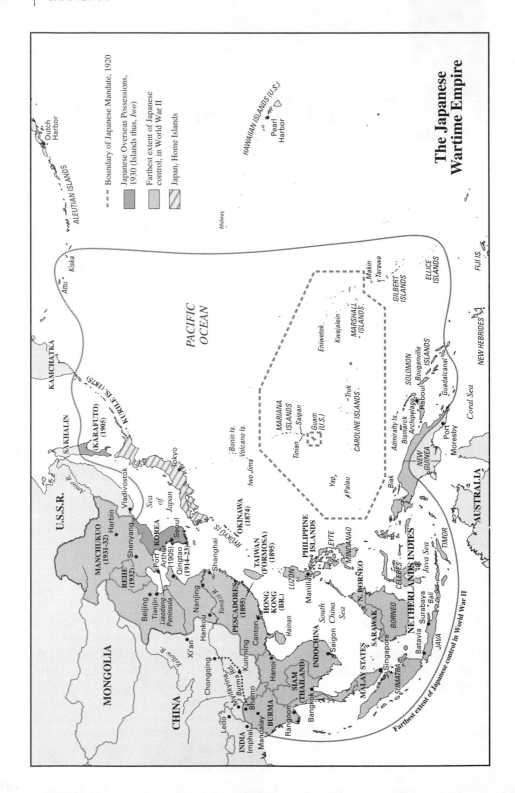

The Japanese Wartime Empire

Boundary of Japanese Mandate, 1920

Japanese Overseas Possessions, 1930 (Islands thus, *Iwo*)

Farthest extent of Japanese control, in World War II

Japan, Home Islands

centering on Japan that would include French Indochina, the Dutch East Indies, and other European colonial territories as well as Manchukuo and China. "The countries of East Asia and the regions of the South Seas are geographically close, historically, racially and economically very closely related to each other," announced Foreign Minister Arita Hachirō. "They are destined to cooperate and minister to one another's need for their common well-being and prosperity, and to promote peace and progress in their regions."[1] More an afterthought than a visionary blueprint, the Co-Prosperity Sphere was described as a self-sufficient economic bloc linking the industrial economy of Japan with the semi-developed areas like Manchukuo and north China and the colonial economies in Southeast Asia. It was a response to growing anxiety that the world was fragmenting into large economic regions under the control of the Americans, the British, the Germans, and the Soviets.

The announcement of the Greater East Asia Co-Prosperity Sphere coincided with a major shift in strategic policy. In late July 1940, after consultations with the army, the Konoe cabinet decided to strengthen ties with the Axis powers and to set up military bases in French Indochina. The army wanted a foothold in Southeast Asia as a staging area for an invasion of China from the south to cut off Chiang's supply routes, and the navy wanted it as a jumping off point to seize the rich natural resources of the European colonies—rubber, tin and oil resources—needed to sustain the war effort. After receiving the assent of the pro-Nazi Vichy government in France, Japanese troops moved into northern Indochina in September 1941. A few days later, the government signed the so-called Axis Pact, a tripartite mutual defense treaty with Germany and Italy that aimed at deterring the United States, the only major non-belligerent world power, from intervening either in the European War or the Sino-Japanese conflict.

This turn of events, which firmly wedded Japan to Axis aggression in Europe, set Japan on a collision course with the United States, where sympathy for the "brave Chinese" and support for the Chiang regime was on the rise. The Roosevelt administration, continuing the policy of its predecessor, had made clear its disapproval of Japanese aggression in China. While Japanese leaders spoke of "liberating" Asia, in his famous "quarantine speech" of October 1937 the American president spoke of stopping an "epidemic of world lawlessness." Hindered by strong isolationist sentiment in Congress and among the general public, the Roosevelt administration was unable to offer direct aid to the Chinese government. Instead, it adopted a slowly escalating program of economic sanctions to force Japan to abandon its aggression in China.

By the mid-1930s, the United States supplied nearly one-third of all Japanese imports, including goods critical to military mobilization. This made Japan vulnerable to American economic pressure. In the summer of 1938, Washington placed a voluntary "moral embargo" on shipments of aircraft, arms, and other war material to Japan; in July 1939, it abrogated its commercial treaty with Japan in anticipation of expanded economic warfare; and in 1940, the president restricted the export of aviation motor fuel, scrap iron, and steel to Japan. The American economic sanctions perplexed and irritated the Japanese leaders, who could not understand why the United States favored China, where it had only limited economic or security interests. Failing to appreciate the self-righteous idealism behind the American actions or the growing American concern that the global spread of democracy was threatened by a virulent new authoritarian nationalism, they could only conclude that the United States was moved by arrogance, a sense of racial superiority, or a selfish hypocrisy.

Although the Americans loomed as a major stumbling block to a successful military solution of the China problem, the Konoe cabinet nurtured a desperate hope that the United States might help Japan in pressuring Chiang to accept Japan's terms. In any case, it wanted the Americans to lift the economic embargo. In April 1941, Nomura Kichisaburō, a special ambassador, arrived in Washington to carry on negotiations with Secretary of State Cordell Hull. His initial proposals indicated Japanese willingness to disengage from the war in China on certain conditions: a negotiated withdrawal of Japanese troops from China; Chinese recognition of Manchukuo's independence; a merger between the Chiang government and the pro-Japanese puppet regime at Nanjing under Wang Jingwei (Wang Ch'ing-wei); and a joint Sino-Japanese anti-Soviet pact. Needless to say, these conditions would have left Japan in a hegemonic position on the continent if the hostilities ended.

From the outset, however, the Americans were as unresponsive to Japanese overtures as the Japanese were uncomprehending of American goals. For President Roosevelt and Secretary of State Cordell Hull, the China war was a simple case of "totalitarian aggression." They were not inclined to make any concessions to the Japanese at a time when Nazi armies had occupied most of western Europe and the fate of England was hanging in the balance. In response to Nomura's proposals, Hull replied that negotiations could not move forward unless Japan agreed to certain basic international principles: respect for the territorial integrity of other nations, respect for the principle of non-intervention in the affairs of other countries, respect for the principle of equality among nations, and the non-disturbance of the status quo in the Pacific except by peaceful means. Acceptance of these high-flown principles would require Japan to abandon all its de facto territorial gains since 1931. In effect, while the Japanese wanted to talk about existing realities, they found the Americans willing to talk only about international law. This did not augur well for the future of the negotiations.

In the meantime, the Konoe cabinet tried to mend fences with the Soviet Union, which the army still regarded as a major threat. The Kwantung Army's humiliating rout at the hands of Soviet troops on the Manchukuo border in the summer of 1939, however, prompted second thoughts about the wisdom of going to war with the Soviet Union. Fear of the Soviet Union abated when Stalin, to the surprise and shock of many Japanese leaders, signed a "non-aggression" pact with Hitler in August 1939, but as army leaders prepared for a move into Southeast Asia they continued to worry about the vulnerability of their northern flank. In April 1941, the two countries finally concluded a neutrality pact. It was the German invasion of the Soviet Union two months later, however, that most eased Japanese fear. With Soviet troops diverted from the Manchukuo border to the European front, the Japanese ceased to worry about another Japanese-Soviet confrontation.

Relieved of this anxiety, in July 1941 the Konoe cabinet, under pressure from the army and navy, moved troops into southern Indochina as preparation for operations against the Dutch East Indies. Faced with the new evidence of Japanese intransigence, the Roosevelt administration froze Japanese assets in the United States and imposed an embargo on oil exports to Japan. Great Britain, the British Commonwealth nations, and the government of the Dutch East Indies soon followed suit, cutting 90 percent of Japan's petroleum imports. Without oil, the Japanese war machine was bound to come to a halt in China and elsewhere within a matter of months. The government quickly denounced the oil embargo as part of an "ABCD (American-British-Chinese-Dutch) encirclement" of Japan. The Konoe cabinet was left with the hard choice of seizing the oil fields in the Dutch East Indies or abandoning its gains in China. A Japanese attack on the Dutch East Indies was certain to provoke war with the United States, a conflict that many leaders, especially the navy high command, thought would be hard to win. But the alternative of submitting to the demands of the "white imperialists" was hard to stomach.

Although the escalation of American economic warfare was intended to deter further Japanese territorial advances, it had precisely the opposite effect. The navy high command, which had urged caution and restraint in dealing with the Americans, concluded that it would be better to open hostilities quickly before the country's precious oil reserves were exhausted. The army leadership, who had a much less acute sense of Japan's military limitations and economic vulnerabilities, were in full agreement. In early September 1941, an imperial conference decided to go to war by late October, pending a final attempt at negotiation with the Americans. Prime Minister Konoe even proposed a direct meeting with President Roosevelt, but when the American government rebuffed him, he decided to resign. Anticipating the outbreak of war, the *jūshin* nominated as his successor, War Minister Tōjō Hideki, an ardent spokesman of the army's hard-line position, who had played a key role in the military buildup of the 1930s.

As a last gamble, the Tōjō cabinet sent Washington a proposal to withdraw from Indochina if the United States agreed to end the oil embargo, help Japan get oil supplies from the Indies, and assist Japan in achieving a diplomatic end to hostilities in China. In November 1941, the Roosevelt administration once again indicated that it would accept nothing less than a return to the pre-1931 status quo, the withdrawal of Japanese troops from China, Manchuria, and Indochina, and Japanese recognition of the Chiang Kai-shek government. The irresistible force had met an unmovable object. Faced with the diplomatic stalemate, the Tōjō cabinet decided to make a preemptive strike against American forces in the Pacific. On Sunday, December 7, while secretaries in the Japanese embassy at Washington rushed to finish typing a translation of the final note breaking off relations with the United States, carrier-based Japanese planes swept out of the sky in a surprise attack on the naval base at Pearl Harbor, inflicting heavy damage on the American Pacific fleet. What one scholar has called a "wanted, unwanted war" had begun.

The decision for war with the United States, as Roberta Wohlstetter has put it, was "forced by the more terrible alternative of losing status or abandoning the national objectives."[2] It was the result less of deliberate long-term planning than of a decade of incremental decisions: acceptance of the Kwantung Army's fait accompli in Manchuria, miscalculation about the strength of Chinese resistance, a failure to understand the moralism driving American foreign policy, and an escalation of official rhetoric about national goals. Cumulatively these decisions backed the government into a corner. As one high official observed in November 1941:

> It is impossible from the standpoint of our domestic political situation and of our self-preservation, to accept all of the American demands. . . . If we miss the opportunity to go to war, we have to submit to American dictates. Therefore I recognize that we must decide to start war against the United States. I will put my trust in what I have been told: namely, that things will go well in the early part of the war; and that although we will experience increasing difficulties as the war progresses, there is some prospect of success.[3]

As this comment suggests, the Japanese leadership was not enthusiastic about war with the United States, but the alternative was to accept national humiliation and demotion to status as a second-rate power, which was not acceptable.

WAR IN THE PACIFIC

The Japanese leadership did not enter the war with the United States as blindly as they had stumbled into the China war. Long-range strategic plans envisaged a limited war similar to the one that ended in victory in the Russo-Japanese war. Counting on the advantages of surprise and superior preparation, the plans aimed at forcing the larger and stronger United States to the negotiating table before it could mobilize its full strength. A series of lightning-fast amphibious operations were to establish a defensive perimeter stretching south and westward from the Marshall Islands in the Central Pacific down through the Indonesian archipelago to Malaya and Indochina. Once secured, this perimeter was to be held against American counterattack while German armies completed the conquest of Europe. Japanese planners expected that when the United States was faced with the overwhelming Axis victories in both Europe and Asia, its leaders would be ready to negotiate a peace settlement that would leave Japan in control of the Greater East Asia Co-Prosperity Sphere.

The Japanese strategy was bold and dangerous, but at first it seemed to succeed. In the early days of war, Japanese planes swiftly neutralized Anglo-American naval and air forces in the Pacific by the devastating attack on Pearl Harbor, air strikes against the American air base at Clark Field in the Philippines, and the sinking of the British warships, the *Prince of Wales* and the *Repulse*. With control of the sea and the air established in the western Pacific, the way was open for a series of amphibious landings in the Philippines, the Dutch East Indies, and Malaya, and an overland thrust from Indochina across Thailand to Burma. A succession of early victories proceeded like clockwork—the British naval base at Singapore fell in February 1942; the Dutch East Indies were under Japanese control by the end of March; the last American redoubt at Bataan in the Philippines was taken in early April; and the Burma Road supplying China from the south had been cut by the end of May. By the spring of 1942, amphibious operations had established a string of island bases in the Southwest and Central Pacific—Guam, Wake Island, the Solomons, the Gilberts, the Marianas, and northern New Guinea. Japanese troops had even established a tiny foothold in American territory on the westernmost tip of the Aleutian chain in Alaska. The defensive perimeter was now complete.

Conquering this vast territory had been relatively easy, but welding it into a Greater East Asia Co-Prosperity Sphere was far more difficult. Although the Japanese already had their hands full trying to control nearly 300 million Chinese in Manchukuo and occupied China, they now had to deal with another 130 to 140 million people in Southeast Asia. In November 1942, a Greater East Asia Ministry was established to deal with local governments within the sphere, but real control remained in the hands of Japanese occupying forces, whose activities often contradicted the government's goals. To obtain collaboration, the Japanese authorities stressed their "anti-imperialist" goals of driving Western colonialism out of Asia. Wherever convenient, Japanese forces promoted local anti-colonial nationalist movements, encouraging indigenous leaders to set up independent regimes. In November 1943, for example, pro-Japanese leaders from occupied China, Manchukuo, Thailand, the Philippines, and Burma assembled in Tokyo for a summit conference—the Greater East Asia Conference—to reaffirm the vision of Pan-Asian solidarity. On the other hand, Japanese military and naval forces were more interested in extracting crucial resources such as oil, tin, and rubber from the newly occupied areas to supply the war effort. Military necessity forced the Japanese to practice what they had preached against, and soon they took over the roles of the European colonial officials, policemen, and plantation managers they had ousted. As this contradiction became increasingly evident, the Japanese turned from cooperation with local regimes to coercion.

The Japanese occupation severely disrupted the lives of the occupied peoples. Even before the invasion of Southeast Asia, the military high command had decided that their forces would live off the land, obtaining food and other supplies locally without relying on the home economy. The Japanese military commandeered what they needed, demanding forced delivery of supplies and paying in military currency that rapidly lost value. The local populations found themselves faced with chronic shortage of foodstuffs and other basic goods, and the inevitable result was rapid inflation, black marketeering, and widespread corruption. To remedy manpower shortages, the Japanese lured or dragooned hundreds of thousands of male workers in Southeast Asia into labor service battalions to build roads, construct air strips, or lay military railway lines. Often given barely enough to eat, let alone adequate medical care, and subjected to brutal discipline, many of these forced laborers died far from home. Following a policy already adopted in China, the Japanese military also "recruited" tens of thousands of Korean, Chinese, Filipino, and other women as "comfort women" in military brothels, where they served the sexual needs of Japanese officers and soldiers. These exactions in flesh, life, and dignity belied official propaganda slogans touting the "liberation" of Asia.

Quite apart from this gap between rhetoric and practice, the Japanese simply did not have the economic and material strength to control and defend the Co-Prosperity Sphere. Japanese planners had envisaged fighting on interior lines, maintaining the great defensive perimeter by moving mobile forces to fend off Allied counterattacks, while it extracted resources from newly conquered territory. But Japanese economic and material capabilities were severely overextended. The Japanese merchant marine fleet was barely adequate to maintain supply lines to the Pacific outposts let alone carry oil, tin, rubber, and other resources back to Japan. As one businessman lamented to an American reporter after the war:

> Here was Japan's problem. We lacked coal, iron, and oil, the very guts of modern industry. When the war started we got the sources of these things, but we could not bring them to Japan. To have brought in all the needed raw materials from the captured lands of the south we needed thirteen million tons of shipping. But we started the war with only seven and a half million and that was rapidly cut down.[4]

To make matters worse, in every essential war industry—steel, aircraft, automotive, munitions—Japan's productive capacities were grotesquely outstripped by the American enemy's. Even before the war started, the United States was producing four times as many airplanes as Japan, and as the war progressed the gap grew wider. Although the Japanese leaders were well aware of the economic imbalance, they entertained optimistic predictions that Japanese war production could grow and that any material deficiencies could be covered by "Japanese spirit." Production did expand, but at a much slower rate than that of the United States, and the Japanese also lagged behind the Americans in developing new tools of war like radar and long-range bombers.

The assumptions behind the Japanese war plans began to crumble in the summer of 1942. The critical turning point came with the battle of Midway in June. The Japanese naval high command had planned to lure the Americans into a decisive naval battle that would smash the remainder of the American

Comparison of U.S. and Japanese Fighting Strength During World War II

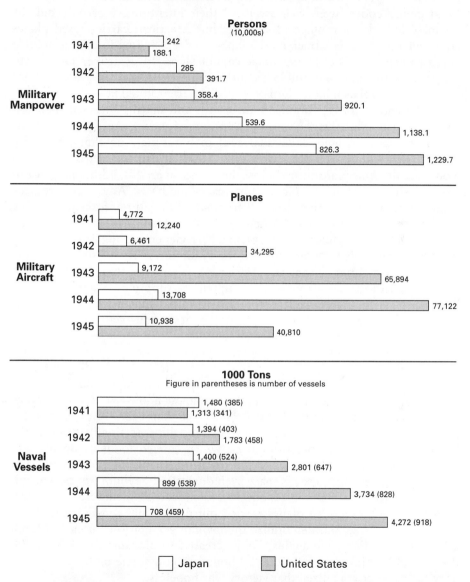

Persons
(10,000s)

Military Manpower

Year	Japan	United States
1941	242	188.1
1942	285	391.7
1943	358.4	920.1
1944	539.6	1,138.1
1945	826.3	1,229.7

Planes

Military Aircraft

Year	Japan	United States
1941	4,772	12,240
1942	6,461	34,295
1943	9,172	65,894
1944	13,708	77,122
1945	10,938	40,810

1000 Tons
Figure in parentheses is number of vessels

Naval Vessels

Year	Japan	United States
1941	1,480 (385)	1,313 (341)
1942	1,394 (403)	1,783 (458)
1943	1,400 (524)	2,801 (647)
1944	899 (538)	3,734 (828)
1945	708 (459)	4,272 (918)

☐ Japan   ▨ United States

Source: Based on Sakamoto Shōzō, *Shinsen Nihonshi zuhyō*, Tokyo: Daiichi gakusha, 1985, p. 157.

Pacific fleet, including the aircraft carriers that had escaped destruction at Pearl Harbor. As luck would have it the Americans, who had broken Japanese naval cipher codes, were well aware of their intentions. Not only did the Japanese lose the advantage of surprise, but American carrier-based planes launched a devastating attack on the Japanese fleet, sinking four irreplaceable aircraft carriers and crippling other capital ships. In a stroke, Japan's supremacy on the high seas and in the air was shattered, and its strategic plans started to unravel as military initiative shifted to the United States

By the end of 1942, American air, naval, and marine forces launched a counteroffensive against the weak outer points of the Japanese perimeter. After capturing the island of Guadalcanal in bitter fighting that left nearly 25,000 Japanese troops dead with only 1600 Americans killed and 4250 wounded, the Americans thrust across the Pacific in an "island-hopping" campaign. Instead of attacking Japan's forward island bases, American forces attacked to their rear, cutting them off from supplies and reinforcements. One arm of the counteroffensive, backed by the American navy, arched through the central Pacific while another, planned by General Douglas MacArthur, struck out from New Guinea toward the Philippines. To the surprise of the Japanese, who thought that the Americans regarded submarines as inhumane, American undersea warfare disrupted the supply lines within the Co-Prosperity Sphere. The Japanese were unable to produce merchant vessels as fast as they were sunk, and as a result Japanese industrial production declined steadily after reaching a plateau in 1943.

By mid-1944, it appeared that victory, even one negotiated at the bargaining table, was beyond Japan's grasp. In June 1944, the Allied landing in France foreclosed the possibility of German domination in Europe, and the American capture of the island of Saipan put the Japanese home islands within range of American bombers. In the fall of 1944, when American B-29s launched a major strike against the Yawata steel works, the war finally reached the home islands. The American bombers, which carried loads of up to eight tons, flew at high altitude beyond the reach of Japanese fighter planes and boldly penetrated Japanese air space even during the daylight hours. The initial targets were military installations and industrial facilities, but by the spring of 1945 American planes carried out night-time incendiary raids intended to terrorize and demoralize the civilian population. In early March 1945, an incendiary raid against Tokyo created a holocaust that left 78,000 dead, 43,380 injured, and 1,500,000 homeless in a single night. Even ordinary Japanese now realized that victory was hopeless.

THE HOME FRONT

The outbreak of war with the United States, which the government promptly designated as the "Greater East Asia War," had been met with wild public exhilaration. The population had been saturated with anti-Western propaganda during the spiritual mobilization campaigns of the late 1930s, but confrontation with the United States let loose a new flood of emotion. As reports of early victories blared over radio loudspeakers, the population was swept up in a heady mixture of pride, anger and optimism. Takamura Kōtarō, a well known poet, celebrated the attack on Pearl Harbor with the following poem:

> Remember December eighth!
> On this day the history of the world was changed.
> The Anglo-Saxon powers
> On this day were repulsed on Asian land and sea.
> It was their *Japan* which repulsed them,
> A tiny country in the Eastern Sea,
> Nippon, the Land of the Gods,
> Ruled over by a living god.[5]

Like many others, the poet was certain that Japan was launched on a grand enterprise destined to change the course of human history. It did, but not quite in the way expected.

In a sense, war fever helped to reintegrate a society scarred by the social conflict of the 1920s and the economic hardships of the early 1930s. Galvanized by a new sense of national mission, the population pulled together behind the war effort in a mood of dedication and self-sacrifice. The press called on the "nation of one hundred million" to "act in the spirit of belonging to one great family," and the schools called on children to become "little patriots" willing to give all for their country. Despite tightening government controls over every aspect of daily life, public morale remained high in the early stages of the war. All over the country, family and friends waved good-bye to new recruits at the train station with banners and banzais, and neighborhood associations mobilized young and old to pitch in with ration distribution, war bond sales, collections of scrap metal and other valuables, air raid drills, and the like. Patriotic voluntary activities renewed a sense of community solidarity, and neighborhood associations often challenged the status quo by elevating less affluent community members to positions of responsibility.

With the escalation of the war effort came changing roles for women, whom Prime Minister Tōjō called the "warm fountainhead" of support for the front lines. To be sure, the "good wife, wise mother" ideology remained in place, but women were mobilized in new ways. Brandishing the slogan "Be Fruitful and Multiply for the Prosperity of the Nation," the government adopted a pro-natalist policy of urging women to have large families. Boy babies, who would become soldiers one day, were the most important kind of war material. The welfare minister, among his other duties, presided over "healthy baby contests" to encourage mothers to nurture their infants properly. In 1938, the Diet, under pressure from women's political organizations, passed a law providing state protection for a mother and her children if her husband were killed, became ill, or deserted the family. With fathers often absent on military service, mothers became the main authority figure within many families, and everywhere women took greater control of their households.

Wartime mobilization meant expanded public roles for women as well. Indeed, many feminist leaders like Ichikawa Fusae supported the war effort as an opportunity for women to gain greater power and freedom through service to the state. While quasi-official organizations like the Patriotic Women's Association were run by male officials, at the local level housewives whose husbands had gone off to war played a key role in the activities of the neighborhood associations, doing much of the legwork and sometimes providing informal leadership. The government was reluctant at first to mobilize women for factory work, but growing manpower shortages eventually forced it to do so. By the end of the war, three million women, including hundreds of thousands of middle school girls, made up a substantial proportion of the work force, especially in the munitions industry. Many women, especially young unmarried women, however, were either conscripted or pressured to join "volunteer labor groups," and their pay scales were substantially lower than that of male workers.

The government did its best to boost the morale of men and women alike through the new popular media. Movies were as powerful a tool for keeping up patriotic spirit as they were in the United States and other belligerent countries. Films like *The Story of Tank Commander Nishizumi*, whose honest and straightforward hero dies while trying to protect the safety of his men, celebrated the humble virtues of dedication and self-sacrifice expected of all the emperor's subjects, military and civilian alike. Others exalted the comradeship among soldiers at the front, the patriotism of female factory workers, or the bravery of traditional heroes like the "forty-seven" samurai of Akō who died after avenging the death of their lord. Interestingly, few wartime films reveled in the violence of the battlefield or depicted the American enemy in graphic terms as subhuman monsters (perhaps because there were no actors to portray them.) On the other hand, pan-Asianist films, such as *China Night*, which depicted a romance between a Japanese sailor and a Chinese war orphan, encouraged their audiences to imagine an Asia sympathetic to Japan's mission.

The government also kept the public's wartime morale high by keeping them ignorant of how the war was actually going. News was subject to heavy censorship, and government officials were rarely candid in their reports on the progress of the war. Official spokesmen for the military high command, for example, portrayed the rout at Midway as a victory and the endless setbacks on the Pacific perimeter as tactical withdrawals. Not only did the government keep the full truth from the public, newspapers bombarded the population with patriotic slogans and stories of heroism at the front. Even when the American air raids made it self-evident that the war effort was not going well, editorials urged the "one hundred million" Japanese to prepare themselves for a final defense of the homeland. Without any other sources of information, the population had little choice but to accept the official version of the war.

While the country's leadership maintained a facade of patriotic unity, squabbling and in-fighting continued among the political elite. In public,

Prime Minister Tōjō was self-effacing, insisting he was merely an ordinary citizen doing his job at the emperor's request, but in fact he was an adept bureaucratic politician who gathered power into his own hands. Not only did he retain control of the War Ministry, he was ex officio president of the Imperial Rule Assistance Association. In November 1943, he headed the new Munitions Ministry, established to supervise a total mobilization of the war economy, and in early 1944 he also assumed the post of army chief of staff. Ruthless in disciplining his military critics, usually by sending them off to the war zone, he placed his personal clique in key positions throughout the government. But Tōjō was not a popular figure, nor did he have the full confidence of the *jūshin*. When the tide of war began to turn against Japan, they had no hesitation about easing him out of power

Even in the midst of war, other political forces continued to defend their turf. The politicians in the Diet found themselves under new attack in the general elections of 1942, when the government set up a system of official recommendation to weed out liberal candidates and support nationalistic ones. Even so, nearly one-fifth of the nonrecommended candidates won seats, and the old political parties, though officially dissolved in 1940, retained shadow organizations and links with their local constituencies. The bureaucrats guarded their pre-war prerogatives too. When new wartime ministries, such as the Greater East Asia Ministry or the Munitions Ministry, were established, older ministries fought to protect their jurisdictional boundaries. And perhaps most surprising of all, rivalry between the army and the navy intensified. The services fought over strategic planning, the allocation of strategic materials, and even the standardization of equipment. An otherwise identical item, for example, might require left-hand threaded screws if supplied to the navy and right-hand threaded screws if supplied to the army.

By late 1944, the worsening military situation in the Pacific, the American sea blockade, and American bombing raids brought rapidly deteriorating conditions on the home front. Places of public entertainment were closed down, and prostitutes were pressed into service as factory workers; rations of meat, fish, and fresh milk had all but ceased; widespread malnutrition brought a rise in the incidence of tuberculosis, rickets, and eye disease; taxes soared, prices increased, and black markets flourished; and even university students, once exempted from conscription, were finally mobilized for military service. As American air attacks increased in intensity, life in the cities grew ever more desperate. Nearly 10,000,000 Japanese, out of fear or out of necessity, evacuated to the countryside to stay with friends or relatives, and urban households with a roof over their heads counted themselves as lucky. The bombed-over sections of Tokyo were so desolate that even stray dogs disappeared from the streets—those that had not been eaten simply starved to death. Except perhaps in the urban mansions and country villas of the elite, a democracy of suffering prevailed.

The social fabric nevertheless continued to hold. Many Japanese grumbled in private or confided complaints to their diaries, and a few bold souls even scrawled revolutionary or anti-war graffiti in public places. But political or social discontent never erupted into riots, demonstrations, or anti-war rallies, nor did there emerge a domestic underground movement or a domestic conspiracy such as the one that nearly cost Hitler his life in July 1944. To be sure, the Special Higher Police and the military gendarmerie (*kempeitai*) were relentless watch dogs, rounding up suspected radicals and tracking anti-war elements with paranoid efficiency, but the bonds to emperor, nation, and kokutai, so carefully cultivated by the government over the previous decades, continued to undergird Japanese society as it slid into devastation. As one journalist later recalled,

> Despite the fact that there wasn't even one article which seemed believable throughout the entire wartime Japanese newspapers, we tried to force ourselves to believe and to be ready to die. If a parent were on the verge of bankruptcy and told a transparent and painful lie, would it be possible for a child to expose the secret? All the child could do would be to die silently with this parent, submitting to his fate.[6]

Even as the devastation of the country seemed more and more certain, fresh-faced young pilots hurled themselves in bombed-loaded *kamikaze* planes at American naval vessels, and housewives, old people, and children trained themselves to use sharpened bamboo spears in preparation for the inevitable American invasion.

THE SURRENDER OF JAPAN

The Japanese leadership found the Pacific War no easier to bring to an end than the China War. As it became clear that victory was out of the question, a few high officials, including the *jūshin*, the imperial household bureaucracy, and the former prime minister, Konoe Fumimaro, raised the possibility of a compromise peace. The military and naval high commands resisted the idea vigorously. After the fall of Saipan, when Tōjō was finally forced to resign as prime minister, responsible officials might have made approaches to the Allies. But the army leadership, whose pride and honor were at stake, was determined to continue the war even under obviously unfavorable circumstances. In public, the new prime minister, General Koiso Kuniaki, uncompromisingly announced the unanimous determination of the "Yamato people" to fight the Anglo-American enemy to the end.

What conservative civilian leaders feared was that deteriorating economic conditions might lead to social breakdown. In early 1945, Prince Konoe sent the emperor a long memorial arguing that with each passing day the conditions necessary for a "communist revolution" were growing and that since defeat seemed inevitable, the war should be ended through negotiation as quickly as possible. In November 1943, however, the American, British, and

Chinese leaders had declared at the Cairo conference that they would accept only an "unconditional surrender" from the Japanese. Since the Japanese leadership, whatever their individual views on the desirability of continuing the war, insisted on the preservation of the imperial institution as a minimum condition for peace, the Allied position was a formidable stumbling block to any negotiation. The Soviet Union still remained neutral, however, so the Koiso cabinet, despite its bellicose public rhetoric, made secret diplomatic feelers toward Moscow to persuade it to serve as a go-between with the other Allies.

In the spring of 1945, the war situation went from bad to worse. In April, American forces made landings on Okinawa, finally bringing the war to the home islands. Desperate resistance by Japanese army forces, who were as ruthless toward the Okinawan population as toward the American enemy, made it clear to all that the defense of the homeland would be a bloody one. Civilians were forced to commit mass suicide rather than surrender to the enemy, and between 100,000 and 150,000 lost their lives in the fighting. Events in the outside world also turned to Japan's disadvantage. The Soviet Union announced in April that it did not intend to renew its neutrality pact with Japan, and the following month Germany surrendered after Hitler committed suicide in his Berlin bunker. This left Japan to fight the Allies all alone. Confronted with this unpromising turn of events, the *jūshin* nominated Admiral Suzuki Kantarō, an advocate of an honorable negotiated peace, as prime minister, but the military and civilian leadership remained divided about what to do next.

On the one hand, the Suzuki government, bending to the wishes of the military high command, decided to make preparations for a final decisive "battle for the homeland" that would inflict enough damage on American invading forces to force abandonment of the Allied policy of unconditional surrender. (An official *People's Handbook of Combat Resistance* instructed its readers to attack the Americans with "hatchets, sickles, hooks or cleavers" or to aim karate kicks at their stomachs and testicles.)[7] On the other hand, civilian leaders continued to urge negotiations with the Allies. Kido Kōichi, a top imperial court official, argued that Japan would lose all capacity to fight by the end of 1945 if American bombing continued and that popular unrest was likely to result. As a sop to these sentiments, the Suzuki cabinet authorized another quiet approach to the Soviets, asking for help in mediating with the Allies, but Moscow was not very responsive. Unknown to the Japanese, in February 1945 Stalin had already agreed at the Yalta Conference to enter the war against Japan within three months of the German surrender.

The last chance for a negotiated peace came in July when President Harry Truman and Prime Minister Clement Atlee issued the Potsdam Declaration, calling on the Japanese government to surrender unconditionally or face "utter destruction." Fearful that unconditional surrender would compromise the survival of the imperial institution, Prime Minister Suzuki chose to "silently ignore" (*mokusatsu*) the proclamation, dashing the hopes of a negotiated peace once and for all. Had the Americans held out guarantees for the emperor, it might have been possible to strike a bargain, but such a move would have been unacceptable to the American public, who put Hirohito in the same category as Hitler and Mussolini. In Japan, on the other hand, top civilian leaders were unwilling to bargain the fate of the "national polity," and the army high command was determined to fight to the last civilian in defense of its lost cause. With the Japanese leaders unwilling or unable to surrender, the end game was left to the Americans, who were anxious to end the war as quickly as possible.

The American government had several choices. Military plans had been drawn up for two amphibious landings on the Japanese home islands, one on Kyushu in the late fall of 1945, and a second in the Kanto region in early 1946, but since American casualties were likely to be high, perhaps in the tens of thousands, the Truman administration hoped to avoid this alternative. Neither were American leaders particularly anxious to wage a war of attrition against Japan, escalating air attacks and intensifying the naval blockade until the Japanese economy came to a complete halt and the Japanese population reached the point of starvation. The American public was tiring of the war effort, and American troops in Europe were anxious to return home rather than fight in the Pacific theater. The successful explosion of an atomic device in the New Mexico desert in late July meant that neither invasion nor blockade would be necessary to end the war.

American officials had debated whether to use the atomic bomb against a real target, whether to give the Japanese government a forewarning, or whether to demonstrate its power on an uninhabited piece of land, but President Truman reached the final decision to drop the bomb with relatively little hesitation. Not to have used such a powerful and expensive weapon to end the war quickly, especially since the Soviet Union was soon likely to join the fighting, would have been politically difficult for any American leader. (After the war ended, some senior military leaders expressed the view that the bomb might not have been necessary to end the war, but at the time none of the President's closest advisors counseled against it.) To ensure the maximum psychological impact, the targets chosen were cities with military industrial concentrations that had escaped heavy conventional bombing: Kokura, Niigata, Hiroshima, and Nagasaki. The first atomic bomb fell on Hiroshima on August 6. The explosion, which created an enormous fire ball several million degrees centigrade at the center, set off shock waves and sheets of fire that left the city a flattened pile of rubble, charred corpses, and dying wounded. Every combustible object, including human bodies, within a two-kilometer radius of ground zero was incinerated. Three days later a second, more powerful bomb was dropped on Nagasaki, a major ship building center, but fortunately for its population hilly terrain protected some of the city from massive destruction. Estimates of those immediately killed by the blast in Hiroshima range from 78,000 to 140,000, while those for Nagasaki range from

Atomic victims in Nagasaki sharing water from a bottle
the day after the blast in August 1945.

27,000 to 70,000. If those who later died from radiation sickness, injuries, or
related illness in later years are included, the estimates go much higher.

Although the Japanese authorities were not quite sure what the new weapon
was, or how many the Americans might possess, military observers dispatched
to Hiroshima sent back reports of its enormous power. The dropping of two
atomic weapons, however, may have been less a shock to the Japanese leadership than news that the Soviet Union had declared war on Japan and that Soviet troops had crossed the border into Manchukuo. The "utter destruction"
flamboyantly threatened in the Potsdam Declaration was at hand. Nevertheless, military leaders still resisted the idea of unconditional surrender. The
war minister and the chiefs of staff, who argued that the Allies intended to
enslave the country and debase the "national polity," insisted that conditions
be attached to American demands. Their resistance crumbled only when the
emperor, coached by peace-prone civilian advisers, announced at an imperial
conference that it was against his wishes to subject the people to further suffering. When the Japanese government asked the Americans for a guarantee

that surrender would not affect the emperor's prerogatives, however, Washington replied that his eventual fate would be determined by the Japanese people. This ambiguous response brought renewed army objections, but on August 14 the emperor soberly urged surrender. Only he could dare to make the final decision to end a war that he had declared, that had been fought in his name, and that had cost the lives of 2.7 million of his subjects.

On August 15, 1945, as adults stood with heads bowed and children listened half-comprehending to his high-pitched voice crackling over radio loudspeakers, the emperor announced that the war had not "developed to Japan's advantage" and called upon the people to "endure the unendurable and suffer what is insufferable." The words "defeat" and "surrender" were never uttered, but nearly everyone understood that the Great East Asia War, fought to drive the "Anglo-American imperialists" from East Asia, had ended in a humiliating defeat at their hands. One Tokyo resident confided to his diary:

> All of us sank into silence and didn't say a word. I felt in a daze, exasperated, and tears of resentment began to flow. . . . [E]ight long years of ceaseless hard work, with Japan's fate in the balance, have ended up in unconditional surrender. Every aspect of the people's daily lives had been whipped into line on behalf of winning the war. They had been forcibly paraded about, compelled to persevere through unending tensions, hardships and privations. . . . I keenly felt a sense of cruel grief.[8]

All the wartime sacrifice, suffering, and hardship was suddenly rendered meaningless. It was a devastating moment, etched in the memory of all who lived through it.

The significance of the Pacific War has been debated ever since it ended, and it is likely to be debated for generations to come. During the wartime years, most Americans regarded the conflict with Japan as part of a global struggle between the forces of "fascism" and "democracy." This view obscured the large differences between the Japanese leaders and their Axis allies. Oddly enough, the Japanese political system, for all its repressive apparatus, was at least as "democratic"—and certainly more "constitutional"—than America's wartime allies, China and the Soviet Union. While General Tōjō could be forced out of office in the middle of the war, Mussolini and Hitler could be removed only by assassination or defeat. And while Hitler sought permanent German domination of Europe, the grandiose vision of a Greater East Asia Co-Prosperity Sphere was an afterthought to the more pragmatic Japanese leaders, who probably would have been content with limited gains on the Asian continent had they been able to negotiate a peaceful settlement with the Guomindang.

On the other hand, the wartime Japanese view that they were fighting to liberate the oppressed peoples of Asia from "Anglo-American imperialism" or to protect them against the "threat of Bolshevism" is even less convincing. To be sure, the war weakened the Western colonial empires and stimulated anti-colonial independence movements in Southeast Asia, but the Japanese

Japanese War Casualties

Military fatalities

China War, 1937–1941	185,647
Imperial Army, 1941–1945	1,140,429
Imperial Navy, 1941–1945	414,879
	1,740,955

Civilian families in air raids

Tokyo	97,031
Hiroshima	140,000
Nagasaki	70,000
63 other cities	86,336
	393,367

Other fatalities

Civilians in Okinawa	150,000
Civilians in Saipan	10,000
Soldiers and civilians in Manchuria (winter of 1945–1946)	100,000
POWs in Soviet Union	300,000
	560,000

Total Japanese war dead	2,694,322

Servicemen reported ill or injured (1945)	4,470,000
Servicemen receiving disability pensions	300,000

Source: John W. Dower, *War Without Mercy: Race and Power in the Pacific War* (New York: Pantheon, 1986), pp. 297–299 and accompanying annotations. The mix of precise official data and general estimates is unavoidable.

military thrust into the region was prompted less by an anti-imperialist mission than by its strategic and economic needs. And it seems likely that had the Japanese won the war they would have been no less oppressive (and possibly even more efficient) overlords than Western colonialists had been. Except for collaborators who staked their political futures on the Japanese, few in the occupied territories were sorry to see the Japanese leave in 1945. Indeed, bitter memories of the war experience—the brutality of Japanese soldiers, the arrogance of civilian officials, the massacre of innocent civilians, the cruel suffering of the "comfort women" and forced laborers, and the destruction of property—were to remain alive in Asia for more than a generation to come.

What can be said with certainty is that defeat changed the country's direction dramatically. After nearly fifty years of territorial expansion overseas, the country shrank back within the boundaries of the archipelago. The defeat shattered the myth that Japan had a mission to create a new order in Asia, and it destroyed any illusion that war was uplifting or ennobling. While a few retrograde nationalists later remembered the war with nostalgia, most of those who lived through it did not. Instead, the wartime generation was soon to see defeat as an opportunity to make a fresh historical start. After years of traveling through a "dark valley," it was time to rebuild at home not pursue the senseless folly of overseas conquest. And as they turned inward once again, the Japanese were to discover that the benefits of peaceful interaction with the outside world far outweighed any they had enjoyed while helping to build the Greater East Asia Co-Prosperity Sphere.

ENDNOTES

1. *Nihon gaikō nenpyō oyobi shuyō bunsho,* vol. 2 (Tokyo: Hara shobo, 1965), 433–434.

2. Roberta Wohlstetter, *Pearl Harbor: Warning and Decision* (Stanford, Cal.: Stanford University Press, 1962), 353.

3. Nobutaka Ike, *Japan's Decision for War* (Stanford, Cal.: Stanford University Press, 1967), 236.

4. Clark Lee, *One Last Look Around* (New York: Duell, Sloan and Pearce, 1947), 55.

5. Quoted in Donald Keene, "Japanese Writers and the Greater East Asian War," *Journal of Asian Studies* 23, no. 2 (Feb. 1964), 213.

6. Masuo Kato, *The Lost War: A Japanese Reporter's Inside Story* (New York: Alfred A. Knopf, 1946), 157.

7. Quoted in Alvin D. Coox, *Japan: The Final Agony* (New York: Ballantine Books, Inc., 1970), 98–99.

8. Quoted in Thomas R. H. Havens, *Valley of Darkness: The Japanese People and World War Two* (New York: W. W. Norton and Co., 1978), 192–193.

IV

Peace, Prosperity, and Stability, 1945–Present

15

Occupation, Reform, and Recovery

T he arrival of American occupying forces in late 1945 plunged Japan into a period of rapid change, unprecedented since the Meiji Restoration. Flush with victory, the Americans came determined to transform their former enemy into a "democratic" and "peace-loving" country that would no longer threaten its neighbors or international peace. To that end, they sought to transform Japanese society from top to bottom, much as the Meiji leaders had done. But Japan was not a *tabula rasa*, nor could the Americans reinvent it overnight. While Occupation officials might draw up blueprints for reform, they had to be carried out by Japanese politicians, bureaucrats, and experts. Indeed, the most durable American reforms succeeded because they served the interests of some Japanese or because they rested on foundations already laid in the pre-war period. Nevertheless, by the end of the Occupation in 1952, the Americans had dramatically altered the political, social, and economic landscape of Japan.

POSTWAR JAPANESE SOCIETY

The war's sudden end left many Japanese psychologically devastated. Prime Minister Higashikuni urged the people to "repent" for their failure to bring the war to a successful conclusion, but most ordinary Japanese were more likely to be feeling anger, relief, apprehension, or lethargy rather than repentance. Wartime censorship had concealed military and naval setbacks, so few people realized just how badly the war had been going. Not surprisingly, many were indignant at having been so monstrously misled, and their confidence in the nation's leaders from the emperor on down was exhausted. Most ordinary Japanese had little time for recrimination, however. Unconditional surrender was humiliating, the more so for being unexpected, but the end of the fighting also meant a return to some semblance of normal life—no more blackouts, no more bombing, no more nights spent in air raid shelters. The majority of the civilian population, especially the women and children, were relieved that the long ordeal was finally at an end. What the future held could hardly be worse than the war itself.

The war's effects nonetheless lingered on. The country was prostrate economically, its factories at a standstill, and its food supplies barely sufficient to keep the population alive. About one-quarter of the country's physical capital had been destroyed, and nearly a third of the population had lost their homes. Major cities like Tokyo and Osaka had been turned into wastelands of ash and ruin by American strategic bombing. Children orphaned by the bombing slept on the sidewalks, and homeless families took refuge in old air raid shelters, shacks built from rubble, and even burned-out streetcars. In early 1946, a Western reporter described the once thriving port of Yokohama as a "man-made desert."

> The skeletons of railway cars and locomotives remained untouched on the tracks. Streetcars stood where flames had caught up with them, twisting the metal, snapping the wires overhead, and bending the supporting iron poles as if they were made of wax. Gutted buses and automobiles lay abandoned by the roadside. . . . all was a man-made desert, ugly and desolate and hazy in the dust that rose from crushed brick and mortar.[1]

The ragged inhabitants of the city, seemingly indifferent to the devastation surrounding them, shuffled through the debris.

For millions of city dwellers, the overwhelming preoccupation was putting food on the table. As the result of fertilizer and tool shortages, the 1945 rice harvest was two-thirds its normal size, reducing food stocks to dangerously low levels. By the end of 1945, the average Japanese was consuming only about 1800 calories per day, close to the starvation level and well below the amount required to sustain even light labor. Hundreds died of starvation, and malnutrition was widespread. Children growing up in the immediate postwar years were shorter and smaller than those a few years older or younger, and many young adults fell victim to tuberculosis and other diseases that preyed on the physically weakened. While the Americans shipped in emergency food supplies, continuing shortages provoked public anger. In May 1946, a crowd of nearly 250,000 demonstrated in front of the imperial palace demanding food. "We are starving," shouted one of its leaders, who pointed toward the emperor's residence. "But what about him?"[2]

The repatriation of more than 6 million civilians, soldiers, and sailors, who had been trapped in the far-flung empire at war's end, added to the impact of wartime destruction. In the fall of 1945, they began arriving home, often with little more than the clothing on their backs. The economy had not

A mother and her children walk through the devastation of post-surrender Tokyo.

only to feed and house them but to provide them work too. The industrial sector of the economy, particularly heavy industry, had ground to a halt, however, and most firms were laying off production workers not hiring them. The government, dominated by conservative senior politicians and bureaucrats, was more interested in helping the industrialists than their workers, and in the months after surrender, it paid out enormous indemnities to large industrial firms for losses suffered in the war. The amount was equal to nearly one-third of what the government had spent for military purposes since the outbreak of war with China in 1937. As a result, the money supply increased from ¥28.6 billion in August 1945 to ¥60.5 billion in February 1946, and the resulting inflation hurt the middle class as well as workers.

Economic suffering brought a breakdown of the public order that had held firm even during the darkest days of the war. Many who were desperate to make ends meet turned to crime. In a society that traditionally astonished outsiders by its high level of public honesty, ordinary robbery and pilfering became common, and violent crimes like rape, murder, and armed robbery increased. (In one sensational case, a serial killer arrested in 1945 for the rape and murder of seven women confessed that he had lured them with promises of food. "It was easy," he said.) With legitimate work so scarce, criminal gangs had little trouble recruiting demobilized soldiers or persuading destitute women

to work as prostitutes. Even law-abiding citizens, unable to subsist on official rations, regularly visited the bustling black markets. Defeat, it seemed,
had brought not only national humiliation, but a breakdown in public
morals as well. Indeed, one novelist argued in a 1946 essay that the lower the
Japanese sank toward the depths of morality, the more likely they were to
overcome their "spiritual vanity" and recover their basic "humanity"—a
bleak vision indeed.

On the other hand, psychological and material devastation also made the
population susceptible to change. The defeat raised doubts about every aspect of national life, but especially about patriotic values. "All the official
slogans and high ideals of the Empire became a laughing stock," one young
critic later recalled. "Everything public became meaningless."[3] With the old
national leadership discredited, and the wartime dream in shambles, most
Japanese were ready for any change that promised a better, more peaceful,
and more stable life. For some, that meant turning toward religion, especially
the "new religions" that proliferated rapidly after the war's end, as a legion
of sect leaders promised their followers worldly success or otherworldly so-
lace; for others, it meant plunging into new mass movements that attacked
the entrenched elites and championed radical political and social ideals. But
for most ordinary Japanese, the pursuit of change meant following the lead
of the Americans. While the American presence caused much resentment,
many Japanese found themselves attracted by American ideas and culture,
whether that involved championing democracy, learning English, or wearing
aloha shirts.

THE AMERICAN OCCUPATION

Confident that the United States would ultimately win the war with Japan,
the Roosevelt administration began to make plans for a defeated Japan as
early as 1942. The "surprise attack" on Pearl Harbor and the bitter fighting
in the Pacific inclined the president and his advisors toward a harsh and ret-
ributive peace that would punish the Japanese for starting the war. Indeed, so
strong was anti-Japanese sentiment among the American public that in a 1944
Gallup Poll 13 percent of the respondents favored a complete extermination
of the Japanese people after the end of the war. On the eve of the Japanese
surrender, however, the breakdown of wartime cooperation with the Soviet
Union, especially in occupied Germany, persuaded many American officials
that a vengeful peace would serve no long-term purpose.

Post-surrender plans drafted in the late summer of 1945 tempered the urge
to punish with an emphasis on constructive reform. The policy-makers in
Washington decided that the best way to ensure that Japan would never
again become a menace to the United States or its Asian neighbors was to
turn it into a "peace-loving democracy." But the Americans never lost sight

of Japan's potential military and strategic significance. The destruction of the Japanese fleet had turned the Pacific into an "American lake," and officials in Washington were determined to keep it that way. Even though Japan was to be disarmed and democratized, postwar strategic planning assumed that it would play a role in supporting the United States as the dominant power in the western Pacific. As the occupation unfolded, reform efforts were sometimes difficult to reconcile with this strategic goal.

During the first two or three years of the occupation, the drive toward reform predominated. The American occupying forces arrived in Japan with an easy optimism about the malleability of the Japanese and an absolute confidence in the superiority of their own culture. In their view, the American victory over "fascism" and "militarism" had proven the superiority of the "American way of life," and they saw their country's military triumph as an advertisement for democracy and freedom. No one embodied this outlook more thoroughly than General Douglas MacArthur, the Supreme Commander for the Allied Powers (SCAP), who symbolized the American Occupation to most Japanese. Believing that the Americans could tutor the politically "immature" Japanese in democracy just as they had prepared the Filipinos for independent self-rule, he seemed to delight in bringing radical change to Japan. As he confided to a group of American journalists, "Why I could be shot if I tried to do some of the things at home that I am doing over here. . . . Of course I'm simply carrying out orders. But it's practically revolution, gentlemen, revolution!"[4] In public, MacArthur struck a pose as a benevolent but unapproachable leader, more distant than the emperor himself. An official photograph of their first meeting showed a casually dressed MacArthur, hands tucked in his pockets, confidently towering over Hirohito, who looked tense in his formal cutaway coat and striped pants. It left no doubt about who was in charge.

Perhaps the best advertisement for reform was the presence of several hundred thousand American soldiers and civilians, the largest influx of foreigners Japan had ever experienced. Wartime propaganda had portrayed the Americans as "beastly" brutal racists, and immediately after surrender the government quickly organized "recreation centers" (mainly dance halls, cabarets, and brothels) to protect "daughters of good families" against violation by the Americans. But ordinary Japanese were surprised at how kind and friendly the Americans turned out to be. While the record of the Occupation troops was marred by some rapes and assaults against Japanese citizens, most American soldiers acted differently from Japanese soldiers in wartime Asia. Children were delighted at the chocolate bars and chewing gum the GIs handed out so freely, and their mothers and grandmothers were surprised at how polite the Americans were. The demonstrable affluence of the Americans made an equally deep impression on the Japanese. Despite four years of warfare in the Pacific, the Americans were able to bring thousands of trucks, tanks, airplanes, and pieces of heavy weaponry into Yokohama and other ports, and to stock their PXs with an abundance of consumer goods and

Official photograph of the first meeting between General Douglas MacArthur and Emperor Hirohito in October 1945. (Two other versions were discarded because MacArthur's eyes were closed or the emperor's mouth was open too wide.)

appliances. These startling glimpses of American economic strength were unsettling. If the United States could fight for four years and still command such material wealth, then perhaps "American democracy" had lessons for Japan.

The American revolution from above could not have succeeded without Japanese cooperation. Not surprisingly, many liberal, social democratic, and left-wing academics and politicians, who had been active in the 1920s but had been driven into silence or retirement during the wartime years, were now eager to help the Americans in building a democratic new Japan. Perhaps the most eager were those on the extreme left, including the reorganized Japanese Communist Party, whose leaders the Americans released from political prisons shortly after the occupation began. In October 1945, the Communists, whose program for postwar Japan had much in common with the Americans', issued a statement thanking the Americans for making "democratic revolution" possible in Japan. But SCAP officials found themselves more comfortable with moderates like Ichikawa Fusae, a longtime advocate of women's rights; Ōzaki Yukio, a Diet politician once known as the "god of universal suffrage"; and Shidehara Kijūrō, the internationalist foreign minister of the 1920s. Indeed, Shidehara, who spoke excellent English, was persuaded to head the first postwar cabinet, which also included leading businessmen, academics, and politicians thought to have opposed the war effort.

Ultimately, however, it was the civil bureaucracy whom the Americans needed the most. Since the war had ended without an invasion, the existing administrative apparatus remained intact. The Americans decided to control the country indirectly, relying on Japanese officials rather than an American military government to carry out the reform program. In the immediate postwar years, SCAP headquarters overwhelmed the ministries with a flood of reform directives that perplexed and often horrified Japanese officials. To modify what they regarded as radical policies, officials often stalled or bargained with SCAP headquarters, subtly changing reform measures as they moved through Japanese government channels. Although SCAP officials and American journalists saw this as an attempt by reactionary forces to sabotage the American reform effort, it was an inevitable consequence of the fact that the United States had neither the human nor financial resources to govern the country directly. Few Americans in Japan knew much about the country, and fewer still could even speak the language.

DEMILITARIZATION AND POLITICAL DEMOCRATIZATION

The American occupation moved quickly to dismantle the "emperor system," the institutional structure that American analysts thought had sustained wartime aggression. Not only did SCAP dissolve the Imperial Army and Navy, and abolish the War Ministry and the General Staff, it also swept away the apparatus of political repression. All political prisoners were released; the Peace Preservation Law and other laws constraining freedom of speech were abrogated; the Special Higher Police were disbanded; and censorship was ended. For the first time in more than a decade and a half, it was possible to act and speak without fear of reprisals by the police. With the lifting of censorship, new magazines and journals with names like *Jiyū (Freedom)*, *Shinsei (New Life)*, and *Sekai (World)* poured out a flood of criticism toward the wartime regime and its leadership, and debated why Japan had gone so wildly astray.

To weed out those suspected of "militaristic" tendencies or collusion with the military, the Occupation began a bloodless political "purge" in early 1946. Nearly 210,000 business executives, journalists, right-wing activists, school teachers, university professors, civilian officials, and former military personnel were barred from public office or other positions of public responsibility for alleged support of wartime aggression. According to one estimate, about one out of every four top business executives was forced into retirement. Fearful that voters would return to office Diet members elected in 1942, when the Tōjō cabinet had tried to pack the House of Representatives with pro-army candidates, the Occupation also barred more than three hundred incumbents from running in the first postwar election in 1946. The only pre-war elite to survive this draconian purge largely unscathed was the civilian bureaucracy, whose services were needed to run the country. Just how much the purge contributed to the democratization of Japan is difficult to say, but there is no doubt that it opened the way for new leaders in many spheres.

The Americans were equally determined to punish those directly responsi-ble for the outbreak of war. The most obvious culprits were war leaders like Tōjō Hideki who were accused of having plotted war against China and the United States. In the fall of 1945, American authorities rounded up several dozen wartime political and military leaders on charges of "crimes against peace" and "crimes against humanity." Twenty-eight were brought to trial before an international tribunal of judges representing the Allied powers. Like the trial of Nazi leaders at Nuremberg, the Tokyo war crimes trial was staged as a moral drama to teach the Japanese public the consequences of militarism and international aggression. Few members of the Japanese public paid much attention to the tribunal or regarded the convictions it handed down as anything more than "victor's justice"—punishment inflicted by the winners on the losers. Trials of nearly 6000 lesser war criminals, mostly ac-cused of atrocities against civilians or POWs, were held in Yokohama or in the countries where the crimes had been committed.

The long-run impact of the Tokyo trials is difficult to assess. On the one hand, the trial judgments reminded the Japanese public that their country had been responsible for the war and that they should remain vigilant against attempts to revive militarism. On the other hand, by suggesting that the war was the work of a militarist cabal who had duped the Japanese people into following them, the trial judgments absolved the ordinary Japanese from any complicity, even though the majority had supported the war effort, often with enthusiasm. Indeed, placing all the blame on the wartime leaders de-flected a debate over popular responsibility for the war and laid the ground-work for later claims that the Japanese had been "war victims" as much as the Asian peoples under Japan's wartime domination or the Allied fighting men who died in the war. As direct memories of the war faded, the sense of victimization grew stronger.

In the midst of this massive assault on the wartime leadership, the position of the emperor himself seemed in doubt: was he to be included among the war guilty or not? During the war, a vocal group of American politicians and officials had advocated trying the emperor as a war criminal, a view that was echoed by the postwar radical left in Japan. The imperial court bureaucracy was well aware of this possibility, and in the emperor's early encounters with the foreign press, he took care to distance himself from his generals and blame them for war. In fact, the emperor and his inner circle had little cause to worry. Joseph Grew, the last pre-war American ambassador to Japan, had already succeeded in convincing policy-makers in Washington that abolishing the imperial institution or prosecuting the emperor would stir up political and social unrest that might thwart democratic reform. Since intelligence reports based on Japanese POW interrogations suggested that popular loyalty to the monarch was deep, MacArthur had decided to keep the emperor in his position. The only price exacted was a complete demythologization of the imperial institution and a reduction of its constitutional importance. On New Year's Day 1946, the emperor reaffirmed the Meiji emperor's "commitment" to democracy and renounced all claims to divinity.

Just as the Meiji leaders had turned the emperor into a symbol of "civilization and enlightenment," imperial household officials did their best to reconstruct Hirohito as a "democratic" civilian monarch, modeled on the royal families of contemporary Europe. During 1946 and 1947, Hirohito toured the country in a rumpled business suit, meeting his subjects in factories, hospitals, and mine shafts in an effort to establish himself as a thoroughly human, if somewhat awkward, public figure. Photos of the imperial family chatting in their parlor or enjoying a seashore vacation appeared in the popular press as well. The teen-aged crown prince, Akihito, was provided with a new "democratic" education, including English lessons with a Quaker schoolmarm from Philadelphia. The decision to keep Hirohito in his position may have been useful to reduce domestic tension in the short run, but his continued presence as a public figure proved awkward in the long run. As long as he remained emperor, the unresolved question of war responsibility lingered on, making it difficult for postwar leaders to apologize to their Asian neighbors for the wartime destruction and havoc.

The constructive phase of political democratization centered on revision of the Meiji constitution. At MacArthur's prompting, the Shidehara cabinet drew up a revised constitution in late 1945, but the SCAP government section judged it far too cautious. It made few changes in the emperor's powers, permitted the restriction of basic civil rights by statute law, and retained the armed forces as an institution. In early February 1946, after working six days and resting on the seventh, SCAP staff officials produced their own draft, written first in English, then translated into Japanese. Although Prime Minister Shidehara and other high government officials were aghast at the extreme changes the Americans proposed, they had little choice but to accept it as an "amendment" to the Meiji constitution. After four months of debate, the newly elected Diet approved the new constitution with only minor changes. Despite its obviously American origins—ironically the preamble begins with the phrase, "We the Japanese people"—it has remained the fundamental law of the land ever since.

The revised constitution completely overturned the emperor-centered and state-centered document written by the Meiji leaders. It declared that sovereignty lay in the people of Japan not in the imperial institution. By reducing the emperor to a mere "symbol of the state and the unity of the people," it restored the imperial institution's pre-Restoration role as a purely ceremonial office, concerned with public rituals. By guaranteeing a long list of "fundamental human rights," the new constitution also curbed the powers of the state to interfere in the lives of its citizens. Interestingly, many of these rights, such as collective bargaining or the equality of women, were not to be found in the American constitution. To safeguard these rights, the constitution established an independent judicial system, headed by a supreme court with the power of judicial review.

The most radical feature of the new constitution was its explicit rejection of military force as an instrument of national policy. Under Article Nine, the constitution renounced war as a sovereign right of the nation and force as a means of resolving international disputes, and it pledged that to that end Japan would not maintain "land, sea and air forces as well as other war potential." Even today, it is not clear whether Shidehara or MacArthur first proposed this provision. There is little doubt, however, that MacArthur strongly supported it. Having emerged from the war as a victorious general, he wanted to secure a place in history as a magnanimous man of peace. Even though Article Nine appeared to strip Japan of a basic right of national self-defense, there was less public debate over this clause than over the question of whether "popular sovereignty" undermined the concept of a special "national polity" (*kokutai.*) It seems likely that many Japanese politicians and officials expected that Article Nine could be revised or eliminated once the occupation ended.

The new constitution revamped the Diet by adopting the principles of parliamentary supremacy and cabinet responsibility that liberal politicians and political activists had advocated since the 1880s. A new, publicly elected House of Councilors replaced the old House of Peers, and the House of Representatives was given control over the cabinet. The prime minister was to be elected by a majority in the House of Representatives, and the majority of the cabinet were required to be Diet members. If the lower house passed a vote of no confidence, the prime minister was obliged to resign from office or hold new elections. The lower house was also given the power to approve the national budget, and it could override decisions of the new House of Councilors by a two-thirds vote. Under accompanying legislation, the status of Diet members was elevated by giving them salaries equal to the highest ranking bureaucrats.

While the restructured central government followed the British parliamentary model, the local government system looked more like the American federal model. In a very basic way, the Americans equated the devolution of power from the center as a way of spreading democracy to the grass roots. To break the hold of the central ministries on local government and to nurture a new tradition of self-rule, the constitution provided for the public election of prefectural governors, and it created prefectural assemblies popularly elected and directly responsible to the voters. To buttress the autonomy of local governments, other laws increased prefectural and local-government power to raise taxes, placed control over local police forces in their hands, and established publicly elected school boards.

Although the Occupation reforms overturned many basic features of the pre-war state, it left the civil bureaucracy untouched. To be sure, ministerial bureaucrats were declared to be "public servants" rather than "servants of the emperor," but their status and powers were little affected. Some central agencies and ministries, including the once powerful Home Ministry, were abolished, but their officials simply moved to newly created agencies. Elitist recruitment procedures remained in place, and so did bureaucratic immunity from political appointments. All American attempts at major civil service reform met with firm bureaucratic resistance. Occupation officials did not press the issue, since they were so heavily dependent on the existing administrative structure. As a result, morale remained high among the civilian bureaucrats, who continued to believe that their education, expertise, and connections were indispensable to the country. Indeed, with the disappearance of the military establishment, once powerful rivals in making national policy, they enjoyed greater freedom of action than they had had before the war.

DEMOCRATIZING JAPANESE SOCIETY

The American public blamed the war on Japan's unscrupulous military leaders, but Occupation planners found its origins deep in the Japanese social structure. The "emperor system," in their analysis, was sustained by a "feudal" hierarchical social order that repressed women, peasants, and factory workers and by a "monopolistic" economy that concentrated wealth in the hands of big landlords and big businessmen allied with the military and "fascist" elements. To prevent a resurgence of Japanese militarism would require transforming Japan into a democratic society. Creating such a society, however, was more complicated than writing a new constitution. There was hardly any aspect of ordinary life that the Occupation officials did not consider changing. (Some even wanted the Japanese to shift to the Western alphabet so that they would think more "rationally" and "democratically.") Reforms emerged in a piecemeal fashion. Some SCAP officials introduced reforms to bring about a more equitable distribution of wealth, while others tried to build popular social forces to defend democracy against conservative reaction after the Occupation ended. What all these policies had in common was an attempt to foster personal individualism, political independence, and social equality.

To bring democracy into the family, for example, SCAP authorities backed a revision of the civil code that had made the samurai family a model for the rest of the society. The revision, completed in 1947 in face of strong conservative opposition, gave priority to the rights of individual family members and weakened the enormous legal powers placed in the hands of the household head. It also eliminated the gender balance embedded in the old code. The family property was to be shared by all survivors, and daughters were given the same inheritance rights as sons. The practice of male primogeniture was abolished. Since the revised constitution proclaimed marriage to be based on mutual consent between husband and wife, the new legal code also gave wives more power to initiate divorce proceedings. Not surprisingly, the divorce rate took a sudden upward jump after the new code was promulgated. Some American officials thought that the new code did not protect the rights of women and children as strongly as it might have, but it clearly swept away the patriarchal underpinnings of the old one.

In the countryside, the Occupation sought to end rural poverty, which many Americans thought had been a breeding ground for militarism. In early 1946, the Shidehara cabinet, hoping to increase food production by creating a larger class of independent cultivators, had proposed a land redistribution program to the Diet, but the landlord interests, who still had influence in the Diet, weakened the bill by spreading the redistribution over a five-year period and limiting its effects to only about one-third of all cultivated land. Under pressure from SCAP officials, who demanded more sweeping measures to end "feudal oppression" in the countryside, the Diet passed a second land reform bill compelling all absentee landlords to sell their land, limiting the holdings of village landlords to 1 *cho* (2.45 acres), and placing an upper limit on the size of all landholdings. Its intent was to promote rural prosperity by creating a new owner-cultivator class.

By and large, the land reform program achieved its goals. Under its provisions, a massive economic leveling took place in the countryside. About 4.3 million farmers, or roughly 70 percent of the total, many of them former tenants, acquired new land at bargain basement prices, often with low interest government loans. Tenancy was virtually eliminated. Only 10 percent of all cultivated land was still farmed by tenants in 1950. In the wake of land reform, the countryside was dominated by small-scale independent farmers working the land for themselves instead of paying rent to landlords. With new incentives to make a profit, farmers sought to improve productivity with new tools and new techniques. By the early 1950s, most farm households were living quite comfortably, enjoying a much higher living standard than in the pre-war period. By contrast, the pre-war landlords lost most of their landed assets, and statutory limits on the size of land holdings guaranteed that landlordism would not return in the future. Nevertheless, residual social prestige meant that former landlords often continued to play a role in local community organizations—village assemblies, local school boards, and agricultural cooperatives—out of proportion to their numbers.

To democratize the industrial sector, SCAP officials adopted a program of "economic deconcentration" to curb the power of large business enterprises, especially the zaibatsu, who had profited from wartime aggression. After dissolving the zaibatsu holding companies in 1945, SCAP officials set up a commission to dispose of their assets by public sale. The breakup of the complex networks of zaibatsu-affiliated firms, including the great trading companies, struck a severe blow to the pre-war plutocracy, but it created a more competitive business environment. To prevent reconcentration of economic power, SCAP backed an anti-monopoly law in 1947 that forbade (1) the formation of trusts or holding companies, (2) excessive share holding by financial institutions, and (3) the creation of cartels and or other monopolistic organizations. As one top business leader noted two decades later, by opening opportunities for other firms, dissolution of the zaibatsu was a major factor behind postwar economic growth.

Since American Occupation plans identified strong labor organizations as "schools for democracy," SCAP tried to build an independent union movement free from employer pressure or government harassment. Under SCAP guidance, in 1945 the Diet passed a new labor union law guaranteeing the right of workers to organize, strike, and bargain collectively. Fired by a missionary zeal to breathe life into the union movement, SCAP officials made the rounds of factories, shipyards, and workshops with union organizers in tow. Many pre-war labor activists, including Communist Party members, joined in the effort, and so did younger organizers with no pre-war experience. The result of the recruiting campaign was a sudden explosion in the scale of the labor movement. Total union membership rose from 420,000 at the end of 1945 to nearly 5,000,000 (or about 40 percent of the industrial labor force) a year later. Since recruiting all workers in a single factory or work place was the easiest way to organize a union, many new unions were firm-based "enterprise unions" that included both white and blue collar workers.

Many workers joined unions to avoid being laid off, but as Occupation policy-makers had hoped, others saw union membership as a way to protect themselves against the arbitrary power of their employers. At the national level, the new union movement was dominated by two large federations: Sōdōmei, led by moderate labor leaders; and Sanbetsu, led by Communist Party members. Both federations pursued political as well as economic goals, but the more politically militant Sanbetsu was the larger of the two, nearly double the size of its rival. For the first time in modern history, the working class seemed poised to assume a central role in the country's social and political life.

EDUCATION AND IDEOLOGICAL CHANGE

The American post-surrender plans included "re-education" of the Japanese people as one of its major goals. In the fall of 1945, SCAP set to work destroying the ideological structures thought to have buttressed militarism and authoritarianism. It ended state financial support for Shinto shrines, which the Americans regarded as sites for propagating nationalistic beliefs, and the use of wartime terms like the "Greater East Asia Co-Prosperity Sphere" was strictly prohibited. School courses on ethics, Japanese history, and geography were suspended until new textbooks could be written under American supervision, and school children were required to brush out passages in their readers that referred to imperial divinity, Japanese racial superiority, or patriotic myths and legends. To ensure that public discourse remained untainted by further "propaganda" (and to control public criticism of the United States or its policies in Japan) the Occupation instituted close censorship of the press, radio, and movies.

The Americans hoped to implant the political values of freedom, individualism, and democracy in the heads of young Japanese. "Democratic education" would teach children to become independent-minded individuals, aware of their own rights and committed to the ideals of democratic self-government. New courses in "social studies" showed students how to become responsible "democratic citizens," and the election of "class committees" gave them their first experience in the mechanics of democratic procedure. To overcome gender inequality, coeducation was introduced at all levels, from first grade through high school, often with a good deal of giggling in the classroom during the transition. But education was easier to democratize on paper than in the schools. Teachers trained under the pre-war system often enforced quasi-military style discipline in their classrooms or turned their students out to bow respectfully when the emperor came through town. Even so, children who started elementary school in the immediate postwar years absorbed an understanding of democracy as probably no other generation before or since.

Educational reform focused on opening up the pre-war system of higher education that had been designed to prepare a small number of male students for elite positions. On the advice of visiting American educational experts, SCAP authorities promoted a new system that allowed all students to rise as far and as fast as their abilities permitted. Compulsory education was extended through middle school (i.e., the ninth grade), and an American-style single-track system replaced the old multiple-track school system. To expand higher education, public teachers' colleges and other local institutions were upgraded as prefectural universities. (Since they seemed as ubiquitous as the *bentō* lunch boxes for sale at every train station, cynics nicknamed them "lunch box universities.") Although these new institutions did not rival the older national public and private universities in prestige, they did make it easier for young women as well as young men to enter higher education.

To curb the power of the ministry of education, whose officials controlled every aspect of the schools from textbook selection to teacher evaluation, SCAP reforms shifted power to local communities. Publicly elected school boards were given administrative control over local schools, and parents were encouraged to become involved in school life by joining new PTA organizations.

The educational bureaucracy, among the most conservative of all the ministries, escaped the effects of the purge, but many school teachers retired in the immediate postwar years, opening the way for idealistic young people, often just out of the university, to enter the profession. Within a few years, this postwar cohort of teachers, many of them imbued with radical new values, were locked in culture wars with the education bureaucracy.

Like many members of their generation, these young people were swept up in the atmosphere of ferment, dissent, and debate that blossomed in the postwar years. Freed from the constraint of wartime censorship, the intelligentsia joined the Occupation authorities in attacking the "emperor system" and all that it stood for. Not only did they criticize the wartime leadership, they analyzed the pathology of pre-war society with its "feudal" and "absolutist" elements. But the debate over what democracy meant and what values postwar Japan should adopt revealed deep lines of fracture within the intellectual community. For some literary figures like Dazai Osamu, a self-confessed "decadent" who wrote novels about self-destructive protagonists, "freedom" seemed to mean self-indulgence; and for others it implied nihilistic license to do what was once forbidden, whether it was going to striptease shows, writing pornography, or experimenting with drugs.

The main split was between "modernist" liberals, who argued that the Japanese needed to develop "personal autonomy" (*shutaisei*), and Marxists, who wanted to raise the class consciousness of the oppressed. Maruyama Masao, a liberal who wrote essays analyzing the pathologies of pre-war ultranationalist thought, called on the Japanese to judge society by moral standards higher than those defined by the state. What Japan needed, he argued, was not simply institutional reforms imposed by the Occupation but a psychological or spiritual revolution that would turn Japan into a community of "autonomous" individuals. Marxists, on the other hand, were less concerned with individual autonomy than with collective solidarity, and they called on "progressive elements" to carry out a complete social, economic, and political leveling that would put an end to domination by the capitalist class.

Since the Marxist left, particularly the Communists, had most consistently opposed the wartime regime, Marxism had an especially powerful appeal to the intellectual, academic, and journalistic communities. Professors hounded from their posts as Communist sympathizers returned to their campuses as heroes of resistance, and there was hardly a university student who did not read (or at least claim to read) the *Communist Manifesto* or *Das Kapital*. The core concepts of Marxism—the inevitability of class struggle, capitalist exploitation of labor, the economic necessity of imperialism—all seemed to make sense of Japan's recent historical experience. So too did the idea of social revolution: only if the masses united could they oust, peacefully or by force, the entrenched ruling classes who thwarted the growth of true democracy. While most students did not join the Communist Party, university campuses were continually agitated by strikes and protests staged by radical leaders of Zengakuren (All Japan Student Federation). Many newspaper reporters, journalists, and film makers also identified themselves with Marxist ideas.

THE SHIFT TO THE LEFT

The Occupation's "revolution from above" encouraged a visible political shift toward the left. The election of 1946, which was carried out under a revised election law that lowered the voting age to 20 and gave women the right to vote, swept a new generation of politicians into office. About 80 percent of the newly elected Diet members, including thirty-nine women, had never served before. Even more striking were the gains of the left. At the height of their pre-war strength in 1937, the "proletarian parties" had held no more than thirty-seven seats, but as a result of the 1946 election left wing parties—rechristened by the press as "progressive parties"—controlled nearly one-fifth of the lower house. This increase was much less dramatic than those made by the Socialists and Communists in postwar Western Europe, but some SCAP officials hoped that the newly strengthened left wing, especially the Socialist Party, would emerge as the central force in the new democratic politics.

The electoral base of the left centered in the rapidly burgeoning labor movement, whose leaders had adopted radical new tactics in the work place. In late 1945 and early 1946, many new unions pursued "production control," the practice of locking out non-union personnel and white collar management. Instead of going out on strike, the workers kept the plant or enterprise going so that wages could be paid. Their goal was to challenge the authority of managers who had supported the war effort or refused to give workers their fair share of the profits. Japanese officials declined to condemn the practice as illegal, but SCAP officials, who saw "production control" as a threat to private ownership, expressed disapproval. The major labor federations, especially the Communist-dominated Sanbetsu, then shifted to mounting strikes in essential industries to achieve model wage and working settlements. Their targets were enterprises like the national railway system or the major power companies whose services were needed to keep the economy running.

What union leaders sought was a "living wage" based on workers' needs rather than their output. This concept, inspired by a Marxist idea—"from each according to his abilities, to each according to his needs"—reflected the desire of ordinary workers for wages that took into account age, seniority, and family size and provided enough real buying power to support a family. But union leaders, who wished to wrest power from management, also demanded greater control over the evaluation of individual workers, the setting of wages, and even promotions, and they insisted on ending the status system—different entrance gates, dining halls, bonuses, and the like—that separated blue collar workers from white collar. The electrical and national railway workers unions also secured contracts that guaranteed no dismissals, in effect establishing the principle that workers had a permanent right to their jobs. These successes built rank-and-file support that put enormous leverage in the union leaders' hands.

Conservative politicians, disturbed that strikes and excessive labor demands were straining an already prostrate economy, were bitterly hostile toward the left wing and their allies at SCAP headquarters. In January 1947, Prime Minister Yoshida Shigeru publicly denounced striking workers as "trouble makers" and rejected wage hike demands from the national public employees union. A "joint struggle committee" backed by both Sōdōmei and Sanbetsu flung back the gauntlet by announcing plans for a general strike that would shut down the whole economy. Moderate left-wing leaders wanted to force Yoshida out of office, but more radical elements, including many Communists, hoped to provoke a "revolutionary crisis" that would bring a "people's government" to power. The pending general strike forced SCAP to choose between the "democratic" union movement and the conservative government. MacArthur, who feared massive social unrest might threaten the stability of the Occupation, chose to back Yoshida by ordering the strike to be called off.

Although the failure of the general strike was a blow to the radical activists, the moderate left continued to make political gains. In the 1947 election, the Socialist Party won nearly a third of the lower house, making it the plurality party. Their victory not only reflected widespread popular economic discontent, it also demonstrated the effectiveness of the large labor federations in mobilizing votes. The Socialists cooperated with two centrist conservative groups to form a coalition cabinet under Katayama Tetsu, a moderate Christian socialist, but the left-wing Socialists, who were committed to orthodox Marxism, refused to participate. Nonetheless, supporters of the new cabinet had high hopes that it marked a major historical turning point. In the heat of the election campaign, Katayama had declared that a socialist government would begin the transition from capitalism to socialism, and the party program promised the nationalization of heavy industry.

In fact, the country's first left-wing cabinet did little more than preside over the passage of SCAP reforms. The only item accomplished on its own agenda was passage of a law to control the coal industry. Left-wing Socialist leaders like Suzuki Mosaburō accused Katayama of insufficient enthusiasm for a socialist economy, but the moderates in the party realized that the party's position was weak. Since the Socialists had won only one-quarter of the popular vote, they had to cooperate with their conservative coalition partners. As intra-party squabbling grew more intense, small factions from both right and left defected, weakening it still further. In early 1948, the left Socialists voted against a cabinet budget proposal that hiked postal and railroad rates to fund official salary increases, forcing Katayama to resign. The coalition government continued under Ashida Hitoshi, a centrist conservative, but it eventually collapsed in a cloud of scandal when cabinet members and high officials were accused of accepting bribes from a Showa Denkō, a chemical fertilizer company seeking loans from a government bank. In the 1949 election, there were signs that the left was beginning to polarize. While the Socialists suffered heavy losses, and even Katayama lost, the strength of the more radical Communists jumped from four seats to thirty-five.

As Japanese voters swung to the left, some Occupation officials questioned whether it was wise to continue encouraging the unions. What the Americans had hoped for was a labor movement that protected the workers' interests but did not interfere in politics. In 1948, SCAP urged the Ashida cabinet to deny public workers the right to strike and set up a system for mediating labor disputes in the public sector. With help from visiting American union leaders, Occupation officials tried to promote American-style "business unionism" with goals limited to improving wages, hours, and working conditions. Moderate Japanese union leaders, who deplored the tactics of militant confrontation as reckless and irresponsible, organized "democratization leagues" within Sanbetsu to wrest power from "elitist" Communist elements. In 1950, with direct SCAP support, these "democratization leagues" joined with several Sodomei unions to form Sōhyō, a new national labor federation.

RECONSTRUCTING THE ECONOMY

While American "democratization" reforms moved forward, the top priority of centrist and conservative Japanese leaders was economic reconstruction. (As Yoshida Shigeru told General MacArthur in 1945, democracy was a product of affluence: to build it, people had to be fed and given jobs.) In the last months of the war, a small group of technocrats, bureaucrats, and academicians led by Ōkita Saburō, later known as the "father of the economic miracle," met secretly to make plans for the postwar economy. Borrowing lessons from the wartime control system, they proposed an economic revival based on the development of technologically advanced large-scale industries managed by private firms that were guided by government "indicative planning." Business leaders also shifted their sights to peacetime production. As Matsushita Konosuke, head of a major electrical goods firm, told his employees as few days after surrender, the highest mission and responsibility of the company was to "rebuild its factories and strive to increase production of household appliances as quickly as possible."[5]

While General MacArthur requested food and medical supplies to prevent disease and unrest, at first the Americans did little to relieve the bleak economic situation. "The plight of Japan is the direct outcome of its own behavior," noted the Occupation planning document "and the Allies will not undertake the burden of repairing the damage."[6] Indignant at Japan's harsh wartime exploitation of the areas it conquered, many American officials advocated a punitive economic policy. In 1946, an American mission headed by Edwin W. Pauley recommended that part of Japan's industrial plant be dismantled and sent as reparations to countries that had suffered Japanese occupation. The Japanese, he said, had no right to higher living standards than their Asian victims. This proposal, which was a great shock to the Japanese business world, created an atmosphere of uncertainty that impeded new investment. MacArthur, who feared the social and political consequences of a drastic reparations, chose to stall on implementing the policy, and in the end only a few factories were dismantled and sent abroad.

Even without the burden of heavy reparations, the task of economic recovery was formidable. Nearly all heavy industrial production had come to a halt, and the output of coal had plummeted. Massive unemployment and shortages of consumer goods created enormous inflationary pressures, and so did the speculative hoarding of wartime raw material stockpiles turned over to private enterprises at the war's end. To make matters worse, the Japanese government fueled inflation further by running up budget deficits and printing currency to cover its debts. Although these chaotic conditions filled the pockets of speculators, profiteers, and black marketeers, they stifled the recovery of the legitimate economy.

The main champion of an aggressive recovery policy was Finance Minister Ishibashi Tanzan, an early advocate of a Keynesian policy of government-stimulated full employment. By focusing investment in key industries such as coal, steel, fertilizer, and housing construction, he hoped to lift the economy by its own bootstraps. Critics argued that his policies would only create more inflation, but Ishibashi countered that it was more important to provide jobs for repatriated soldiers and other unemployed workers than to worry about consumer prices. In late 1946, the Reconstruction Finance Bank, which channelled government credit to key industries, adopted an investment strategy known as the "priority production system." The idea was to boost coal production to provide fuel to the steel industry, whose output could be used to make mining machinery and other industrial equipment, eventually leading to a general recovery of production. At SCAP's direction, the government also established an Economic Stabilization Board to administer price controls, ration goods, and subsidize the production of basic consumer goods. Although these new agencies put enormous power in the hands of the economic bureaucracy, they were welcomed by business leaders.

By 1947, Washington took a more active interest in promoting economic recovery and stability. The shift in policy grew out of American domestic politics and American fear that the "cold war" was spreading to Asia. Conservative business interests had begun to criticize the radical character of the Occupation program, and the Republican majority in Congress complained about the cost of sending food and other aid to Japan. As Chinese Communist armies moved closer to victory in their civil war with the Guomindang, George Kennan, chief of the State Department's policy planning staff, argued that Japan ought to be turned into an ally against "Communist expansion" in East Asia. The result was a gradual shift in Occupation priorities from economic "democratization" to rebuilding Japan as the "chief factory of Asia." Since industrial revival required large-scale, technically-advanced firms, the "economic deconcentration" program was slowed down, and the list of firms targeted for break up was sharply cut. Restrictions on trade with the outside world were lifted, and imports of American raw cotton helped revive the textile industry. SCAP also abandoned its hands-off policy toward inflation, black markets, and the wage-price spiral that hindered stable growth. In 1949, an economic mission headed by Joseph Dodge, a self-made banker who had helped shape American policy in Germany, recommended economic stabilization based on a balanced budget, more efficient tax collection, tighter inflation controls, and a foreign-exchange rate favorable to building trade. In place of Ishibashi's inflationary program of government investment and subsidies to private enterprise, the Yoshida government switched to fiscal conservatism and the revival of a free market economy. Following Dodge's commission recommendations, it balanced the budget, cut back all subsidies to private industry, and curbed the activities of the Reconstruction Finance Bank.

The Dodge Commission's recommendations proved a useful weapon in the conservative struggle with the left wing. As part of its retrenchment efforts, the government dismissed 250,000 public employees, among them many union activists, and private industry followed suit by "rationalizing" its work force. Responding to the conservative counter-offensive, the radical left, including many university students, staged demonstrations all over the country in late 1949, often engaging in violent clashes with the police. Far from weakening the Yoshida cabinet, however, this new round of left-wing militancy gave SCAP an excuse to carry out a so-called "red purge" against Communist Party activists and other radicals. The ousting of radical activists from the mass media as well as industry was a severe blow to the far left. Although the Communists had regarded the Occupation as an army of liberation, they now saw SCAP in league with political reactionaries and ruthless capitalists to crush the revolutionary masses.

Many historians, both Japanese and American, have argued that in response to the Cold War the American occupation embarked on a "reverse course," abandoning the lofty goals of 1945 and aborting "true" democratization. The term, which is more appropriately used to describe conservative policies of the 1950s, suggests that the Americans abandoned their original goals, but this was not the case. While economic and labor policy underwent a shift, the other major reforms—constitutional revision, land reform, educational democratization, revision of the civil code, and so forth—remained unaltered, creating the basis for a more democratic Japan, however imperfect that democracy might be. The Occupation reforms left few Japanese nostalgic for a return to the pre-1945 system, and the empowerment of new political forces, especially the left wing, checked the resurgence of a militaristic or authoritarian Japan. While disappointed "progressives" became increasingly shrill in their attacks on American policy, it was the Occupation that had created a political and social environment in which their dissidence and opposition could flourish.

ENDNOTES

1. Mark Gayn, *Japan Diary* (Tokyo and Rutland, Vt.: Charles E. Tuttle Co., 1981), 1–2.

2. *Fifty Years of Light and Dark: The Hirohito Era* (Tokyo: The Mainichi Newspapers, 1975), 217.

3. Oda Makoto, "The Meaning of 'Meaningless Death,'" *Journal of Social and Political Ideas in Japan*, 4, no. 2 (Aug. 1966), 76.

4. Edgar Snow, *Journey to the Beginning* (New York: Random House, 1957), 391.

5. Konosuke Matsushita, *Quest for Prosperity: The Life of a Japanese Industrialist* (Tokyo: PHP Press, 1988), 42.

6. Raymond Dennett and Robert K. Turner, eds. "Initial Post-Surrender Policy for Japan," vol 8. of *Documents on American Foreign Policy, 1945–1956* (Boston: World Peace Foundation, 1948), 267–273.

16

The Politics of Confrontation

The invasion of South Korea by the Soviet-backed North Korean regime in June 1950 brought the Cold War to East Asia with a vengeance. Coming less than a year after the Communists took power in China, the Korean War seemed to American leaders a dangerous escalation in the advance of "International Communism." The Truman administration immediately dispatched troops to the peninsula under the auspices of the United Nations, and in late 1950, the Chinese sent in an army of "volunteers" to help retreating North Korean forces. The outbreak of the Korean War provided an economic boost for Japan, which became a logistical base for American forces, but it also sharpened the focus on two critical questions: First, what was Japan's role to be in the Cold War world? Second, once the Occupation ended, what direction should the "New Japan" take domestically? The debate over these issues was heightened by a lack of domestic political consensus, compounded by complex political fractionalization. Not only were the conservatives pitted against the left wing, but both camps were divided within. The result was an era of political contention that lasted nearly a decade.

THE PEACE SETTLEMENT

Even as SCAP relentlessly pressed forward with its reform program, both Americans and Japanese had begun to think about what would happen to Japan after the Occupation ended. In 1947, General MacArthur, who argued that a long military occupation was likely to generate anti-American sentiment, announced that it was time for the Americans to leave Japan. Once the country had been restored to full sovereignty, he said, its security could be guaranteed under the protection of the United Nations. As one of the authors of the "peace constitution," MacArthur was committed to turning Japan into the "Switzerland of Asia." These ideas generated little enthusiasm in Washington, where the foreign policy and defense establishments had reached a consensus that Japan should be a regional platform for American power. The American navy wanted to retain bases at Yokosuka and Sasebo on the island of Honshu, and American army leaders wanted the Japanese to build up their military forces so that they would not be completely dependent on the United States for security after independence. In 1949, the American Joint Chiefs of Staff made it clear that they were opposed to a peace treaty with Japan unless the United States was able to maintain bases there and unless the Japanese rearmed themselves in preparation for a possible third world war. The deadlock between MacArthur and policy-makers in Washington was not resolved until the eve of the Korean War.

In the meantime Japanese leaders had been trying to speed the return of independence by signaling their willingness to align themselves with the United States in the Cold War conflict. In 1947, Prime Minister Ashida sent a secret memorandum to Washington, hinting that Japan might accept an international guarantee of the country's security and a strengthening of domestic police forces to maintain internal law and order, but nothing much came of his proposal. By early 1950, Prime Minister Yoshida, aware that the dispute between SCAP and Washington over Japan's future was stalling peace negotiations, dispatched Finance Minister Ikeda Hayato to Washington with the message that Japan would agree to the stationing of American troops on the main islands after the end of the occupation. (As Yoshida jokingly told an American diplomat, Japan might become an American "colony" for a time but eventually would pull ahead of the United States just as the Americans had pulled ahead of the British.)

What Yoshida hoped for was a return to a foreign policy based on economic expansion and cooperation with the Anglo-American powers, very much like that pursued by Shidehara Kijūrō in the late 1920s. The humiliating defeat demonstrated the folly of reconstructing Japan as a military power. The only sensible alternative was to entrust the security of the country to the United States. As Yoshida later wrote, it was not "a question of either dogmas or philosophy" but "merely the quickest and most effective—indeed the only way—to promote the prosperity of the Japanese people."[1] There was by no means consensus on this position within Japan. When it became clear that Yoshida was planning a "separate peace" with the United States and its "Free World" allies, other voices called for a "comprehensive peace" with all wartime belligerents, including the Soviet Union. In 1950, the Peace Problems Study Group, a group of prominent liberal and left-wing intellectuals, announced opposition to a peace treaty that excluded the Soviets. They argued that the cold war was not going to last forever and that Japan should commit itself to neither side. Their "four peace principles"—comprehensive peace, no foreign military bases, neutrality in international affairs, and no rearmament—won support from the Socialist Party and its affiliated labor federation, Sōhyō, as well as from the "progressive" intelligentsia.

Despite the public clamor, Yoshida carried on negotiations with John Foster Dulles, a prominent Republican lawyer representing the American government, but the two men could not agree on Japan's future strategic position. Yoshida was willing to accept American bases, but he balked at Dulles' suggestion that Japan build its own force of 300–350,000 men by the mid-1950s. Since the United States was likely to come to Japan's defense in an international crisis, Yoshida saw no need to maintain conventional military and naval forces, nor was he willing to sacrifice economic recovery to American strategic needs. As he told Dulles, the economy was still too weak to afford rearmament. Only when the Americans appeared to hold the peace negotiations hostage did Yoshida finally agree to a limited and gradual build up of Japanese defense capacity.

The upshot of Yoshida's negotiations with the Americans was a delicate compromise between American strategic interests and Japanese economic recovery. The peace treaty signed in San Francisco in September 1951 granted Japan full independence, with no reparations, no punitive economic restrictions, and no commitment to massive rearmament. On the other hand, Yoshida also signed a Mutual Security Treaty with the United States, which not only gave the Americans the right to station forces in Japan, but left the United States in full administrative control over the Ryukyu Islands, gave the Americans the right to deploy their forces in Japan without consulting the Japanese government, and permitted American forces to be used in dealing with domestic disturbances within Japan. In short, the security treaty placed Japan on the forward line of the American defensive perimeter in East Asia.

The Japanese had to make another important concession to the Americans as well. Yoshida, whose diplomatic career began in Manchuria, felt that China was more important to Japan's future than the United States. Not only was China a natural market for Japan, it was also an important source of raw materials. The Chinese were not "real Communists," he thought, and in any case Japan had to maintain close ties "whether China was red or green." Once the occupation ended, Yoshida had expected to establish normal diplomatic relations with the new People's Republic of China, just as the British had. To ensure ratification of the peace treaty by the United States Senate, however, Yoshida was forced to recognize the Guomindang government on Taiwan as the only legitimate government of China. By solidly wedding Japan to the American strategic bloc, Yoshida had mortgaged its diplomatic independence as well.

Although Yoshida's personal popularity reached its peak when he returned from the peace conference at San Francisco, the settlement met with dissent both on the left and the right. The Japanese Communist Party, predictably enough, rejected the settlement completely. The party platform announced that Japan had come under the domination of American imperialism. The

Socialists, on the other hand, were so divided in their reaction that in late 1951 the party split apart. The right Socialists accepted both the peace settlement and the security treaty, but the left Socialists argued that Japan should have signed a comprehensive peace with all the wartime belligerents, including China and the Soviet Union. Nor were all conservatives satisfied with the settlement. Even members of Yoshida's own political party criticized the security treaty as an "unequal treaty" that compromised Japan's sovereignty.

Out of deference to American wishes, the newly independent Japanese government began to build a limited military force. The first step had already been taken shortly after the outbreak of the Korean War when the Yoshida cabinet created a 75,000 man National Police Reserve. No debate took place in the Diet, nor was there any international consultation. Organized with American help and staffed by former Imperial Army officers, this embryonic army was ostensibly organized to deal with domestic disturbances as American troops left Japan for the war front in Korea. When the Korean War ended, the United States hoped to shift some of the burden for the containment of Asian Communism to a NATO-like regional collective security including Japan, Taiwan, and South Korea. The Yoshida cabinet protested that further rearmament was constitutionally impossible and politically dangerous, but it finally agreed to transform the National Police Reserve into the National Self Defense Force with full land, air, and sea capabilities. By a further agreement, the United States began a program of military assistance, supplying the new military force with training and arms, and providing aid to build up domestic military-related industries.

Initially the policy of limited rearmament enjoyed support among a public uneasy at the thought of a completely disarmed and defenseless Japan. Fear that the world was on the edge of war was high in the early 1950s, and public opinion polls showed that a majority of respondents favored rearmament. But once the Yoshida cabinet began organizing a new military, support began to plummet. With bitter memories of wartime suffering still fresh, the sudden appearance of Japanese in uniform again was profoundly disturbing. Few wished to repeat recent history. A popular domestic peace movement, sustained by anti-nuclear sentiment, support for the "peace constitution," and growing anti-American sentiments, slowly gathered force.

Rice roots opposition to the presence of American troops generated a nationwide anti-base movement. The seamy atmosphere of tawdry bars, open prostitution, and occasional crime in towns near the bases caused local resentment. So did appropriation of agricultural land by the Americans. As early as 1949, for example, local fishermen in Chiba prefecture staged a protest against the use of the local coast as an American firing range. When the number of American bases expanded under the new security arrangements, anti-base "struggles," as they were called by the left, increased in frequency and spread throughout the country. Local protestors were supported by local government officials, peace movement activists, radical students, and left-wing politicians. Newspapers were filled with pictures of demonstrators, many of them women, staging vigils or sit-ins outside the gates of American bases, confronting American military police, or blocking joint American-SDF maneuvers. Activists also filed suits to block the expansion of American air-fields and other facilities.

What gave the peace movement a strong impetus in the early 1950s was a pervasive "nuclear allergy" among the Japanese public. While the Occupation had suppressed any public discussion of the atomic attacks on Japan, once Japanese regained independence Hiroshima and Nagasaki became powerful symbols for a new anti-nuclear movement. With the lifting of American censorship, an "atomic bomb literature" of novels, personal reminiscences, and critical essays described the horrors wrought by weapons of mass destruction and reminded the public that the Japanese were the first people to suffer atomic attack. The anti-nuclear movement expanded rapidly in early 1954 when a Japanese fishing boat, the Lucky Dragon 5, was contaminated by the fall out from an American hydrogen bomb test at Bikini atoll in the Pacific. After one crew member died, a popular movement to ban all nuclear weapons was organized in Tokyo, and on the anniversary of the first atomic attack a new anti-nuclear organization, Gensuikyō, held a national rally at Hiroshima. The notion that the Japanese had been victims as well as aggressors in the war gained currency as the public reflected on the uniqueness of Japan's experience with atomic warfare.

THE "REVERSE COURSE"

While most Japanese had benefited from the American-initiated reforms, the sweeping American assault on pre-war institutions upset conservative political elements, who continually grumbled about the Occupation's "excesses" and "injustices." By the time the Occupation ended in April 1952, they were in a position to do something about their grievances. After the fall of the Socialist-backed Ashida cabinet, Yoshida Shigeru returned to power, determined to hold elections that would break the left-wing momentum. In the 1949 elections, his party (Democratic Liberals) won a landslide victory. Capturing a 58 percent majority in the lower house, Yoshida organized the first majority government since the end of the war. The election also brought into office a number of retired high officials like Ikeda Hayato and Satō Eisaku, who were recruited to revitalize the party. Impressed by Yoshida's victory, members of another conservative group defected to his party, which was renamed the Liberal Party. Facing a weak opposition, divided among the two wings of the Socialists and two centrist conservative parties, Yoshida had little difficulty in retaining a hold on the government for the next five years.

A vigorous and domineering man who suffered neither fools nor rivals gladly, Yoshida was known as a "one man" leader, conspicuously contemptuous of journalists, arrogant toward the public, and high-handed in his po-

Yoshida Shigeru, who negotiated the San Francisco Peace Treaty and signed the Mutual Security Treaty with the United States in 1951. He served as prime minister five times between 1946 and 1954.

litical tactics. Although the peace negotiations consumed much of his energies, Yoshida was determined to modify Occupation reforms that he thought to be hastily conceived, administratively inefficient, and inappropriate to Japanese society. Even the Americans had realized that the Japanese would reevaluate Occupation reforms after the return to independence. General Matthew Ridgeway, who succeeded MacArthur after he was relieved of his command by President Truman, indicated that the United States would have no objection if the Japanese did so. It was no surprise that Yoshida set up a private advisory committee, headed by Ishizaka Taizō, a powerful business leader, to consider revisions of the American reform program. This was the beginning of a conservative "reverse course" led by politicians and business leaders nostalgic for the pre-war order and determined to curb the power of the left.

The term "reverse course" was coined by a Japanese newspaper in late 1951 to describe the sudden revival of pre-war nationalist rituals—the imperial garden party, patriotic songs like the "Navy March," or visits to the Yasukuni Shrine where the war dead were commemorated—but conservative goals were much broader. First, the Yoshida government envisaged an intensification of "anti-subversive" measures. It had already set up an agency to gather intelligence on the Communist Party and other left-wing groups, but in April 1952 the government proposed a Subversive Activity Prevention Law that gave officials the power to prevent general strikes, establish a press code, and prohibit public assemblies and demonstrations. The bill met with strong opposition in the upper house, where debate likened it to the pre-war Peace Preservation Law, but a milder version established a Public Security Investigation Agency with the power to recommend the dissolution of groups advocating or using political violence. Second, the Yoshida government attacked the antitrust laws passed during the Occupation. It pushed through the Diet a 1953 revision of the Anti-Monopoly Law that loosened restrictions on joint directorships and joint share holding and permitted the formation of cartels to deal with recessions or to introduce new productive technology. Third, the conservatives passed laws abolishing prefectural police forces, recentralizing the police under a newly established National Police Agency, and putting all high-ranking police national officials under the direct control of the prime minister. And finally, the Yoshida government called for a return to the pre-war elitist multi-track school system, but it backed down when it became clear that the mass education system introduced by the Americans remained intact.

Although the conservative "reverse course" left the Occupation's basic political and structural reforms intact, opposition was emotional and intense. The leadership of the Communist Party, heavily hit by the "red purge" in 1950, called on its members to stage "armed resistance" to overthrow the "reactionary" Yoshida cabinet. On "bloody May Day" in 1952, clashes between demonstrators and police left two dead on the imperial palace plaza. During the summer, naive young party activists, hoping to establish a new "people's government," retreated to rural mountain areas to prepare for guerrilla warfare against the authorities. The tactics of confrontation carried over into the Diet, where the "progressive" parties, including the Socialists, feared that the Yoshida conservatives were trying to turn Japan back to the bad old days. Their distrust deepened when a number of purged pre-war politicians were returned to the Diet in the election of 1951. The Socialists, making no pretense of being a loyal opposition, deliberately disrupted the Diet proceedings by boycotting committee hearings or floor debates, occupying the speaker's chair to prevent the passage of bills, or slowing down floor votes by "ox walking" toward the ballot box. For their part, the conservatives, exercising what the press called "the tyranny of the majority," rode roughshod over all objections to their proposals. With so little consensus on the rules of the parliamentary game, let alone on substantive issues, many outside observers wondered whether political democracy would survive in Japan.

Confrontations in the Diet were paralleled by confrontations in the work place, where a different kind of "reverse course" was taking place. While some Japanese business leaders accepted the emergence of a newly strength-ened labor movement, many wished to roll back concessions made in the early postwar strikes. With the support of the Yoshida government, the busi-ness community, represented by the newly organized Employers' Federation (*Nikkeiren*), launched a campaign to retrieve management prerogatives lost to the unions and to regain control over the workers. In 1950, a wave of fir-ings in the name of improving productivity brought the dismissal of many radical union organizers and leaders. When unions demanded the renewal of contracts signed in the early postwar years, management refused their de-mands and simply shut down operations. Unemployment was still high in the early 1950s, and managers knew that they could afford long strikes better than the workers could. The result was a wave of intense disputes in the au-tomobile, mining, and steel industries. To break the power of the existing unions, management also encouraged the formation of "second unions" led by moderate workers upset at the radical tactics of left-wing union leaders. Often managers used persuasion, telling workers that their best interests lay with the firm, but sometimes they resorted to bribery and coercion as well.

To protect moderate workers and promote loyalty to the firm, managers accepted the principle of job security, implicitly creating a system of "lifetime employment" that persisted over the next decades, and they also accepted a system of seniority-based pay that gave experienced workers higher wages than younger ones. But managers used confrontational tactics to reverse many concessions made to the postwar labor movement. For one thing, they insisted that wage settlements be pegged to company profit and labor pro-ductivity rather than to worker needs. While management accepted "base-up" agreements, guaranteeing an overall rise in wages, they refused automatic cost-of-living raises or any formula based solely on worker needs. For an-other thing, management made sure that individual wages and promotions were determined not by union officials or worker representatives but by man-agement supervisors. In part, this change was aimed at the feather-bedding that often resulted from union control over personnel practices, but it also had the effect of encouraging workers to compete with one another for raises. The result was a new model of corporate paternalism in labor-man-agement practices that modified but did not eliminate all the union gains of the Occupation period.

The union movement saw these management victories as major setbacks, but the leaders of Sōhyō, the largest labor federation, were divided over how best to respond to the management counter-offensive. One faction, under Takano Minoru, advocated a broad campaign of local strikes that would unite workers and their families with local communities in a political strug-gle against the entrenched political and economic establishment. By contrast, an opposing faction, led by Ōta Kaoru and Iwai Akira, favored allying with Sanbetsu, the other large national federation, in a national campaign focused on economic issues. After a prolonged debate, the two factions compromised in 1956 on a "spring offensive" to coordinate wage negotiations undertaken by local enterprise unions. The ultimate goal was to achieve wage levels comparable to those of Western countries. By presenting a united front, the union leaders also hoped to check any further erosion of union power. By the late 1950s, the "spring offensive" had turned into a national collective bargaining session that established overall goals for annual wage increases. Settlements reached by the unions in one key industry, such as steel or railways, provided a benchmark for negotiations in other industries.

While the "reverse course" of the early 1950s accelerated a shift in the national political mood from left to right of center, it did not bring a return to pre-war institutions and policies. The Japanese public was too jealous of the gains made under the Occupation to accept such a drastic reversal. Most ordinary Japanese, whether newly prosperous farmers, factory workers, or members of the growing white collar class, were aware of how they had benefited. To be sure, the central government reasserted its authority at the expense of local autonomy, and the central ministerial bureaucracies expanded their jurisdictions, but they did so in an environment that was drastically different from pre-war Japan. The political opposition forces created by the Occupation reforms, especially the militant left, were able to check the most reactionary impulses of the conservative right, and a critical and unfettered press had no compunctions about attacking government policy. The postwar culture of dissent and distrust of authority remained vital. As a result, the "reverse course" orchestrated by conservative political and business leaders proved quite modest.

CONSERVATIVE CONSOLIDATION

The "reverse course" was marked not only by intense conflict between right and left, but also by confusion and divisions within both camps. The Socialists, who had split apart over the peace settlement in 1951, remained deeply divided over basic ideology and political tactics. The right Socialists included both Marxist and non-Marxist social democrats, but the left Socialists were committed to "scientific Marxism." These basic differences were papered over during the Occupation, but right Socialists never felt comfortable with their more radical colleagues. While the right Socialists wanted to build a mass "working man's party" with broad popular support, the left wing wanted to become a true "class party" representing the interests of the proletariat; and while the right Socialists favored a gradualist approach to socialism relying on the ballot box and the parliamentary process, the left Socialists were willing to use extra-parliamentary tactics if necessary to bring about a socialist revolution.

The conservatives were equally divided, though less by ideological or tactical issues than by conflicting ambitions and personal differences. Yoshida had managed to establish his domination of the conservative camp, but his position was challenged by the return to politics of a number of "depurged" pre-war politicians. The most powerful was Hatoyama Ichirō, a former Seiyūkai leader who had relinquished leadership of the Liberal Party to Yoshida when he was purged in 1946. Not only did he feel Yoshida had usurped his rightful place in the political world, he thought Yoshida was turning Japan into a powerless client of the United States. Other returned leaders resented Yoshida's favoritism toward former bureaucrats like Ikeda and Satō, and they disliked his dictatorial leadership style. After toying with the idea of forming a new party of their own, they decided instead to foment an anti-Yoshida movement within the Liberal Party.

The Hatoyama faction backed Yoshida's "reverse course" legislation, but they sought to undermine his political position in any way they could. In 1953, they even joined with the Socialists in a no-confidence vote that censured Yoshida for calling a left-wing deputy a "damn fool." Unfortunately, the ensuing election ended the Liberal absolute majority. By contrast, both wings of the divided Socialists picked up new seats, and so did the Communist Party. Those gains were due in large measure to the backing of national labor federations, Sōhyō and Sanbetsu, but they also reflected growing public doubts over the government's rearmament program. Many voters were swayed by the powerful appeal of Suzuki Mosaburō, a left Socialist leader: "Youth, do not take up arms! Women, do not send your spouses and children to the battlefield!" The left Socialists, who gained more seats in the election than the right Socialists, felt the "correctness" of their position had been vindicated.

Under relentless attack by a press sympathetic to the "progressive" parties, Yoshida's popularity plummeted. "One man" rule had been acceptable when Yoshida stood as a buffer between SCAP's good intentions and the complexities of Japanese society, but it was not so popular once the Occupation ended. Neither was Yoshida's testiness, his reliance on an inner circle of cronies, or his contemptuous treatment of the Diet. In early 1954, the cabinet was tainted with scandal when Yoshida blocked the arrest of his chief lieutenant, Satō Eisaku, for accepting bribes from shipbuilding companies. This egregious misuse of official power roused general indignation. Public opinion polls showed a dramatic decline in support for the cabinet, and the conservative opposition led by Hatoyama finally merged into a new party, the Democrats. In December, the new party joined the Socialists in voting for a no-confidence resolution that finally forced Yoshida to resign after more than seven years in power.

Although the departure of this domineering figure from the political scene did not bring an end to political confrontation, it did pave the way for the consolidation of both the Socialists and the conservatives, or the establishment of what some have called "the 1955 system." What galvanized both camps was recovery of Socialist electoral support in the 1953 election. Leading business executives, in the midst of their struggle to roll back the power of the unions, were alarmed at the slow but steady rise in the left-wing vote.

The prospect that the socialists seeking a "dictatorship of the proletariat" might be voted into power was alarming. Shortly after the election, the leaders of the four largest business organizations, led by Keidanren, urged conservative leaders to bury their differences. Given the intensity of the hostility between Yoshida and Hatoyama, that was not likely to happen, but many conservatives, including Kishi Nobusuke, wanted to build a conservative majority party large enough to continue the "reverse course" and revise the constitution into the bargain.

When Hatoyama became prime minister in 1954, it was the left wing's turn to worry. Fearing that the reverse course was likely to accelerate under his leadership, both wings of the Socialist Party decided to wage the 1955 election campaign under the joint slogan of "protecting the peace constitution." The result was new gains for the Socialists. The left wing, including the Communists secured more than one-third of the seats in the lower house, enough to block any conservative-backed constitutional revision. The divided Socialists, even though unable to resolve internal ideological differences, rejoined in October 1955 to consolidate their electoral gains. Within a month, the three conservative parties countered by merging into the Liberal Democratic Party, a unified conservative force that controlled a firm absolute majority in the lower house. In hindsight, the establishment of the Liberal Democrats ushered in a period of one-party dominance that was to last a generation, but no one anticipated that at the time. What was more visible was an escalation of political confrontation between left and right.

In contrast to Yoshida, whose main goal was the rebuilding of the Japanese economy, the leadership of the new party was dominated by those with a strong nostalgia for the pre-war days, when Japan was a great power in a military and diplomatic sense. Not surprisingly, the party platform had a strong anti-left, anti-American, and anti-Yoshida tinge.

> While democracy and liberalism, stressed during the occupation, should be respected and defended as the guiding principles of the new Japan, the initial occupation policies were directed mainly to the goal of weakening Japan, with the result that . . . the concepts of state and patriotism were unjustly suppressed and state power was excessively fragmented and reduced.[2]

A major goal of the LDP leaders was revising the constitution to eliminate Article Nine, to restore the emperor as head of state, and to give the cabinet new emergency powers. As long as the left wing controlled one-third of the Diet seats, however, the prospects for basic constitutional changes remained remote.

To break the power of the left, the LDP decided to change the election law by replacing the multiple-member electoral district that returned three to five Diet members with a small, single-member district system that favored majority or large party candidates. In 1956, the LDP proposed an electoral reform bill that not only introduced the small district but redrew district boundaries to eliminate Socialist electoral bases. Denouncing this "Hato-mander," the

Socialists retaliated by adopting "ox walk" voting tactics, forcing the LDP to emasculate the bill and finally kill it in the upper house. The conservatives, however, continued their campaign to strengthen central bureaucratic controls. In 1956, the system of publicly elected local school boards, introduced under the Occupation, was replaced by a new system of school boards appointed by the ministry of education. When the education minister ordered the new boards to make evaluations of teaching staff, presumably with an eye toward eliminating "trouble-making" radical teachers, the left struck back. With the backing of the Socialists and the major labor federations, the national teachers' union, Nikkyōso, responded with a massive opposition campaign that forced the government to back down and accept a compromise that allowed for self-evaluation.

The acrimony between the political left and right was exacerbated by left-wing frustration at failure to return to power. Despite lingering internal divisions, the reconsolidated Socialists looked forward to the 1958 election as a chance to rebuild power, and they announced their goal of capturing a majority in the lower house. In fact, although the left vote increased at about the same rate as the conservative vote declined, the Socialists were disappointed to find that they had won only six new seats. After a bruising debate about how to reconstruct the party after this "defeat," the Socialist leaders decided to continue a program of strident opposition to the LDP's continuing "reverse course." Indeed, left-wing leaders of all stripes were looking for a cause to bring an end to the continuing domination of the conservatives.

THE SECURITY TREATY CRISIS

The politics of confrontation culminated in 1959–1960 in a great national debate over Japan's relationship with the United States. Throughout the 1950s, the conservative government had faithfully followed Washington's lead in foreign policy, maintaining correct but distant relations with the Soviet Union, continuing to recognize the Guomindang regime on Taiwan, and occasionally trying to open dialogue with the Syngman Rhee regime in South Korea. The United States repaid this loyalty by sponsoring Japan's return to the international community. To enhance its respectability, the United States backed Japan's efforts to become a member of the United Nations, and to facilitate its participation in the world market, the Americans sponsored Japan's entry into international economic organizations like the International Monetary Fund (IMF), the World Bank, the General Agreement on Trade and Tariffs (GATT), and the Organization for Economic Cooperation and Development (OECD). The American government also gave Japanese producers full access to the American domestic market, and it did what it could to encourage the recovery of the Japanese economy.

Even under the Hatoyama government, the conservatives did not stretch their tether to the United States. Hatoyama's chief foreign policy goal was a peace agreement with the Soviet Union, which had refused to sign the San Francisco treaty in 1951. By achieving a détente with the Soviets, Hatoyama hoped to reduce Japan's dependence on the relationship with the United States. But when the Russians refused to return the so-called "northern territories," four islands in the southern Kuriles occupied by Russian forces, Hatoyama decided to shelve the idea of a peace treaty. Instead, in December 1956 Japan signed an agreement reestablishing normal diplomatic exchanges with the Soviet Union, arranging for the return of Japanese POWs from the Soviet Union, and reopening trade. The Japanese also secured a promise of Soviet support for Japanese membership in the United Nations. Even while pursuing this "independent diplomacy," however, the Hatoyama government was in constant consultation with the United States.

During the late 1950s, the debate over foreign policy focused on the security treaty, which was to come up for renewal in 1960. As many conservatives complained, the original agreement gave priority to American security needs over Japanese sovereignty. In early 1957, a new LDP prime minister, Kishi Nobusuke, announced his intention to negotiate a treaty revision with the Americans. Kishi, however, was a controversial political figure who had built his pre-war reputation as one of the architects of the planned economy in Manchukuo, then as a member of Tōjō's wartime cabinet. Indeed, his signature was on the declaration of war against the United States. Although Kishi was arrested as a Class A war criminal after the war, SCAP decided not to bring him to trial. After election to the lower house in 1953, he quickly emerged as a leader of the conservative right wing, playing a key role in founding the LDP. Had more senior LDP leaders like Ishibashi Tanzan or Ōgata Taketora not succumbed to illness, he might not have become prime minister, but when he came to power the left wing was immediately on its guard.

LDP leaders like Ikeda Hayato did not see much advantage in revising a treaty that served Japan's defense needs, and even Kishi himself knew that a renewal of the treaty would provoke intense public debate, but the new prime minister was determined to open a "new era of United States-Japan relations." He made a highly visible trip to the United States, where he played a round of golf with President Eisenhower, received a Yankees cap from Casey Stengel, and appeared on the cover of *Time* magazine. The Eisenhower administration, warned by the embassy in Tokyo that anti-American sentiment was on the rise, agreed to consider a complete overhaul of the treaty. It was better to make concessions to Japan than to risk its shift toward a "neutralist" foreign policy.

Negotiations produced a draft that restored parity between the two countries. First, while the original treaty contained no explicit American commitment to come to the defense of Japan, the revision did. American forces stationed in Japan were to be mobilized not only for the defense of the "Far

East" but of Japan as well. Interestingly, the revised treaty did not impose on Japan a reciprocal obligation to come to the defense of the United States. Second, while the original treaty gave the Japanese government no control over how American bases in Japan were to be used, the revised treaty provided for "prior consultation" between the two governments in the event of major changes in the deployment or armaments of American forces, or their dispatch outside Japan. In theory, this provision allowed the Japanese to veto the introduction of nuclear weapons into Japan or the use of American bases for military operations in the rest of Asia. Third, while the original treaty gave the United States the right to intervene in the case of "large-scale internal riots and disturbances," the Japanese insisted on the abolition of this clause as incompatible with Japan's status as an independent nation. Finally, a ten-year limit was set on the treaty, giving either side could abrogate the treaty after giving a year's notice.

Although the revised treaty put Japan on a more equal footing with the United States, it was not popular. As the American ambassador had correctly observed, the public mood had changed in Japan during the middle 1950s. After the Korean War ended, the Cold War seemed to thaw a bit, and fears of a third world war retreated. In their place, new doubts arose about the wisdom of aligning with either side in the Cold War, and the appeal of neutrality grew. The left wing proposed a neutrality that leaned toward the Soviet bloc, but many Japanese preferred complete non-alignment with either of the Cold War superpowers. Public opinion polls showed that after 1955 support for the Mutual Security Treaty plunged, opposition to revision of the constitution increased, and more people were opposed to rearmament than favored it. Indeed, an NHK public opinion poll in 1959 showed that more than half the respondents preferred a neutralist foreign policy and only 26 percent favored continued alignment with the "Free World."

The new public mood was not simply the result of the peace movement's campaigns. It also reflected a new assessment of the United States as an ally. While America had loomed large as a military power in the early 1950s, its relative status declined over the decade. Not only had the Soviet Union broken the American nuclear monopoly by producing a hydrogen bomb, it successfully launched its Sputnik satellite in 1957. A few months later, the first American satellite rocket exploded on its launching pad. It appeared that the Soviet Union might be moving ahead of the Americans in military technology, raising doubts about whether Japan had picked the best and most reliable ally. At the same time, resentment of the American military presence in Japan intensified. When William S. Girard, an American soldier, shot and killed a Japanese farm woman salvaging spent ammunition casings on an American firing range, the public was shocked to learn that Japan had no legal jurisdiction to try him for murder. In effect, the American military forces were protected by a kind of extraterritoriality. Incidents like this, though rare, incited public indignation, creating a public mood ripe for an explosion of anti-American sentiments.

Anticipating large-scale protests, in 1958 the Kishi government, to the surprise and alarm of some of its ministers, introduced a bill to enlarge police powers to conduct investigations and searches, seize material evidence, and intrude on private property. Protesting that the bill was "undemocratic," and fearing that it would be used to crack down on domestic dissent, the Socialists boycotted the Diet proceedings for nearly a month, forcing the LDP to withdraw it. Angered at Kishi's cavalier tactics, the Socialists, Sōhyō, Zengakuren (the national student organization), and several other left groups decided to mount a massive public campaign against renewal of the security treaty in the fall of 1959. Public anxieties were heightened when the Soviet Union threatened to keep the "northern territories" if the treaty were ratified. During the spring, the left parties stalled the treaty debate in the Diet, but the crisis did not come to a head until May 1960. The Kishi government tried to force ratification of the treaty through the Diet by prolonging its session. When Socialist deputies seized the speaker's dais to prevent this, police were called in to remove them forcibly. In response, the Socialists decided to boycott the vote. Despite the absence of the main opposition party, the LDP majority rammed through approval of the revised treaty.

An outraged press attacked the government for its flagrant disregard for the rules of parliamentary democracy, and a storm of protest erupted in Tokyo. Radical students snake-danced through the streets of Tokyo where they fought pitched battles with the riot police; millions of workers went on strike; and huge crowds including ordinary citizens, housewives, salaried workers, and nonradical students surrounded the Diet building. The demonstrations, spontaneous and unparalleled in size and scale, led many to fear a complete breakdown in the political process. While some conservatives saw the country on the verge of revolution, many on the left feared a right-wing coup. What sustained the demonstrations, however, was not the security treaty itself or hostility toward the United States or even the mass mobilization tactics of the left, but rather outrage at the "undemocratic" tactics and policies of the Kishi government. The prime minister's association with a war that had come to be regarded as a monstrous mistake fed deep fear and distrust of his cabinet, and his use of the police, his support of repressive legislation, and his open advocacy of constitutional revision seemed like the return of a bad dream.

The denouement of the crisis came in June 1960 when James Hagerty, the American president's press secretary, arrived in Japan to arrange a visit by President Eisenhower. At Haneda airport, Hagerty's automobile was surrounded by several thousand radical student and union demonstrators, and he had to be rescued by helicopter. A few days later, Kamba Michiko, a female student at Tokyo University, was killed in a clash between the police and Zengakuren students at the Diet building. Her death shocked the public, forcing Kishi to withdraw his invitation to Eisenhower and submit his resignation. While the demonstrations failed to block the ratification of the revised Security Treaty, they marked an end to the politics of confrontation, which were soon to give way to the politics of complacency.

TOWARD ECONOMISM

With Kishi's departure, the veterans of pre-war politics saw their power within the LDP gradually fade. In their place emerged a new generation of postwar leaders unencumbered by political baggage linking them to the past and unenthusiastic for the policies of the "reverse course." Many were the former bureaucrats recruited by Yoshida, who was still a formidable influence behind the scenes. These younger LDP leaders were oriented toward the future, not the past, and they wanted to broaden the party's electoral base by avoiding divisive issues like the security treaty, constitutional revision, and rearmament. The left-wing leaders, who had been shaken when the demonstrations got out of hand, also wished to withdraw from the brink of political chaos. At the height of the anti-treaty demonstrations, even the Communist leadership had vetoed extremist proposals to attack the prime minister's residence. But the main changes took place in the Socialist camp, which once again split in two. The right Socialists formed the new Democratic Socialist Party, which supported the treaty revision, leaving the left Socialists in control of the party. But younger leaders within the Socialists were restless at the party's embrace of doctrinaire Marxist political formulas, and they too called for a party program aimed at a broader electorate.

The end of the anti-Treaty movement coincided with a major setback for organized labor, the failure of the Miike Coal Mine strike, an epic struggle that lasted nearly nine months. For the mine workers, the issue was worker cutbacks brought on by a national policy of switching the energy base from coal to oil; for mine management the issue was its power to make business decisions based on company profitability rather than worker welfare. The big business community, major banks, and other large enterprises backed the mine company, providing financial help to tide over the work stoppage, while the large labor federations, including Sōhyō, pitched in on the side of the strikers, raising funds to support their families and mobilizing hundreds of thousands to man their picket lines. In the end, the striking workers were defeated by economic reality: technological change and government policy had made coal a declining industry. In August 1960, shortly after the treaty crisis ended, the strike was settled by a mediation that reduced worker dismissals but permitted the company to make lay offs in the long run.

The shift away from the politics of confrontation was launched by Prime Minister Ikeda Hayato, who, much to the surprise of the press and the public, assumed a "low posture" toward the opposition. In contrast to the combative attitude of conservative leaders since Yoshida, Ikeda announced that he intended to show "patience and generosity" toward the opposition. Even more important, he announced an "Income Doubling Plan" to increase average household income by 100 percent over the next decade. It was a promise that Ikeda and his advisors knew would be easy to keep. Between 1954 and 1959, the national income had grown at an average annual rate of 10.8 percent, making the dramatic promise to double income a safe one. Indeed, it understated the economy's potential considerably. Since the general public was unfamiliar with concepts like "GNP" or "national income" and worried about the country's economic weakness, the announcement of the "income doubling plan" brought a surge of support for the conservative government. No other postwar cabinet had achieved as high a popularity rating as the Ikeda government. More important, the new policy spread a healing balm on a public bruised and battered by constant ideological and policy warfare. As the LDP adopted a policy of "economism" focusing on economic growth and popular affluence, a calmer and more moderate political atmosphere settled over the country. Indeed, critics later suggested that this new policy anesthetized the public.

ENDNOTES

1. Masatake Kosaka, *A History of Postwar Japan* (Tokyo: Kodansha International, 1982), 106–107.

2. For a slightly different translation, see Masumi Junnosuke, *Postwar Politics in Japan, 1945–1955,* trans. Lonnie Carlisle (Berkeley: Institute of East Asian Studies, 1985), 312.

17

The Economic Miracle

The promise to double the national income seemed a pipe dream to most Japanese, who still thought of their country as poor and semi-developed. A 1961 Economic Planning Agency survey showed that nearly two-thirds of respondents in Tokyo and Osaka doubted that Japan could catch up with European living standards within the next decade. In reality, the economy had already begun to take off. During the "special procurements boom" of the Korean War, economic recovery accelerated when American forces fighting on the peninsula bought trucks, jeeps, uniforms, and other military supplies in Japan, and by the end of the war industrial production had more or less reached pre–World War II levels. Between 1955 and 1973, the real GNP surged forward at an annual average rate of about 10 percent, much faster than any other advanced industrial economy in the world, and by 1968 the economy surpassed in size those of Great Britain and Germany.

THE BASIS OF RAPID GROWTH

The transformation of Japan from a nation humbled in defeat into the third-largest industrial economy in the world seemed nothing less than an "economic miracle" at the time, but rapid growth was far less miraculous than many thought. Since the turn of the century, the Japanese economy had been expanding faster than most other industrialized countries, and despite postwar economic collapse it did not have to be rebuilt from scratch. While many factories, mills, and power stations had been destroyed, the plant capacity of the chemical and heavy industries was larger in 1945 than it had been at the beginning of the war. Oddly enough, wartime bombing may even have contributed to postwar growth by leveling plant and equipment made obsolete by technological advance in the Western wartime economies. The most important legacy from the pre-war period, however, was the country's abundant human resources—a highly educated population, a pervasive achievement ethic, ubiquitous institutions of social discipline, widely diffused technical skills, experienced managerial and entrepreneurial classes, and an activist economic bureaucracy—which made it easy for Japan to absorb new technologies, increase productivity, and innovate in the marketplace once postwar recovery ended.

It should also be pointed out that Japan was not alone in breaking records in the 1950s and 1960s. As one economist has put it, Japan's "economic miracle" was an extreme case of a general phenomenon. During the years of Japan's "economic miracle," nearly all the economies of Western Europe grew at a much faster rate than they had before World War II. Indeed, the whole world economy was growing at an unprecedented rate. In contrast to the 1930s, when the depression had led the advanced countries to adopt beggar-thy-neighbor economic polices, the postwar world economic order encouraged trade through the removal of trade barriers and the reconstruction of the international monetary system. At the Bretton Woods conference in 1944, the wartime Allies agreed to establish a system of stable currency exchange rates, and the General Agreement on Tariffs and Trade (GATT) signed at Geneva in 1947 aimed at creating a "freer and fairer" international economy by reducing tariffs, encouraging multi-lateral economic relations, and establishing universal rules for world trade. These new international institutions, intended to promote collective economic security, provided a hothouse atmosphere for international economic growth.

The end of protectionism meant that Japan was no longer faced with high tariff or other barriers to its exports, nor did it have difficulty in obtaining the raw materials needed to keep its industrial engine churning. It could buy metal ores and other basic resources wherever it could make the best deal, and like other industrialized countries it had access to the cheap petroleum pumped out of the newly developed oil fields in the Middle East. What is striking about the Japanese is that they took advantage of this favorable new international environment more effectively than the other advanced economies. While everyone else was growing, Japan simply grew faster.

One reason no doubt was the emergence in the 1950s and 1960s of a powerful political commitment to give priority to economic growth. While the postwar left-wing parties focused on fairer distribution of the national wealth, conservative politicians, business leaders, and top bureaucrats aimed at increasing it as rapidly as possible. In this sense, postwar growth was a continuation of the long-term drive to "catch up" with the Western countries. In contrast to the pre-war period, however, catching up no longer meant building an empire or maintaining a strong military. As conservative leaders like Yoshida and Ikeda realized, the Mutual Security Treaty allowed Japan to limit its military outlays. In 1938, about 16 percent of Japan's GNP had been absorbed in military expenditure, but in 1968 only about 0.8 percent was. Capital, skills, and energy that might have been channeled into national defense were devoted instead to expanding the civilian economy. This gave Japan an advantage over the United States, which assumed an enormous financial burden as the military leader of the "Free World."

During the 1950s, civilian economic bureaucrats, drawing on their wartime experience with state economic management, put commitment to growth into practice. While Japan did not have a "command economy" that allowed the government to allocate resources by directive, ministries like the Ministry of Finance (MOF), the Ministry of International Trade and Industry (MITI), and the Ministry of Construction, guided private enterprise by a complex mixture of "indicative planning," informal persuasion, "administrative guidance," and regulatory control. The Economic Planning Agency, an outgrowth of the wartime control system, periodically issued plans announcing the most desirable direction for the economy to take. Although these plans were not enforceable, private firms often relied on government forecasts in making their own plans for investment, hiring and output; and conversely private firms often had a hand in shaping the government plans. The economic bureaucracy and the business community worked closely with frequent public consultations, and even more frequent behind-the-scenes negotiations. Relations were not always harmonious, and often businessmen fought against bureaucratic decisions, but business-government cooperation gave the outside world the impression that the country was being run as a gigantic corporate enterprise—"Japan, Inc."

What made official "guidance" possible was an expansion of the bureaucrats' legal powers. During the 1950s, almost unnoticed in the confrontations over the peace treaty, rearmament, and security questions, the Diet had passed laws drafted by the economic bureaucracy that gave it enormous powers to shape and regulate private investment: preferential allocation of foreign currency to import raw materials and machinery; controls over access to the world market through export and import licenses; regulations limiting foreign investment; tax breaks for the introduction of foreign technology; subsidies, grants, and low interest loans to targeted industries and the development of local infrastructure; and the power to permit the formation of cartels. These laws also permitted the government to protect domestic "infant industries" against foreign competition and to prevent foreign capital from dominating key industrial sectors. Only a very few foreign ventures, usually those not seen to be competing with Japanese industries, entered the Japanese market in the 1950s and 1960s.

Protectionist measures, though providing breathing space for private enterprise, were less important than "industrial policy" in spurring targeted industries. The economic bureaucrats hoped first to build basic industries, then a manufacturing sector able to compete with imported foreign manufactured goods, and eventually to create export industries to earn dollars and other hard currency. The goal was to achieve economic independence from the United States. By contrast, the government provided little help to older industries regarded as inefficient, not competitive in the world market, or on the verge of decline. In the early 1950s, industrial policy promoted electric power, steel, shipbuilding, and coal production. Nearly 80 percent of the loans from the government's Industrial Development Bank financed modernization of technology in these four industries. While the policy succeeded in making Japan the world's largest producer of merchant ships in 1955, and the second-largest producer of steel by 1958, it was less successful in the coal industry, where mines were running deeper and deeper into the ground, making domestic coal too costly to compete with imported petroleum.

By the mid-1950s, the list of targeted industries expanded to include oil refining, chemical fertilizers, plastics, petrochemicals, machine tools, electronic goods, automobiles, and artificial fibers like nylon. The economic bureaucrats were betting that as incomes rose, demand for these producer and consumer durable goods would increase. Since many of these industries were new to Japan, it was possible for them to deploy the latest manufacturing techniques quickly and cheaply. A backlog of technological know how had built up in the United States and Europe during the wartime and postwar years, providing a happy hunting ground for Japanese businessmen searching for up-to-date machines, methods, and processes. In the open postwar atmosphere, few countries were consumed by technological nationalism. Indeed, many American companies saw the export of American know how as a powerful weapon in the Cold War. Japanese firms usually found them willing to make licensing arrangements or other tie-ups for new technologies at a fraction of the cost it took to develop them.

The Income Doubling Plan announced by Prime Minister Ikeda in 1960 triggered a bullish economic mood full of excitement about the future. Assured that the domestic market was going to expand as household incomes rose, businessmen were confident that heavy investment in new plant and equipment would pay off in the long run. The plan to create a major industrial belt stretching along the Pacific coastline, from Tokyo-Yokohama in the east to northern Kyushu in the west, spurred public investment in infrastructure as well. During the 1960s, new roads and bridges, superhighways, high-speed railroad lines, harbor facilities, and industrial plant sites sprouted all along the Pacific corridor. Preparations for the 1964 Olympics, the first ever to be held in Asia, provided an opportunity for construction of subways, freeways, hotels, and sports facilities in Tokyo as well as the realization of a pre-war plan to link Tokyo with Osaka by the world's fastest railway line, the so-called bullet train.

It should be no surprise that the public enthusiastically supported the commitment to rapid economic growth. From the outbreak of the war with China in 1937 until the end of the Occupation, the Japanese had been starved for ordinary consumer goods like food and clothing. This tremendous pent-up consumer demand was intensified in the early postwar years by the presence of the Americans, whose PXs overflowed with products that few Japanese had ever seen before, let alone thought of buying. Even those who had no direct contact with the Americans learned of their life style through radio broadcasts, weekly magazines, Hollywood movies, and even comic strips. When *Blondie* ran in a major Tokyo newspaper toward the end of the Occupation, its readers were astounded to see that an ordinary middle-class family like the Bumsteads lived in a house filled with electrical appliances and had separate bedrooms for themselves and their children. If political leaders wanted to catch up with the advanced economies to restore Japan's international prestige, ordinary workers and their families were envious of the affluent living standard that foreigners like the Bumsteads enjoyed.

Ordinary households not only provided the domestic demand that fueled growth, they also supplied the work ethic that kept it going. After decades of economic hardship, most people were determined to work hard and save money to achieve a "brighter," more comfortable life. From the 1950s into the early 1970s, the six-day week was the rule in nearly all companies and government offices, and overtime was normal. The overall average work week for those employed in large enterprises was 47.5 hours including overtime. Office lights in Tokyo and Osaka burned late into the night, and factory workers rarely took their full allotted vacation time. The model worker was the "fanatic company man" (*mōretsu shain*), who put all his energies into company work and thought of little else. As one American observer put it, Japan seemed to be a "nation of compulsive overachievers."

Ordinary Japanese were also "compulsive oversavers." With memories of economic uncertainties still fresh, most Japanese households saved as a hedge against the future. To be sure, other factors were at work as well: one was the lack of a universal social security system, which put a premium on saving for old age; another was the lack of easy credit for consumers, which created a need to put money aside for big purchases. The practice of giving employees semi-annual bonuses, often amounting to a quarter or a third of a household's annual income, made it easier to save. In any case, the rate of savings out of disposable household income was about 7 percent in the 1950s, but as incomes rose it had reached 23 percent by the 1970s. Private savings in turn created a vast pool of capital available for investment in further industrial growth, making it possible for the "fanatic company man" to work more efficiently and save even more. This "virtuous cycle" played an important role in sustaining economic expansion.

In sum, what made possible the rapid growth from 1955 to 1973 was a combination of many factors—a favorable international environment, an emerging political consensus on the priority of economic growth, an activist economic bureaucracy, pent-up consumer demand, and a rising savings rate. To single out any one of these as the "secret" of Japan's economic success is futile. Even economists are uncertain about the relative importance of these factors. While it is possible to estimate the contribution of measurable factors like savings, investment, wages, technology, and the like to the growth rate, the role of "residual factors," i.e. those that cannot be measured, is extremely high. What this suggests is that "culture," "psychology," and "history" may have been as important as any quantifiable factors.

CORPORATE CAPITALISM

Although industrial policy was important for economic growth, the government's role was indirect— setting priorities, offering incentives, and making rules. The economy remained a private enterprise system, driven by competition among large-scale corporate firms who made the basic decisions on what goods to produce, what technology to use, and what prices and wages to set. These firms sustained the continuous innovation that made the "economic miracle" possible. One by-product of rapid economic growth was the emergence of "corporate capitalism" as a major social force. While the military had provided a model for organizational behavior in pre-war Japan, the large corporation played a similar role in postwar Japan. A job with a large corporation became the most sought-after type of employment, and the corporate salaried worker enjoyed a life style that others sought to emulate.

The Occupation purges and the break-up of the zaibatsu combines opened the way for a new generation of business leaders. A handful of top pre-war managers tried to resume their positions after "depurging," but the economic climate had changed so much by the early 1950s that their skills, knowledge, and connections often were no longer relevant. The most visible members of the postwar business elite were self-made men like Matsushita Kōnosuke and Honda Sōichirō, who built large new firms in the consumer goods industries. The more typical corporate leaders, however, were organization men, university or technical school graduates who had worked their way up through the corporate hierarchy. Higher education not only provided them with technical or intellectual skills but also with access to "old boy" networks— classmates or college mates in other large firms, in the bureaucracy, or in politics. The new corporate leaders were "white collar" professional managers. Unlike pre-war zaibatsu executives, who owned large holdings of their company's stocks, their outlook was less "capitalistic," focusing more on expanding the assets and output of their firms than on paying high dividends. Growth was as important as profit, and often they cut profit margins to expand market share or raise the firm's ranking. Most large firms constantly plowed profits back into expansion of plant and productive capacity. Indeed, no peacetime private-enterprise economy had reinvested such a high share of current output into future growth. Public and private fixed investment rose from 20 percent or so of GNP in the early 1950s to 37 percent in 1973.

In the bullish climate created by rapid growth, corporate leaders were more inclined to take risks than their counterparts in the United States and

Europe. Often, they were also bolder than sober-sided economic bureaucrats who constantly clucked about the dangers of economic "overexpansion" or "overheating," particularly when imports of new technology and raw materials gobbled up foreign exchange reserves too fast. In the early 1950s, for example, MITI officials were reluctant to let the Sony Corporation import the transistor technology developed by the Bell Laboratories for fear it had limited commercial applications, and officials at the Bank of Japan were skeptical about large-scale projects like the new Kawasaki integrated steel mill in Chiba. But as one boom succeeded another, the optimistic gambles of the corporate leaders paid off more often than the pessimism of the bureaucrats.

Corporate willingness to invest heavily was not simply a question of psychology or mood. It reflected the sources of corporate capital. During the 1950s and 1960s, corporations relied less on the public capital market, as they had before the war, than on the sale of shares to other corporations or loans from banks and other financial institutions. As a business economist would put it, most corporations were "highly leveraged" or had a high "debt-equity ratio." This meant that corporate leaders answered not to brokerage firms or individual stock holders but to bankers and other corporate creditors. When a firm faced short-term difficulties—overexpansion or a drop in sales—lenders were likely to stand by it until the crisis was resolved. What mattered to both parties was not short-term performance but long-term relationships and long-term results. Indeed, most annual corporate stockholder meetings lasted but a few minutes. By the 1960s, management sometimes hired agents known as *sōkaiya*, often linked with criminal gangs, to intimidate stockholders who had the audacity to question company policy.

Not surprisingly, when the Occupation ended, the corporate world began to reconcentrate, often with explicit or implicit official encouragement. What emerged were alliances of firms known as "enterprise groups" (*keiretsu*). During the early 1950s, for example, the zaibatsu affiliate firms split apart by the Occupation, like Mitsui and Mitsubishi, began to regroup, buying each other's stock, arranging regular meetings for their top managers to exchange information, exchanging directors, and receiving preferential treatment from group-related banks, insurance firms, and general trading companies. Other "enterprise groups" formed around major private financial institutions like the Sanwa or Dai-Ichi Banks that made loans to its members or bought their shares. Since they lacked a common history or common name, these groups were much looser and less disciplined than the reconstituted zaibatsu groups. There were also "enterprise groups" dominated by large manufacturing firms like Hitachi, Toyota, or Matsushita Electric that controlled a network of subsidiaries, affiliates and subcontractors. By the early 1970s, six large "enterprise groups"—Mitsubishi, Mitsui, Sumitomo, Fuyo (formerly Yasuda), Sanwa, and Dai-Ichi Kangyō—accounted for 21.9 percent of all the share capital in Japan.

While some feared reconcentration of corporate power marked a "return of the zaibatsu" the postwar "enterprise groups" were quite different in character, strategy, and structure. The bank or industrial concern that stood at the center of these groups had no absolute control over the policies and personnel of affiliated firms, nor did these firms stay within the group if they could find more advantageous sources of capital, credit, and cooperation elsewhere. Even the postwar Mitsui and Mitsubishi enterprise groups were not under the central control of a holding company, nor were they under any legal or other constraint to do business only within the group. What bound these alliances of firms together were ties of mutual interest and convenience: the sharing of information, technology, personnel, marketing strategy, and finance. And in contrast to the pre-war zaibatsu who often stifled competition by dominating a particular industry, the postwar "enterprise groups" were intensely competitive. As one MITI official later recalled the competitive energy of the steel industry:

> If one company said it was going to do something, then [another] said we will do it too. . . . That kind of initiative was remarkable. If there were six companies, then six blast furnaces would be built all at once . . . even without an increase in demand.[1]

This oligopolistic competition was not limited to investment; it also involved keeping prices lower, product quality higher, and market share larger than firms in other "enterprise groups."

The ideology of the corporate capitalism during the 1950s and 1960s centered on the notion that the firm was a collective enterprise in which all employees shared and from which all benefited. To put the labor strife of the 1950s behind them, corporate managers promoted the notion of the firm as a "community." Postwar worker demands for recognition of equal status encouraged managers to adopt a leadership style that stressed solidarity. As the head of the Sony Corporation observed, "The most important mission for a Japanese manager is to develop a healthy relationship with his employees, to create a family-like relationship with the corporation, a feeling that employees and managers share the same fate."[2] The working day in most large firms began with morning calisthenics and the company song, and managers made gestures like eating in the company cafeteria or wearing the same company uniform as blue collar workers. While the rhetoric of Japanese business leaders often struck foreign observers as naive or hypocritical, it should be remembered that they (and most of their older employees as well) had gone to school at a time when elementary education inculcated pupils with collectivist values.

Since the typical union in a large firm was an "enterprise union" embracing all employees, both blue collar or white collar, it was easier for Japanese workers to identify with their companies than it was for workers in the United States and Great Britain, where a tradition of independent and adversarial unionism was much stronger. By the last 1950s, management tried to encourage this sense of identity by offering "regular workers" an implicit guarantee of lifetime employment, wage increases linked to seniority, and benefits like company housing and health insurance. (To be sure, most firms also hired part-time workers, often women, who were laid off when market demand weakened.) To give "regular workers" a sense of participation in the company's success, management also organized the workers into small groups to discuss how to improve productivity (QC circles) or reduce defects (ZD movement). Often innovations or improvements in the production process came from the shop floor rather than the management's offices, but these small groups also encouraged workers to compete against one another as each strove to work the most efficiently or produce the least defects.

Wages rose steadily during the period of rapid growth, averaging around 15 percent a year (or 10 percent in real terms) in the principal industries. The "spring wage offensives" initiated by the large labor federations in the mid-1950s became a mechanism for negotiating orderly wage increases. Every spring, with much fanfare, the labor leadership would target a particular industry for an increase in the basic wage rate. If the demand succeeded, unions in other industries would use it as a target for their own demands. In a sense, the spring offensive was a collective negotiation between big labor and big management. The strikes that accompanied it were usually short and symbolic, occurring before negotiations to remind managers of what might happen if negotiations broke down. Since production and profits were rising, and labor shortages were becoming more common in the early 1960s, management usually gave workers a wage settlement that boosted their incomes to meet inflation and then some. Indeed, managers were aware that the spring offensives provided a stable setting for dealing with labor and reduced worker time lost through strikes. Large firms also established long-term relationships with the union leaders, strengthening the sense of the company as a community. With the exception of West Germany, no other industrial economy was as free of crippling labor disputes as Japan in the 1960s.

The emergence of "corporate capitalism," however, did not push smaller enterprises out of the picture. In 1970, about 40 percent of all manufacturing workers were employed by small firms and workshops with less than fifty workers. Often, they served as subcontractors to manufacture parts or assembly components for large firms. The Toyota automobile company, for example, surrounded itself with a cluster of smaller firms producing windshields, headlights, clutches, and other parts assembled in Toyota plants. Since workers in small firms received lower wages, subcontracting allowed large firms to keep down their labor costs as a buffer against business fluctuations. Since manufacturing technology was more complex than in pre-war times, large firms often provided their small subcontractors with technical help and sometimes capital and personnel as well. Workers in these enterprises, however, were rarely unionized, and few enjoyed the lifetime employment guaranteed to workers in large firms. Indeed, they often resented the "regular workers" in large manufacturing corporations or in large-scale public enterprises like the national railway system.

"MIDDLE CLASS SOCIETY"

By the middle of the 1960s, most ordinary Japanese were enjoying the benefits of rapid economic growth. The economic boom brought with it an unprecedented popular prosperity. The fear of joblessness, so acute in the postwar years, had all but vanished. The rapid pace of industrial expansion, coupled with a sudden drop in the birth rate, wiped out labor surpluses. Wages and personal income also rose at a precipitous rate, exceeding even Ikeda's promise of doubled household incomes. In 1960, the average worker in firms with more than 30 employees earned ¥24,400 per month, by 1970 this had more than tripled to ¥75,700. Labor shortages reduced wage differentials between big enterprises and small, between white collar workers and blue collar workers, and between younger workers and older; and the wide gaps in household income, so characteristic of pre-war society, leveled off as well. Indeed, by the early 1970s, distribution of income (if not of assets) in Japan was far more equitable than in any other industrial economy.

As popular affluence spread and household incomes rose, most Japanese were growing more and more content with their places in society. A 1965 government survey that asked respondents to compare their living standard with that of the general public found that 72 percent thought they were "in the middle"; by 1973 90 percent did. These polls showed that most people felt they were neither much better off nor much worse off than their neighbors, but they also suggested the growth of "middle-class consciousness." Indeed, some commentators began to celebrate Japan as a "classless society," where poverty had been eliminated and everyone belonged to the middle class. In fact, pockets of poverty persisted, particularly among the old, the less educated, and the self-employed, and a new wealthy class of successful entrepreneurs, business leaders, politicians, and land owners was emerging. But in the heady atmosphere of rapid growth, these persisting discrepancies were overlooked by most people, who took pride in the economic accomplishments of the country and grew increasingly confident that a better economic future lay ahead for themselves and their families.

To most Japanese, the ideal life style was that of the "salary man"— the white collar worker employed by a large corporation. During the early years of rapid growth, "salary men" enjoyed not only higher incomes than blue collar workers or farmers but higher status as well. With the spread of lifetime employment practices, their jobs also seemed more secure. In the 1950s, popular films often glamorized the life of the salaried worker as carefree and easy. Not surprisingly, white collar parents expected their children to follow in their footsteps. Even more significantly, however, surveys showed that most blue collar mothers wanted their sons to become "salary men," and most farm housewives wanted their daughters to marry one. It was, after all, the white collar household that seemed to enjoy the "bright new life" with ample income and leisure to enjoy an active consumerism.

For the average Japanese, the most tangible evidence of national prosperity was their ability to buy more and better consumer goods than ever before. In the mid-1950s, companies like Matsushita Electric and Toshiba began marketing electrical household appliances like rice cookers, washing machines, refrigerators, vacuum cleaners, and television sets— the wonderful machines that Americans seemed to enjoy as a matter of natural right. As household disposable incomes rose, so too did the proportion devoted to consumer durables, and as demand for these goods increased, mass production brought their cost down, making it possible for even more families to buy them. A fourteen-inch television set that cost ¥140,000 (or several months' wages) in 1953 dropped to ¥40,000 in 1960.

The 1959 economic white paper, noting a 60 percent increase in expenditure on household appliances, announced that a "consumer revolution" was beginning in Japan. After years of relative material deprivation, it was an exhilarating experience. As one Japanese recalled,

> The first evening we turned on the television set we were so excited that we could not sleep. When the refrigerator arrived we kept opening and closing the door until Mother scolded us, and we sat transfixed watching the electric rice cooker after it was switched on. How "high class" it was to live like this, we thought, eating bread browned in the toaster and spread with butter.[3]

"Keeping up with the Tanakas"— what economists call the "neighborhood effect"— was an important stimulus to the revolution, particularly among white collar workers, who regarded the acquisition of electric appliances, pianos, and eventually automobiles as status symbols. So was the artificial creation of demand.

The American model of mass marketing taught Japanese manufacturers how to sell consumers goods they did not know they needed. During the 1960s, expenditures on newspaper and television advertising shot up much faster than the GNP, and children learned to recite the latest commercial jingles as easily as their multiplication tables. Many firms set up local retail chains to sell their products or created door-to-door neighborhood organizations to canvass customers. Large corporate manufacturers also pursued the tactics of "planned obsolescence," quickly changing models to make older appliances out of date. Even if consumers did not wish to buy a new appliance, they often discovered that replacement parts were difficult to find when their old model broke down and were forced to buy the newest one. As the market became more and more saturated with consumer durables (and housing space overflowed with them), manufacturers relied increasingly on catchy slogans or better design to attract business away from their competitors. By the early 1970s, Dentsū, the advertising agency that handled about one quarter of the Japanese market, had become the largest in the world.

The "consumer revolution" had an enormous impact on the lives of women. In many urban households, the wife had control over the family finances, taking control over her husband's pay envelope and deciding how to spend it, often to buy the new electrical appliances that helped rationalize her housework. As the result of rural electrification, even farm housewives could do the family laundry in a washing machine and prepare the day's rice in an automatic cooker. Manufacturers, well aware that women made key buying decisions, took care to win them over by whatever means possible. The Matsushita Electric Company, for example, provided research money for women students writing graduation theses in home economics and awarded its own products as prizes to the winners. While women remained at a disadvantage in politics or the work place, no one doubted their sovereignty within the household. Since most families were able to get by on the husband's income alone, women's participation in the workplace also declined, reaching its lowest point in 1965. To be sure, some housewives used their freedom from housework to earn extra money to buy more consumer goods or accumulate more savings for a house or the children's education, but many also spent more time with their children or simply enjoyed their new leisure.

The pursuit of affluence turned the interests of ordinary Japanese inward toward private concerns. When a 1973 government survey asked people what gave meaning to their lives, 49 percent said "home and children," 30 percent said "work," and 9 percent said "hobbies and sports." The older ethic of service to country or society embodied in the wartime slogan of "self-sacrifice for the good of the whole" (*messhi hōkō*) gave way to "my-home-ism" (*maihomushugi*), a catch phrase that summarized a new focus on the narrow world of family and work place. What the "typical" Japanese sought was the pursuit of a "middling" life style centered on the household— a cozy apartment or house filled with shiny new appliances, a happy family life punctuated by an occasional vacation trip, and perhaps even an automobile to polish on the weekend. In a sense, "my-home-ism" was the little man's version of the "GNP nationalism" embraced by the political, bureaucratic, and business elites. But it also reflected a rejection of the encompassing claims that the pre-war state had made on the population.

The new affluence had its impact on other values too. On the one hand, the morality of personal frugality, long prompted by government in its efforts to build the state and economy, was a casualty of the consumer revolution. As most Japanese sought to acquire every creature comfort they could afford, habits of thrift and saving changed. While overall household savings were on the rise, the family nest egg was more often spent on family consumption than on family emergencies. By the early 1970s, the introduction of the credit card made the acquisitive life less painful, and so did small finance companies (*sarakin*) specializing in high interest loans to white collar workers. A small but perceptible decline in the savings rate signaled the change. On the other hand, affluence seems to have reinforced and intensified the popular belief in the importance of study, learning, and education as the gateway to middle-class status, career success, and personal affluence.

As aspirations for white collar status spread, so did a "mania for education." Parents of all socioeconomic strata wanted their children to climb as high as they could on the educational ladder, and the most ambitious pressured them from kindergarten onward to enter schools that would prepare them for entry into a "good university," the key to a white collar career. The rate of college or university attendance went up dramatically, from about 10 percent of the appropriate age cohort in the 1950s to about 38 percent in 1975. The popular press made fun of the "education-minded mother" (*kyōiku mama*), herding her children from school to English tutor or piano teacher to evening homework, but most parents felt a personal responsibility to push and prod their offspring. By the early 1970s, as more and more children and teenagers struggled to climb aboard the educational escalator, competition intensified. Despite its cost in money, frustration, and family tension, "examination hell"—preparation for high school and university entrance tests— became a normal part of adolescence. Family spending on children's education increased, and so did the number of students attending private cram schools (*juku* or *yobikō*). Late in the evening, commuter trains carrying tired white collar workers home after a long day at the office were often filled with their equally tired offspring returning from several hours of after-school instruction at cram schools.

URBANIZATION

During the war, Japan had experienced a temporary deurbanization. As the result of Allied bombing and the evacuations that accompanied it, most major cities had shrunk in size. In 1950, even after the postwar return of millions of repatriates and evacuees, the proportion of the urban population remained lower than it had in the pre-war period. With the revival of heavy industry and the building of new factories and offices, however, the trickle of population back into urban areas turned into a flood. While new births accounted for some of the urban population increase, the main cause was new employment opportunities. The city with its bright lights, rising wages, fixed hours, and relative social freedom lured young people away from the long hours and heavy work on the farm, and every spring firms faced with growing labor shortages brought newly recruited middle school graduates into the cities by the train load. Between 1955 and 1970, people were pouring into the six major cities (Tokyo, Yokohama, Osaka, Nagoya, Kyoto, and Kobe) at an average rate of 1 million a year, with the biggest surge in growth during the early 1960s. On the eve of the 1964 Olympics, Tokyo became the first city in the world to claim a population of 10 million. By the early 1970s, the large cities along the Pacific Coast had spilled over their old boundaries into huge sprawling suburbs, creating a chain of vast metropolitan concentration that came to be known as the "Tōkaidō megalopolis" or the "Tōkaidō corridor."

It took time for urban infrastructure to catch up with this rapid influx of population. Unlike many European countries, Japan had no national policy to provide affordable rental housing for employed workers, and unlike the United States it did not encourage home ownership by allowing income tax deductions for mortgage payments. While the central government established a public corporation in 1955 to build low-rent apartment buildings, most urban newcomers had to rely on the private housing market. In their effort to attract workers, large corporations (and even small-scale firms) provided company-owned housing for both white collar and blue collar workers, but private railway companies and other urban developers built most new housing in the sprawling suburbs that gobbled up the rural hinterland around Tokyo, Osaka, and other large cities.

As the single young people who moved to the city got married, their dream was to find a 2DK (kitchen, dining room, two bedroom) apartment in a newly built multi-story apartment complex (*danchi*). In contrast to other residential housing stock, the *danchi* apartments were conveniently designed, easy to keep warm and clean, and boasted flush toilets. These amenities made the "apartment tribe" (*danchizoku*) the envy of other urban residents in the late 1950s and 1960s. But as children got bigger, the new ideal became a detached house with separate rooms for the children, a yard, and parking space. The construction industry responded by the mass production of prefabricated houses, built in factories and assembled on the family lot. The result was unplanned development, often turning rural communities into suburbs without an adequate urban infrastructure—paved streets, water, sewage, schools, and parks.

Accelerating urbanization, coupled with economic growth, had its impact on the size and structure of the family unit. While a postwar "baby boom" from 1946 to 1948 produced a sudden spurt in the birth rate, it fell off dramatically thereafter. Ordinary Japanese, who wanted to provide their children with better lives than what they had known during the war and the depression, now produced smaller families. This was made easier by the 1948 Eugenics Protection Law, which legalized abortions for economic as well as medical reasons. (SCAP officials, worried that "overpopulation" had been an important reason for rural poverty and overseas expansion in prewar Japan, promoted its passage.) By the late 1950s, the population was growing at only 0.9 percent per year, about two-thirds the rate of the 1920s, and the birth rate fell steadily. Abortion remained an important means for controlling family size, but other means of contraception soon surpassed it. In 1950, fewer than 20 percent of all married women under 49 used contraceptive methods, but by 1970 more than half did.

The fall in the birth rate meant that per capita incomes could grow at more or less the same rate as the GNP, permitting a rise in living standards. By limiting family size, families not only reduced population pressure on the whole economy but increased their personal affluence as well. As a 1955 ad for spermicidal jelly noted, "Fewer births bring an affluent life." The new ideal became the small nuclear family consisting of the parents, one "princess," and one "only son." While the average family size remained steady at a little under five persons from the 1920s down through the mid-1950s, it dropped to 3.45 in 1975. With more time to spare for child care, and with the urge to acquire white collar status so strong, families became more and more child-centered.

The growth in urban population also brought a drop in the number of three-generation households, where grandparents lived with children and grandchildren. Urban dwellings, particularly the 2DK apartments, were simply too small to accommodate Grandma and Grandpa. Adult children no longer had to take care of sick or aging parents, as they were expected to in pre-war days, and the transmission of cultural knowledge across generations also broke down. The urban housewife was more likely to turn to friends or neighbors for advice about cooking or housekeeping than to ask her mother. Indeed, the number of "how to" manuals on everything from sex to child-rearing increased noticeably in the 1960s as the cross-generational gap widened.

As the urban nuclear family pattern became more common, the notion of the family as a continuing corporate household (*ie*) went into rapid decline. Symbolic of the change was the fact that few urban families maintained Buddhist family altars (*butsudan*) containing the family's ancestral tablets. Neither did the family any longer revolve around the father, who in the pre-war period had large responsibilities as the household head. For one thing, postwar legal reforms put an end to the practice of primogeniture, requiring instead that family property be inherited among all the children according to a legally fixed formula, making the notion of a family head no longer important. In any case, confiscatory inheritance taxes often left little household property to pass on to children, making investment in their education far more important. While parents tended to devote more attention to the education of sons, relationships among siblings became more egalitarian over time.

The separation of workplace and living place also weakened the father's position within the family. During the heyday of growth, the father often worked overtime or spent the evening with company colleagues, coming home late at night after the children had gone to bed. The television "home dramas" so popular by the middle 1960s, usually depicted a warm and loving family, cozily tucked around the dining table, with the wife rather than the husband at its center. The "absent father" usually left most of the major financial, child-rearing, and other responsibilities to his wife, and relations between husband and wife became more egalitarian than in the pre-war period. Employment opportunities for middle-class women outside the home were usually limited, but if the wife did earn some outside income as well, her voice in family affairs was even stronger.

In the urban setting, individuals were much more isolated and anonymous than in the small-town atmosphere of villages and provincial towns. No

An apartment complex (*danchi*) on the outskirts of Osaka. Note the sleeping mattresses (*futon*) airing on the balconies and the forest of television antennas on the roofs.

longer were they embedded in a stable community where their families had lived for generations. Men found their most important circle of friends in the workplace, office, or factory; and women turned to neighbors living in the same apartment house or the local PTA for contacts outside the family. If people felt connected with society beyond the workplace or family circle, it was usually through the new mass media. After 1959, when most Japanese rushed to buy black and white television sets to watch the marriage of Crown Prince Akihito to his popular "commoner" fiancee "Michiko-san" (Shōda Michiko), nearly every household was linked together in a new national "electronic village." By the mid-1960s, television had surpassed movies in popularity. Children were more likely to talk with their classmates about the shows they had seen the night before than about other topics, and many grown-ups felt closer to television celebrities than to other public figures.

Television was only the most visible manifestation of a new popular culture emerging in the cities. Large publishing houses turned out mass-circulation weekly magazines (*shūkanshi*), heavily loaded with gossip about entertainers, politicians, and businessmen, as well as consumer advice on the best restaurants, stores, travel opportunities, and products. What appeared on television was often echoed in these weeklies, and vice versa. Trends in fashion, entertainment, and consumption came and went at a dizzying speed. For children and young adults, there were dozens, then hundreds of new comic magazines, often with circulations that reached into the hundreds of thousands.

In contrast to the United States, comic books often carried influential cultural messages, not unlike the ethics textbooks banned by the Occupation. By reading about fledgling baseball players or judo wrestlers, boys absorbed lessons about personal determination, patience, and friendship, and by reading syrupy romances, girls could retreat into a world where femininity, gentleness, and passivity prevailed. By the late 1960s, university students were as likely to bury their noses in the latest melodramatic comic book (*gekiga*) as in the works of Karl Marx.

The new mass culture was very different from pre-war popular culture. Its production was centralized in Tokyo, where the headquarters of all the major television, publishing, and film companies were located. This made the media more susceptible to pressure from the large corporations that supplied their advertising revenues. As a result, news organizations often soft-pedaled stories embarrassing to political figures or business leaders. On the other hand, since official censorship had come to an end (except with respect to hard-core pornography and nudity), the flood of information and ideas pouring out of the new media was difficult to control. What the public saw or read in the mass media competed with what the government told it, and determined journalists could and did expose official scandals. The mass media also competed with textbooks and the class room as a source of information, making it far more difficult for the government to shape young minds. While some critics complained about the vulgarity or vapidity of the mass media, others began to speak of Japan as an "information society" (*jōhō shakai*).

THE CHANGING COUNTRYSIDE

The obverse side of urbanization was the diminishing social and economic importance of the countryside. In the early 1950s, the same number of people were employed in agriculture as in 1940, but the rapid expansion of the manufacturing and service sector drew labor out of agriculture. The farm population, which accounted for half the total population in 1950, shrank to 19 percent in 1970. The number of farm households, relatively constant since the Meiji period, declined as well, breaking the balance between countryside and city. After 1955, over half the country's prefectures, especially the most rural ones, steadily lost population. In some poor and remote mountainous areas, abandoned villages were left with no one but those too old to move, and even in more prosperous areas cultivable fields of only marginal productivity were often abandoned. As young people moved away, it often became difficult to support traditional village ceremonies and festivals, and in the northeast some village shops closed down during the winter months for lack of business. Nostalgic journalists lamented that rapid economic growth had cost the country the "destruction of the village."

Changes in Occupational Structure, 1920–1985

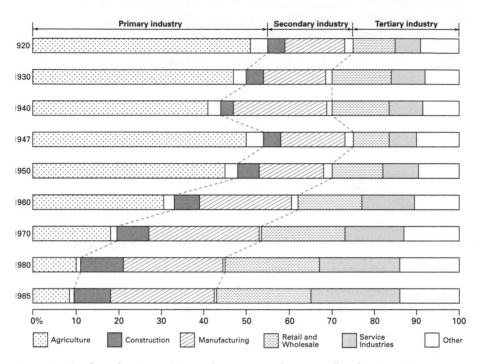

Source: Based on figures from National Census of Japan, Bureau of Statistics, Office of the Prime Minister.

The perspective from the countryside was quite different. Economic growth and population drain erased the abiding cultural differences that had separated city and country for centuries. As the urban market for foodstuffs expanded, farmers began to mechanize cultivation, increasing their output and productivity by using mass produced small-scale farm machinery— at first power cultivators or miniature tractors, then tiny threshing combines and eventually even rice-planting machines. By the mid-1970s, Japan led the world in the amount of mechanized power used per unit of cultivated land. The result was that farming became a part-time occupation, indeed even a weekend activity, releasing the husbands in farm families for other employment. Often they took jobs as seasonal workers in construction or manufacturing. Manufacturers set up factories and workshops in rural areas to tap the stable but inexpensive rural labor pool, making it possible for farmers to become part-time or full-time commuters as well. The bulk of the farm work was left to the farmer's wife and parents, who could handle heavy work more easily by relying on machines. This work style, known as "mama-grandma-grandpa agriculture" (*sanchan nōgyō*), was most common in the regions near Tokyo and Osaka, where alternate employment opportunities for men were most abundant. By the late 1960s, only a minority of farm households relied exclusively on agriculture for their income.

To be sure, farmers were also the recipients of generous government largesse. After the Socialists captured 20 percent of the rural vote in 1947, conservative politicians strove to win back the countryside by increasing agriculture subsidies. The Yoshida cabinet offered farmers government money to reclaim land, improve existing fields, and introduce better seed varieties and new crops; and it spent heavily on rural public works, creating jobs for part-time farmers and improving rural quality of life. From the early 1960s, the LDP governments hiked the official price paid to farmers for rice, subsidizing their incomes as well. The price of Japanese rice diverged from the world price so rapidly that by the end of the decade it was three times more expensive, and government rice storehouses held several years' supply. Other high value-added crops, from livestock to mandarin oranges, were subsidized as well, making the level of government agricultural support the highest among all industrial countries. While these political favors made agriculture the most heavily protected and least efficient sector of the economy, they also contributed substantially to rural prosperity. By the 1970s, farm households enjoyed incomes that on average surpassed those of their city cousins. Taxes on agricultural land were relatively low, and in any case farmers were more easily able to evade taxes than salaried workers with their paycheck deductions. The farm population repaid the government's largesse by voting steadily for the LDP.

The new rural prosperity allowed farm communities to participate in the "consumer revolution" along with the urban dwellers. As one farmer told a foreign visitor:

> Before the war, you could work and work and work and you never saved money, could never eat delicious food, couldn't even eat enough. Now even without working your guts out you have money left over—well, not that much left over, but enough so we don't feel in need—and our life is sheer luxury compared with what it used to be.[4]

Indeed, farmers were more likely to rank themselves "middle class" than white collar or professional workers, and often their life style was more affluent. The diffusion of family automobiles, for example, began in the countryside in the 1960s, and many farm families used their new affluence to replace their traditional thatched-roofed dwellings with sturdy and spacious concrete structures equipped with all the amenities of urban housing. The rate of rural house ownership was much higher than in the cities. Even in Tokyo, only 40 percent of all households owned their own residences in 1975.

The gap between city and country was also closed by the spread of mass culture, particularly television. Since everyone was watching the same programs and commercials produced by a Tokyo-centered media industry, the homogenization of popular culture accelerated. Local dialects declined as

Levels of Socio-Economic Attributes

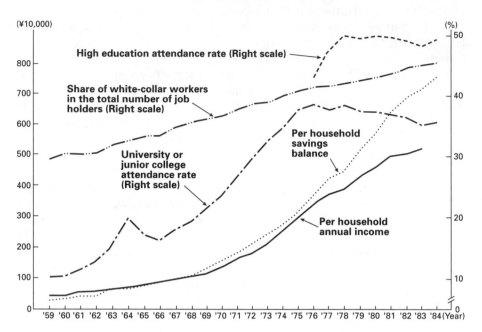

Source: National Economic Planning Agency, *Annual Report on National Life for Fiscal 1985*, p. 255.

television announcers and actors brought "standard Japanese" into every home, and when local festivals were broadcast on the television they were less community celebrations than vicarious tourist events. As advertising diffused the consumer information throughout the country, a distinctive rural life style gradually disappeared. Rural housewives were as likely to serve their families "instant noodles" as urban ones did, farmers wore work caps and jackets just like those of factory workers, and their offspring worshiped the same "rockabilly" stars as their city cousins did.

With signs of prosperity everywhere, the Japanese entered the 1970s in a mood of growing optimism and self-confidence—a quiet pride that Japan had emerged as the world's third-largest industrial economy. The most tangible symbol of the new mood was EXPO '70, an international exposition dedicated to the "progress and harmony of mankind" held on the outskirts of Osaka. Foreign tourists visited the exposition by the tens of thousands, but the Japanese visited it by the millions, enthralled as much by their own technological and economic accomplishments as by the foreign exhibitions. It was not difficult to imagine that the twenty-first century might well be the "Japanese century" as the twentieth had been the American century or that a Japanese "superstate" would be the world's most affluent country one day.

ENDNOTES

1. Itō Masanori, *Kōdō seichō kara "keizai taikoku"* (Tokyo: Iwanami shoten, 1988), 23–24.

2. Akio Morita, *Made in Japan* (Tokyo: Weatherhill, Inc., 1987), 130.

3. Itō Masanori, *Kōdō seichō kara "keizai taikoku"* (Tokyo: Iwanami shoten, 1988), 36–37.

4. Ronald P. Dore, *Shinohata: A Portrait of a Japanese Village* (Berkeley: University of California Press, 1994), 65.

18

The Price of Affluence

The Liberal Democratic Party was the main political beneficiary of the "economic miracle." Buoyed by steady economic growth, the party tightened its hold on power. The resulting conservative hegemony confounded the expectations of Ishida Hirohide, a maverick LDP member, who predicted in 1963 that as more and more people moved to the cities and as more and more workers shifted from agriculture to manufacturing, the country's voters would shift to the left. But the LDP continued to control an absolute majority in the House of Representatives, and it did so despite growing public uneasiness at the social strains, contradictions and dislocations generated by economic growth. As the ebullient atmosphere of the 1960s gave way to a more sombre mood in the 1970s, many again predicted the imminent demise of conservative rule. However, the party proved flexible enough to weather declining popularity by addressing many of the new problems that the economic miracle brought in its train.

THE "IRON TRIANGLE"

By shifting public attention to the national goal of "GNP growth" and "income doubling," Prime Minister Ikeda Hayato and his successor, Satō Eisaku, put behind them the divisive rhetoric and strident confrontations of the 1950s but there was more to building a conservative hegemony than adopting a policy of "economism." While the left wing appealed to the interests of the "proletariat" or "working class," the LDP catered to a much wider spectrum of voters. As individual Diet members built up their own electoral bailiwicks, the party leadership used its majority in the House of Representatives to weave to-gether a powerful network of political connections and economic interests. What emerged was the "iron triangle," a circle of political insiders who exer-cised preponderant influence on the formation of national policy.

At the base of the "iron triangle" were the political networks of individual Diet members. When the LDP was established in 1955, its local organization was weak—indeed, nearly non-existent. To consolidate a local base (*jiban*), local politicians organized "support associations" (*kōenkai*) that included not only ordinary voters but local men of influence—small businessmen, pre-fectural assembly members, bankers, local businessmen, agricultural cooper-ative leaders, and others. The glue holding these associations together was the distribution of political favors. Indeed, most provincial LDP politicians were as busy servicing their constituents as debating national policy or for-mulating legislation. They arranged for their constitutents to meet with gov-ernment officials, found jobs for their offspring, attended weddings and funerals, and occasionally took supporters on excursions to nearby resorts or hot springs. For women voters, the support associations arranged folk dance classes, sewing lessons, and even cooking schools. The cultivation of warm personal ties with voters was the key to political success. When election time came around, a Diet member was more likely to talk about his personal serv-ice to the constituency than burning national issues.

The LDP national leadership, by contrast, leveraged the party's Diet strength to build ties with a broad range of interest groups, promising policy and legislation that favored them and opposing policies that did not. The core of the party's support lay in the countryside. At election time, the LDP relied on local agricultural cooperatives to turn out the vote just as the left parties relied on the national labor federations. In return for heavy LDP gov-ernment spending on rural roads, improved irrigation systems, rice price sup-ports, and generous subsidies for other crops, the party expected the farmers to back its candidates. In the late 1950s, the LDP also tried to win the alle-giance of small business groups (such as barbers and bathhouse operators), professional associations (such as physicians and dentists), and single-issue pressure groups (such as war veterans, expropriated former landlords or the bereaved families of war dead.) The LDP was rapidly becoming a "catchall party" that represented a diverse complex of interest groups.

The most important single interest group backing the LDP was the big busi-ness community: national business federations like Keidanren and Nikkeiren, large industrial companies and corporations, and big banks and financial firms. Business had been the major source of funds for the conservative and centrist political parties ever since the 1920s, but the LDP leadership courted its support even more aggressively than their prewar predecessors had. The cost of politics escalated rapidly in postwar Japan. Under the multimember electoral district system (three to five members), LDP candidates often had to compete with one another as well as opposition candidates. Conservative politicians needed ever larger war chests to finance their electoral campaigns and their never-ending outlays on wedding gifts, funeral condolence offerings, public receptions and excursions. In the 1969 election, for example, it was said that a candidate could win with ¥100,000,000 but would lose if he spent only ¥70,000,000.

The ability to raise money made all the difference to a political career. Diet members relied for help on local backers, but most also belonged to large intraparty factions (*habatsu*) whose leaders supplied them with electoral funds and secured them offices in the party or in the cabinet. At any one time there might be six to eight major LDP factions, whose leaders competed for the party presidency, a position that led automatically to the prime ministership. Big business federations like Keidanren or Nikkeiren made political contributions to the party headquarters but individual firms, special business associations, and individual businessmen and executives gave money directly to faction leaders or to their followers. Many top LDP politicians formed close personal ties with corporate leaders, top executives and other wealthy supporters who provided them with free houses, stock market tips, and other lucrative favors. Whenever the party presidency was contested, money flowed freely to reward old faction members for their loyalty, to attract new ones, and to cement coalitions with political allies.

In return for political funds, business and corporate donors expected privileged access to the party leaders and their political networks. As the LDP consolidated its hold over the Diet, it was able to exert greater influence over the central bureaucracy, which continued to play a central role in policymaking. Bureaucrats, for example, drafted nearly nine out of every ten bills presented to the Diet. In this respect Japanese democracy bore less resemblance to American congressional politics than to European parliamentary politics. The longer the LDP stayed in power, however, the greater became its power to set the legislative agenda. Top ministerial officials had to consult with the party's Political Affairs Research Committee (PARC), whose approval or disapproval could determine the fate of a bill in the Diet, and party influence over policy-making grew as more and more former officials decided to run for the Diet as LDP candidates. Indeed, by the 1960s about one quarter of all lower house members were ex-bureaucrats, who had retired early to run for office. Not only did they bring specialized expertise needed to the party but they maintained personal connections with former colleagues in the central ministries.

The "iron triangle"—the LDP, key interest groups, and the central bureaucracies—constituted a narrow political arena, where most important policy decisions were made. It was not so much a stable coalition of political forces as a circle of political insiders linked by long-term relationships. Important discussions about legislation, discretionary regulatory actions, and the use of public funds took place behind closed doors with little or no public debate, making it difficult for opposition groups to have much voice in public affairs. Neither the labor unions, nor public interest lobbyists, nor even the intellectual community had much sway in Diet politics. Instead, political insiders fought among themselves. For example, physicians demanding higher health insurance payment might be on one side while firms who paid premiums for their employees were on the other, farmers might lobby for higher rice subsidies while business firms argued that agricultural protection should be ended, and right wing LDP politicians calling for more patriotic textbooks might find themselves at loggerheads with foreign ministry officials. These policy debates often took place out of the public view. Newspaper and television reporters were reluctant to report on their details for fear of losing access to their inside sources.

Decisions made within the "iron triangle" were often influenced by "gift-giving," kickbacks and other insider favors rather than by debate over the merits of a particular policy. Political scandals, dubbed "black mist" by the press, erupted with increasing frequency in the late 1960s. LDP members in the Tokyo municipal assembly were indicted for receiving bribes; LDP cabinet ministers were forced to resign after being accused of official malfeasance; and several LDP Diet members were charged with blackmail, fraud, tax evasion, extortion and bribery. Public opinion polls revealed rising discontent toward the "structural corruption" that seemed part and parcel of LDP rule. When a weekly magazine asked a number of Tokyo residents what came to their mind when they heard the word "politician," the replies—"tax thieves," "two-faced," "rotten," "greedy," and the like—indicated a rising level of political cynicism.

THE DIVIDED OPPOSITION

Although the LDP continued to control the cabinet, as Ishida Hirohide predicted, changing demographic patterns were shrinking the LDP's traditional rural electoral base. In rapidly growing metropolitan areas where voters were younger and cut off from their village or provincial roots, they were less susceptible to community pressures to vote conservative. In the 1967 election, the party failed to win a majority of the popular vote for the first time. The decline reflected a growing number of young white collar voters who thought of themselves as attached to no particular party. What enabled the LDP to maintain a Diet majority despite a declining popular vote was the electoral districting system, whose boundaries had not been redrawn since the early postwar period when half the population still lived in rural areas. Even though the LDP's rural constituency was shrinking in size, it carried a weight in the electoral process that far outstripped its numbers. For example, in one of the most rural districts (Hyōgō 5th), it took only 81,400 votes to win a Diet seat in the 1982 election, but it took 326,350 votes in a heavily urbanized urban district on the outskirts of Tokyo (Chiba 4th). In other words, the voter in the most rural district had a voice three times as strong as the voter in the most urban district. This imbalance between the weight of rural votes vis-à-vis urban votes checked the electoral gains of the left-wing parties. But even had Diet seats been apportioned more fairly to reflect population change, it is unlikely that the left could have dethroned the LDP.

The Socialists, who had thought power was nearly within their grasp, saw their own popular electoral support stagnate, then decline in the 1960s. The defection of the right Socialists to form the Democratic Socialist Party in 1960 had weakened the party at the polls, but a more basic reason for the decline in the socialist vote was a shift in popular attitudes toward the policies and ideas they represented. As wages and living standards rose, ordinary working men were no longer interested in the ideological or foreign policy issues that preoccupied the Socialist leaders, nor were they as susceptible to gloomy predictions about the future of "monopoly capitalism." Marxism was losing its appeal. In other parts of the world, regimes based on orthodox Marxist-Leninist ideas did not seem to work very well. The split between the People's Republic of China and the Soviet Union in 1961, for example, shattered the myth of "international solidarity," and the Soviet crackdown on the "Prague Spring" in Czechoslovakia in 1968 demonstrated that socialism did not guarantee democracy.

Within the Socialist Party, Eda Saburō, inspired by changes in the European socialist movements, attempted to refurbish the party's image by calling for a less ideological and more moderate program with broader popular appeal. In 1962, he presented his "vision" of a new Japanese socialism, different from that of either the People's Republic or the Soviet Union. Instead of calling for "revolution," he said, the party should aim at "structural reform" that would achieve American standards of living, a Soviet-style social insurance, and a British model of parliamentary politics under the aegis of the Japanese "peace constitution." Whether this pragmatic attempt to combine the best of the "free" and "socialist" worlds would have won the sympathy of voters remains moot. Left-wing Socialists, incensed at Eda's apparent acceptance of the capitalist system, ousted him from the party leadership.

The Socialists also suffered from their unwillingness to repudiate the increasingly shrill and violent tactics of the radical student movement whose demonstrations disrupted university campuses in the late 1960s. Radical students continued to oppose the Security Treaty as well as the growing American involvement in Vietnam, but from the mid-1960s they took up campus issues such as tuition increases, overcrowded classrooms, or control over student facilities. After the 1960 anti-treaty riots, however, Zengakuren had split into a welter of factions, who constantly fought bitter and often byzantine battles over tactics. Helmeted students, armed with rocks, Molotov cocktails, and wooden (later metal) staves and wearing face masks to disguise their identities, engaged in increasingly violent confrontations with riot police or rival student factions. The public, confused by what seemed to be meaningless factional struggles, gradually lost sympathy, then lost patience with the radical students, especially when they took to the streets, blocked traffic, or disrupted commuter rail service. The final straw came in early 1969, when radical Tokyo university students, barricaded in a central auditorium, were dislodged by riot police using tear gas and siege machinery. The dramatic clash played on nearly every television screen in the country.

While the Socialists and the Democratic Socialists floundered at the polls, other opposition parties gained strength. The Japanese Communist Party recovered support by trading its militant revolutionary stance for a more moderate position as a benign, fair-minded, and pragmatic party, less interested in the ideological orthodoxy than in improving the lot of the masses. Communist election posters in the early 1950s had depicted militant factory workers flexing their biceps beneath red banners, but by the mid-1960s they displayed smiling youths looking confidently toward the future or cheery grandparents cuddling bright-eyed grandchildren. The party, which sought to gain voter support by becoming more nationalistic, asserted its "independence" from the international Communist movement by cutting ties with Moscow in 1963–1964 and with Beijing in 1966–1967. The party newspaper *Akahata* gained a wide readership by publishing exposés of official corruption and other political scandals, and gadfly Communist Diet members enlivened parliamentary proceedings by posing embarrassing questions to LDP cabinet ministers. While the Communists won few seats in the Diet, their share of the popular vote rose to around 9–10 percent in the 1970s. Many were protest votes cast against the ruling party.

The other opposition party that gained strength was the Kōmeitō (Clean Government Party) organized in 1964 as the political arm of the Sōka Gakkai, a Buddhist-linked "new religion" that quickly built an enormous membership among people who felt displaced or disconnected during the years of rapid urbanization in the 1950s. Maintaining rigid discipline over its members, and subjecting them to intensive indoctrination, the Sōka Gakkai constituted a core electoral base for the Kōmeitō. But the party sought broader support by advocating policies that made left-wing slogans more palatable to urban lower middle-class and working-class voters. Its platform promised "humanitarian socialism" in domestic policy (i.e., free enterprise tempered by greater social justice and fairer distribution of wealth), and it favored "strict neutrality" in relations with the outside world.

The fragmentation of the opposition enabled the LDP to maintain its grip on power and weakened opposition leverage on the government and bureaucracy. To a certain extent, however, the opposition parties, particularly the left-wing parties, acted as advocates for groups marginalized by social discrimination or ethnic prejudice. The *burakumin* liberation movement, representing the former outcast group, struck alliances with both the Socialists and the Communists to fight for greater social and political equality. In Kyoto, where the left controlled city hall, the local government mounted "assimilation" programs to educate the public against prejudice, and financed programs to provide burakumin neighborhoods with new schools, building community centers and better public services. Since the burakumin were excluded from the "iron triangle," however, little was done to overcome systematic discrimination in housing, employment, and education on a national level. Companies, landlords, and even universities routinely rejected prospective employees, tenants, and students if background checks uncovered burakumin origins.

Members of the resident Korean community, who numbered 638,000 in 1974, often turned to the left-wing parties for help in overcoming similar difficulties. Although the majority of the resident Koreans were second- or third-generation inhabitants of Japan, who had neither visited Korea nor learned the Korean language, the naturalization law, which was based on parentage rather than place of birth, excluded them from citizenship and benefits such as social security, public housing, and even health insurance. Naturalization was not impossible but it entailed giving up one's Korean identity by adopting a Japanese personal and surname. To make matters worse, systematic employment discrimination forced many resident Koreans to earn their livelihood in low-status or socially marginal jobs. Many were proprietors or employees of *pachinko* (pinball) parlors, small restaurants, cheap cabarets, and massage parlors—and often members of organized criminal gangs. A few resident Koreans succeeded as pop singers, film actors, or professional athletes, but only at the cost of concealing their ethnic identity.

Deep splits within the resident Korean community, mirroring the division of Korea itself, made concerted political action difficult. Residents who chose to affiliate with North Korea (even though their families might originally have come from the south) adopted a separatist strategy, creating a self-contained network of schools, universities, banks, credit unions, and other businesses. They built a self-segregated community where it was possible to live "outside" Japanese society. Not surprisingly, this group aligned themselves politically with the Communists and the Socialists. Those who identified with South Korea, on the other hand, were more likely to build connections with conservative politicians. Efforts to pass legislation against anti-Korean discrimination made little headway, however, and Korean community activists often turned to the courts to challenge discrimination in employment or public education.

THE STRAINS OF GROWTH

While the opposition made little headway in challenging the LDP hegemony, public discontent was rising, as economic growth created new and unanticipated problems in Japanese society. The industrial complex built up in the 1950s and 1960s was concentrated in a belt stretching along the Pacific coast from Tokyo to northern Kyushu. To reduce costs and increase efficiency, huge industrial sites (*kombinato*) brought together oil refineries, petrochemical plants, power generation plants, and heavy industry in concentrations all along the coastline. Cramming much of the world's third-largest economy into a narrow strip shorter than the California coastline made Japan one of the most polluted countries in the world. The shores of Tokyo Bay, once lined with shell-gathering and bathing beaches, slowly disappeared under landfills and factory zones; a soupy veil of smoke, smog, and exhaust fumes lay heavy in the skies along the industrial corridor; industrial effluents dyed rivers dark

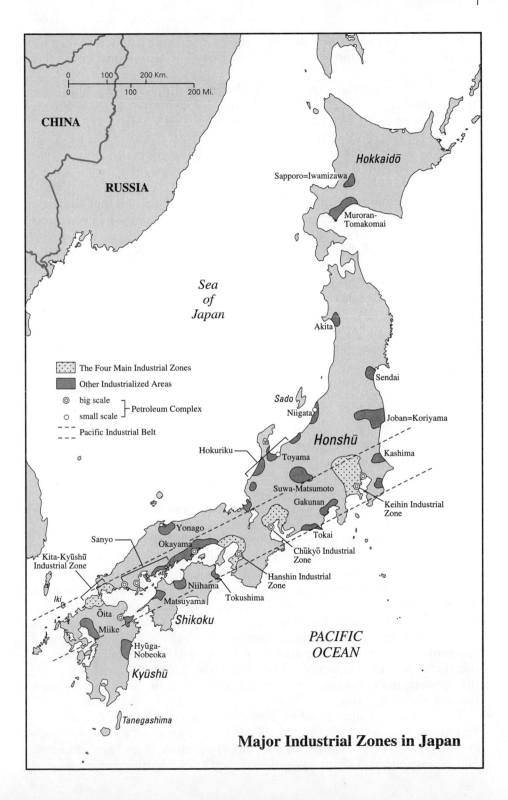

CHINA

RUSSIA

Hokkaidō

Sapporo=Iwamizawa

Muroran-
Tomakomai

*Sea
of
Japan*

Akita

Sendai

The Four Main Industrial Zones

Other Industrialized Areas

◎ big scale ⎤
○ small scale ⎦ Petroleum Complex

– – – Pacific Industrial Belt

Sado

Niigata

Joban=Koriyama

Honshū

Hokuriku

Toyama

Kashima

Suwa-Matsumoto

Gakunan

Keihin Industrial
Zone

Yonago

Sanyo

Okayama

Tokai

Kita-Kyūshū
Industrial Zone

Chūkyō Industrial
Zone

Niihama

Hanshin Industrial
Zone

Iki

Matsuyama

Tokushima

Ōita

Shikoku

Miike

Hyūga-
Nobeoka

*PACIFIC
OCEAN*

Kyūshū

Tanegashima

Major Industrial Zones in Japan

unnatural colors and flaked off-shore waters with foamy patches of chemical scum; and in the Inland Sea, tides of "red algae" destroyed once active fishing grounds.

Public attention was focused on environmental pollution by local cases that dramatized its cruel effects. In the mid-1950s, mercury-filled effluents from a Nippon Chisso Corporation plant in Kumamoto prefecture had worked their way into the human food chain, accumulating in fresh fish caught by nearby fishermen. The result was an outbreak of mysterious symptoms that came to be known as the "Minamata disease." Its victims, mainly from poor and low-status fishing households, suffered extreme neurological disorders—numbness of limbs, loss of speech, convulsions, partial blindness, and congenital mental retardation. In 1965, a similar disease affected residents near a plant of the Shōwa Denkō Corporation in Niigata, and in 1968 cadmium-filled effluents from a Mitsubishi Mining Corporation refinery in Toyama were discovered to be the cause of the *itai-itai* (literally, "It hurts, it hurts") disease that made human bones so brittle that sufferers broke them simply by moving their bodies. The corporations owning these polluting plants at first denied any responsibility, claiming instead that the afflictions were caused by vitamin-deficient diets or poor sanitation. Officials in several central ministries, including the ministry of health and welfare, did their best to obstruct research in university laboratories testing for evidence of industrial pollution. Shut out of the "iron triangle," the victims of local pollution were backed by left-wing activists, and public-interest lawyers brought law suits against the polluting corporations. In all three of these cases, as well as in another dealing with heavy air pollution in Yokkaichi, the courts awarded the victims compensation, eased the rules of proof for victims, and made it clear that companies had a legal responsibility to prevent pollution. These law suits, which publicized the miserable plight of the victims, raised general consciousness of the need to protect public health and the environment.

Environmental pollution was not simply the result of irresponsible corporate action, however. It was also a consequence of the changing life style of the Japanese. Rapid urbanization in Tokyo and other metropolitan areas had lunged forward without much attention to building an infrastructure for sanitation. Even in 1980, only 28 percent of all households in Japan were hooked up to public sewer systems. When human waste was a commodity, dealers made a flourishing business hauling it from the cities to the surrounding agricultural villages, but that market disappeared as farmers turned to the use of chemical fertilizers. Urban sewage had to be pumped out of cesspools and dumped into nearby waterways, usually after purification but sometimes not. On major coastal beaches where Tokyo residents flocked in the summer, the concentration of intestinal bacteria in the sea water often reached alarming levels.

The problem of what to do with solid waste was even more daunting. As "miraculous growth" accelerated, Japan had become a "throwaway society." In 1962, the average per capita daily production of garbage was about 500 grams, but by 1975 it had doubled. Not only was there an increase in volume but the "quality" of garbage was changing too. The "packaging revolution" accompanying the "consumer revolution" brought increased use of non-biodegradable plastic and vinyl containers, creating mountains of trash that could only be disposed of in offshore dumps. In 1965, residents of Kōtō Ward in Tokyo began to complain about the swarms of flies that throve on "Dream Island," a nearby waterfront landfill where the rest of the city dumped its garbage, and in the early 1970s a local "garbage war" broke out when they blockaded the passage of garbage trucks from other wards.

The highly rational network of bus, subway, and railway lines built in the 1950s and 1960s to service the growing cities was overwhelmed by the continuing influx of population. During the rush hour in Tokyo, "pushers" jammed commuters into overflowing train and subway coaches, and passengers were barely able to move their limbs. (Occasionally an unfortunate rider was crushed to death.) The rapid diffusion of the automobile—a rare sight in the early 1950s when only 2 percent of all roads in Japan were paved and an auto trip outside the cities was high adventure—also added burdens to urban life. With a sudden surge in the number of trucks and private passenger cars,

Station staff (called "pushers") packing passengers into a commuter train during rush hour in Tokyo in 1968.

the major urban areas were afflicted by increases in automotive smog and noise levels, road congestion, and traffic accidents. Worries that Japanese industry could not build an automobile fast enough to take advantage of the new interurban freeways soon disappeared in the haze of exhaust fumes hovering over their clogged lanes. One economist suggested that the automobile was turning Japan into a "battlefield" with pedestrians playing the role of unarmed combatants.

At first, ordinary Japanese were willing to put up with the inconveniences, dislocations, and distortions that accompanied growth. They saw them as sacrifices that had to be borne for the sake of the economic future. When voters discovered that the future included environmental deterioration, rising land prices, crowded public facilities, and unwanted development projects, they began to turn away from LDP candidates at the local government level. In 1967, Minobe Ryōkichi, a Tokyo University professor supported by the Socialists and Communists, won the governorship of Tokyo with a campaign that promised "Blue skies over Tokyo." The election of left-wing mayors and governors in Osaka, Kanagawa, Saitama, and other heavily urbanized areas in the late 1960s and early 1970s indicated how strongly local citizens resented the national government's neglect of the "distortions" of growth. Indeed, hoping to revive the flagging fortunes of the left, an association of left-wing mayors organized in the early 1970s and proposed that "progressive" local governments "encircle" the LDP-controlled central government.

Popular protest also found an outlet in "citizens' movements" or "local residents' movements" that sought to solve local congestion, pollution, or development problems. Unlike the massive left-wing "struggles" of the 1950s, these local movements were non-ideological, nonpartisan, and organized from the bottom up. Relying on petitions, sit-ins, demonstrations, and local election campaigns, their participants sought to block pollution by local factories, excessive noise from overflights by civilian and military jets, construction of freeways or high-speed rail lines through their neighborhoods, and even high-rise apartments that cast daytime shadows over neighboring houses. Although the leaders of these movements were usually men, their rank and file were predominantly women, often non-working wives of white collar workers, who had the time and energy to do organizational leg work. To be sure, these women often took a "not in my backyard" attitude, but more often they were moved by palpable concern at how a dangerous intersection, heavy smog concentrations, or increased traffic might affect their children or grandchildren. While their husbands were absent at the office or factory all day, it was they who were most affected by "public nuisances" (*kōgai*). Like the victims of pollution or members of discriminated minorities such as the resident Koreans, local citizens' movements often took their grievances to court, where they frequently won the public relations battle if not always a legal victory.

This rising swell of public protest, amply reported in a sympathetic press, forced the LDP government to abandon its laissez-faire indifference toward the environmental problem. Annual government economic plans in the late

1960s shifted away from a fixation on growth to visions of a comfortable pollution-free society. In 1968, the Diet passed an antipollution law setting standards for air, water, and noise quality, and requiring polluting enterprises to pay compensation for damage inflicted on local communities. Under pressure from industry, the law also included a clause mandating that environmental protection be pursued in "harmony" with economic growth. After a heated Diet debate two years later, the "harmony" clause was deleted, and in 1973 the government set up a compensation system for pollution-related health problems. By the 1970s, the government had instituted the toughest automobile standards in the world, and spending on pollution control amounted to a higher percentage of the GNP than in any other advanced industrial country.

The antipollution campaign, which required new industrial investment in pollution-control devices, soon produced visible results. By the late 1970s, Tokyo residents were able see Mount Fuji for more than a handful of days per year, and public complaints about pollution declined slightly but steadily. Strict controls over industrial waste improved water quality; regulations on industrial and automobile emissions cut air pollution; and new sewer systems and purification facilities eased the disposal of organic waste. While these policies slowed down the rate of environmental deterioration, they could not reverse much of the damage already done to the natural environment. In small but telling ways—the disappearance of crawfish and frogs from suburban ditches or the decline in fish catches in the Inland Sea—the landscape had changed unalterably.

The LDP-dominated government also came under attack for its failure to pay enough attention to national welfare policy. In their rush to expand the GNP, conservative politicians and economic bureaucrats had concentrated on raising average living standards rather than ensuring that everyone, including the weak, infirm, and elderly, enjoyed the benefits of growth. Compared to other industrialized countries, including the United States, the level of social welfare benefits such as pensions remained quite low, and workers not employed by large firms or corporations were often left outside the system. As one major newspaper noted,

> Our country's economic policy in the past has emphasized high production, but there is no reason, internal or external, why this emphasis must be continued. The most urgent task Japan faces today is to shift to an economy which emphasizes social welfare, one that will solve long-term inadequacies in our social environment, and will provide equal social guarantees to all citizens.[1]

The left-wing and other opposition parties took up the cry, calling on the LDP to cut military spending and use the money saved to improve social welfare programs.

In responding to this criticism, the LDP initially took the position that the best social welfare policy should be based on self-help. People should be encouraged to save for the future, and big corporations should be encouraged to provide solid pensions for their employees. Party leaders eventually realized, however, that boosting the GNP was not the only way to win votes, and that redistributive policies could yield political dividends. In the early 1970s, government pension benefits for the elderly were tripled, free medical care was extended to the elderly, and health insurance systems were improved. As with environmental policy, national social welfare policy was executed mostly by local governments, which often instituted their own local systems as well. In any case, social security expenses per capita more than doubled between 1970 and 1980, as did the portion of national income spent on social security. Political consensus agreed that the government had a responsibility to ensure citizens minimum standards of well-being, but the notion of a "welfare state" never took hold as it did in England, western Europe, and to a lesser extent in the United States.

THE END OF RAPID GROWTH

Ironically, just as the LDP-dominated government was coming to grips with the social effects of economic growth, rapid growth itself came to a sudden and unexpected end. During the 1960s, the economy had motored along at an average annual growth rate of about 10 percent, but in the mid-1970s it had slowed down to half that. Even more striking, in 1974 the economy shrank rather than grew. In a sense, none of this should have come as any great surprise. Economic growth always moves in spurts and cycles, and no society has ever experienced accelerated economic growth indefinitely. What shocked the public was the abruptness of the change—and the inability of either the LDP government or the central bureaucrats to head it off. While its consequences were not as dramatic or drastic, the slowdown revived memories of the 1929–1930 depression.

The end of rapid growth was in large measure the result of events outside Japan. The international environment that had facilitated the boom times of the 1950s and 1960s was changing, bringing an end to stable exchange rates, inexpensive energy imports, and minimal trade barriers. Japanese economic success had also generated frictions with the other industrial economies, particularly the United States. As Japanese industrial productivity rose, its manufactures were able to compete with foreign goods in the world markets as well as the domestic. When European countries like West Germany and Holland had increased their productivity in the 1960s, their governments had revalued their currencies, but in Japan, where the drive to catch up remained an idée fixe, discussion of revaluation was taboo. Since the dollar-yen exchange rate remained at the ¥360 = $1.00 rate set in 1949, the prices of Japanese exports were artificially lower than they should have been.

Reluctance to devalue the yen irritated not only the Europeans but the Americans, whose share of world trade had fallen steadily due to declining industrial productivity of American industry, heavy dependence on military production, and historic indifference to foreign markets. By the late 1960s, the United States was beginning to run a chronic trade deficit with Japan, and American businessmen were complaining about Japanese competition. Textile manufacturers in the South, for example, asked President Richard Nixon to persuade Japan to restrict its textile exports to the United States. After a delay of two years while Japanese manufacturers fought against the move, export ceilings were finally imposed in 1970. But the problem of an undervalued yen remained.

In the summer of 1971, the Nixon administration, faced with the first overall trade deficit the United States had experienced in more than eight decades, adopted policies to combat domestic inflation and cut the trade imbalance. Washington announced the imposition of a 10 percent surcharge on all imports and cut the dollar loose from the fixed international exchange rate. Although intended to deal with a general problem, there was no doubt that these measures were aimed at reversing unfavorable trade balances with West Germany and Japan. While the European countries immediately responded by floating their exchange rates, the Japanese government desperately clung to the old rate, until it was clear that the postwar system of fixed exchange rates had come to an end. In the wake of this "Nixon shock," the value of the yen rose steadily, igniting fears among Japanese manufacturers that their goods would no longer be competitive in the world market. In hopes of stimulating domestic demand, the Satō Eisaku cabinet increased overall spending and loans to private firms, but business gloom persisted.

In 1972, Tanaka Kakuei, a dynamic new prime minister, came into office with a plan to "rebuild the Japanese archipelago" by promoting industrial development in the provinces. Brash and rough-hewn, with only a technical school education, Tanaka was an exuberant self-made man who first made his personal fortune in the construction business, then used his money and wits to struggle to the top of the LDP hierarchy. Known as the "computerized bulldozer" because of his hard-driving intelligence, he maintained an extensive personal network in the bureaucracy and boasted a spectacular reputation as a political fund raiser. Tanaka's economic vision, which echoed the Ikeda "income doubling" plan, called for a network of small provincial industrial centers linked by high-speed railways and superhighways, that would bring economic growth to regions lagging behind the Pacific coast industrial corridor. Its optimistic projection of a 9 percent growth rate over the next decade set off a temporary boom, marked by speculative corporate investment in land and other commodities in preparation for a new wave of government and private investment. As a result, inflation, the constant companion of growth during the "miracle," began to rise ominously.

In the midst of this uncertain situation came the "oil shock" of 1973. The petroleum-producing nations in the Middle East, Africa, and Latin America, seeking a fairer share of world prosperity, had been trying to raise oil prices during the 1960s. When the fourth Middle East War broke out in the fall of 1973, the Arab oil-producing countries placed an embargo on oil exports to countries siding with Israel, and the Organization of Petroleum Exporting

States (OPEC) jacked up crude oil prices fourfold. The sudden disruption of oil supplies and the rapid increase in prices plunged Japan into a panic. The shift from coal to oil fuel that began during the 1950s and 1960s had made Japan dependent on the outside world for more than 80 percent of its energy. The OPEC price hike made the Japanese hostage to an international conflict in which they had no interest and over which they had no control. With memories of wartime and postwar shortages still fresh, consumers suddenly started buying up goods, and wholesalers began hoarding their inventories. Housewives in Osaka and other major cities, alarmed by rumors that the nation's toilet paper supply was running out, stripped store and supermarket shelves of every roll. By early 1974, wholesale prices were nearly one-third higher than they had been the year before.

The combined impact of the "Nixon shock" and the "oil shock" set in motion the worst recession the economy had experienced since the end of the war. Prices continued to rise; industrial production dropped; and corporate profits plunged. Nearly half the country's corporate enterprises reported losses. The sudden slowdown reminded the public of how fragile their prosperity was. According to one estimate, if industries like steel and petrochemicals continued to grow, by the 1980s they would require nearly one-third of the world's oil supplies. In other words, imported natural resources like oil, on which "miraculous growth" had rested, might someday be too scarce or too expensive for Japan to acquire. Clearly the "miracle" could not continue as it had, and many Japanese began to doubt whether their living standards would continue to rise. Not surprisingly one of the most popular best sellers of 1973 was *Submerging Japan (Nihon chinbotsu)*, a science fiction novel describing the disappearance of the Japanese archipelago in a cataclysm of earthquakes, volcanic eruptions, and tidal waves.

Middle-class hopes for a "bright life" faded as the economic slowdown hit family budgets. The household savings rate, which had grown steadily through the 1950s and 1960s, peaked in 1974, then began a noticeable decline that continued into the next decades. As the price of land rose, many *danchi* residents had to give up their hopes of buying a little house in the suburbs. In 1950, it was possible to buy a house at a cost equal to one year's income, but by the mid-1970s it had risen to five or six times as much. Those who did buy houses took on a heavy debt burden, sometimes even mortgaging their pensions, and still found themselves far from the city core, often with a one- or two-hour commute to work every morning and evening. Since big firms cut back managerial and executive positions as the economy slowed down, white collar workers found their chances for advancement and promotion more limited than before. Many were routed to make-work jobs "sitting by the window"(*madogiwazoku*) until retirement. At the same time, more and more women were finding their way into the work force as low-paid part-time workers to supplement the family income.

By the mid-1970s, the overwhelming majority of the population felt they were no longer better off than they had been in earlier years. Many felt their situation was getting worse. For all the promise of the economic miracle and for all the foreign admiration of the Japanese achievement, increasing numbers of ordinary Japanese felt themselves to be leading lives of quiet—albeit comfortable—desperation. As popular expectations about the future diminished, so too did enthusiasm for the conservative leadership of the country. During the 1970s, public opinion polls showed a decline in the support rate for the LDP and a rise in the number of those who supported no political party at all. The revelation of new political scandals further tarnished the party's image.

In 1973, a major monthly magazine, *Bungei shunjū*, published an exposé showing how Prime Minister Tanaka had used his government positions to attract public money to his election district, parleyed insider political connections to accumulate a huge political slush fund, and built a large and powerful LDP faction through profligate distribution of money. Tainted as a symbol of "money politics," Tanaka's popularity quickly faded, and he was finally forced to resign as prime minister. Even more sensational was his arrest in 1976 for accepting bribes from the Lockheed Corporation to persuade a domestic air line company to buy its planes. Coming at a time when most middle-class families were increasingly gloomy over the future, the Lockheed scandal angered the general public. After a small faction of younger members split from the party in protest, the LDP was barely able to maintain its majority in the lower house. Many thought the end of LDP hegemony was in sight, and even promises of political reform by his successor, Miki Takeo, who was known as "Mr. Clean," did not dispel such predictions.

RESTRUCTURING THE ECONOMY

For all the public gloom, the economic slowdown of the mid-1970s was mild compared to the pre-war depression. It was difficult, however, for the government to surmount these problems through fiscal policy. While prices usually fall in a depression, the economy was experiencing a period of "crazy prices." If the government tried to revive the economy by heavy spending, inflation was sure to accelerate, making life even harder for ordinary consumers. Instead, the government pursued a policy of fiscal stringency, cutting back on the budget and restricting the money supply. Only when inflation began to slacken in the late 1970s did the Fukuda Takeo cabinet, under pressure from Keidanren, the leading national business association, increase spending on public works and other public investment to stimulate demand. But instead of raising taxes to do so, the government increased its borrowing, issuing "red ink" bonds to cover the gap between income and outgo.

The main task of adjusting to the economic slowdown was left to private enterprise, whose managers struggled to adopt "lean management" policies as profits plummeted. Manufacturing firms reduced inventories, borrowed less money, used less fuel, and introduced robotics on the assembly line. Cutting the work force could increase productivity, but it had to be accomplished without violating the guarantee of lifetime employment for regular company workers. Big corporate firms tried at all costs to avoid layoffs that would hurt worker morale or spark labor troubles. Often they called on older workers to take "voluntary retirements" or did not replace those who retired or quit. Redundant workers were transferred from plants or offices to short-handed work sites, even if this meant uprooting their families, or they were sent to work for affiliated subcontracting firms. If new workers were needed, companies hired part-time or temporary workers who could be laid off during slack periods. Many "part-time" or "temporary" workers, especially middle-aged women, stayed on the jobs for years, doing the same work as permanent employees for lower wages and benefits. Since the labor market was so tight, labor unions willingly accepted wage settlements that matched or slightly exceeded the inflation rate. It made more sense to accept a moderate real wage increase than make demands that might threaten the whole enterprise.

Only the public sector workers, including national railway system employees, demonstrated any militancy. Since the 1950s, these workers, who were forbidden to strike under a law passed after the failure of the 1947 general strike, had been trying to have this restriction lifted. To leverage its demands for better pay, increase control over the workplace, and have a larger say in promotions, the public sector union had resorted over the years to work slowdowns and other devices. In 1975, in the midst of the economic slump, one million public workers staged a "strike for the right to strike." Significantly, however, the strikers attracted little outside support. Public resentment of the railway workers had been piqued when a slowdown by national railway workers two years before had caused rush hour delays, and angry white collar commuters had beaten up drivers at several stations. Many ordinary workers, including those employed in the non-unionized small enterprises, regarded the railway workers as lazy and overpaid. Labeling the strike as an infringement on the "human rights" of the rest of the population, the government had little difficulty staving off union demands and punishing the strike's leaders. The failure of the strike marked the steady decline of militant labor activism.

The ensuing labor peace rested on an increasingly conservative public mood. A government survey, for example, showed that a majority of workers felt that it was better for labor unions to carry on negotiations than to stage long-lasting strikes, that it was not necessary for unions to belong to a national federation, and that the best strategy for workers was to cooperate with employers. Indeed, formal membership in union organizations stagnated in the 1980s, and the unionization rate dropped from 35.4 percent of the work force in 1970 to 25.2 percent in 1990. Radicalism was in decline on university campuses too. Not only had the public become hostile to disruptive radical students tactics, but as the economy slowed down young people grew more anxious about their future employment prospects. Middle school and high school students spent more and more time preparing for entrance examinations, and university students were reluctant to engage in political activities that might spoil their chances for a decent job.

Hardest hit by the economic slowdown were the "smokestack" heavy industries that had led the "economic miracle": steel, shipbuilding, petrochemicals, aluminum, and the like. Heavily dependent on cheap oil and imports of raw materials, these industries scrambled desperately to survive the crisis. Many firms set up manufacturing operations in Southeast Asia or China, where labor costs were lower and pollution controls less rigorous. But the heavy industry sector as a whole stagnated or fell into decline. By the 1980s, the huge coastal industrial complexes in northern Kyushu or along the Inland Sea were becoming rusting relics of a more optimistic era. MITI, which had done so much to promote these industries, worked to ease their decline with a law that allowed firms in "depressed industries" to form rationalization cartels or scrap excess plants and machinery. The government also extended unemployment insurance benefits and provided financial relief for industrial cities and towns hard hit by the recession. The philosophy of "economism," which stressed the centrality of economic prosperity in politics, was now extended to industries on the way down as well as those on the way up.

The economic picture was not entirely bleak, however. What officials and journalists called "knowledge-intensive" industries—electrical machinery, precision machinery, machine tools, clocks and watches, cameras, and medical equipment—were growing. These industries depended less on imported fuel and raw materials, whose costs were rising, and more on highly educated skilled workers using advanced technology. The electronics industry, in particular, held great promise for the future, luring new investment in plant and technology. Japanese manufacturers were quicker to develop the production of semiconductors and employ them in integrated circuits than foreign firms. Soon they launched a "microelectronics revolution" that introduced the world market to a whole new generation of consumer products, from videotape recorders to personal computers. The technological gap between Japan and the West was finally beginning to close, and the outside world began to realize that Japan was a technological as well as an economic superpower.

As employment in manufacturing and mining leveled off, new jobs were also being created in commerce, finance, and other service industries. By the early 1980s, white collar (including "office ladies") employment was growing smartly. Banks, insurance companies, and financial firms continued to expand; software manufacturers sprang up as the computerization of office work accelerated; industrial waste disposal firms helped large companies comply with the new pollution control regulations; cram schools expanded to shepherd students through "examination hell"; and consultants offered advice on everything from city planning to fashion design. Not all the new businesses in the service sector were very sophisticated, nor did all the new jobs required high levels of skill or education. Colonel Sanders arrived in

Japan in 1970, followed shortly by Mister Donut, McDonald's, and Shakey's Pizza. Japanese imitators like the Mossburger or Lotteria chains soon sprang up, offering fare such as the "rice burger," a sandwich of burdock root, bacon, and seaweed compressed between two grilled rice buns. Fast food technology was also applied to more familiar fare such as noodles and rice dishes.

During the late 1970s, manufacturers of consumer durables like electrical appliances, television sets, and automobiles shifted their sights from domestic sales to the world market. During the post–oil shock recession, many Japanese firms tried to sell abroad what they could not market at home. Japanese exports took a sudden upward surge, pouring automobiles, color television sets, audio equipment, or other high tech products into the world market at an astonishing rate. Exports rose faster than overall production, from $19.3 billion in 1970 to $129.8 billion in 1980, more than a sixfold increase. What made Japanese goods so desirable to foreigners was not simply their price. Where once the label "Made in Japan" had signified cheap and shoddy goods, it was now an imprimatur of quality. For example, modestly-priced Japanese-made compact automobiles, known for their fuel economy and low defects, were becoming a common sight in the United States, Western Europe, and many Southeast Asian countries as well. By the mid-1970s, nearly half the country's automobile production was being built for export.

The shift away from heavy industry helped reduce Japan's dependence on imports of oil and other raw materials. A second "oil shock" occurred in 1979 when OPEC tripled its prices in the wake of the revolution in Iran and the outbreak of war between Iraq and Iran, but the Japanese were able to weather the crisis better than the other industrial countries. No toilet paper panic seized the public, nor did prices rise as precipitously as they had during the first oil shock. By contrast, in the United States and other industrial countries, where industrial restructuring had not taken place, output continued to stagnate, unemployment remained high, and inflation continued to rise into the 1980s. The reaction overseas to this contrast in economic performance was mixed: while many foreign observers held up Japan's managerial practices and economic policies as models for the advanced nations, politicians, businessmen, and officials in the advanced industrial countries began to complain about Japan's one-sided trade practices.

ENDNOTE

1. Quoted in *The Wheel Extended*, 3 no. 4 (Spring 1974), 33.

19

The Conservative Resurgence

B y the mid-1970s, it was clear to the rest of the world that Japan had become an "economic superpower" if not a political one. When the first
economic summit of advanced industrial countries convened at Versailles
in 1975, Japan was invited to join as one of the "big five" industrial nations.
This new international recognition, buoyed by an ever expanding Japanese
share of the world market, laid the foundation for a new surge of nationalism.
At the same time, the LDP leadership sought to revitalize the party's sagging
fortunes by proposing a "new conservatism" at home and "internationalization" abroad. After three decades of docilely following the American lead in
foreign policy, it appeared that Japan was finally overcoming the low international profile it had maintained during most of the postwar era.

CULTURAL NATIONALISM

National self-esteem had suffered in the early postwar years under the impact
of defeat, occupation reforms, and relentless self-criticism by "progressive"
intellectuals. In 1951, a government public opinion survey found that 47 percent of the respondents thought that the Japanese were inferior to Westerners, and in 1955 about the same percentage said they did not think the
Japanese economy could survive without aid from the United States. As the
material gap with the Americans and the other Western economies closed,
however, these feelings of inferiority faded rapidly. By the late 1960s and
early 1970s, polls showed that a substantial majority of the Japanese public
felt that as a people the Japanese were superior to any other in the world, and

an even more substantial majority thought Japan was equal or superior to the countries of Western Europe in technology and "economic power." The only area where the majority thought Japan still lagged behind was in standard of living. As national self-esteem rose, more and more Japanese thought their country was moving once again toward the top of the international hierarchy.

Conversely, respect for the major Western countries, especially for the United States, plummeted. While the Security Treaty was renewed automatically in 1970 without widespread public objection, political relations with the United States became strained as the Americans bogged down in the Vietnam war. Daily television broadcasts, especially scenes of American bombing raids in North Vietnam, reminded the Japanese public of their own wartime sufferings. A nonpartisan anti-Vietnam War movement centering on Beheiren, a "citizens movement" led by several prominent Japanese intellectuals, promoted the idea that the Americans were waging a ruthless war against other Asians for no good reason. When President Nixon urged America's Asian allies to increase their military capabilities, many Japanese took this as a sign that the United States was no longer willing to guarantee the security of its allies in East Asia. Needless to say, the American decision to devalue the dollar in 1973 also eroded public confidence in the United States as a world leader. The popularity of the United States, usually ranked highest in opinion polls about the public's "favorite foreign country," dropped behind countries like France and Switzerland.

As respect for the United States declined, many Japanese began to reevaluate the meaning of World War II. Revisionist histories of the war had already appeared in the 1960s. In 1963, Hayashi Fusao's *Affirmation of the Great East Asia War (Dai Tō-A sensō kōteiron)* argued that Japan's wartime goals had been the "liberation of Asia" and portrayed the United States-Japan conflict as the last phase of a "hundred years' war" with the West. This interpretation of the war, echoed from time to time by prominent LDP politicians, appealed to members of the older generation who had not come to terms with the defeat, but it also found an audience among those too young to remember the war. Accustomed to a Japan that was peaceful and prosperous, those born after the war often found it difficult to understand what Japan had to be ashamed of, nor were they inclined to be as self-critical as those who had lived through defeat. The school curriculum placed little emphasis on the study of recent history, and their understanding of Japan's wartime expansion was rather dim.

The mass media encouraged a softening of war memories too. War movies in the 1950s had emphasized the brutality of the Japanese military and the havoc wrought on other Asians, but by the 1970s films and television shows were more likely to portray the comradeship of the wartime troops, the heroism of the *kamikaze* pilots, the steadfast solidarity of the home front population, and the suffering of civilians at Hiroshima and Nagasaki. In 1978, with the support of the Association of War Bereaved Families, whose votes were ardently cultivated by the LDP, the spirits of General Tōjō and thirteen others convicted of "war crimes" by the Tokyo trials were quietly enshrined at the Yasukuni Shrine. Even the trials themselves came in for reinterpretation. In 1983, Yamazaki Toyoko's *Two Homelands (Futatsu no sokoku)*, a novel portraying the anguish of a Japanese-American interpreter who finds the trials so arbitrary and unjust that he commits suicide, became a best seller, and was then adapted as a yearlong evening drama series on the national broadcasting system.

The suicide of Mishima Yukio, one of the country's leading novelists, was the most dramatic expression of this nostalgic patriotism. Upset by the spread of pacifism and radicalism, Mishima began writing essays and fiction that glorified the samurai ethic and romanticized the radical right-wing officers of the 1930s. In 1970, accompanied by members of the Shield Society, a private paramilitary group outfitted with designer uniforms, Mishima "occupied" the NSDF headquarters and called for a coup to "restore the emperor." When the NSDF failed to take action, Mishima committed ritual suicide. Few took Mishima's "coup d'état" seriously or thought it anything more than the act of someone psychologically unbalanced, but it demonstrated that the extremist nationalism was not entirely dead. Indeed, all through the 1970s and 1980s small groups of right-wing extremists patrolled the streets of Tokyo with sound trucks blaring out old army and navy songs, and self-appointed "patriotic" activists threatened violence against those they accused of sullying the national honor.

The patriotic right, however, remained a tiny minority, albeit one whose political influence behind the scenes outweighed its numbers. The majority of the public had no wish to return to the extremist nationalism of pre-war days. International polls showed that Japanese young people expressed far less willingness to sacrifice themselves or die for their country than their contemporaries in the United States or the United Kingdom. Nor did the pre-war symbols of nationalism—the national flag, the national anthem, the imperial shrine at Ise, or the imperial throne itself—retain their emotional appeal, particularly among the young. To be sure, spectators were moved to see the "rising sun" flag unfurled for medalists at the Olympic Games or other international sports events, but the flag roused no deep feelings of devotion to the state or its national mission. Rather it represented a Japan that was finally making its way back to international respectability.

While a majority of Japanese continued to support the imperial institution, they showed little interest in a restoration of the pre-war monarchy. Few, if any, regarded the emperor as a "living god," and the number of those wishing to expand his political emperor's powers steadily dropped all through the 1960s and 1970s. Most expected the emperor to perform his postwar role as a constitutional monarch, presiding over public ceremonies, receiving foreign visitors, and making occasional tours through the country. An imperial wedding, birth, or death aroused momentary public interest in the royal family, more out of human interest than any identification of the emperor with the nation, but indifference toward the imperial family steadily rose. Indeed, to many younger Japanese, Hirohito was known as "Ten-chan" ("Empie"), a sobriquet that would have brought a prison sentence if uttered publicly in pre-war Japan.

Economic nationalism based on pride in Japan's material success, rather than state-centered patriotism or nostalgia for the "good old days," provided the impetus behind the new nationalism. What interested the Japanese public was why their economy was doing so well. In the early 1970s, a rash of works by foreign observers such as Herman Kahn, who predicted the imminence of a "Japanese century," pointed out the superiority of Japanese economic organization and management practices over those of the Western economies. Many Japanese authors took up the theme, suggesting that it was perhaps time for foreigners to learn from Japan rather than the other way around. One of the biggest best sellers was *Japan as Number One*, the translation of a work by an American sociologist, Ezra Vogel, who suggested that the Japanese were better in everything from crime prevention through party politics to school sports. (He even pointed out that the world record for hitting home runs was held by Oh Sadaharu, a Japanese baseball star, rather than by an American player.)

The most popular expression of the new cultural nationalism was a boom in books on "Japanese national character" (*Nihonjinron*) or "Japanese national culture" (*Nihon bunkaron*). Ranging from abstruse discussions of traditional philosophy to chatty comments about daily customs and manners, the *Nihonjinron* literature offered a positive and self-congratulatory evaluation of Japanese tradition, history, culture, and thought. To be sure, the boom produced pseudo-scientific works that discussed the difference between the "Japanese" brain and the "Western" brain or hypothesized that "Japanese bees" were less aggressive than "Western" ones, but works such as Nakane Chie's *The Vertical Society (Tate no shakai)* (1967) or Doi Takeo's *The Structure of Dependence (Amae no kozo)* (1971) were serious exercises in cultural comparison. What all of these books had in common was an emphasis on the "homogeneity," "uniqueness," or "distinctiveness" of the Japanese in comparison with Westerners. In a sense, the *Nihonjinron* echoed ideas about Japanese national identity put forward in the 1890s, when the country was emerging from another period of intense development dependent on borrowing from the outside world.

The *Nihonjinron* literature emphasized qualities that modern Japanese had always admired in themselves: industriousness, tenacity, politeness, and kindness. In reaction to postwar self-criticism, *Nihonjinron* writers also asserted that social values condemned by the American Occupation as "feudal" were positive virtues. As one high school principal remarked, "Pre-war nationalism went too far and led the country to war. After the war, we went too far again, this time in the opposite direction, denying values of anything that had to do with the pre-war system and thereby leaving the nation with only its outward form and without its heart."[1] While the American Occupation had said that "traditional values" like social harmony, cooperation, and obedience stifled democracy, individualism, and freedom, many Japanese now argued that they helped to account for the "economic miracle." Traditional values enabled the Japanese society to manage complex human relationships with a minimum of conflict and made Japan safer and more secure than other industrial societies. Not surprisingly, by the 1970s and 1980s opinion polls showed that an increasing number of respondents ranked "filial piety" and "repaying a benefactor's kindness" as more important than "respect for individual rights" or "respect for freedom."

The *Nihonjinron* literature turned primarily on cultural comparisons between Japan and the West. Few Japanese made much of Japan's "Asian" identity or stressed common interests with Asia. Indeed, the Japanese public paid very little attention to their neighbors. Until the late 1970s, the People's Republic of China, South Korea, and North Korea all remained (along with the Soviet Union) the countries "least liked" by the Japanese public. The image of these countries as "backward" or "less developed" was compounded by political criticism of the repressive military regimes in South Korea and the undemocratic totalitarianism in China and North Korea. When diplomatic relations were reopened with China in 1972, most thought of it as an opportunity to open up the huge Chinese market to Japanese goods. And when economic development accelerated in so-called new industrializing economies (South Korea, Taiwan, Hong Kong, and Singapore) in the 1980s, these countries were seen not as societies with strong cultural ties to Japan but as promising outlets for Japanese investment or as sources of cheap labor for Japanese manufacturers. As tourists, the Japanese were much more likely to visit the United States and Western Europe than any neighboring country. In their hierarchical vision of the world, they still ranked Asia behind Japan and the West.

Oddly enough, resurgent cultural nationalism was accompanied by a new public interest in "internationalization," a contradictory slogan that sometimes meant opening Japanese society up to foreigners but more often meant promoting Japanese culture in the outside world. To some extent, this was a natural consequence of the increased flows of goods, people, and information to the outside world. Zen meditation centers, sushi, bars and judo academies were sprouting up in New York, Los Angeles, and Paris, and American and European children were watching Japanese animated television programs like *Atom Boy* and *Speed Racer*. But the government hoped to promote "understanding" of Japan by expanding student exchange programs, establishing fellowship funds to promote Japanese studies abroad, and making it easier for foreign students to attend Japanese universities. The goal, however, was not simply to advertise Japan's cultural heritage but to suggest that Japan might provide a model for the rest of the world.

THE "NEW CONSERVATISM"

By the late 1970s, the steady economic recovery buoyed not only a cultural nationalism, but a recovery of the LDP's political fortunes as well. In the

1980 election, the party regained the Diet majority it had lost in 1976. Except for a slight downward blip in 1983, it increased that majority for the rest of the decade. The party also regained control over local governorships that had been occupied by opposition-supported incumbents in the 1970s. Undoubtedly, renewed optimism about the economic future, as well as concern that the opposition parties would be poor managers of the economy, paved the conservative comeback trail. But the nature of LDP popular support had changed. As the result of a 1985 Supreme Court decision that existing electoral districts unfairly denied urban votes a weight equal to rural votes, district boundaries were redrawn and new seats were created. Older voters, particularly those in the countryside continued to support the party, but the LDP was increasingly dependent on the support of younger and more independent urban white collar voters. These voters were fickle, supporting the LDP because they associated the party with affluence but were ready to be lured away if a more attractive alternative political force were to emerge.

Despite the LDP's electoral success, divisions over basic policy orientation were emerging within the party. For two decades, mainstream LDP leaders had given priority to a doctrine of "economism," putting GNP growth and limited rearmament at the center of national agenda. Many party members wondered whether economic growth was a sufficient national goal. As Prime Minister Ōhira Masayoshi noted in 1979:

> In the thirty-odd years since the end of the war, our country has sought economic prosperity, and by moving forward with our eyes fixed on that goal, we have accomplished remarkable achievements. . . . However, it can not be said that we have paid sufficient attention to the harmony between man and nature, the balance between freedom and responsibility, a sense of worth deeply rooted in the inner spirit. Material civilization itself, rooted in urbanization and rationalism, has reached its limits.[2]

It was time, he concluded, to define new domestic and international goals. This sense that the country had reached a turning point laid the grounds for a "new conservatism."

Although launched by Prime Minister Ōhira, the new conservative program was most closely associated with Prime Minister Nakasone Yasuhiro, who took office in 1982. In contrast to his low-key predecessors, Nakasone was a flamboyant public personality, given to grandstanding and bold gestures. A natural public speaker with a histrionic presence and a surfeit of self-confidence, Nakasone was the first LDP leader to make astute use of television press conferences. Indeed, many thought his style was "presidential," more like a Ronald Reagan or a Francois Mitterand than the usual Japanese prime minister. Since he had come to power with the help of the Tanaka Kakuei faction, few thought his cabinet would last very long. In fact, Nakasone remained in power for nearly five years, bringing a change in the political mood in Japan and reviving LDP popularity. Promising to render a "general settling of accounts in postwar politics" he announced an intention to move beyond politics as usual. But his tenure in office proved how difficult it was for the ruling LDP to abandon "economism" or extricate itself from the "iron triangle."

The domestic agenda of the "new conservatism" drew inspiration from Thatcherism in England and Reaganism in the United States. Many LDP leaders argued that their own central government had become too large, gobbled up more and more taxes, made its citizens dependent on welfare benefits, and robbed them of individual initiative. But the domestic program of the new conservatives quickly ran into trouble. The Ōhira cabinet attempted to limit spending on welfare programs by calling for a "Japanese-style welfare society" that would create "strong and stable individuals" by reducing their dependence on the state. Politically, this was difficult to carry out. For one thing, welfare programs were far more modest in Japan than in the United States or Europe. For another thing, increased expenditures on old age pensions, expanded medical benefits, education, and other social services had proven popular with the voters. Any attempt to cut social welfare benefits while large corporations were enjoying high profits and low taxes was likely to meet with a public outcry. Since many LDP members were reluctant to tamper with these programs, the effort to build a "Japanese style welfare state" faded rather quickly.

The new conservatives instead touted plans for "administrative reform," a program to reduce the size of government. It was packaged as protection against the "advanced country disease": a combination of declining work ethic, reliance on government borrowing, and expanding public debt. In fact, the call for administrative reform was a reaction against Keynesian policies of the late 1970s, when the government borrowed heavily to stimulate growth through increased spending on government construction and public works projects. Big business leaders and MOF officials, two powerful elements in the "iron triangle," backed "administrative reform" most enthusiastically. The MOF wanted to check growing government indebtedness by raising taxes, and corporate leaders wanted the government to rationalize itself, as business had, by adopting "lean management" after the oil shock.

It was difficult, however, to overcome vested interests who opposed budget cutbacks. For all the talk about the need to end deficit spending, it was clear that the Japanese central government was neither as bloated nor as inefficient as many Western governments. Opponents of drastic retrenchment argued that the Japanese government was already relatively lean: the number of public officials per capita was low, and so was the overall tax rate. Political opposition to administrative reform came primarily from ministerial bureaucracies who wanted to protect their budgets and LDP politicians who wanted pork barrel projects to build voter support. Many powerful interest groups also opposed a tax increase. The national business federations made clear their opposition to any rise in corporate taxes, and the small business community, especially retailers who solidly supported the LDP, raised their own objections. In short, resistance within the "iron triangle" produced deadlock on new conservative plans for "administrative reform."

When Prime Minister Nakasone came to power, he soft-pedaled the issue of tax increases, making "privatization" of public enterprises the centerpiece of his domestic program instead. His main target was the national railway system, which had been under government ownership and management since 1906. The system constantly ran at a loss, even though its fares were higher than on private railway lines. The railway workers' union, the most powerful of the public sector unions, had resisted any efforts to improve efficiency by reducing featherbedding, absenteeism, and redundant hiring. Conservative politicians and businessmen wished to break the railway union's power, and large corporations feasted their hungry eyes on the national railway system's real estate assets, particularly in major urban centers like Tokyo. In 1986, after a long struggle with both railway management and unions, the Diet passed a law breaking the system up into six regional private companies. A government corporation took over the old system's debts, and the new companies proved successful very soon. Holding up "privatization" as a model for the benefits of "small government," the Nakasone cabinet also converted the national telephone and telegraph system into a private corporation and ended the government monopoly on the sale of tobacco and salt.

A sweeping LDP victory in the 1986 election demonstrated the popularity of Nakasone's leadership, but a post-election attempt to raise taxes brought his downfall. During the election campaign, the prime minister had pledged not to introduce any new taxes. Once the election was over, he proposed a new sales tax to the Diet. Needless to say, the public outcry was immediate, enabling Nakasone's intraparty rivals to force his resignation. In 1988, his successor, Prime Minister Takeshita Noboru, succeeded in engineering the passage of a European-style VAT (value-added tax) system by reducing income taxes, corporate taxes, and local residency taxes at the same time. The move was unpopular nevertheless, particularly among housewives, who felt the impact on their household budgets immediately. Since prices were no longer denominated in neat multiples of five, the one yen pieces cramming their purses constantly reminded them of the new tax burden. The opposition parties, determined to garner political support by mounting an anti-tax movement, picked up enough votes in the 1989 House of Councilors election to win a majority, making it more difficult than ever for the LDP to press forward with the new conservative domestic program.

"INTERNATIONAL CONTRIBUTION"

In foreign affairs, the new conservatives hoped to define a role for the newly prosperous Japan. For all its importance in the world market, the country had yet to make much impact on world politics. Down through the 1970s,

Japanese foreign policy had been passive and reactive. The Japanese government took few initiatives in international affairs; its leaders were unassertive at international gatherings; and its military forces were prohibited from possessing nuclear weapons or taking part in overseas operations. Like the United States during its isolationist period, Japan was a reluctant giant, unwilling or unable to involve itself deeply in international politics. This disparity between Japan's economic strength and its international role spurred mounting criticism abroad. In the United States, many politicians and journalists accused Japan of getting a "free ride" by failing to take full responsibility for its own defense. Some American congressmen talked of revising the Security Treaty, levying a "security tax" on Japan, or even asking NSDF vessels to patrol the Indian Ocean.

Stung by American and other foreign criticism that Japan did not carry its share of the burden in preserving international stability, the new conservatives argued that unless Japan made a good faith effort to increase its "international contribution" to world peace and prosperity, it might well bring on a collapse of the free trade system. But there was no consensus on what form Japan's "international contribution" should take. One alternative was to open Japan's market wider to imports from other industrial countries, either by stimulating internal demand or reducing import restrictions and other non-tariff barriers to trade; a second alternative was to assume a larger share of the cost of international stability by increasing Japanese aid to the less developed world; and a third alternative was to take on greater responsibility for Japan's self-defense by raising military expenditures and defining an expanded role for the NSDF. Since opening the domestic market wider threatened business and bureaucratic interests allied with the LDP, this alternative was politically dangerous. The new conservatives concentrated instead on overseas development aid (ODA) and military expenditures.

In an effort to rebuild a tight relationship with the United States, the LDP governments of the 1980s shifted away from a "multi-directional" foreign policy adopted by LDP cabinets in the late 1970s. For the first time, Japanese leaders began to speak of the relationship with the United States as an "alliance." In part, this was a response to the eruption of a "new" Cold War after the Soviet invasion of Afghanistan in 1979. The Carter administration canceled its participation in the 1980 Moscow Olympics as a gesture of protest, and President Reagan denounced the Soviet Union as an "evil empire." For their part, Japanese officials, businessmen, and politicians close to the defense establishment used the breakdown of détente between the Americans and the Soviets to beef up Japan's own defenses. The Japanese public, never fond of the Soviet Union, was reminded of its refusal to return the "northern territories," and the Japanese press began to carry stories about a Soviet force buildup in the "northern territories," the expansion of the Soviet Pacific fleet, and Soviet support for the Vietnamese invasions of Laos and Kampuchea.

The possibility of a renewed Soviet military threat in Asia undoubtedly made the public uneasy. The conservative leadership seized it as an opportunity to buttress the military relationship with the United States. In 1979, Prime Minister Ōhira responded to American requests for greater "burden sharing" by agreeing to defray part of the expenses of the American bases in Japan, an offer that no NATO country had made. On the other hand, Ōhira countered American pressure to increase defense by proffering the notion of "comprehensive security," a policy of protecting Japan not simply by military force but through a combination of diplomacy and economic measures as well. In practice this meant an increase in expenditure on ODA (overseas development assistance). Between 1980 and 1990, Japanese grants and loans to developing countries more than tripled. Not surprisingly, substantial amounts were initially directed toward countries on the periphery of the Soviet Union— Pakistan, Turkey, and China—but much aid also went to Southeast Asia, where Japanese private investment was growing.

The rhetoric of "international contribution" encouraged some right-wing LDP members to suggest the time had come to revise the "peace constitution." Centrist and moderate LDP leaders, however, were aware that public support for the constitution had grown over time. In 1980, Prime Minister Suzuki Zenkō affirmed that his cabinet had no intention of revising the constitution. Indeed, he called it a "splendid code" that was in many ways superior to other constitutions in the world in its commitment to the principles of pacifism, democracy, and fundamental rights. Even the hawkish Nakasone was reluctant to tamper with the national consensus on the constitution. What he wanted was not a return to full militarization but the building of a more "equal" military relationship with the United States.

As prime minister, Nakasone made a conscious effort to establish himself as a world leader, visiting thirty-seven countries on twenty-three overseas trips, including seven visits to the United States, a record that made him the best traveled Japanese prime minister in postwar history. A great deal more at ease in dealing with Western leaders than his predecessors had been, he managed to capture attention in the outside world. On his first visit to the United States, he gave speeches in English, established a first-name relationship ("Ron" and "Yasu") with President Reagan, and stood at the American president's side when photographs were taken at the Williamsburg summit. To the shock of many back home, including members of his own cabinet, he also referred to Japan, with its American air bases in Okinawa and elsewhere, as an "unsinkable aircraft carrier" for the United States. It was not an image that most Japanese, with their strong commitment to the peace constitution, found comfortable.

To establish closer military ties with the United States, the Nakasone cabinet promised in 1983 to make an exception to a long-standing policy against exporting military technology by allowing such exports to the U.S. Following up on the Suzuki government's promise to defend sea lanes up to 1000 nautical miles from Japan, his government also indicated willingness to blockade the main straits around Japan in the event of an emergency. These efforts to forge closer military links with the United States led to a 1987 agreement allowing Japanese companies to participate in the development of the Reagan administration's SDI (Strategic Defense Initiative) and other anti-missile programs. In all these ways, the Japanese were able to demonstrate growing willingness to participate as an active partner in the security relationship with the Americans.

On the home front, Nakasone hoped to increase Japanese defense expenditure, both to placate the United States and to buttress Japan's position as a military presence in East Asia. After the first "oil shock" in 1972, the military budget had been cut. From the outset Nakasone's goal was to break the 1 percent of GNP limit placed on arms defense expenditures by the Miki cabinet in 1976. The brief resurgence of the opposition in the 1983 election posed a temporary stumbling block to his plan, but more important was resistance from moderate LDP leaders who sensed little public support for the measure. After the LDP won a substantial majority, however, Nakasone was finally able to break the 1 percent limit in the 1987 budget, though only by the slight margin of .004 percent. Since the GNP was still growing, by the end of the 1980s Japan had become the third-largest military spender in the world after the United States and the Soviet Union.

The expansion of the military budget had a strong support among heavy industrial firms. NSDF forces amounted to only about 240,000 men in the late 1980s, well below its authorized strength, but these forces were very well equipped, with as much firepower per man as any military force in the world. The NSDF was also the most sophisticated non-nuclear military power in East Asia. Using most of the budget increases to buy state-of-the-art military hardware, from tanks to missiles, the NSDF was a hearty customer for a growing domestic arms industry. Indeed, 90 percent of its equipment was domestically produced, including sophisticated equipment dependent on the microelectronic technology at which Japan excelled. By the late 1980s, the Japanese were planning production of a domestically designed fighter plane, the FSX. Much to the disappointment of MITI and business leaders, the government bent to pressure from the American government, which wanted to protect its own domestic aircraft industry, and agreed to a joint development project with an American company.

The enhancement of Japan's military capacities played well in Washington, but it was not so welcome in the capitals of East Asia, where memories of Japan's imperialist past remained vivid. Although both South Korea and the People's Republic of China received development aid and enjoyed growing economic ties with Japan, basic distrust of Japanese intentions made relations complex and sensitive. Attempts to resuscitate Japan's military position were seen as potentially dangerous. The Chinese and the Koreans were upset by the so-called textbook controversy in 1982 when the Japanese press reported that history books approved by the ministry of education had substituted the word "invasion" for "aggression" in describing Japan's attack on China in 1937. Protests from Asian countries poured in again in 1985 when Prime Minister Nakasone, in a diplomatically feckless effort to revive the symbols of patriotism, officially participated in ceremonies at Yasukuni Shrine to pay respect for the war dead, including convicted and executed war criminals. The Chinese, the Koreans, and other Asians were also outraged when high-ranking LDP politicians and cabinet ministers made public statements justifying Japan's imperialist activities in Korea and on the continent. In this context, the scrapping of the 1 percent ceiling seemed a step on the way to rebuilding Japan as a military power. In 1987, the PRC minister of defense advised his Japanese counterpart that development of Japan's military potential should be limited "in light of the tragic lessons of history."

For all Nakasone's flamboyance in the international arena, in the end his foreign policy gestures remained well within the basic framework of the post-1960 political consensus on security issues. Although Nakasone had supported revision of the peace constitution in the 1950s, he showed no inclination to do so as prime minister. While American and Japanese military worked out more detailed plans for joint operations and intensified joint training maneuvers in the late 1980s, both sides still saw the relationship as a defensive one and assumed that the United States would come to Japan's aid in the event that it was attacked. A handful of right-wing politicians and business leaders mooted the idea of developing a Japanese nuclear capability, but the LDP leadership also remained firmly committed to the "three nonnuclear principles" enunciated by Prime Minister Satō in 1967, well aware that more votes were likely to be lost than won by abandoning them. In any case, the signing of a nuclear arms reduction treaty between the United States and the Soviet Union in 1987 suggested that nuclear weapons were losing their value as an instrument or symbol of national strength. With a renewed thaw in U.S.-Soviet relations in the late 1980s, the concerted effort to build up conventional forces lost much of its rationale as well.

TRADE FRICTION

The strengthening of security ties with the United States, however, was counterbalanced by a growing rift over trade issues. In 1960, Japan's exports had accounted for a little less than 3 percent of the world's total, but by the mid-1970s they reached the level of about 6 percent, then shot up to nearly 10 percent in the mid-1980s. Imports rose at a much slower rate, however. As a result, the country's trade surpluses and foreign exchange reserves began to swell. Hardest hit by the tide of Japanese exports was its biggest customer, the United States, whose industrial sector was lagging behind Japan's in growth of investment and productivity. During the 1980s, Japan's trade surplus with the United States nearly quintupled, and the bulk of its exports were manufactured goods that Americans had once excelled at producing: automobiles, heavy machinery, and electrical goods. The increase in Japan's defense expenditures and U.S.-Japan joint military planning had little effect on growing American irritation over the large and growing trade surpluses with Japan.

As Japan's trade surpluses mounted, friction with the United States assumed a repetitive pattern: Japanese exports of a particular product such as steel or automobiles would suddenly increase; American manufacturers and labor unions would call on Washington to limit the influx of Japanese goods; the American government would present Tokyo with a demand for voluntary limitations; the Japanese bureaucracy would respond slowly, trying to protect the interests of the Japanese producers; and soon the trade problem would escalate into a high-level political problem. When the Americans accused the Japanese of "unfair" competition, dumping goods in the American market at prices lower than in Japan or of subsidizing industry, the Japanese would respond that their goods were better in quality, their workers more industrious, and their industrial productivity higher than Americans. Tempers flared on both sides. Ugly incidents such as the 1982 murder of a Chinese-American mistaken for a Japanese by an unemployed Detroit auto worker confirmed the Japanese public's impression that the Americans were acting

The Japan - U.S. Trade Imbalance

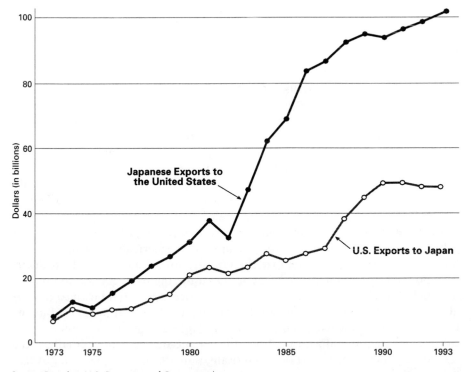

Source: Based on U.S. Department of Commerce data.

unreasonably and emotionally. But the apparent reluctance of the Japanese bureaucratic and political elite to reduce the trade surplus convinced many Americans that Japan was engaging in "adversarial trade."

Trade friction began with steel and cotton textiles in the late 1960s, shifted to television sets and other electrical appliances in the early 1970s, hit full stride with automobiles in the late 1970s, and accelerated with micro-electronics and semi-conductors in the 1980s. During its early phases, trade friction was smoothed over by voluntary export restraint (VER) agreements prompted by the threat of possible American trade sanctions. Often, these agreements did not produce expected results. For example, even though Japanese automobile manufacturers cut their exports to the United States in the early 1980s, they marketed more profitable expensive models, and American manufacturers raised their own prices instead of improving quality.

As protectionism gathered support from both American labor and American business, the U.S. Congress passed an Omnibus Trade Act in 1988. Its "Super 301" clause gave the American president the right to take retaliatory action against countries deemed to engage in unfair trade practices. To deflect growing anti-Japanese sentiment, however, the American government urged the Japanese to open up their market by reducing "non-tariff barriers" such as non-competitive bidding on construction contracts, opaque administrative regulations, and insider relationships among Japanese firms. If Japanese goods were allowed to compete freely and openly, the American government insisted, then it was only fair that American goods should be provided a "level playing field" in Japan. With European backing, the Americans urged the Japanese government to stimulate imports through expansion of domestic demand. Prime Minister Nakasone showed that his heart was in the right place by ostentatiously buying foreign-made neckties in a Tokyo department store, but this made little impression on the outside world.

The Reagan administration began "market-oriented, sector-selective" (MOSS) negotiations aimed at increasing imports of American goods in particular sectors. In 1986, for example, an agreement was reached to increase Japanese imports of American-made semiconductors by 20 percent. More often, however, the Americans met with a slow response or no response at all. While American officials accused the Japanese of deliberate foot-dragging, complex struggles within the "iron triangle" delayed market opening, as one set of bureaucrats and their allied interest groups fought with one another behind the scenes. For years, for example, the Americans had pressed the Japanese government to liberalize the importation of agricultural products. This policy was supported by Keidanren and the big business community, as well as by MITI officials, who feared that the rice issue would lead to retaliation against Japanese manufactured goods in the American market. But the Japanese farm lobby, backed by the LDP and allied with the ministry of agriculture, resisted liberalization. When the Japanese government finally lifted restrictions on the import of beef and oranges in 1988, the American government complained that the move was "too little and too late."

By the end of the decade, trade friction had become a chronic issue. The Bush administration moved in the direction of managed bilateral trade by launching the so-called Structural Impediment Initiative (SII) aimed at removing "non-tariff barriers" or "structural barriers" to the Japanese market. For its part, the Japanese government argued that the basic reasons for the trade deficit were that American consumers spent too much and saved too little, and that American business pursued short-term profit instead of long-term strategy. Nor were Japanese politicians reluctant to point out that ethnic diversity, high crime rates, low educational standards, and a declining work ethic also hurt American economic growth. Although the Japanese government promised to expand domestic demand by spending more on public works projects, the trade imbalance between the two countries continued to grow.

THE BUBBLE ECONOMY

Ironically the trade deficit allowed the Japanese to finance the growing budget deficit produced by Reaganite "supply-side" economic policy. By cutting taxes while increasing military expenditures to deal with the "new" Cold War, the Reagan administration plunged the American government into a rising pool of red ink. Responding to rising interest rates in the United States, Japanese investors recycled dollars produced by the trade surplus by lending money to the American government through the purchase of government bonds and securities. As a result, by 1985 the United States had become the world's largest debtor nation, and Japan the largest creditor. To make matters worse, the Reagan government insisted that a strong dollar was a sign of the country's economic health. In fact, a strong dollar made it more difficult for American goods to compete in the world market.

By the mid-1980s, the Reagan administration finally realized that unless the dollar was devalued to a more realistic level the American economy would be faced with growing problems. In late 1985, at a meeting in the Plaza Hotel in New York, the finance ministers of the five major industrial countries, including the United States and Japan, agreed to support the appreciation of other currencies against the dollar. The Plaza Accord, as it came to be known, brought a brief economic slowdown as the price of Japanese goods in the world market rose sharply. But the rising yen also brought down the cost of oil and other raw materials purchased in dollars. Electric power companies, gas utility companies, and industrial firms that relied heavily on such imports enjoyed sudden windfall profits. Instead of passing the benefit on to consumers through price cuts or to the workers through wage increases, these firms chose to invest their profits in new ways.

In the late 1980s, Japanese investment abroad surged. While continuing to practice "lean management," many firms cut production costs by investing in overseas production facilities, especially in Southeast Asia, where labor was cheaper and pollution regulations less strict. More and more "Japanese" radios, television sets, and tape recorders were being made in Thailand, Malaysia, Singapore, and elsewhere. Even those manufactured at home were assembled from parts made outside Japan. The rising yen also made foreign real estate, stocks, and securities relatively cheap. New investment in Asia was dwarfed by a sudden spurt of new investment in Europe and the United States, where Japanese firms were assiduously courted by local governments hoping to create new jobs. By the late 1980s, Japanese automobile plants were springing up in Ohio, Tennessee, and California. But it was Japanese-owned resort hotels and golf courses in Hawaii, and the purchase of such visible popular cultural icons as Columbia Pictures and Rockefeller Center by well known Japanese firms that brought home to the American public just what an economic powerhouse Japan had become.

For most Japanese businesses, the rising yen was associated with a new boom: the "bubble economy." To stimulate the economy, the government had increased public spending and eased interest rates. With their pockets full, many Japanese firms embarked on speculative investments in real estate, office buildings, stocks, and securities. Indeed, by plunging headlong into "financial engineering" (*zai-tech*) even manufacturing corporations like Toyota acted like banks or securities companies, buying stocks and other high-yielding financial assets or investing in real estate. In response to this sudden flood of investment funds stock prices soared (the Nikkei index rose from ¥12,000 in 1985 to ¥39,000 in 1989), encouraging businesses to raise money by selling stock rather than borrowing from banks. Real estate prices soared too, setting off speculative investment in land, buildings, and construction. Since corporate firms were no longer as interested in borrowing money, banks became less disciplined. They lent money to small firms and real estate companies, including pure speculators with dubious credit and credentials. Bathed in a warm glow of optimism that the good times would roll on forever, even sober-sided executives engaged in financial sleight of hand.

The giddy upward spiral of the economy prompted an orgy of conspicuous consumption symbolized by the purchase of major European art works such as Van Gogh's *Sunflowers* by Japanese corporations. Even ordinary Japanese splurged as the rise in the yen made foreign travel cheaper. Between 1985 and 1990, the number of Japanese traveling abroad jumped from 5 million to 11 million, helping to bury a bit of the trade surplus with tourist dollars. But not everyone shared in the sudden expansion of wealth brought by the "bubble." To many working people, blue and white collar alike, the rising per capita income figures often seemed like a mirthless statistical joke. In relative terms, many ordinary households found themselves no better off than before. During the 1960s, everyone had seemed to benefit more or less equally as the economy grew, but the expanding "bubble" seemed to widen the gap between the very affluent and the not so affluent. In contrast to the Western industrial economies, income distribution still remained fairly even in Japan, but there was a growing inequality in household assets. As land prices surged, households owning houses or apartments became dramatically wealthier than those who rented, and the assets of Tokyo residents grew faster than those in the rest of the country. To be sure, much new wealth existed only on paper. Even so, those with real estate could borrow more easily from banks to play the stock market or engage in *zai-tech* themselves.

Neither did the rising value of the yen benefit the Japanese consumer. It made the cost of living much higher in Japan than elsewhere in the developed world. According to one estimate, in 1992 it was 1.3 times as expensive to live in Tokyo as in New York, the most expensive city in the United States. (Oddly enough, although a loaf of bread cost about the same in both places, a sack of rice was twice as expensive in Tokyo.) Foreign imports should have become cheaper, but corporate profiteering kept their prices relatively high, as did a marketing and distribution system that placed many layers of agents, wholesalers, and retailers between the foreign producer and the Japanese consumer. In effect, consumers were giving invisible subsidies to this unproductive sector by paying prices well above world market levels. And since export industries, faced with the need to keep their plants running and their workers employed, lowered their prices abroad while keeping them high at home, the consumer was subsidizing them as well. As long as price levels in Japan were higher than in the outside world, the affluence of the bubble economy was illusory. Oddly enough, however, despite general complaining about prices, interest groups representing consumers were few and far between. Indeed, many ordinary Japanese consumers worried that a reform of the distribution system might bring widespread unemployment and that lifting agricultural subsidies would hurt the farm population.

WOMEN, WORK, AND FAMILY

As the economy expanded, more and more women entered the labor market. During the early postwar years, when the "good wife, wise mother" ideology remained strong, the ideal woman had been the housewife who sacrificed personal aspirations to devote herself to husband and children. Popular women's magazines like *Fujin kōron* argued that a stable family should have priority over a woman's desire to pursue a career and enjoined women to find fulfillment in the successes of her family at school or at the office. The welfare bureaucracy, charged with supervision over family issues, warned that the welfare of the nation's children would be put at risk by rising employment of women. Indeed, as household incomes rose in the 1960s, the percentage of women in the work force dropped off noticeably.

As the economy slowed down in the 1970s, however, more and more women sought jobs to supplement the family income. Between 1975 and 1985, female employment grew nearly twice as fast as male employment.

Wholesale and retail sales, traditionally a female-intensive industry, accounted for some of the growth, but even more important was the burgeoning of banking, finance, and other knowledge-based industries that required clerical workers, data-processors, low-level managers, and other specialized workers. Educated women, especially those with post-secondary degrees, found themselves in demand. Firms once reluctant to hire women eagerly sought them out. Electrical appliance makers, automobile manufacturers, clothing and fashion firms, and other companies producing consumer goods hired women to participate in product development and marketing. And even high tech firms recruited women with engineering training to develop software and other information technology.

Women were better able to fill high-skilled jobs than they had been two decades before. In 1965, only a very few women entering the job market had post-secondary education, but by the late 1980s over 40 percent did. Indeed, by 1989 a slightly higher proportion of women (36.8 percent) than men (36.6 percent) pursued their education after high school. To be sure, higher numbers did not mean that women were better educated than men. Less than half the 1.86 million students in four-year institutions were women, while nearly all those in two-year institutions were. While most male students majored in the social sciences or in engineering, women students clustered in the home economics, education, and humanities departments. Clearly, higher education was preparing men and women for quite different roles in society. For most young women, education was intended to make them better marriage partners, not economically self-sufficient career women. And even those who sought careers found themselves shunted into "female" roles. In elementary education, for example, nearly two-thirds of the teachers were women, but hardly any principals were. Women, it appeared, were allowed to nurture the young in the classroom, but not thought suitable to manage the school.

Not all employed women in the 1980s were first-time job seekers. The expectation remained that young women would work for four or five years, then get married. As family size shrank, young mothers were able to return to the work force once their children left for school. Often they sought extra household income to make a down payment on an apartment or a house, to cover the rising costs of children's education, or simply to keep pace with the proliferation of new household appliances, home entertainment products, and other upscale goods. Many middle-aged wives, reluctant to rely on their children for old-age support also worked to build a nest egg to supplement their husbands' retirement payments and government pensions. This two-phase employment pattern was comfortable for most women, but those who reentered the work place usually ended up in part-time jobs, either because they were still responsible for child care or because employers did not offer them anything else.

Whether entering the job market for the first time or returning to it after the early years of marriage, few women could expect to secure positions of importance or responsibility in large business firms. A "glass ceiling" kept

Attitudes Toward Gender Roles

Opinion poll responses to the question:

"How do you feel about the mentality that, 'husbands should go out to work and wives look after the home'?"

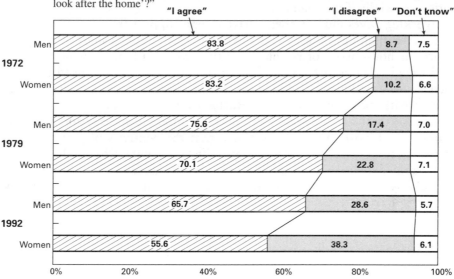

	"I agree"	"I disagree"	"Don't know"
1972 Men	83.8	8.7	7.5
1972 Women	83.2	10.2	6.6
1979 Men	75.6	17.4	7.0
1979 Women	70.1	22.8	7.1
1992 Men	65.7	28.6	5.7
1992 Women	55.6	38.3	6.1

0%   20%   40%   60%   80%   100%

Source: Based on public opinion surveys conducted by the Office of the Prime Minister.

them from getting the same promotions as men did, and usually they received lower wages or salaries for doing the same work. In 1988, on average women's wages were only 50 percent of men's. An active but fragmented feminist movement, inspired by the "women's lib" movements in the United States and Europe in the 1960s, had attacked gender discrimination in the work place, but its membership in the movement was small, as was its influence. Politicians and bureaucrats, however, did respond to growing international pressure, especially from United Nations' sponsorship of an "International Woman's Decade." In 1980, the government ratified an international treaty to end sexual discrimination, and in 1985 the Diet passed an equal employment opportunity law.

While the new law aimed at reducing discrimination against women and other gender inequities in the work place, it had little effect on actual business practices. The law did not prohibit many forms of discrimination, nor did it grant women new rights. Rather it set up a mediation system to resolve disputes over discrimination. At the same time, to assure equity with men, the law removed the special protection given to women with respect to hours, overtime, and shift work in postwar labor standards laws. In response, a few firms created a two-tier structure for women employees: a "general track" for women in less complicated clerical jobs, and a "career track" for those in management positions. Women on the "general track" did not expect promotions nor did many of them expect to stay with the firm very long. But even women in "career track" positions, who could expect to rise in the company hierarchy, found it awkward to be transferred to other cities, especially if they had families.

Working wives did not always have strong support from their husbands, who were often unwilling to undertake more than a token share of responsibility for house work or resented that they were no longer the household's sole bread winner. Perhaps this is why opinion surveys continued to show that a substantial majority of women (and needless to say, a majority of men) agreed with the proposition that "Husbands work outside the home; wives take care of the household." The idea of different spheres for men and women died hard, and so did the idea that the woman's place was in the home. Despite a strong feminist critique, the "good wife, wise mother" ideology retained its hold on the adult population. Conservative gender and family values showed a tenacity in Japan that they did not in many other highly industrialized societies.

ENDNOTES:

1. Kosaka Yoshino, *Cultural Nationalism in Contemporary Japan: A Sociological Inquiry* (New York: Routledge, 1992), 213.

2. For slightly different translation, see Satō Seizaburō et al., *Postwar Politician: The Life of Former Prime Minister Masayoshi Ōhira* (Tokyo: Kodansha International, 1990), 451.

20

Japan in the 1990s

T he death of the Emperor Hirohito in early 1989 marked the end of an era for those who remembered Japan's kaleidoscopic changes during his reign. The imperial funeral rites, attended by the leaders of 160 nations, were a testimony to the postwar transformation of the country from international pariah to a respectable world power. But other events in 1989 suggested that the country was once more on the verge of important transformations: for the first time in three decades the LDP lost a general election to the upper house; the stock market index buoyed by the bubble economy reached a historic peak only to crash a few months later; and the Berlin Wall crumbled under the picks, hammers, and chisels of Germans from both sides. These events, though unrelated in origin, signaled the emergence of a world quite different from the one the Japanese were used to. As old certainties gave way to new uncertainties at home and abroad, the future no longer seemed comfortably predictable.

THE POST-BUBBLE ECONOMY

The "bubble economy" burst suddenly in early 1990 when the Bank of Japan, under the guidance of the ministry of finance, raised interest rates. As credit tightened, the stock market collapsed, ushering in a prolonged economic slowdown. The real growth rate of the GNP dropped steadily, and so too did the index of industrial production. Large corporations cut hiring, and new high school and university graduates, who had been so much in demand just a few years before, suddenly scrambled to find jobs. Women graduates faced even greater difficulties than men. In the face of economic uncertainty, consumer spending dwindled, and so did capital investment. Owing to the drop in domestic demand, even the much vaunted automobile industry cut its output. In 1993, it surrendered Japan's position as the "world's Number One car maker" to the United States for the first time in more than a decade. The recession seemed to go on interminably, longer than any since the beginning of rapid economic growth. To make matters worse, as the value of the yen continued to appreciate, reaching roughly ¥80/$1.00 in early 1995, Japanese manufactured goods became less and less competitive in the world market. And while Japan's economy was foundering, its neighbors in East Asia, including the People's Republic of China, were enjoying "economic miracles" of their own.

The sudden slowdown after the sybaritic years of the "bubble economy" indicated long-term as well as short-term problems. The optimistic view was that Japan could recover from economic setback as it had from earlier recessions. Pessimists, on the other hand, speculated that growth rates were likely to remain low over the long haul, comparable to those in the United States and other advanced industrial countries. In the short term, most agreed, the bloated corporate structures built in the late 1980s needed paring down. As the result of bubble investment fever, many industrial firms were saddled with excessive plant facilities, and many financial institutions were weighed down with bad loans to unsuccessful speculative enterprises. By the mid-1990s, firms like Matsushita and Mitsubishi shed their highly visible but unprofitable investments in the United States. While some pundits continued to predict that economic recovery was just around the corner, business confidence plummeted.

What worried pessimists about Japan's economic future were long-term changes at home and overseas. Although Japanese industry had been highly successful at importing and commercializing new technologies during the 1960s and 1970s, the technological gap between Japan and the other advanced industrial countries had closed. It was by no means clear where future technical innovation would come from. Since "technological nationalism" was on the rise in the other advanced economies, it was no longer easy or cheap to acquire new product ideas or production technologies from abroad. The technicians, scientists, and engineers who worked for Japanese industry were among the finest in the world, but as corporate profits dropped so did spending on research and development. By the early 1990s, Japan was lagging behind in the development of telecommunications, computer software, microprocessors, and other areas on the high-tech frontier. Even when Japanese did make innovations, such as in the field of "high resolution" television, they found themselves leapfrogged by technical developments abroad or faced with international technical standards different from their own. For the first time in several years, commentators talked once more about the need to learn from the United States.

Despite the low official level of unemployment, many Japanese firms suffered from "in-house unemployment." Companies continually improved blue collar productivity by investing in new equipment and new technology, but the white collar work force, particularly in the growing service sector, was enormously inefficient. For one thing, the Japanese continued to travel in the slow lane of the new international "information highway." Many Japanese white collar workers performed tasks that could be done faster and better by computer. (While service was polite and pleasant in a Japanese bank, for example, withdrawing a small amount of money might require a fifteen-minute wait.) The lifetime employment system also made it difficult to increase white collar work efficiency by laying off unneeded or redundant workers. Employees were furloughed instead of fired or given make-work projects that contributed little to the firm's profitability. In 1994, the major national employer's federation (Nikkeiren) even issued a report proposing major changes in corporate personnel practices, ending the practice of lifetime employment and introducing a more flexible employment system that linked wages and benefits to performance instead of seniority.

The corporate structure itself prompted other worries about the economic future. The mere size of many corporations seemed to lead to bureaucratization, a decline in management risk-taking, and greater inflexibility in corporate decisions. It was common to criticize "the big enterprise disease," an organizational hardening of the arteries that threatened Japanese business dynamism. Excessive reliance on long-term relationships with other firms also checked an inclination to explore new opportunities, and a corporate culture based on teamwork seemed to stifle innovation. While corporate conformity, homogeneity, and discipline of corporate management worked well when the economy was expanding, these qualities appeared counterproductive in times that demanded change. No one advocated the kind of ruthless corporate restructuring pursued in the United States but neither were they confident that large business firms could continue operating as they had since the end of the war.

The problems of the economy extended beyond business practices and management techniques. As income and education levels rose, so did the personal expectations of those entering the labor market. Few young men and women were interested in jobs that were "dirty, dangerous, or demanding." An increasing number of foreign workers, lured by higher wage levels, migrated to Japan from South and Southeast Asia, Latin America, and the Middle East to take on these undesirable occupations, and Southeast Asian women were brought in to work in bars, cabarets, and massage parlors. For the first time since the pre-war Korean migration, ordinary Japanese were startled to find in their midst a large group of ethnic and cultural aliens who were neither interested nor able to assimilate easily into Japanese society. Their numbers seemed likely to grow as the pool of potential domestic workers shrank. The birth rate had fallen below the level needed to maintain the population at its current size, and in 1993 it hit the lowest point ever recorded.

The shrinking work force had other long-term implications. As affluence and improving health care helped Japanese live longer, the population was "graying" at a rapid rate. Indeed, the average age at death steadily rose, to give Japan the highest levels of longevity in the industrial world, and the country was expected to become the world's "most aged society" by 2005. While one might expect this to be a matter for congratulation in a society that traditionally revered filial piety, it was a source of social concern. The growing ranks of the elderly would have to be supported by a shrinking cohort of younger, productive (i.e., income producing) persons. According to some estimates, as the postwar baby boomers reached retirement age, the older "nonproductive" population was predicted to reach one-quarter of the total population by 2020. Unless people were encouraged to work beyond the normal retirement age or unless more and more women took jobs, this meant a growing economic burden on the work force.

The concerns of the pessimists were real, and so were the problems that worried them. But the more optimistic took a calmer view, pointing out that the economy's fundamental social and economic base was still sound. By any standard, the Japanese economy was a strong one, no matter how bleak the short-term outlook seemed. The euphoria of the 1980s simply made things appear worse than they really were. The potential for continued growth remained, as long as corporations made the hard decisions required of them and as long as the government shifted policy to deal with the country's new problems. Indeed, by early 1996 the growth rate had rebounded slightly; stock prices were up; and corporate profits rose again, as large firms restructured themselves. But even optimists had to admit the intransigence of the country's basic economic problems—a listless growth rate, a bearish stock market, and a banking system weighed down by bad loans equal in value to the Australian GNP. "Japan stands at a crossroads," warned Toyoda Shoichiro, the Keidanren chairman. "If we take no action and let these problems linger on, the Japanese economy will be headed for catastrophe and will be left out of the world's prosperity in the twenty-first century."[1]

THE END OF LDP HEGEMONY

If the economy seemed to have gone slightly off track in the early 1990s, the political world was completely derailed. For years, public apathy, cynicism, and disillusion with the political world had been on the rise. In the 1950s, when the future shape of postwar democracy seemed to be at stake, popular interest in politics was high, and a majority felt that the Diet in some way or other reflected the "will of the people," but as the "iron triangle" tightened its grip on the political process, public trust declined. By the late 1970s, polls showed that only 40 percent of the respondents thought that the Diet represented the people. The advantage of incumbents in winning re-election meant that fewer new faces were coming into politics. Many younger Diet members were "second generation" politicians who "inherited" their seats from their fathers. With the conservative political establishment so firmly entrenched, many voters thought it pointless to go to the polls at all. Voting rates in national elections declined steadily, especially among the young. The number of voters identifying themselves as "independents" rose from 7 percent in 1960 to 30 percent in 1980, and by the early 1990s perhaps half the electorate no longer felt strong ties to the established parties. Indeed, in the 1995 gubernatorial elections in Tokyo and Osaka, voters shocked conventional politicians by electing two "non-party" candidates who had begun their careers as television comedians.

What turned voters away from the LDP was rising disgust at the "structural corruption" that seemed to accompany the party's long hegemony. It was striking, for example, that the party's largest and most influential faction was led by Tanaka Kakuei, the former prime minister convicted for receiving bribes from the Lockheed Corporation. Political power, it seemed, depended on the ability to raise political funds by fair means or foul rather than by taking a stand on principle or policy. During the years of rapid economic growth, the voters had forgiven the LDP leadership for its scandals, considering them a lesser evil than the incompetence of the opposition. But as the economy headed into hard times, the public was no longer convinced that the party was indispensable to national prosperity. And with the end of the Cold War, the LDP embrace of the United States in foreign policy no longer guaranteed voter support either.

Popular disgust with back-room maneuvering was fed by a new series of political scandals. In the summer of 1988, it was revealed that Recruit Cosmos, a real estate firm, had sold its unlisted stock at bargain basement prices to several politicians and bureaucrats, allowing them to make huge profits when the stock was sold publicly. Although no major LDP leader was indicted, former Prime Minister Nakasone was questioned by investigators, and Prime Minister Takeshita Noboru resigned when it was revealed that his secretary had received cash and stock from the company. To contain growing public outrage, the LDP promised political reforms to bring an end to "money politics." An electoral reform commission came up with a plan to reduce the number of Diet seats, replace the multiple-seat (three to five members) electoral district with a single-seat system, and elect 40 percent of the lower house by proportional representation. The shift to the small district was intended to end the costly electoral battles between fellow LDP candidates, and the introduction of proportional representation was intended to protect the interests of the smaller parties like the Socialists or the Komeitō. But neither Prime Minister Kaifu Toshiki, an engaging figure with an image as a "clean" politician, nor his successor Miyazawa Kiichi was able to overcome intraparty resistance to the legislation.

In early 1992, as the debate over political reform continued, a new and even wider scandal was revealed. Prosecutors arrested the president of Sagawa Kyūbin, a major fast-delivery trucking company, for passing on political donations to nearly 100 politicians through firms linked with a major underworld organization. The vice premier, Kanemaru Shin, who had succeeded to the leadership of the former Tanaka faction, admitted receiving bribes. When investigators discovered ¥5 billion in bank bonds and ¥1 billion in cash and gold bars hidden away at his residence, Kanemaru was arrested for tax evasion as well. The scandal set in motion an intraparty revolt that led to the disintegration of the LDP.

Younger conservative political leaders, many of them "second generation" politicians, who were frustrated by the inertia of the LDP leadership and the bureaucratization of its organization, were impatient for change. In anticipation of electoral reform, they wanted to redraw the political landscape. On the eve of the 1992 house of councilors election, Hosokawa Masahiro, the telegenic descendant of a famous daimyo house, bolted from the LDP to form the Japan New Party, which won several seats in the election. Desertions from the LDP accelerated in the summer of 1993, when several younger faction leaders joined a no-confidence vote against the Miyazawa government, forcing a snap general election for the lower house. Even before the election returns were counted, it was clear that the LDP majority was doomed. A group headed by Takemura Masayoshi, who had risen from local politics, split off from the LDP to form the Sakigake (Harbinger) Party, and another headed by Ozawa Ichirō, a former Tanaka faction leader, formed the Japan Renewal Party.

The big loser in the 1993 election was not the LDP, which remained the plurality party, but the Socialists, who lost nearly half their seats. The voters wanted a change but not a radical shift in national leadership. What the voters got, however, was a political landscape crowded with strange new political alignments and alliances. In the wake of the 1993 election, a coalition of eight anti-LDP factions, including the Socialists, the Komeitō, and the conservative splinter groups, ended the era of LDP hegemony by backing a new cabinet headed by Prime Minister Hosokawa. The major accomplishment of the Hosokawa cabinet was final passage of a political reform bill that provided that three hundred Diet seats be elected from single-member districts with the remaining two hundred to be chosen by proportional representation. The law allowed businesses and other groups to make contributions to individual politicians, so it was unlikely to have much effect on "money politics." But there was no doubt that the new law would force a major party realignment in the long run.

The coalition backing Hosokawa fell apart when he announced a plan to replace the unpopular 3 percent consumption tax with a new 7 percent "social welfare" tax, and his successor lasted only two months. Unsettling as this rapid turnover was, an even stranger development came in the summer of 1994. While many expected that LDP would form a new majority government in alliance with former LDP defectors, it allied instead with the Socialists and the Sakigake Party behind a cabinet headed by the Socialist leader Murayama Tomiichi. This strange alliance—between two parties that had been locked in conflict for decades—demonstrated how hungry the Socialists were for a taste of power and how desperate the LDP were to regain it. Even more surprising, the Socialist leaders reversed many long-standing policies by recognizing the constitutionality of the NSDF forces, affirming the Mutual Security Treaty with the United States, rejecting a foreign policy based on neutrality, and recognizing the rising sun flag and the national anthem. These views brought the Socialists into line with the majority public opinion but they undercut the party's *raison d'être*—to serve as a check on the conservative forces. Whatever the results of political reform, party divisions would never be the same again.

Just what would emerge from this political turmoil, and how the party politicians would align themselves, depended very much on the outcome of the first election to be held under the political reform bill. Few were willing to predict what new party lines would look like or how long it would take them to solidify. The reformed electoral system, however, was stacked in favor of large conservative or middle-of-the-road parties. The Socialists, who had jettisoned their long-standing policies, seemed to have little future even with the introduction of proportional representation. Most predicted that the Socialists would be squeezed out of existence by two or three large centrist or conservative parties recruited from the LDP, the conservative splinter groups, and the Komeitō. Indeed, in late 1994 the Japan New Party joined with the Komeitō and the other LDP defectors to form the New Frontier Party, and in the spring of 1995 the Socialists floated plans to disband in order to create a new "liberal" group.

For all its troubles, the LDP still occupied the largest bloc in the Diet. After Murayama's resignation in early 1996, a coalition centering on the LDP continued to control the cabinet, and nearly 40 percent of potential voters expressed support for the party. All things considered, it seemed likely that the LDP would remain the largest party after elections under the new electoral system. The New Frontier Party, which called for a two-party system, tried to carve out policy positions distinctive from its rival, but its leader Ozawa Ichirō, a former member of the Tanaka faction, was distrusted as a wily insider, adept at maneuvering behind the scenes. When the election finally came in 1996, the LDP won a plurality of the vote. Indeed, it came within a whisker of winning an absolute majority in the Diet, enabling the party to return to power under Prime Minister Hashimoto Ryūtarō, a cocky "second generation" politician. But the party was not out of the woods. Its future depended on its ability to deal with the country's economic woes.

THE TROUBLED BUREAUCRACY

The collapse of the LDP hegemony in the early 1990s brought a temporary upsurge in the influence of the ministerial bureaucracies. The short-lived coalition cabinets that moved in and out of power after 1993 were unable to exercise strong leadership or develop clear policies. Although this gave the bureaucrats a free hand they had not enjoyed under the discipline of LDP hegemony, it did not augur well for major institutional change. Whatever the defects of LDP hegemony, the party was sensitive enough to public sentiment to know when a shift in policy directions was appropriate. The bureaucrats, on the other hand, never worried about the lash of voter discontent and remained confident that they knew what was best for the country. Whatever the outcome of the party realignments, they expected the "iron triangle" to remain in place.

By the mid-1990s, however, public confidence in the bureaucracy was waning. For one thing, officials in MITI, the MOF, and the Bank of Japan no longer seemed able to work the policy magic that spurred the "economic miracle." Blame for the prolonged economic slump rested heavily on the shoulders of the bureaucracy. As many critics pointed out, the economic bureaucrats had not only created the bubble economy but had then deflated it too suddenly. For all their fabled expertise, they seemed unable to pull the economy out of its post-bubble doldrums either. Indeed, many suggested that excessive bureaucratic supervision of the economy, arcane and arbitrary regulatory procedures, and cozy alignments between bureaucrats and interest groups were making the economy far less competitive than it should be.

By the mid-1990s, many business, academic, and political leaders called for "deregulation" of the economy. In part, this was a response to foreign criticism. The American government had long complained that excessive regulation constituted a "non-tariff barrier" to the Japanese market, and so did American businessmen. In early 1995, the United States proposed a set of general principles to guide deregulation in all the advanced countries. But ordinary Japanese had their own good reasons to complain about the thicket of economic regulations. Not only did heavy regulation protect weak enterprises or declining industries from market failure, it favored the interests of producers and sellers over those of consumers. Regulations forced home owners to buy appliances, building materials, and even furniture at prices higher than a completely unregulated market would have allowed; they permitted trucking companies to charge almost identical rates with little or no competition; and they limited the spread of large discount retail stores offering a variety of consumer goods at low prices. The web of regulations reduced the overall competitiveness of the economy while keeping consumer costs high.

The numerous public corporations set up by various ministries as intermediaries with private business interests also came under heavy criticism. Many of these corporations performed important functions such as electric power development or management of regional freeway systems, but some overlapped with other special corporations or served only marginal public purposes. The general public was well aware, however, that public corporations offered comfortable post-retirement jobs for high government officials who "descended from heaven" (*amakudari*) to run them. Businessmen, downsizing to cope with economic slowdown, resented this bureaucratic feather-bedding, and reform-minded politicians criticized them as a wasteful drain on the national budget. With the ministerial bureaucracies and LDP "policy tribesmen" allied to resist change, plans to streamline or consolidate public corporations fizzled, but the demand for smaller government did not disappear.

The Hanshin earthquake of 1995, which killed several thousand people and leveled large sections of Kobe, made it clear that the bureaucracy was not adept at managing major domestic crises either. The widespread destruction, especially the collapse of urban freeways certified as "earthquake proof," was shocking. Even more shocking was the response of both the central and local government to the disaster. Not only was Tokyo slow to set up an emergency headquarters, it failed to mobilize NSDF forces for disaster relief quickly. Bureaucratic regulations also thwarted efforts by foreign relief agencies to send help. Foreign doctors dispatched by an international emergency organization, for example, were not allowed to provide medical treatment to earthquake victims because they lacked Japanese medical licenses, and search dogs, brought from abroad to find victims in the rubble, were quarantined too long to be of any use.

During the mid-1990s, daily newspapers and nightly television broadcasts continued to headline reports of bureaucratic incompetence, inflexibility, and corruption. MOF officials were blamed for shoring up failing credit unions and housing loan companies with public funds; regulatory officials covered up the troubles of supposedly "bankruptcy-proof" banks; health and welfare officials were accused of allowing AIDS-tainted blood plasma to be given to hemophiliacs. Public trust in the bureaucracy was probably at its lowest point since 1945. It seemed likely, however, that the bureaucracy would survive as long as no strong political leadership was able to carry out regulatory reform. In 1996, the Hashimoto cabinet announced a strong commitment to deregulation and bureaucratic restructuring, but the general public was skeptical that it could bring about fundamental reform. More likely were slow but incremental changes in rules, procedures, and administrative practices that would diminish bureaucratic regulation but leave ministerial autonomy and bureaucratic self-confidence intact.

THE END OF THE COLD WAR

The end of the Cold War brought new uncertainties in Japan's relations with the outside world. With the final disintegration of the Soviet Union in 1991, the superpower confrontation that had long defined Japan's international niche came to an end, giving the Japanese an opportunity to forge a new and independent role in the international arena. As politicians, journalists, and intellectuals had urged for more than a decade, it was time for Japan to speak up for itself. A country so important to the world economy could no longer react passively to initiatives taken by other powers. Indeed, Ishihara Shintarō, a novelist turned LDP Diet member, teamed up with Morita Akio, the head of the Sony Corporation, to publish *The Japan That Can Say No*, a best-seller that called for more independence in foreign policy. The country's political leadership, however, had difficulty not only in finding Japan's voice but in deciding whether it was better to say "No" than "Yes."

Securing a permanent seat on the UN Security Council was about the only issue on which the politicians, bureaucrats, and the public seemed to agree. Beyond that, opinions about Japan's international role were wide-ranging. The general public seemed to favor a larger economic role—contributing to the healthy development of the world economy, cooperating with developing countries, or promoting scientific, technological, and cultural exchange. Those on the left wanted Japan to take a stronger, more vocal stand on other issues, such as human rights, environmental protection, population control, and international trade that affected the whole world. But many conservative and centrist politicians urged the government to wield greater political and military clout. A country with a large stake in international stability, they argued, should take responsibility in maintaining it, whether through military burden-sharing with the United States and its allies or through participation in United Nations peace-keeping operations.

The difficulty of deciding how to make a greater political-military contribution was revealed in the debate over Japan's response to the Gulf War in 1990. Since the oil shock, Japan had been careful not to offend the oil-producing countries of the Middle East on which the country was so heavily dependent. When the Saddam Hussein regime invaded Kuwait, however, the Kaifu cabinet quickly joined in the economic boycott against Iraq, demonstrating a willingness to put international stability ahead of national economic self-interest. Instead of sending troops to join the United Nations military build-up against Iraq, however, the Japanese government pursued "checkbook diplomacy" by offering $4 billion in aid to Iraq's neighbors. Since Japan was a major consumer of Kuwaiti oil, the United States and other countries committing troops and money to the United Nations effort expressed disappointment at the amount. Stung by this criticism, the Kaifu cabinet proposed legislation permitting the dispatch of NDSF forces to the Middle East, but it met with strong opposition, inside and outside the Diet, on the grounds that it would violate the letter and spirit of Article Nine.

While Japan ultimately contributed $13 billion to the countries that sent military forces to the Gulf, its failure to act quickly and decisively renewed concerns abroad about its reliability as a world leader. In 1992, after a long and fractious debate, the Diet finally passed a law that allowed NSDF forces to join United Nations PKO (peace keeping operations) in a non-combatant role. Since the legislation required the Diet to give specific approval in every case, it guaranteed a national debate whenever the issue arose. In the fall of 1992, NSDF engineering units were dispatched to Cambodia to repair roads and bridges destroyed in the long civil conflict there, and other non-combat units went to Mozambique in 1993 to deal with refugee problems under UN auspices. But a large segment of the public and the political community remained uncomfortable with the idea of sending Japanese troops abroad. The dispatch of an NSDF water-purification team to Rwanda in 1994, for example, prompted a Diet debate on how many machine guns they might carry for their own protection. It was clearly going to take time before the Japanese public fully understood just what was involved in making a "contribution" to international security.

The debate over peace-keeping operations, coupled with the end of the Cold War, raised questions about Japan's defense policies. Few voices were heard in favor of abolishing the NSDF forces after the collapse of the Soviet Union. Even the Socialists finally recognized their constitutionality. But the changing international situation opened the question of whether or not to reduce defense spending. By 1992, the Japanese defense budget was the third largest in the world. Few countries were likely to attack Japan, many argued, so it was time to make defense cuts. Others countered that the political instability of East Asia was increasing, since the Soviet Union no longer served as a check on China or North Korea, the two most unpredictable and potentially dangerous countries in the region. If Japan were to cut its defense expenditures or reduce military capacities too quickly, it might find itself unprepared for an unanticipated crisis; and in any case increased commitment to international peace-keeping operations required Japan to maintain its level of defense spending.

The end of the Cold War also put Japan's relationship with the United States into a new context as the focus of United States foreign policy shifted to questions of trade and economy. It was clear that American political leaders of all stripes were irritated by Japan's growing trade imbalance with the United States. In early 1992, for example, President George Bush traveled to Japan with the heads of the three big automobile companies in tow. While he managed to extract a promise from Japanese automakers to increase purchases of American-made auto parts, enforcing this promise was left to his successor. To strengthen the American bargaining position on trade questions, President Bill Clinton announced his intention to impose unilateral sanctions against countries that pursued unfair trade practices against American products. In the spring of 1995, when American negotiators failed to secure an agreement over the import of American automobile parts, Washington announced it would impose punitive tariffs on Japanese luxury automobiles and charge Japan with unfair trading practices at the new World Trade Organization. While the dispute was resolved by a political compromise, it was clear that similar disputes would continue. Indeed, new disputes were already brewing over the import of American photographic film to Japan and the use of Japanese airport facilities by American courier delivery companies.

While public opinion polls showed that most Americans felt friendly toward Japan, and that an even larger majority of Japanese felt the same toward the United States, the rhetoric of hostility escalated on both sides of the

Pacific. Most ordinary Americans admitted that the Japanese worked hard and produced high-quality goods, but they had difficulty understanding why the Japanese were so reluctant to buy American goods or why important sections of the Japanese market were closed to foreign firms. Given that the United States guaranteed Japan's military security and supported Japan on other issues, the Japanese attitude seemed ungrateful at best, arrogant at worst. The situation was made no better by the "America-bashing" of Japanese politicians who criticized the United States as a whining cry-baby or a declining power unable to hold its own in the world market.

For their part, many Japanese resented the continuing presence of American troops in Japan. The military relationship suffered a severe shock in September 1995 when three American marines were arrested and convicted in a Japanese court for the rape of a twelve-year-old Okinawan girl. The incident provoked new debate in Japan over just how valuable the Security Treaty was to Japan and what its costs were to ordinary Japanese citizens. Feeling against the American presence ran most strongly in Okinawa, where most American forces were concentrated. The prefectural governor supported efforts by farm households that had been displaced by the American bases to retrieve their land when lease agreements with the Americans expired. The Hashimoto cabinet did its best to smooth over the incident and to reassure the American government of its commitment to the mutual security arrangement, but basic doubts lingered among the general public.

THE NEW ASIANISM

As relations with the United States grew testier, new interest kindled in Asia. Trade had been growing with the region since the 1980s, and businessmen were finding profit margins higher in Asia than in the United States and Europe. Indeed, by 1993 the volume of Japanese trade with Asia had surpassed that of trade with the United States. The Asian market provided an outlet for Japanese pop culture as well as Japanese goods. For example, an NHK television drama depicting the life of a poor pre-war farm woman attracted large Chinese audiences who identified with her perseverance, courage, and hard work. Business journals and newspapers, sensing an opportunity to expand overall trade and foreign investment, carried articles calling for the "re-Asianization" of Japan or touting growing "Japanization" in the rest of Asia.

Stronger links with Asia were seen as a way to diversify the country's diplomatic ties and reduce its heavy dependence on the United States. The development of regional organizations aimed at greater trade and economic integration, such as the Asian Pacific Economic Conference (APEC) founded in 1989, offered new opportunities for Japan to act as a regional leader. Indeed, the Malaysian government invited Japan to play a central role in an East Asian Economic Conference (EAEC) that would exclude the United

States. But the Japanese were reluctant to lead an exclusively Asian club. The United States government, anxious to strengthen its own ties with the rest of Asia, made clear to the Japanese that it wanted to be included in any regional economic organization, and countries with long-standing ties to the United States like South Korea, Taiwan, and the Philippines were reluctant to participate in a regional bloc potentially hostile to American interests.

In building closer ties with their Asian neighbors the Japanese faced other barriers. While trade and investment continued to grow, lingering memories of Japanese colonial rule and wartime expansion were difficult to erase. During the early 1990s, for example, Korean, Chinese, and Filipina women who had been dragooned to work in wartime Japanese military brothels demanded compensation from the Japanese government. While the Murayama government established a government-subsidized private fund to help the women, the effort failed to extinguish embers of resentment. Even more troubling to many Asians was the continuing reluctance of Japan's leaders to express clear-cut remorse about the war or to make any apologies for the suffering inflicted on the rest of the region. Indeed, older LDP politicians, including cabinet ministers, continued to express their undoubtedly sincere belief that the war had not been a war of aggression but a war to "liberate" Asia.

In 1995, the country's political leadership agonized over how to mark the fiftieth anniversary of the war's end . Centrists and leftists in the Diet insisted that the government make a formal apology to the world, especially to the countries of Asia, but conservative leaders like former Prime Minister Nakasone objected that such action would not be appropriate. In the end, the Diet passed a resolution expressing "deep remorse" for "acts of aggression" in Asia. But the resolution squeaked through only after considerable debate, and several dozen Diet members absented themselves. On August 15, 1995, Prime Minister Murayama unambiguously offered an official "apology" for the wartime suffering Japan had caused, but Asian doubts about what the Japanese really thought about the war lingered. A government-financed project to build a "war memorial museum" in downtown Tokyo, for example, included plans to commemorate Japanese victims but not those of the Asian or Allied countries.

Ties with the Southeast Asia countries—Indonesia, Malaysia, the Philippines, Singapore, and Thailand—were less complicated than elsewhere in Asia. Over the years, Japanese ODA funds helped build basic infrastructure in all these countries, and Japanese investment in manufacturing facilities created new jobs as well. Inevitably, the Japanese economic presence brought local resentment. Japanese firms sent their own managers from Japan to run operations, gave local employees only limited initiatives, and were reluctant to transfer their technology to the recipient country. On balance, however, Japanese investment was viewed as positive. Neither was there very great apprehension in Southeast Asia that Japan might emerge once again as an assertive diplomatic or even military power. Most leaders in these countries were more concerned about the threat of China than they were about Japan.

By contrast, Japanese relations with the two Koreas were diplomatically correct but politically wary. While North Korea courted the Japanese to counterbalance the rising prosperity and stability of South Korea, its peculiar regime was no more friendly to Japan than it was to any other foreign country. (Indeed, its main economic tie with Japan was the flow of hard currency secretly remitted by the pro-Pyongyang Korean residents, who waged a constant struggle against ethnic discrimination.) A slight thaw occurred in relations with South Korea at the time of the Seoul Olympics, when books on Korean culture and history enjoyed a small boom. The South Korean government was also pleased when the Japanese government eased the requirement that Korean residents in Japan be fingerprinted periodically. But a generation of colonial rule had left a residue of distrust toward Japan that was hard to erase. Both the government and the press in South Korea were quick to support the grievances of the comfort women, to criticize any sign of Japanese remilitarization, including participation in UN peacekeeping operations, and to remind the world that Japan showed no official remorse for its earlier aggression in Asia. (Needless to say, when a former Japanese foreign minister asserted that the two countries had joined "harmoniously" in 1910, a vigorous protest from Seoul forced a retraction.)

Relations with the People's Republic of China were equally delicate. The vast Chinese market was as alluring to the Japanese in the 1990s as it had been a century before. The country's slow but irreversible move toward "market socialism" promised broader opportunities for Japanese trade and investment, and billboards in Shanghai and Beijing carried colorful advertisements for Japanese television sets and refrigerators. As a friendly gesture to the Chinese government at a time when the other advanced industrial countries treated it as a pariah for its brutal crackdown on the democratic movement in 1989, the new emperor Akihito and his consort traveled to China, the first time a Japanese monarch had ever done so. While some critics questioned using the emperor as an instrument of foreign policy, supporters argued that isolating China did no good and that growing affluence in China was bound to lead to political liberalization. The question of war responsibility continued to cloud the relationship, however, as did the growing belligerence of the Beijing government. When the Chinese conducted missile practice off the coast of Taiwan in early 1996, in an apparent effort to intimidate voters in the first democratic election there, the Japanese were reminded of China's capacity to cause mischief and upset regional tranquillity.

The "new Asianism" reflected the same impulses that inspired the "multidirectional" foreign policy of the 1970s—a desire to emerge from under the shadow of the United States. But Asian regionalism seemed to hold no great promise in the short term. Japan was, after all, a global economic power that benefited enormously from free world markets and had a large stake in maintaining cordial economic and technological ties with the Western industrialized countries. While closer ties with Asia had an undoubted emotional appeal, political, bureaucratic, and business elites continued to feel that

Japan's best interests were served by cordial relations with the Western countries, especially the United States. While some continued to worry about the "Canadaisation" of Japan, the complex web of economic, military, and political interdependence made that a more likely future for Japan than emergence as a regional leader in East Asia. Indeed, the economic slowdown at home, coupled with evidence of immense vitality in the rest of Asia suggested such leadership was no more than a pipe dream.

THE POST-POSTWAR GENERATION

As the new millennium approached, Japan's prospects remained unclear in many ways, but it took no crystal ball to see that the future ultimately rested in the hands of the generation born after economic growth began in the 1960s. Unlike their parents, who could remember the hard times of the wartime and early postwar years, this new cohort of Japanese seemed so different that the media referred to them as a "new breed" (*shinjinrui*). Shuffled onto the educational escalator at an early age, hustled to after-school cram schools and carefully protected during "examination hell," they had been carefully raised to enter the corporate society built by the older generation. While this generation was able to work "by the manual," many commentators feared that young people lacked the mettle and boldness to keep the economy going, let alone deal with the myriad other problems the country faced.

The main complaint about the "new breed" was that they were less devoted to work than their parents. At the Seoul Olympics in 1988, for example, journalists lamented the "spineless, lackadaisical attitude" of young Japanese athletes who did not seem to care whether they won or lost but were satisfied merely to have participated. Certainly, Japanese athletes brought home fewer medals than their American, Chinese, or even Korean contemporaries, but obituaries for the Japanese work ethic were premature. By comparison with youth in the Western industrial countries, the "new breed" were much more likely to see work as their main interest in life, and most expected to be employed as long as they could. Neither were they much less inclined than their parents to work overtime or to spend time after hours with work mates. It was hard to shake habits of self-discipline drilled into them by the long hard climb up the educational escalator.

But in other ways, their attitudes toward life and society were significantly different from the older generation's. Unlike their parents, who grew up in families of four or five children, the "new breed" came from smaller, child-centered households. The average family in the 1960s and 1970s had less than two offspring, meaning that many children grew up with no brothers or sisters. The experience made them much more self-centered and self-contained than the older generation. Instead of spending after-school hours playing with neighborhood friends, they commuted to cram school, sat at their desks doing home work, or played video games on the family television set. Their sense of social and communal responsibility was much weaker than that of earlier generations. University students were as likely to amuse themselves with solitary computer games as join social and athletic clubs, or plunge into political organizations. The "new breed" was more atomized, if not more individualistic, than previous generations.

In the work place, this change brought a marked decline in loyalty toward the firm and an even greater decline in willingness to make personal sacrifices for it. The "new breed" was more inclined than their parents had been to take holidays, switch to new companies, or even embark on new careers after several years. The collectivist ethic remained strong, but it was no longer directed primarily toward the company. For most young people, work was not an end in itself but a means to some other end: leisure, consumption, or personal fulfillment. In contrast to parents who had scrimped and saved most of their lives, they had grown up accustomed to instant gratification. No longer did they feel that years of hard work and effort were necessary to reach a distant goal. Their weekly allowances had been generous, and their parents had bought the toys their children craved. As these children grew older it was only natural that they expected to buy or do whatever they wanted.

The "new breed" lived not by an ethic of scarcity but by one of acquisition. Bombarded from childhood with television commercials, they were eager connoisseurs of "name brands." Their avid consumerism provided a widening market for new weekly magazines stuffed with information about clothes, computers, electronic gear, rock shows, restaurants, and just about anything else that money could buy. Indeed, manufacturers talked about the shift from mass production to "micro-markets" or "micro-masses" as young consumers sought highly novel or specialized products, whether designer shoes or exotic beers. The huge weekend crowds of young people in the Harajuku section of Tokyo, a concentration of trendy boutiques and fast food shops, demonstrated their eagerness to bury themselves in the market place. While some pointed out that "individualism" was on the rise among young people, it seemed to be an individualism best symbolized by the personal credit card.

The "new breed" looked forward to marriage no less than their parents had. Surveys showed that young men supported the institution more enthusiastically than young women, but marriage rates remained high. Since more young people spent their early twenties enjoying their freedom, dating or even living with several possible partners, however, the marriage age rose. Arranged marriages, where family, friends, or neighbors brought young couples together, were also on the decline. Young people preferred to find partners on their own, and once married, they seemed to enjoy an easier and more intimate relationship with one another than older couples. While the younger generation was more tolerant of divorce than their parents, couples

Young shoppers checking out sneakers at a store in Harajuku, a trendy shopping district in Tokyo, in 1988.

in their middle age were most likely to split, particularly when newly retired husbands began spending more time at home than they had while working.

Oddly enough, for all their materialism, many members of the "new breed" were attracted to the "spiritual" side of life. According to public surveys, young people were far less likely than the older generation to proclaim a personal religion, especially an established religion like Buddhism, Shinto, or Christianity, but were far likelier to believe in the existence of spirits, deities, and other supernatural forces. According to one hypothesis, the "new breed" had difficulty distinguishing fantasy from reality because they had grown up watching television. While the idea may seem farfetched, it does appear that many found the occult as plausible as the scientific. During the 1980s and 1990s, an upsurge in "new religion" sects attracted young people from mainstream middle-class families rather than from the socially marginalized or displaced. While affluence had increased opportunities for self-expression, the goals of "working hard" or "catching up" no longer had the meaning they did for older Japanese. Religious sects offered a sense of purpose that young people had not found in school, university, or workplace, and they satisfied a craving for solidarity, intimacy, and belonging that was no longer satisfied by the firm or company.

The dark side of the new religious cults was exposed dramatically in March 1995 when a deadly nerve gas was released on two major downtown subway lines in Tokyo, killing twelve passengers and sickening 5000 others. Within a few days, police raided the Tokyo offices and rural headquarters of Aum Shinrikyō, a "new religion" founded by Asahara Shoko, a sight-impaired guru who had once been arrested for selling fake medicines. The discovery of toxic ingredients used to manufacture the gas confirmed the sect's involvement. In May, Asahara and other sect leaders were arrested. What shocked the public, who were mesmerized daily by television reports about the sect, was not only the sect's involvement in murder, torture, extortion, and illegal drugs, but the fact that young people, lured by promise of perfecting themselves through meditation and other practices, made up the rank and file of its membership. The leaders surrounding Asahara, moreover, were highly educated, graduates of elite universities, many with advanced scientific or professional training, who avidly carried out criminal acts at his command. Not surprisingly, the incident shook the myth that Japan was the "world's safest country" and raised questions about how a society could have produced such an aberration.

In sum, in the mid-1990s, Japan seemed to be a country adrift, caught up in problems created by its spectacular economic success, but uncertain of what lay ahead. An air of public pessimism prevailed. Public opinion polls showed a steady rise in the number of people who thought Japan was moving in a "bad direction." In early 1997 more than 55 percent did. But pessimism has always galvanized the Japanese public rather than discouraged them. Although the mirage of "Japan as Number One" had faded, it seemed only a matter of time before the Japanese would define a new set of dreams—whether as "life style superpower," "paradise for the elderly," "world leader in environment," or some other comforting identity. A society that had managed to escape colonization by Western imperialism, to rise to a position as a major power only to lose it in an ill conceived war, and then to recover from destruction and defeat to become an economic superpower was clearly facing a better future than it thought it did.

ENDNOTE

1. Quoted in The *New York Times*, 24 Jan. 1997, 1.

Index